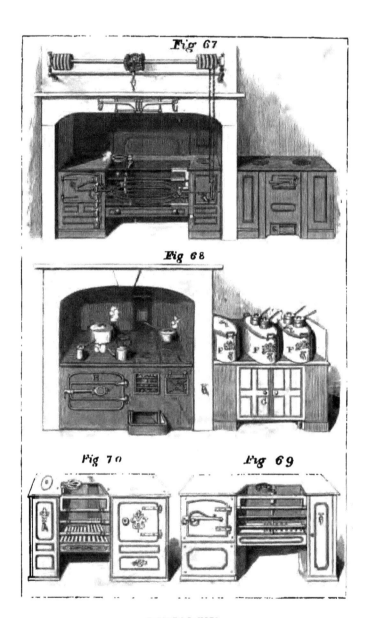

Fig 67

Fig 68

Fig 70

Fig 69

KITCHEN-RANGES.

THE

COOKERY BOO

IN THE

STYLE WITH ECONOMY,

AND

ALL PERSONS IN FULL

CONTAIN

OF THE BEST IN FAMILY

IN APPROVED RULES.

WITH A COMPLETE ANALYSIS

BY AND OF

J. H. WALSH F.R.C.S.

"A MANUAL OF DOMESTIC ECONOMY."

With Engravings.

LONDON

ROUTLEDGE AND CO. FARRINGDON STREET;

AND 18, BEEKMAN STREET, NEW YORK.

1859.

THE

ENGLISH COOKERY BOOK:

UNITING

A GOOD STYLE WITH ECONOMY,

AND

ADAPTED TO ALL PERSONS IN EVERY CLIME.

CONTAINING

MANY UNPUBLISHED RECEIPTS IN DAILY USE

BY PRIVATE FAMILIES.

COLLECTED BY A COMMITTEE OF LADIES,

AND EDITED BY

J. H. WALSH, F.R.C.S.,

AUTHOR OF "A MANUAL OF DOMESTIC ECONOMY."

With Engravings.

LONDON:

G. ROUTLEDGE AND CO., FARRINGDON STREET;
AND 18, BEEKMAN STREET, NEW YORK.

1859.

PREFACE.

THE greater number of the receipts which comprise this *English Cookery Book* form a part of the extended system of *Domestic Economy*, which was published with great success in 1857. They have been compiled with the assistance of several ladies who kindly took an interest in the subject, and who, being at the head of well-conducted establishments, varying in extent and consequent expenditure, may be expected to be good authorities on the value of the receipts they have furnished. A great many of these are from their own family scrap-books, and almost all have had the benefit of an actual trial; so that they may be safely recommended as being adapted to everyday use in our English kitchens. Some of them are selected for their economy, others for their intrinsic value as agents in nutrition, and others again solely for their flavour, or for the sake of variety; but all are practically useful in some shape or other.

The general directions for roasting, boiling, frying, &c., are founded upon the chemical principles which have recently been applied by Liebig, Hassall, and others, to the investigation of animal and vegetable nutritive agents, and for these alone the Editor can take credit to himself. The practical directions for the difficult art of pastry-making are by an experienced cook, who has also carefully examined and comrected the receipts throughout, and the whole have been arranged with a view to a ready discovery of what is wanted on the shortest notice.

The chapters on the department of housekeeping which especially relates to the kitchen, have been added in order to make this book complete in itself; while the directions for carving have not been forgotten, although it is believed that an actual demonstration is required in order to teach this difficult art, so essential to the elegant appearance of the table.

It is hoped that the numerous additions which have been made to the original more contracted plan will render this a most complete system of English cookery, and adapt it to the wants of all families throughout the United Kingdom and the British Colonies.

J. H. W.

September, 1858.

CONTENTS.

THE

PRINCIPLES AND PRACTICE OF ENGLISH COOKERY.

———————◆———————

CHAP. I.—ON FOOD: ITS NATURE, USE, AND ABUSE.

SECT. 1.—ON THE EFFECTS UPON MAN OF THE VARIOUS KINDS OF FOOD USED IN GREAT BRITAIN.

1. THE VARIETIES OF FOOD, the cookery of which is described in
the following pages, are all, more or less, employed in Great Britain,
and may be considered as comprising the full diet-roll of the country.
It is first necessary to examine their effects upon the human system,
and the comparative worth of each, as well in point of absolute
efficiency, as of cost price. But it is impossible to do this with any
thing like certainty, because of the different circumstances connected
with age, sex, temperament, and habits, affecting individuals, and
even the same individual at consecutive periods of his life. All,
therefore, that can be attempted is to calculate the average quantity
of solid food, of the best mixed kind, required by adult men leading
active lives, and then to consider how near any other kind approaches
to this in supporting the full vigour of the system. In this estimate
it is assumed, that in Great Britain an active adult male will consume
about two pounds of solid food, consisting of bread, cheese, meat,
vegetables, and milk; while a healthy female will not require more
than a pound and a half, the average consumption of the two being
one pound and three-quarters per head daily. In all cases, therefore,
when a larger quantity than this of any article is required by healthy
individuals, it may be considered that it is not of the average degree
of nutritive value; and, on the other hand, when a less amount is
sufficient, it is then, by the same rule, above the line. In support of
this calculation, the diet of the navy may be adduced, which is noto-

35

B

riously on a most liberal scale, and intended for very robust and hard-working men, exposed to all weathers. It consists daily of one pound of biscuit (or one pound and a quarter of soft bread), with one pound of fresh meat and half a pound of vegetables (or one pound of salt pork and half a pint of peas, or one pound of salt beef and nine ounces of flour, three ounces of suet, and one ounce and a half of currants). In addition to which there is a daily supply of tea, chocolate, sugar, and spirit; and, weekly, a small allowance of spices and oatmeal. If, therefore, it is found that this slight increase above two pounds per day is enough for such men, who are above the average in their requirements, the amount which I have stated may fairly be taken as the average for working-men in general.

2. EVERY KIND OF FOOD will be useful in proportion to the nature and amount of the solid matter which it contains, the fluid particles being comparatively inoperative; and, in the case of some kinds of vegetables, being also greatly in excess of the solid. But not only is this *quantity* of solid matter important, but its *quality* also must not be overlooked; and in this particular chemical science is not always a sure guide, since there are many substances almost identical in ultimate composition which are yet widely opposed in their effects upon the human economy. Thus, the fibres of wood are composed of carbon, oxygen, and hydrogen, in the same proportions as starch, and yet they are perfectly indigestible; while the latter is as readily converted into nutriment as any substance we have. In the same way, horny matter and bones, though readily dissolved by the powers of the dog's stomach, pass through that of man almost unchanged; and yet they are full of nitrogenized ingredients, which, when capable of solution, or after they are dissolved by the aid of water at a high temperature, are of the highest possible value. It follows, therefore, that every substance used as food must be considered under three aspects—1st, as to the nature of its *ultimate elements;* 2nd, as to the *proportion of solid matters* contained in it; and 3rd, as to its *digestibility* by the *human stomach.*

3. THE CHEMICAL COMPOSITION OF THE SOLIDS varies in many particulars, but chiefly in the presence or absence of nitrogen. Almost all articles of food contain the three elementary substances known as carbon, oxygen, and hydrogen, together with more or less of mineral matter, in the shape of salts or earths; but a certain number of other kinds of aliment contain, in addition, more or less of nitrogen or azote; and hence these two divisions are distinguished, as—1st, non-nitro-

genized or non-azotized articles; and, 2nd, nitrogenized or azotized—the terms *nitrogenized* and *azotized* meaning one and the same thing, whilst the term *protein compound*, which is commonly confounded with them, is by physiologists confined to that exact condition or proportion of nitrogen with carbon, oxygen, and hydrogen, which is capable of being converted into albumen, fibrine, or casein, in the process of digestion.

4. THE AZOTIZED COMPOUNDS are required for the repair of the muscular tissue, and for the nutrition of the body generally, and consequently a proper amount of them must be obtained, or the machine will not be maintained in a state of health, nor will it be kept alive without a certain proportion of them. The list of azotized articles of food includes not only many animal substances, as albumen, fibrine, casein, &c., but also some few vegetables, such as the grains of corn, the seeds of leguminous plants, cabbages, mushrooms, &c. As a consequence, therefore, of their containing nitrogen, all these are specially calculated to support the muscular powers, and to keep up the supplies necessary for the general nutrition of the body; and, in whatever form they are introduced into the stomach, they are capable of being converted into the particular material required. So that, by the aid of the digestive powers, wheaten bread is as capable of forming muscle as flesh itself, containing in fact a vegetable albumen identical in composition with that of the animal kingdom. But some other azotized materials are not found already elaborated in the vegetable kingdom—as, for instance, gelatine; and though this may be manufactured in the animal economy out of vegetable substances, yet there is reason to believe that if it is presented to the stomach ready formed, it is more easily applied to the purposes of nutrition; and consequently gelatine, or, in common language, jelly, is a very valuable aid to the food of weakly or invalid persons, though it is ascertained by experiment that by itself it will not support life. It is also doubly useful in this state, because it is at once absorbed by endosmose from the lining of the stomach and intestines without any necessity for the process of digestion and assimilation—an act which, of itself, requires an expenditure of vital power.

5. THE NON-AZOTIZED COMPOUNDS, used as food, are met with in great abundance in the vegetable kingdom, though there are few vegetables which, in their natural state, are wholly deprived of nitrogen. But the manufactured articles of food commonly known as arrowroot, sugar, oil, and some others, are composed of carbon, hydrogen, and

oxygen alone, and are chiefly used in supporting the respiratory process, and thus maintaining the temperature of the body. Among the compounds known as sugar and starch, the amount of oxygen is only sufficient to form water by its union with the hydrogen contained in them, and thus the carbon is at liberty to combine with the oxygen introduced through the lungs, forming carbonic acid, and giving out heat. Again, in the oily matters used as food, the proportion of oxygen is so small that they contain a large surplus of hydrogen as well as carbon, ready to be burned off in the system by union with oxygen obtained from the air. It is generally believed that the most simple of these non-azotized compounds, as sugar and starch, are carried off by the respiratory process within a very short time after they are introduced into the system; while the oily matters, which are taken up by the lacteals, and require a greater amount of assimilative power, are not so readily brought into use, though quite as efficacious when properly prepared. When the amount of respiratory or non-azotized matter is too small for the heat-producing office, a larger amount of azotized materials must be employed to supply its place, in which there is a great waste. Thus, supposing 100 grains of oil to develop a certain amount of heat, then, in order to accomplish the same effect, 240 grains of starch must be used, or 249 grains of cane-sugar, 263 grains of grape-sugar, 266 grains of proof spirit, and 770 *grains of fresh lean meat.* Alcohol belongs to the respiratory class, *and, if properly diluted,* it may be rendered very serviceable when there is a deficiency of heat-producing material, or when the surrounding air is so cold as to call for an extra supply. But if employed in hot climates, or in addition to food already abounding in carbon and hydrogen, it is injurious, from its affording more of these elements than is wanted by the system.

6. IT IS THUS CLEAR that in man, as well as in all other warm-blooded animals but the carnivorous tribes, a mixture of azotized and non-azotized substances is required for his support. Nature has taught him to supply the wants of his system in the most complete manner, as far as general principles are concerned; and all that art can do is to direct him in his search for those particular articles of food which are most readily obtained, or most easily digested and assimilated to his own wants. No substance is more extensively used than bread, either made of wheat, Indian corn, or rye; and there is none met with throughout the world, upon which alone man can subsist for any length of time without injury to health, excepting, perhaps, oat-

meal porridge, which indeed so closely resembles bread in its composition as to be almost identical with it; and milk, which is still more adapted to support life, but is chiefly intended for young animals by nature. With the addition of a moderate quantity of butter, the heat-producing power of bread is rendered quite sufficient to meet the wants of even our coldest winters; while, for the purpose of affording additional muscular support, flesh, albumen, or milk containing casein, must be supplied, together with gelatine in the shape of soups or jellies. But when bread forms a principal article of diet, unless the individual is taking a great amount of exercise, the regular use of meat in large quantities should be cautiously indulged in, being disadvantageous both to the pocket and to the health. On the other hand, when rice, potatoes, or any other vegetable substances, almost wholly free from nitrogen, are the chief articles of diet, either an enormous bulk must be digested in order to obtain a sufficient supply of nitrogen, and to the great waste of the carbon and hydrogen, or else some material containing a large proportion of nitrogen must be added, such as eggs, milk, or flesh. Lastly, the oily kinds of food are chiefly adapted for those who live in very cold climates, and require an extra supply of heat, and who are consequently led to devour train-oil with the greatest avidity. It is said that the Esquimaux will devour thirty pounds of blubber at a meal, and, as it is slowly digested, they are enabled to go for several days without another supply, and in the interval to keep up a temperature equal to their wants when exposed to their severe climate.

7. THE RELATIVE PROPORTIONS of azotized and non-azotized substances in our ordinary articles of food are here appended, on the authority of Liebig; the non-azotized being calculated as starch :—

Article of Food.	Azotized or Blood-making Materials.			Non-azotized or Respiratory Materials.
Veal contains	10		to	1
Hare ...	10		"	2
Beef (lean) ...	10		"	17
Lentils ...	10		"	21
Horse-beans ...	10		"	22
Peas ...	10		"	22
Fat mutton ...	10		"	27
Fat pork ...	10		"	30
Cow's milk ...	10		"	30
Human milk ...	10		"	40
Wheat-flour ...	10		"	46
Oatmeal ...	10		"	50
Rye-flour ...	10		"	57
Barley ...	10		"	57
Potatoes (white) ...	10		"	65
Ditto (blue) ...	10		"	115
Rice ...	10		"	123
Buck-wheat ...	10		"	130

In this table it must be remembered, that several of the items are somewhat different from those used in this country, as, for instance, veal, which in Germany is almost wholly devoid of fat, while in this country it is often sold with a considerable quantity of that heat-producing article. The same will apply to beef, which, as here sold, will in its composition be more nearly like that of fat mutton in the above table. Still it will show the relative properties in each kind of food; and the observer may class them pretty nearly as they are here given in point of azote. It will thus appear that it will take 133 lbs. of rice, or 125 lbs. of blue potatoes, to supply as much muscular tissue as 27 lbs. of lean beef, or 37 lbs. of fat mutton, or 40 lbs. of cow's milk, or 56 lbs. of wheat flour, or 60 lbs. of oatmeal; and consequently the hard-working man, who chiefly expends muscular tissue, must make a double calculation;—1st, what substance will supply him with the azotized materials which he requires, joined with a sufficient amount of respiratory matter; and, 2nd, will that substance give it him at the lowest possible price? It is obvious that the less waste the better—that is to say, that the two classes of substances should, in theory, be exactly proportioned to the wants of the system, and that all beyond this is a waste of digestive power, and of material also; but in practice it sometimes happens that the poor man, being limited in his supply of money, can lay it out to more advantage by purchasing a larger amount of articles theoretically extravagant, but which, though wasting a part of their elements, will still afford him more of what his system demands. Thus, in round numbers, the quantity of potatoes equivalent to bread and meat are respectively four, two, and one—that is to say, that four pounds of potatoes will go as far in affording muscular tissue as two pounds of bread or one pound of meat; and whenever this quantity of potatoes can be purchased for less money than two pounds of bread or one pound of meat, which is almost always the case, they may with advantage be substituted for the two last kinds of food in an economical point of view. But as it is well known that man cannot long live upon one article of diet, and as the four pounds of potatoes would be too bulky for the stomach, and would give the excretory organs too much to do in getting rid of their superfluous carbon and hydrogen, it follows that, in point of health, a diet composed entirely of this root is prejudicial to health in all ways. When mixed, however, with bread and meat, nothing is more wholesome or more economical than the potato; and it is only when its use is carried to excess that it should be condemned as injurious to mankind.

8. BUT THE MINERAL ELEMENTS OF FOOD are no less necessary than those we have been hitherto examining; for, though the chief *bulk* of the body is built up from the four elementary principles which have been investigated, yet we shall find that all food capable of long sustaining life must contain the mineral salts which are met with in the blood. An alkaline condition of this fluid is absolutely essential to the performance of its functions; and every acid which enters it must at once be neutralized and carried off in the secretions or excretions. Thus, the vegetable acids are speedily oxidized in the blood, and become converted into carbonic acid and water, and then appear as alkaline carbonates, while uric acid becomes converted into urate of ammonia, and is discharged with the urine. The mineral ingredients of food are either phosphates and sulphates alone, as in flesh, grain, and pulse, or these salts mixed with silicates and carbonates, as in green vegetables. These are partly soluble and partly insoluble in water; and as the soluble salts of the ashes of the blood are the same as those of urine, and since we can affect the nature of the latter fluid by a change of diet, we may not only arrive at the soluble salts of the blood from examining those in the urine, but we may modify them also by changing the diet. Phosphoric acid and the phosphates, as well as other mineral ingredients, are absolutely necessary to effect the vital changes constantly going on, and hence we see the importance of supplying them in due proportion and admixture. This is the reason why boiled flesh (or fibrine) alone will not support life; and why yolk of egg, cheese, and similar matters, likewise fail when used by themselves. The pure fibre of meat is certainly rich enough in phosphoric acid, but it has lost the alkalies in the juice; the yolk of egg is still richer in the same phosphoric acid, but it, likewise, is deficient in alkali, which is confined to the white. In cheese, again, the same division of these matters has taken place, the whey retaining all the alkali contained in the milk. Hence it is that salt is so usefully added in unusually large proportions to boiled meat, eggs, and cheese. It is for these reasons, that in all boiled meats the broth ought to be eaten with them, or, at all events, used as soup on the alternate days, the system being content to wait for that short time for the supply of the saline materials, especially if common salt is eaten at the same time, as is almost universally practised.

9. GREEN VEGETABLES contain these saline ingredients in large proportion, so that they may be advantageously used with boiled salt-meat in which the alkaline juices have been lost, both in the salting

and in the boiling process. Hence it has been found by experience, that carrots, parsnips, turnips, and greens are advantageously mixed with boiled beef, which, without their addition, or some substitute for them, will in a short time produce that horrible disease known as scurvy. It is not, however, sufficient in such cases to boil these vegetables in large quantities of water, and then to eat them without their juices contained in the water; but they should be steamed in small quantities of water, and this should be taken with them, in order to extract all their virtues, and render them available.

10. THE USE OF TEA, COFFEE, AND COCOA has of late years become almost universal in this country; and as they all contain a principle nearly identical with each other, and acting in the same way upon the system, it is therefore right to consider them as one and the same. They all seem to promote the natural vital changes, and especially muscular and nervous action. It is true, that the precise effect produced cannot be watched; but it is accompanied with a sense of refreshment attended with new vigour, which is very peculiar, and so captivating that it is very rare to find individuals giving up the use of one or the other of these articles after they are once accustomed to them. It is indeed asserted, that no nation has ever ceased to take either tea, coffee, or cocoa, after once taking to them as a general beverage; and this is, perhaps, the highest character which can be given of any article notoriously free from injurious effects upon the morals. A nation may easily be led wrong, by acting on the passions or appetites; but when it is led in any other way, it may reasonably be maintained that the mode of temptation is not only free from harm, but in all probability is in itself good.

SECT. 2.—ON THE ABUSE OF FOOD.

11. In the preceding section it has been shown that a diet of a mixed kind is best adapted for maintaining the health of man, and that the ingredients of which it is composed should be varied from time to time, and also according to the age of the individual. Thus it is right to use animal as well as vegetable food in moderation, and in proportion to the demands of the system; but more than this is an abuse, and should not be encouraged, as it will surely, sooner or later, produce mischief in some organ or organs. Even alcohol is required under certain circumstances, where a great expenditure of heat is going on, and at all times may be indulged in without injury if properly diluted, and in moderate quantities; though at the same time,

in our temperate climate, it is not required by healthy men who can command a sufficient amount of heat-producing solid food. The various abuses of food may therefore be considered as consisting in— 1st, *excess in quality;* 2nd, *excess in quantity;* and, 3rd, *abstinence from the food required.*

12. EXCESS IN QUALITY is chiefly the result of too highly-stimulating food; that is to say, it consists in partaking of articles which in themselves are highly proper as containing the desired elements, but in too concentrated a form. When taken into the stomach they produce disorder of it from excess of proper stimulus, just as an exceedingly strong light injures the eyes, although a smaller amount of it is absolutely essential to vision. From this cause strong extracts of meat when taken by themselves, rich creams, strong alcoholic drinks, and other concentrations of otherwise wholesome foods, are sure to cause indigestion, and, in the case of alcohol, injury to the whole system.

13. EXCESS IN QUANTITY may either be of the whole elements of the food, or of part. It is well known that the gastric juice is essential to digestion, and that it is poured into the stomach, not in proportion to the food swallowed, but in exact relation to the demands of the system; so that if these are small, and yet a large meal is eaten, there will not be sufficient gastric juice to digest it, and, as a consequence, a considerable amount of crude and easily-fermented food is passed on, or rejected by vomiting. In either case this produces some disorder of the system; and, when habitually indulged in, the effect on the stomach, as well as other organs, is very prejudicial. But besides this bad effect of too great a quantity of otherwise proper food, there is also that resulting from too profuse a supply of either of the two kinds required by the system, and described as blood-making and respiratory. The great and prevalent error in this country is that of eating too much blood-making or azotized matter, whether in the shape of animal or vegetable food; for even in the latter there is too large a proportion to bear mixture with much flesh, as in the case of wheat, peas, or beans. On the other hand, the proportion of respiratory matter may be easily rendered too great, and particularly when strong alcoholic liquors are largely imbibed, as unfortunately so often happens. In this kind of abuse the injury is twofold—first, from the excessive stimulus mentioned in the last paragraph; and, secondly, from the enormous preponderance of respiratory matter. By virtue of the strong attraction for oxygen, alcohol is first oxidized, to the

exclusion of the solid food, and even before the absolute and living tissues of the body. If the food is already composed of sufficient starch, sugar, or fat, every drop of alcohol is poisonous to a certain degree; but, on the other hand, when taken with cheese, meat, or eggs, in which there is a large quantity of nitrogen, alcohol in some shape is by no means injurious, unless its stimulating effects are too great from being in a very concentrated form. It is for this reason that our instinct has taught us to take wine or beer with savoury food in preference to sweets.

14. ABSTINENCE FROM THE QUANTITY OR QUALITY OF FOOD required by the system, is just as great an abuse of what is freely offered to us as the opposite extreme. Thus, it is clearly shown that man is an animal designed to live on a mixed diet, consisting of azotized and non-azotized materials in a given proportion. It matters not whether these are obtained from the animal or vegetable kingdom, as far as the effect upon him is concerned. A man may feed as fully, and form more blood, on a vegetable diet composed of peas or beans, than he would do on fat meat. There is no difference, as far as is known, in the power of producing blood, between flesh and bread, if the former is mixed with a proper amount of starch or oily matter. But there is one reason why flesh is superior to all other kinds of food for the purpose of supplying the waste of muscular tissue; and that is, that it is the very substance which it is intended to form, and therefore is more readily built up into the animal machine. The proper rule is to obtain the necessary amount of each kind of food in a state as near as possible to that tissue for which it is intended, and avoiding too highly concentrated a form. The instinct of man has always led him to apply this rule whenever he could; though in many cases, for want of sufficient intelligence, he has been led to confine himself, on the one hand, to flesh alone, as in the case of the American Indians; and on the other, to roots, as in the case of the stunted tribes of the interior of Africa.

SECT. 3.—ON THE RELATION EXISTING BETWEEN THE MARKET PRICE AND THE ALIMENTARY VALUE OF FOOD.

15. By the former of these terms is understood the cost of any article of food in the regular market, while the latter refers to its good effects upon the body. It will generally be found that these two are pretty nearly proportioned to one another; or, in other words, that

mankind have now found out the precise alimentary value of most kinds of food, and have priced them accordingly. Yet this is not always the case, and one great object of the economist in household affairs is to seek out such as are sold below their real value, and use them for their proper purposes. It is a rule generally maintained, that the supply of any article is equal to the demand; but in proportion to the increase of the demand is the price raised, unless the supply is practically unlimited, when the larger the demand the more the price seems to fall. But still it is notorious that whenever it is found out that any well-known article has more useful qualities than have generally been assigned to it, the demand being increased has a tendency to raise the price, and from that time it is no longer beneficially applicable, and gradually again falls out of use. It must be remembered that in several of our aliments as sold in the market there is a large proportion of water, as in butcher's meat, fish, poultry, and green vegetables, including potatoes; while in flour, rice, and other similar articles, the quantity of water is comparatively small. The following table exhibits the quantity of nutritive matter in the ordinary articles of food, as compared with their price :—

COMPARATIVE VALUE OF FOOD IN NUTRITIVE MATTER.

	Nutritive Matter.	Price.
	lb.	£ s. d.
100 lbs. of Butcher's meat contain	85	2 18 4
" " Baker's bread (seconds)	75	0 18 9
" " Home-made bread (seconds)	80	0 17 8½
" " Do. do. (brown)	78	0 13 6½
" " Do. do. (wheat and Indian meal)...	76	0 15 7½
" " Do. do. (wheat and rice)	68	0 14 0½
" " Do. do. (wheat and potatoes) ...	63	0 15 1½
" " Rice and sago	90	1 5 0
" " French beans (dried)...	92	1 10 0
" " Broad beans (green, but mealy)...	81	2 10 0
" " Peas (dried)	93	1 5 0
" " Do. (green)	70 to 78	2 10 0
" " Potatoes	25 to 28	0 6 3
" " Carrots and parsnips...	14	0 10 0
" " Cabbages...	6½	0 8 6
" " Turnips	6	0 8 6

From this table it will appear, that very nearly in proportion to the amount of the nitrogenized matter in the food, and its fitness for digestion, is the price in the market. Thus, butcher's meat stands the highest in price, not because it contains the largest quantity of nitrogenized nutritive matter, but because it is the most digestible of those which are so compounded, and contains, in addition, a liberal supply of those saline matters which are required; it is therefore valued at 1s. 8d. per lb. of nutritive matter. Dried beans and peas, on the other hand, which contain about the same proportion of nitrogen (see table at page 5), are only valued in public estimation at 4d. per. lb. of nutritive matter; the reason being that they are neither so digestible nor so easily convertible into fibrine as meat, and that they do not contain a proper amount of saline matters. Bread, again, which is composed of these elements in a suitable proportion, sells at 3d. per lb. of nutritive matter, and is consequently much cheaper than meat, or even than beans and peas, and very much more so than potatoes, rice, and sago, which, though so much vaunted as a cheap food, are really deficient in every point of view, being actually sold at from 3d. to 3¾d. per lb. of nutritive matter, and that of a kind almost wholly without nitrogen. The exact price of potatoes is 3d., and of rice or sago 3½d. per lb. of nutritive matter. Carrots, parsnips, cabbages, and turnips, vary from 8d. to 1s. per lb. of nutritive matter, and cannot, therefore, be compared in this respect with any of those kinds mentioned above; but from the quantity of saline matter which they contain, they are invaluable adjuncts to meat, bread, and potatoes, and should never be omitted for any lengthened period.

SECT. 4.—ON THE QUANTITIES OF FOOD REALLY DEMANDED BY THE SYSTEM.

16. This subject has been previously alluded to, and it will, therefore, only be necessary here to repeat in a tabular form the average quantities of each kind of food required by a healthy man taking an ordinary amount of exercise :—

(a) AVERAGE DAILY AMOUNT of the BEST KIND of FOOD required by an ADULT MALE :—

									s.	d.
Meat (uncooked)	...	...	...	...	...	...	...	0¾ lb. ...	0	6
Bread	...	...	...	...	...	...	...	0¾ „ ...	0	1½
Potatoes (or green vegetables)	...	...	...	...	...	...	1½ „ ...	0	1½
Cheese	...	...	...	...	...	...	...	2 oz. ...	0	1
Butter	...	...	...	...	...	...	...	1 „ ...	0	1½
Milk	...	...	...	...	...	...	...	2 „ ...	0	0½
Sugar	...	...	...	...	...	...	...	1 „		
Tea	...	...	...	...	...	...	...	0½ „	0	2
Coffee	...	...	...	...	...	...	...	1 „		
Malt liquor	...	...	...	...	...	...	...	1 pint	0	2

1 4

(*b*) CHEAP FOOD, SUFFICIENT TO SUPPORT AN ADULT IN GOOD HEALTH :—

				s.	d.
Bread ...	...	...	1 lb. ...	0	2½
Potatoes ...	...	...	2 ,, ...	0	1½
Peas or beans ...	...	...	4 oz. ...	0	0½
Dripping or lard ...	...	...	4 ,, ...	0	2
Cabbage or greens ...	...	...	1 lb. ...	0	1
Cheese ...	...	...	3 oz. ...	0	1½
				0	9

This amount of aliment, if properly managed, may be made very tolerably palatable. The peas or beans should be well boiled, and then fried in a part of the dripping with the potatoes and cabbages, which will make a savoury mess. Part of the bread is to be eaten with this, dividing the whole into two meals; and the remainder of the bread, with the cheese, makes the third meal. This diet, with a pint and a half of malt liquor, which, if brewed at home, need not cost more than 1d., will keep a man *accustomed to such fare* in good health ; but there can be no doubt that it would disagree with those brought up to the use of meat, fish, and poultry.

(*c*) CHEAP FOOD FOR CHILDREN, SUITED TO THE COUNTRY :—

				s.	d.
Oatmeal ...	...	...	0¾ lb. ...	0	1½
Potatoes and greens ...	...	...	1 ,, ...	0	1
Milk ...	...	...	1 pint ...	0	1
Treacle ...	...	...	2 oz. ...	0	0½
Bacon ...	...	...	2 ,, ...	0	1
				0	5

The oatmeal should be boiled in water for about half an hour, or longer if very coarse ; then add the milk, and this will serve for breakfast and supper with the treacle. The potatoes and bacon make the dinner.

17. THE ABOVE CALCULATIONS are based upon the absolute amount of food which the human machine demands in order to supply its wants, and makes no allowance for changes required by the stomach, nor for the many other accidental circumstances which will always interfere with the cost. But this will show upon what a small quantity of food health may be supported, and will serve to explain the fact, that large families are often maintained upon sums which, by others, are considered inadequate to find food for a single individual not very far removed from them in social position. It is truly astonishing how much is wasted by overfeeding, and how unfortunately it

happens that when this practice has long been continued, it is next to impossible to leave it off. But though these limited quantities of plain food are sufficient to support life and health, yet there can be no doubt that, by proper management and cookery, the same sums, or very nearly so, which will purchase their rude materials, will suffice to procure much more savoury dishes. Compare a dish of plain boiled potatoes and salt with the same articles fried and flavoured only with a single herring and a little lard; and even if they are reduced in weight sufficiently to pay for the extras, they will be much more palatable, and also more serviceable to the system. This is merely a single illustration, but many others might be adduced, depending generally upon the gratification of the instinctive desire for nitrogenous food. In catering for a man with a strong appetite, it matters little what its nature may be, so that either fish, flesh, fowl, milk, pulse, or mushroom, will serve to afford nitrogen in large quantities, and at the same time act as flavouring matter; but for delicate stomachs the effect will vary greatly, and the choice must then be confined to such *well-cooked* kinds as are found by experience to afford this nourishment, while, at the same time, they present a proper stimulus to the stomach.

CHAP. II.—ON THE ADVANTAGES OF A PROPER PREPARATION OF FOOD FOR THE HUMAN STOMACH.

SECT. I.—GENERAL REMARKS.

18. THE following observations from a recent leading article in the *Times* are so much to the point, that I shall extract them *verbatim*. After referring to the amount of ignorance existing among the class of mechanics and servants, in reference to the best modes of procuring the common articles of clothing, &c., the editor goes on to say:—" But the great, the fearful shortcoming is in the science of cookery. Of it they may be said to know nothing; and we fear in that class of life, nothing, or next to nothing, is known of it. Of course, the boys have not been taught any thing about it, though why they should not be nobody can explain; and as for the women, only those who go out to service profess to know about it, and in no case is their knowledge available for a poor man's household. If they are engaged in a rich family, they live on the best joints, eat succulent roast and fat boiled meat, and waste on their own, and waste still more on the upstairs

table, every thing which comes to their hand. They have a notion that there is a divine virtue in being extravagant and thriftless. Thrift and economy they consider mean. Yet a household of this kind, with the full swing of the kitchen and the larder, is too often the sole training that many a woman gets for the duties of a poor man's wife. It should never be forgotten that household service is the only school that many a woman ever passes through, and to many a woman it is a pernicious school. If she has never learned to save in the midst of plenty, she cannot begin to save under the pressure of small means. As she has never had reason for turning small things to account—to make the most of odds and ends—she is often reduced, and reduces her husband to a recurring vicissitude of one day's feasting and three or four days' fasting, with an intermediate day of scraps. And she is utterly ignorant of the thousand ways of dressing vegetables with a little meat or fish, so as to make the absence of a more substantial dish unregretted. And this happens in a million homes in a country which has, on the whole, the finest fish, the richest and most succulent meats, and produces or imports poultry, eggs, and butter to an extent which precludes their excessive dearness at any season. And while this happens with us, the French peasant, with far lower wages, with fewer materials of food, is making savoury dishes and healthy condiments out of the simplest produce of the field and the moor. Who can wonder, then, that while an English army is half-starved, despite numerous appliances and supplies, a French army feeds itself out of the rudest of Nature's gifts? Miss Burdett Coutts and Lord Ashburton, who took the lead which she has so well followed, will have earned the gratitude of the country if they have done nothing more than set people thinking about the amelioration of their cookery, and lead high teachers to consider that the art of feeding is really a science which affects the well-being of some twenty million citizens in England, and may often affect the existence of some quarter of a million soldiers abroad; and our social reformers will do well by following her example, and teaching the people of England that which, to the majority of them, is still a great secret— 'What food to buy, and how to cook it.'" No one who is acquainted with the workings of our everyday life in England, among the middle and lower classes, will refuse his cordial assent to these remarks; and few will be able to call upon their experience for instances of much greater knowledge among the mistresses of families themselves. It is true, that almost every housekeeper knows what meat costs, and how many pounds she consumes per week, and also the price of bread, and the number of quartern loaves, which she pays for at certain periods; but she does not know the amount of nourishment required by the younger and older members of her family respectively, nor the best kinds of food for each, nor even the best modes of dressing what she fixes upon in her blind and careless choice. It is with the last of these subjects that we have now to deal, and consequently to examine into the relative advantages of—1st, *the proper keeping of food;* 2nd, *roasting and baking;* 3rd, *boiling;* 4th, *frying ana broiling;* 5th, *stewing;* 6th, *soup-making;* besides the art and advantages of preparing what are called *made-dishes, sauces,* and also *pastry, puddings,* and other *sweets.* Prior to these divisions, however, it will be better to dilate at some length upon the duties of the cook in this department.

19. THE GRAND PRINCIPLES OF ECONOMICAL COOKERY are universally the same, however they may fall short in practice of ideal perfection. They are—1st, *To render food, as afforded by nature, more digestible by art.* 2nd, *To avoid, as far as possible, any waste of materials in the operation.* 3rd, *To combine with the most nourishing and digestible kinds of food those which shall render them grateful to the palate.* 4th, *To take care and please the senses of sight and smell, as well as those of taste.* And 5th, *To avoid all needless expense in carrying out the above operations.*

SECT. 2.—THE COOK, AND HER GENERAL UTENSILS.

20. Every cook has constantly to deal with four different elements of calculation, three of which are tolerably constant, and therefore to be depended on, while the fourth is unfortunately somewhat changeable. The first or constant elements are *time, quantity,* and *quality;* the second being her own *organ of taste* and that of her employers.

21. TIME is truly a certain and sure element, always to be depended on as a severe but just master. To the *punctual* observer of his laws he accords his favours without measure; and, on the other hand, those who break them are as surely punished by a constant and ever-recurring series of what they sometimes fancy to be misfortunes. As Napoleon could always manage to assemble his troops on a given spot at a given time, from whatever distance they might have been drawn ; so the cook, with a good head for her business, can contrive that all her dishes shall be ready at the same hour, by properly calculating the time they will take to dress, and commencing each in turn according

to its requirements in point of cookery. If this is neglected, one dish has to wait for another, and is, therefore, more or less injured by delay; and the dinner is postponed so long that the tempers of those who partake of it are by no means in a condition to allow them to judge impartially of its pretensions to a correct preparation. Punctuality, therefore, is the first thing to be inculcated; and this implies a proper grounding in the elementary principles of cookery, so as to be aware, without trouble and reference to books, of the time which every article requires. If the cook has to look every day for these particulars, she will lose time when most precious; but still, if she has not the knowledge, she can only gain it by consulting an authority of some kind; and if she is, as she ought to be, a quick reader, she may soon make herself independent on this score. In every case there should be a clock in the kitchen, or within sight of the cook; and when she is not thoroughly experienced, she should have the aid of a table of the times required for the cookery of the more ordinary articles hung up near her fireplace; which, if she cannot herself write in sufficiently legible characters, should be written by master or mistress.

22. QUANTITY comes next to time in importance; and it is an element still more frequently neglected by those who consider themselves professed cooks. Few of these people weigh or measure the ingredients which they use, but compound their dishes by "rule of thumb." This is in some cases of little consequence; but for young cooks at all events it is a very foolish plan, since it so often leads to a failure; whilst for old ones it ensures an early destruction of their organ of taste, which ought to be husbanded with the greatest care. This is obviously the result, because if dishes are made in the careless way to which I have alluded, they must be tasted again and again, until they satisfy the palate of the cook; while, if they are prepared from ingredients of accurately known measure or weight, they will so seldom vary that it is hardly necessary to taste them at all, or at all events only once. From constant tasting the palled organ of taste becomes insensible to all but very strong flavours, and the consequence is that dishes are sent to table which call forth complaints from the heads of the house; and these complaints being conveyed to a servant who has no *certain* guide in the shape of an accurate receipt, she is unable to rectify her mistake, and on the next attempt perhaps falls into the opposite error. Whenever, therefore, a cook works by any receipt not her own, she should follow it closely for her own sake, or if she can improve upon it, let her do so; but then *let her set down the exact varia-*

tion from the original. In this way she will always have a certain guide; and, though she may lose a few minutes a day in measuring and weighing, yet she may console herself that her hand will last much longer than her palate, and that, by the regular adoption of the practice, she will be able to fulfil her duties for many years longer than she would do if she drew upon her delicate nerves of taste every ten minutes. Perhaps she will say that she does not intend to spend all her life roasting herself, but that she hopes some day to be the mistress of a family. If such is her intention, and she is sure of carrying it out, this argument will not apply; but even then I should strongly recommend her to wait until she has secured a competency, and, in waiting, to take care of her stomach; for no one is more miserably situated than a cook so accustomed to rich food that she cannot live upon plain dishes, and yet cannot pay for any thing else. In every way, therefore, *for her own sake,* the cook should study quantity, and carry out her knowledge in practice; while, for the sake of her master and mistress, she can scarcely ever pass an hour without having recourse to her weights and scales. These must, of course, be provided for her; and if they are to be used as here advised, they must be of the kind shown at *fig.* 109, which should always be on a shelf or table ready for use. If the cook has to take out a pair of scales from a closet or drawer, and set them up, before weighing any article, there can be no wonder that she avoids the trouble. The cost of these scales is from 16s. to 25s., but they soon pay for themselves; and as they weigh any thing from one quarter of an ounce to twenty pounds, they serve for every purpose. We all know perfectly well the rudest kind of scales may be made to answer the same purpose, but it will be found that, without making the thing easy, a cook will always shirk this part of her duty; and indeed in every case with servants, unless they have the best tools which can be supplied, they are almost certain to excuse their neglect by laying the fault upon those who will not give them the "proper things" for their business. The various weights and measures will be found given at the end of this volume.

23. WITH REGARD TO QUALITY, the cook has less to do than with the other elements concerned, unless she is also in the habit of going to market. Still, even when she does not purchase the things required in the kitchen, she will be often called upon for her opinion of their quality; and she should then be able to give it to her mistress without hesitation. This, however, requires considerable experience; and if she has not had it, she cannot be expected to be able to guide when

she herself requires a leader. In the *Economical Housekeeper* the cook, as well as the mistress, will however find ample directions for instructing herself in what is required; but, nevertheless, practice is here of far more importance than the best precepts in the world.

24. As a Nice Sense of Taste is the great secret of the first-rate cook, when joined to the observance of the three elements of success already alluded to, so it should be most carefully educated and prized. I have already mentioned that this sense is easily palled or dulled by constantly calling upon it, and that for this reason it should be as seldom taxed as possible. It is well known that even the best judge fails to distinguish port-wine from sherry after a dozen successive tastes of them indiscriminately, when blindfolded and without the sense of smell to aid him. This, therefore, shows how readily the palate is confused, and how necessary it is to husband its powers. But besides this abuse of the sense of taste from satiety, there is also the fact that the taste of every individual is suffering a change, so that we like this year what was perhaps distasteful a few years ago. Hence the cook requires to consider, when she is drawing upon her own resources, *not only whether her concoction is pleasant to herself, but whether it will please her employers.* She must recollect that her organ and their organs are liable to change in the regular course of events, and dependent also upon the seasons, upon health, and sometimes upon the caprice of fashion. A constant necessity, therefore, exists for ascertaining the degree of success of her efforts from day to day, and this can only be done either by means of the mistress or of her fellow-servant waiting at table. If the cook can depend upon the latter, the intelligence will be more regularly conveyed; and not only this, but the servant waiting can detect the *general* success or failure of any dish or dishes with even more certainty than the mistress herself, because the latter is influenced by her own palate in judging of others, while the servant is not. It is obvious that a dish may be liked by all but the mistress, yet it would be condemned by the single dissentient if she were the sole organ of communication with the cook, and in spite of the fact that, if she were aware of her mistake, she would be the last to wish the change made; for I believe most fully, that in nine cases out of ten the mistress of a family willingly sacrifices her own taste to that of the other members, whether husband or children. Let every cook, therefore, while in health, take care to avoid spoiling her taste by over-use; let her also do all in her power to keep in health, which is absolutely essential to preserve the organ

and lastly, let her on all occasions remember that she is preparing her dishes for a variable and uncertain set of palates, and trim her sails accordingly, by looking out ahead for every change in their likes and dislikes.

25. CLEANLINESS AND PROPER VENTILATION, AS WELL AS LIGHTING, are no less important than the above essentials; but they merely require to be mentioned in order to secure attention. With regard to the first of them, it will always be inculcated by the employers for their own sakes; but it is no less advisable for the sake of the cook, who, if she neglects it, will never be able to send her more delicate things to table looking well, however palatable they may be; and as the eye very often leads the palate, she will disgust the latter at once. With regard to ventilation and lighting, it is manifest that, if the cook is oppressed with the heat and steam arising from the chief scene of her labours, her bodily health will suffer, as well as her temper; and we all know by sad experience how completely a loss of the last-mentioned faculty ensures the defeat of the best concerted plans. All this, however, is fully dilated upon in the next page. With regard to lighting also, a strong light is essential to some departments of cookery, and should always be within the reach of the cook; but for many it is by no means necessary, and only adds, when artificial, to the otherwise sufficiently-high temperature of the kitchen.

26. THE COOK'S BOOK is a weekly account kept by her, in small ruled pages, of her disbursements for pot-herbs, or other petty and frequently-recurring items, for which the mistress will not always like to be disturbed. In the country, where there is no shop at hand ready to supply these demands, no such book is generally kept; but in towns it is almost a necessity, though the more it is confined in its operations the better for the pocket of the employer. In many even small establishments this book extends to butter, milk, cheese, and green-grocery; but it is far better to let these articles be supplied from some neighbouring shopkeeper fixed on by the mistress, and to let him send in his bill weekly, to be paid by her. When this is done, there remain very few things indeed which will require a book, for even the herbs should be included in the green-grocer's weekly bill; and therefore, in reality, this book, so much dreaded by mistresses, may be dispensed with altogether if they will only take care to call in their bills weekly, and pay them themselves.

27. A GREASE-POT AND WASH-TUB are allowed in many families as the perquisites of the cook; the consequences often being that a

very large proportion of good dripping is put into the former, and plenty of serviceable vegetables and meat also into the latter. It seems like playing a very selfish part to prevent the cook from selling what would otherwise be wasted, and therefore, if on trial any individual is found to be trustworthy, the practice may be allowed without loss; but in all cases it is better in engaging a cook to arrange with her by stipulating against either the one or the other, leaving the door open for a future relaxation of the rule in case of good conduct. But even then I believe the temptation almost too great, and that very few servants are to be trusted with this discretionary power when their own interest clashes with that of their employers. There are always, in the summer, pieces of meat which may be reclaimed from " going" by care and management, but which may also be as easily condemned to the wash-tub; and this is the first step in a downward course, soon followed, in many cases, by the constant and regular sacrifice of " broken bread," good bones capable of making plenty of stock, and cold potatoes. If, therefore, there is the money to spare, it is better to fix an extra sum for the cook, and give away these doubtful articles to the poor; and if, on the other hand, rigid economy demands a stricter supervision, I am quite sure that no grease-pot or wash-tub ought to be allowed.

28. THE KITCHEN is usually included within the area of the house, though in country houses the contrary is often the case, and with the advantage of avoiding the smell of cooking. But I am not now about to describe the locality of this department, but rather the fittings which are required in order to place the cook in a condition to perform her duties with advantage to herself and her mistress. It is an old adage, that " bad workmen complain of their tools;" and in this case it is applicable, inasmuch as a bad cook is never satisfied with her kitchen arrangements, however good they may be. But, on the other hand, a good cook will scarcely be able to do justice to her powers unless she is allowed to have a proper and sufficient kitchen-range, with the other requisites presently to be detailed. Light in the kitchen, both by day and night, is one very important item that should always be attended to, and also a proper ventilation. If the cook is half suffocated she cannot possibly do her work properly; and her stomach will be so upset, to say nothing of her temper, that she will be incapable of tasting and seasoning her dishes to suit the palates of her employers. Air, therefore, should be supplied by the kind of valve known as Sheringham's valve, which admits air without

a draught. Arnott's valve may also be introduced with advantage, especially with a close grate, as in this there is little ventilation up the chimney, and the only escape for the foul air is through the fire itself. The comparative economy of coal and gas is fully described in "*The Housekeeper*," to which the reader is referred for its particulars. If gas is preferred, it will be necessary to fix the proper apparatus instead of the usual cooking grate. An immense variety of these last is now made by the different ironmongers, without much real or apparent advantage in any one over the rest. The principal points of difference are these, viz.—1st, Open fires, called kitchen-ranges, with oven and boiler; for the three sizes of those suited to different families, see *figs*. 67, 69, and 70. 2ndly, Cooking stoves, being closed or nearly closed fireplaces (*fig*. 68), with hot plate (A), oven (B), boiler and hot closet (C); also steam kettles (F F F) for vegetables, and a large steam closet (G) for airing linen, warming dishes, &c.; E, a slide for regulating the fire. This is a very complete apparatus, and is sold by Burton of Oxford-street, and by Deane and Dray, as well as other makers, at the prices annexed to this section. For large families this is a very economical stove, and a moderate fire will serve for a very large dinner; but it will not send roast meat to table to suit the palate of a *gourmand*, nor will it compete in economy with a cottage range when wanted for a small family. 3rdly, GAS STOVES, which certainly perform their task very well, and from the ventilation they afford they roast to a turn; but, as I have before remarked, scarcely economically in this department, though, as a whole, they may perhaps compete with coal fires. Their forms are given in *fig*. 72, in which A represents a complete apparatus, intended to bake and roast at the same time in the interior, and to steam on the top; B is similar in all respects, only that it will not both roast and bake at the same time, having only one oven. But by means of slides arranging the air-draught it will do either as desired; C is a very convenient little grate, which may be used either with coal or gas, the former being more suited to the winter when warmth is wanted for the kitchen, whilst the latter, if used in the summer, keeps the kitchen cool and comfortable.

29. A HOT PLATE will be wanted for all kitchens where cooking in any degree of refinement is carried on; in close stoves it is generally heated by steam, as shown in *fig*. 68; or by gas, as in *fig*. 72 A. When, however, there is an open kitchen-range, a separate hot plate is heated by a distinct little stove, and is set in any convenient situation (see *fig*. 67).

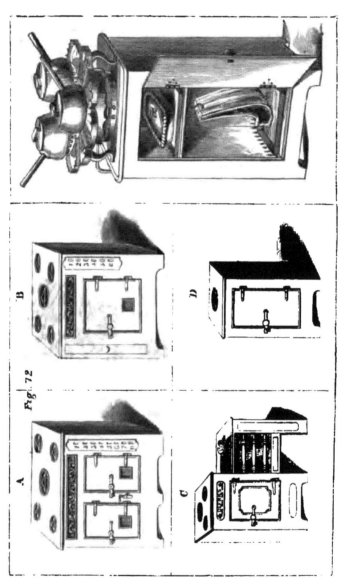

Fig. 72

A   B

C   D

COOKING STOVES HEATED BY GAS.

P. 23.

30. A SMOKE-JACK, as shown in *fig.* 67, is by many considered an indispensable adjunct to the kitchen, while others regard it with abhorrence, on account of the noise which it often makes in its revolutions.

It consists of a circular fan fixed in the chimney flue, about four or five feet above the mantelpiece, which is made to revolve by the smoke, or rather by the heated air as it ascends. Its spindle is connected with the horizontal rod shown in the figure, over the shelf, by simple clockwork machinery, and this again works the spit by means of the chain there shown. Altogether it is a very simple and efficient apparatus for turning the spit, and when the flue can be constructed of a size 14 inches each way, it is the best which can be selected; but in small houses the flues are often limited to 9 inches in one direction, and from them the smoke-jack must be excluded for that reason, its place being supplied by the bottle-jack.

31. DRESSERS AND CLOSETS are required by the cook for her plates and dishes, as well as for her spice-boxes, jars, &c., and should always be provided for her; they are invariably made of wood, either oak or painted deal. Their construction is so simple that they will not require any description here; and the cost only need be given in the annexed table of kitchen fittings, which consists of four separate sets, proportioned to the four houses alluded to at page 4.

PRICE OF KITCHEN FITTINGS.—ESTIMATE No. 1.

Full-sized kitchen-range, complete, with oven and boiler, sliding-cheek, and wrought-iron bars. See *fig.* 67.

ft. in.										£ s.	to	£ s.
4 0	...	...	...	..	...	...	...	...	...	4 12	to	5 10
4 4	...	...	...	...	...	...	...	...	...		...	6 6
4 6	...	...	...	...	...	...	...	...	...		...	7 0
5 0	...	...	...	...	...	...	...	...	...		...	7 17

Smoke-jack complete, with chain, pulleys, spits, &c., wrought-iron main				
wheel, with door and frame for chimney	...	...	...	...£6 10
If outside movement	... ...	...	...	... 18 0
Hot plate, from	... ...	...	...	£2 to 5 0

Or, economic ventilating kitchen range (see *fig.* 68), with hot plate for boiling saucepans, frying, &c.; large oven for pastry, joints, bread, &c.; hot closet for keeping dinners warm, plates, dishes, &c.; sliding front to fire, to act as a blower, or for keeping the heat from the cook when stewing or preserving; steam kettles for vegetables, &c.; and a large steam closet for airing linen, &c.

If with wrought iron boilers, panelled coverings, roller front, and roller slide oven, but not including steam work,—

ft. in.										£. s. d.
4 0	...	...	...	...	...	...	...	...	...	13 10 0
4 3	...	...	...	...	...	...	...	...	...	15 0 0
4 6	...	...	...	...	...	...	...	...	...	16 10 0
4 9	...	...	...	...	...	...	...	...	...	18 0 0
5 0	...	...	...	...	...	—	...	...	...	19 10 0
5 3	...	...	...	...	...	...	...	...	...	21 0 0
5 6	...	...	...	...	...	...	...	...	..	22 10 0
5 9	...	...	...	...	...	...	...	...	...	24 0 0
6 0	...	...	...	...	...	...	...	...	...	25 0 0

Steam closet, with copper bottom: 24 inches wide, £4; 30 inches ditto, £5.

Steam kettles, with pipes, tap, valve, &c.: first kettle, £3; each additional kettle, 30s.

Fixing grates about 6s. per foot in width. The expense of the supply-cistern and pipes depends upon the locality, and is not included in the above estimate.

							£ s.	£ s.
Dresser	...	...	...	...	...	...	5 0	to 20 0
Closets	...	...	...	...	...	...	4 0	to 10 0
Hanging-flap and hooks		...	...	...	...	...	1 0	to 2 0

ESTIMATE No. 2.

Kitchen-range, plan as before, but of reduced size and price, viz. :—

ft. in.									£ s.	£ s.
3 4	...	...	...	...	...	...	...	...	4 5	to 4 17
3 6	...	...	...	...	...	...	...	...	4 7	to 5 0
3 9	...	...	...	...	...	...	...	...	4 11	to 5 4
Smoke-jack	...	...	...	...	...	...	...	...	5 0	to 6 0
Hot plate	...	...	...	...	...	...	...	...	...	... 2 0

Or, economic ventilating kitchen-range, made on the same principle as that above described, with copper boilers, but without the hot closet under the oven, or roller oven shelves,—

ft. in.										£ s. d.
3 0	...	...	...	...	...	...	...	...	...	7 15 0
3 3	...	...	...	...	...	...	...	...	...	8 6 6
3 6	...	...	...	...	...	...	...	...	...	9 7 6
3 9	...	...	...	...	...	...	...	...	...	9 14 0
Dresser of painted deal	...	...	...	...	...	...	...£3	to 5 0 0
Closets	...	...	...	...	...	...	...	...£4	to 6 0 0
Hanging-flap, hooks, &c.	...	...	...	...	...	...	...	1 0 0

ESTIMATE No. 3.

Medium-sized kitchen-range (see fig. 69), with oven and boiler :—

ft. in.									£ s.	£ s.
3 0	...	...	...	...	...	...	...	...	4 0	to 4 10
3 6	...	...	...	...	...	...	...	...	4 3	to 4 13
Dresser	...	...	...	...	...	...	...	2 0	to 3 0
Closets, &c.	...	...	...	...	...	...	...	...	3 0

ESTIMATE No. 4.

Cottage range (*fig.* 70), with oven and cast-iron boiler, and without sliding cheek,—

ft. in.										£ s. d.
2 6	...	...	...	...	...	...	...	...	...	2 0 0
2 8	...	...	...	...	...	...	...	...	...	2 2 0
2 10	...	...	...	...	...	...	...	...	...	2 5 0
3 0	...	...	...	...	...	...	...	...	...	2 7 6
Dresser	...	...	...	...	...	...	...	...	...	2 0 0
Closets, &c.	...	...	...	...	...	...	...	...	...	2 10 0

ESTIMATE No. 5.—FOR GAS STOVES.

			£ s. d.
Cast-iron (roasting, baking, boiling, and steaming) full size ...			26 6 0
Ditto	ditto	smallest ...	16 0 0
Ditto	ditto	third size, Fig. 72, B. ...	8 0 0
Ditto	with open fire also	Fig. 72, C. .	9 0 0
Wrought-iron		small, Fig. 72, D. ...	2 10 0

32. THE BACK-KITCHEN OR SCULLERY, when it is used for brewing or washing, as well as for the ordinary kitchen purposes, should always be external to the house if possible, in order that the steam may escape through the roof. For the water a sink is required, which consists of a flat platform of tiles or bricks, about three or four feet wide, by two feet six inches, with a slightly raised and rounded edge of oak-quartering. This communicates with a drain by means of a bell-trap, over which should be a water-cock if there is a cistern; and when there is a supply of hot water, that also should be laid on. If the house is self-dependent for its water supply, a pump of each sort is generally fixed in the back-kitchen, one of which draws up the spring water from the well, and the other from the soft-water cistern. Besides these pumps, there are usually in well-appointed houses a copper and an open fireplace, to be used as an extra fire when large dinner parties are given, and when, for instance, the close stove is fixed in the kitchen, in which roasting is not capable of being carried on to that degree of perfection which is then desired. Galvanized iron boilers are sometimes set instead of coppers, but they are liable to "iron-mould" linen boiled in them, and they are therefore objected to. In other respects—that is, for brewing or for cooking—this kind of iron is quite equal if not superior to copper, as it is not liable to be dissolved by acids like copper; or, if acted on, it is not injurious to the system, but rather advantageous. The list of back-kitchen fittings, therefore, will stand as under, with the prices according to the nature of the *ménage*:—

BACK-KITCHEN FITTINGS.

	1st.	2nd.	3rd.	4th.
	£ s.	£ s.	£ s.	£ s.
Sink with hot and cold water cocks, bell-trap, &c.	6 10	4 15	8 10	2 10
Well pump	4 10	3 10	2 10	2 0
Soft water forcing-pump	6 10	4 10	8 10	2 10
Washing copper or iron boiler, with furnace grate, set complete	4 10	2 15	1 10	1 0
Plate rack	2 10	2 0	1 10	1 0

33. THE KNIFE AND SHOE HOUSE is a small back office in which boots and shoes are cleaned; and, where a rotary knife-cleaner is not used, a knife-board is fixed for cleaning knives with brick-dust. In most houses, even where the knife-cleaner is used, such a board is wanted in addition, for the purpose of cleaning common kitchen knives when they are stained with vinegar, &c., or for taking out accidental deep stains in the best knives. The cost of this board is only a few shillings, say 5s. to 6s.

34. A DUST-HOLE is also required in all houses to receive the dust and ashes from the house; and in those families where economy is studied, provision is made for the proper sifting or "riddling" of these ashes, by which the cinders are reserved for future use. The circular sieve, with a wire bottom, is a very rude instrument for this purpose; and as, in using it, the housemaid must necessarily be covered with dust, the consequence is, that the ashes are very commonly put away without undergoing this necessary operation. Next to this in utility comes the large and simple riddling machine, which is merely a wooden framed covering to the dust-hole, but having a wire bottom and a handle, by which it may be shaken, while the housemaid stands at a distance. Here, again, however, she is somewhat incommoded, but not so much so as with the hand-sifter. Mr. Kent, the inventor of the rotary knife-cleaner, has patented a CINDER SIFTER also on the rotary principle, which does away with all the housemaid's objections; and, what is still better, *compels* the adoption of the process, because by no other means can the ashes be placed in the dust-hole. Its operation is thus most certain and effective. The unsifted cinders are thrown into the upper part of the machine; a few turns of the handle separate the ashes from the cinders in the most perfect manner, without the least dust or dirt escaping from the sifter; the refuse falls into a moveable box, and the cinders are actually deposited in the coal-scuttle without the possibility of loss, or mixing with the ashes. It is sold at 329, Strand. In houses limited for yard room, this machine is of great service in preventing dust and smell, whilst the whole box

can be removed to the dust-cart and emptied there. In country houses the dust-hole is generally of considerable size, and often communicates with an open cesspool, being intended to absorb the contents as they are discharged into it. This is better than the keeping the two apart, and at the same time exposed to the air; but it is by no means a healthy plan, and is not to be recommended. The cesspool is easily covered in, and may be readily emptied when necessary, by removing a stone set in a wooden or iron frame.

PRICES OF DUST-BINS AND SIFTERS.

Dust-bin with common sifter.

Wooden bin	...	...	...	...	...	...	...	...	£1 10
Sifter	...	...	...	...	...	...	...	...	0 5
									1 15

Dust-bin with sifting cover.

Wooden bin	...	...	...	...	...	...	...	...	£1 10
Sifter with handle	...	...	...	...	...	...	...	...	1 5
									2 15

Kent's patent cinder sifter and dust-bin.

Complete, 1st size	...	...	..	...	...	...	...	...	£3 8
Ditto, 2nd ditto	...	...	...	...	...	...	...	...	4 4

Coal cellars should be built in the most convenient situation for access both from without and from within; and they should, if possible, be of such dimensions as to contain from six months' to a year's consumption, because coal is almost always far cheaper in summer than during the winter season, and therefore a stock should be laid in. It is a good plan to divide this space into separate sections, so that each part shall be cleared off, leaving no small coal, before the next is commenced.

35. THE LARDER, which is the place set apart for keeping fresh provisions in, and also, in most cases, for the salting of pork, beef, &c., should be placed where it can have a thorough draught, and where it is sheltered from the sun. A northern aspect is therefore the most suitable, or, next to that, an easterly one. The thorough draught cannot always be procured directly; but if it cannot in that way, a large air-drain may be carried under the floor to the opposite side of the house, where a grating may be fixed, and thus a free draught may be obtained. Underground larders are seldom efficient for the keeping of meat, because this perfect draught is not attainable except in windy weather, when there is little difficulty in effecting its preservation; but in moist and muggy weather the air is quite stagnant in the basement story of a town house, and consequently, though tolerably cool,

the air is not rapidly changed, and putrefaction goes on without let or hindrance. To fit up a larder for a small house merely requires a number of deal shelves and a door, of which the panels are replaced by plates of perforated zinc, of a pattern sufficiently close to prevent the entrance of flies, and yet large enough to admit the air freely. Where there is also a window, it should in like manner be guarded by similar sheets of zinc.

36. The Utensils required for the cookery of each department, will be fully described under the different heads of Roasting, Baking, Boiling, Stewing, &c.

CHAP. III.—THE PREPARATION OF FOOD BY KEEPING.

Sect. 1.—General Remarks.

36. A Great many Articles of Food are the better for keeping a longer or shorter time, varying, according to their nature, to the state of the weather, and to the place where they are kept. Among the chief of these are—butcher's meat, venison, game, some kinds of poultry, and a few kinds of fish. Even some vegetables are the better for a few hours' keeping after they are brought in from the garden, such as young potatoes and Jerusalem artichokes; but this is an exception to the general rule, which enforces the necessity of dressing vegetables as soon as possible after they are gathered. On the other hand, many fruits require keeping for some time, such as apples, and pears of the kinds called keepers, medlars, and some others. The best mode, therefore, of keeping these several articles will here be given.

Sect. 2.—Essentials for Keeping.

37. The Larder has been described at page 27; and when such a room is well situated, meat, &c., may be kept to great advantage. But in many cases, especially in towns, this cannot be managed, and all that can be devoted to the purpose is a small box of wood with perforated zinc sides, and called a "safe." This is often placed in a small room or closet, perhaps adjoining the kitchen; and then it is not surprising that meat becomes putrid, in warm weather, the day after it comes from the butcher. When there is a back-yard, this safe may often be suspended there with advantage during the part of the day when the sun is shaded off by the surrounding buildings; or per-

manently, if it is entirely excluded. Dry heat is not so injurious as the moist, yet warm, atmosphere, which always prevails in underground kitchens; and even a much higher temperature, if dry, will do less mischief than one comparatively cool, but moist; that is to say, if the latter is above 60 or 70 degrees Fahrenheit, for below that point decomposition does not go on with any degree of rapidity. It must be remembered, that almost all kinds of animal food intended for roasting require a certain amount of decomposition to make them tender, the only exception being those which are, in the first place, sufficiently so when quite fresh; and, in the second, are so prone to rapid decomposition, that they are not to be kept without great risk: such are veal and some kinds of poultry, which in moderately cool weather will not keep more than a few days, and in summer are not always to be depended on for twenty-four hours. For this reason, in frosty weather meat may be kept for an indefinite time without altering its condition; and in long frosts there is scarcely a possibility of getting it into a state fit for the spit. Hence it is always desirable to maintain in the larder a temperature considerably above the freezing point, and below 50, or at all events 60 degrees, with a good current of air free from moisture.

SECT. 3.—DIRECTIONS FOR KEEPING.

38. Whenever these conditions can be obtained, meat, the produce of mature animals, may be kept with advantage, if it is constantly watched and protected from the flies, for a period of time varying, according to the weather, from a few days to three weeks. It must also *be kept dry*, by wiping the moist parts every night and morning, taking care to separate all the crevices and dry them to the bottom. Beyond the above time no meat improves by keeping, if it is not frozen; but in that case nearly the whole period during which it has been in that state must be deducted, and the time calculated independently of it. There appear to be two kinds of decomposition in animal substances, which are quite distinct from each other, and not always depending upon the state of the atmosphere. In the one kind, the change begins in the parts in contact with the air, especially in those which are the most moist. From these it gradually extends to the deeper parts; but so slowly, that very often the surface is quite putrid, and greenish-brown in colour, while the parts round the bone are as sweet as ever, and maintain their original red. This is a true oxygenation, and is the result of keeping healthy animal substances

in a good and proper current of dry air. But in the other kind of decomposition, either the whole mass changes together, or the deep parts go first, and gradually extend their influence to the surface. This is clearly not the result of a union with a fresh supply of oxygen, because that gas would surely affect the surface more than the interior; but it appears to be a new arrangement of the elements already existing in the substance, by which ammonia, and some others of the changeable organic compounds, are evolved. It generally, but not always, occurs in hot and thundery weather, but always with the thermometer above 60 degrees; there is almost always a crackling feel given to the hand in pressing meat when in this state, depending upon the bubbles of gas confined within its meshes; and the smell is of a peculiarly nauseous kind, accompanied with a pungent impression upon the mucous membrane of the nose, which is not very agreeable. When meat is in this state it is very unwholesome, and is even unfit for pigs or dogs. It should, therefore, be buried deeply beneath the surface, out of all risk of affecting the health of the neighbouring inhabitants.

39. WHEN FROZEN MEAT, POULTRY, OR FISH are to be dressed, they should be gradually thawed through their whole substance, either by placing them in a warm kitchen for some hours, or by immersing them in lukewarm water, and keeping it at that temperature by the addition of more warm water as the frozen meat cools it. Meat and poultry are better warmed in air, because the water takes out a certain portion of their juices; but fish will be more easily thawed in water, and without loss of flavour or substance.

40. BEFORE DRESSING MEAT AND POULTRY which have been hung for any length of time, they should be washed with a little strong salt and water; and if any parts of the former are much decomposed, which may be known by their high scent, a little strong distilled vinegar should be rubbed into them, and then, after remaining on the surface for a few minutes, it may be washed off with salt and water Game may be treated in the same way; but even without this precaution it is astonishing how the act of roasting restores the condition of this kind of food. Many people who eat their game with a relish, considering it exactly "kept to a day," would turn from it with disgust if they saw it when preparing for the spit; and therefore the young cook must be careful how she rejects any of these delicate kinds of fare as "too far gone," unless she has the authority of some one competent to judge.

41. THE COOK SHOULD WATCH most carefully all the meat and game under her care, and inform her mistress as soon as she sees the slightest sign by which she may consider it is approaching the proper termination of keeping. Butcher's meat shows its state by the smell, by the touch, and by the look. The slightest taint in warm weather is enough to put the cook on her guard, and especially if the meat begins to feel tender on pressure; if it is turning green on the surface, also, she must consider it as a very sure sign; and especially if, at the same time, the stiffness of the joint is giving way, or bending. Thus, a little practice, with attention to these signs, will soon render her expert, and she may always at first be careful to err on the safe side. In deciding upon the time to keep game, some people hang the feathered kinds up by their tails, and consider they are fit to dress as soon as they drop, and leave their tails behind them. For those who like game "rather high," this is not a bad test in the cool weather of autumn; but in the early part of the season, the feathers adhere too long to give this rule any value, or rather it may be said that, if adhered to, it will cause the spoiling of many brace of grouse and partridges, which will seldom bear much keeping until after the middle of October.

42. FISH will sometimes be the better for a day's keeping, or, in cool weather, even two days will not injure its flavour. It should, however, always be kept in a cool place; and it may generally be hung up with advantage, rather than to deposit it on the floor, as is generally done. If, however, it is of a kind which would be injured by becoming dry—as, for instance, turbot—the latter place is the best; but cod-fish and haddock are better suspended. Ice will always keep fish for an indefinite time, if such is desired; but when it is of a kind which is the better for keeping, the ice will suspend the good effects of that operation, and should not therefore be had recourse to longer than necessary.

43. WHEN MEAT, POULTRY, OR GAME is evidently in a state which will not allow it to be kept until the time when it will be wanted, it may be parboiled or half-roasted, which will postpone its "going" for at least two or even three days. It must be boiled or roasted for nearly half the proper time in the first process; and, in the second, it will generally take about three-quarters of that ordered for it in the usual way.

44. APPLES AND PEARS should be stored in a dry room, not exposed to any draught of air, by which they are dried too much, and become shrivelled on the surface. They should also be kept in the dark, if it

is desired to postpone the time of their becoming ripe. They should be arranged on wooden shelves, in such a way that each apple is distinct from its neighbours—contact with each other being very apt to cause decay. Every week, at least, they should be looked over carefully, and the rotten fruit picked out. Some people keep them in straw or sand, but neither of these modes is equal to the plan described above.

45. Potatoes and Jerusalem Artichokes are kept either stored in a dark and dry cellar, heaped up in a corner or stored in casks; or out of doors, in heaps or "buries" covered over with earth, and sometimes thatched. A shallow trench is first made in a situation free from wet—that is to say, well drained. In this the potatoes are heaped up in a pyramidal form, at as high an angle as they will sustain without falling. The earth removed from the trench is next laid over them, and beaten down with a spade so as to form a smooth sloping surface on all sides, which in some soils is a sufficient protection, but in loose sands will demand the addition of ordinary thatch.

CHAP. IV.—GENERAL REMARKS ON ROASTING AND BAKING.

SECT. I.—GENERAL OBSERVATIONS.

46. Although boiling may appear a more simple operation than roasting, and though it is certainly more easy of application when the utensils are at hand; yet the latter is the first step in the science of cookery, since it requires only a fire, while for boiling a waterproof vessel must be added. In savage life roasting or baking is common enough, a fire of dry branches being first made, and then the meat to be cooked is suspended near it by transfixing it with a straight stick, and supporting this upon two forked sticks stuck in the ground. For baking they scoop a hole in the ground and make a fire in it, then, after thoroughly heating it, the fire is removed, the meat introduced, and covered over with a flat stone, or with branches when this is not at hand. With these rude methods a joint may be cooked with a considerable approach to perfection, quite equalling the most successful efforts of any cook *who does not baste her meat*, an operation which the savage cannot perform, because he has nothing to catch the dripping in, nor, if caught, has he a spoon to baste with.

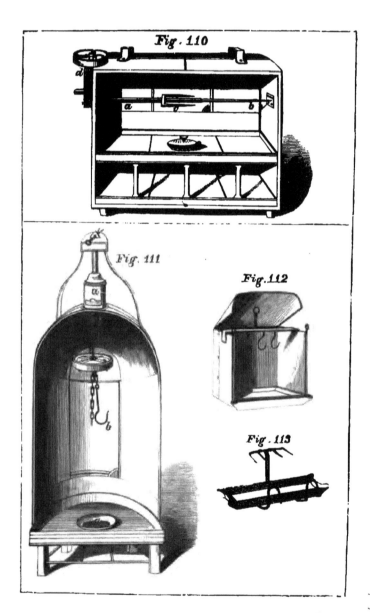

Fig. 110

Fig. 111

Fig. 112

Fig. 113

ROASTING APPARATUS.

SECT. 2.—UTENSILS.

47. FOR ROASTING OR BAKING, the kind of grate is of the utmost importance: it being impossible without a good one to turn out a well-dressed joint to advantage. It may be said that an open fire will always dress a joint of meat: and so it will, but not a large or small one at the choice of the cook, unless the fire is capable of being made narrow or broad, shallow or deep, according to the shape of the joint and its mode of suspension. The various kinds of kitchen-ranges will be found described at page 22; and the comparative cost of fuel, including gas, in the *Economical Housekeeper*. It is therefore unnecessary here to return to the subject; but the reader may be reminded that, when alluding to roasting, I mean at an open fire; and by baking, I intend the process as conducted in an iron oven attached to a grate, or in a baker's oven. Unless, therefore, any specific remarks refer to roasting or baking by *gas*, the above methods of cookery are always to be understood.

48. A SPIT OR HOOK for suspending the meat, with some kind of machinery for turning it, is the next in importance to the fire. Of these, the horizontal spit, worked by the smoke-jack, is the most perfect (described at page 23, and illustrated by *fig.* 67). In every case the article to be roasted is either suspended from above by a hook, or string tied to it, or it is transfixed by a horizontal spit (see *fig.* 110, A B), and kept from turning round upon it by driving the points of the slide (C) into the end; this slide travels freely upon the spit, but the shape of this being angular, and the socket of the slide fitting accurately, it cannot slip round, and consequently when pushed well into the meat it keeps it firmly fixed upon the spit. The next thing is to provide for the regular and constant rotation: this is done in the most simple way by a piece of cord, which, after it has been twisted in one direction, has a tendency to untwist itself, and so keeps up its action for a certain time, but requires constant attention. Next to this comes the bottle-jack (*fig.* 111 A), which, by means of common clock-work, keeps up a constant revolution of any article attached to the hook (B). The objection to this kind is, that a fire can with difficulty be made equally strong at the top and bottom, and, consequently, the joint is roasted either too much or too little in one or other of its ends. But being of a comparatively low price it is often used, and succeeds well enough for poultry, game, or small joints. The horizontal roasting apparatus (*fig.* 110) answers every purpose; and for a small family,

D

not requiring large haunches of mutton or venison to be dressed, it is quite equal to the smoke-jack. The spit shown at *fig.* 110 is the ordinary one, which serves for joints, or for poultry or game; and one on the same principle is used also for these articles with the smoke-jack; but in addition a cradle-spit (see *fig.* 67) is frequently employed, so as to include certain stuffed joints in its embrace without perforating them. It is not, however, very often wanted, and may well be dispensed with. In this kind of apparatus the spit is made to revolve by clock-work at (D), wound up by a key in the same way as the bottle-jack.

49. BESIDES THE SPIT AND JACK, A SCREEN must be used to prevent the loss of heat, which would otherwise occur by radiation. If a smoke-jack is used, a large screen is brought up near the fire, similar in form to *fig.* 110, but somewhat larger, and generally made to hold and warm the dishes and plates intended for dinner. In order to have it of the most perfect kind, it should be made of wood, which is a non-conductor of caloric, and lined with polished tin, which is a good reflector of it; but, in general, it is made of tin, and painted on the outside, which is, however, a bad plan, as the paint increases the tendency to radiate heat. If, therefore, it is not made of wood, it should be left with as much metallic polish as possible *on both sides*. The two forms (*figs.* 110 and 111) are those usually adopted, and answer the purpose exceedingly well, though not quite equal to the large screen adapted for the smoke-jack, because they do not so completely keep off all the cold draughts of air from doors and windows, and these cool the joint almost as much as the loss by radiation.

50. A DRIPPING-PAN AND BASTING-LADLE will always be necessary, the former to collect, and the latter to use the dripping upon the joint. In the dripping-pan a well (*figs.* 110 E, 111 E) is provided to catch the fat and gravy as they fall, the whole surface inclining to it; this well is covered with a hinged-lid, so as to keep any cinders out. The ladle is merely a long iron spoon, tinned.

51. IN THE OVEN attached to grates there is very little to describe, it being a mere chamber of iron (*fig.* 68) with flues conveying the heated products of the fire round it, at the will of the cook. A damper cuts off these, or otherwise; and in many grates the cook is enabled, by raking the hot coals into a chamber provided for the purpose, to increase the heat very considerably. For baking, all the steam is purposely confined; but when these ovens are used for roasting, certain ventilators are opened, and these cause a current of air, which

certainly takes off, in some measure, the peculiarly rank taste generally accompanying this kind of cookery.

52. DUTCH AND AMERICAN OVENS, AND TOASTING OVENS suspended to the bars, are also used to roast certain articles before a small fire, without revolution on the spit. They are very useful for small families. (See *figs.* 112 and 113, which represent the Dutch oven and the toaster.)

53. PRICE OF ROASTING UTENSILS.

	£ s. d.		£ s. d.
Smoke-jack, complete (see page 23)	... 5 0 0	to	10 0 0
Meat-screen for ditto, of wood, lined with tin ...	... 1 10 0	„	3 10 0
Ditto, with hot closet, from	... 4 10 0	„	7 0 0
Dripping-pan and stand	... 0 15 0	„	1 5 0
Horizontal spit and jack, with meat-screen, dripping-pan, and plate-warmer, (see *fig.* 110)	... 3 3 0	„	4 10 0
Bottle-jack and screen, with dripping-pan (see *fig.* 111)	0 18 0	„	1 8 0
Ditto with hot closet	... 1 16 0	„	2 0 0
American oven	... 0 10 0	„	0 15 0
Dutch oven (see *fig.* 112)	... 0 4 6	„	0 6 0
Hanging toaster (see *fig.* 113)...	... 0 1 6	„	0 4 6

SECT. 3.—SPITTING AND TRUSSING.

54. Spitting is merely the insertion of the spit; but even this operation, simple as it appears, requires some little nicety. If the article is to be suspended, it is only necessary to hang it up by its smallest end, because the fire being generally stronger below than above, it will, in this way, be more likely to be thoroughly done. The horizontal spit should be kept very clean, and tolerably sharp, and in introducing it, be careful to pass it as near as possible through the *centre of the joint,* so that, in revolving, it may present all its sides at equal distances from the fire. A neglect of this precaution causes the projecting part to be overdone, or the receding part to be the reverse.

55. THE CRADLE-SPIT is intended to include large kinds of poultry, or rolled and stuffed joints, &c., without transfixing them. It, however, cannot be used without leaving its mark wherever it touches, and is therefore very objectionable on that account.

56. POULTRY AND GAME require to be trussed before they are roasted, which is done with the aid of skewers, trussing needles, and fine twine. When poultry is bought of the poulterer, it is generally sent home ready for the spit. If otherwise, it must be treated as follows :—The skewers are of the ordinary wooden kind, and the needles are merely of iron, similar to packing needles, and sold in the shops as "trussing needles," some being bent or curved, and others straight. Before trussing, it is first necessary that the skin should be

thoroughly deprived of its feathers, and the hairs remaining are to be
singed off with white paper, or gas answers still better; they are next
to be drawn, which is better done after singeing, though some cooks
reverse this proceeding.

DRAWING GAME OR POULTRY.

57. In drawing Game or Poultry, there are two methods of proceeding, depending upon the time during which the birds are to be
kept. Thus, when partridges, pheasants, or poultry are to be kept as
long a time as possible, it is desirable to remove the crop and intestines
without admitting air into the interior: this is done by the method
described below; but the objection to it is, that sometimes, though not
often, the gall-bladder is broken, and causes thereby a degree of
bitterness which is very unpleasant:—Take a wooden skewer, and pass
it into the vent so as to hook the intestine on its point, then withdraw
it with the point on the thumb, and it will bring a part with it inverted,
like the finger of a glove in drawing it off; keep repeating this until a
loop of intestine is brought out, when, by means of the finger using
gentle traction, the whole may be drawn, leaving the gizzard, heart,
and liver behind. The crop should be removed through a small slit
made in the side of the neck, which will admit the finger to grasp it
and draw it out as whole as possible. Some people prefer leaving this
in until the final trussing, and for poultry which have had twelve hours'
fasting it is quite unnecessary to remove it; but in game, and especially in pheasants, the crop is often very full, and, if allowed to
remain, will ferment, and cause the adjacent parts to turn sour.

58. THE USUAL METHOD is to make a transverse opening with a
knife between the vent and the rump. Through this the intestines
are carefully drawn, and *after* they are all out, they should be severed
at the vent; then pass in the fingers and detach the gizzard, liver, and
heart from their attachments, together with the crop, if it has not been
already removed through the neck; but it is better to bring away all
together. After all are withdrawn, stretch the vent with the finger,
and pass it over the rump, which will completely close the opening
The gizzard is now to be detached, and slit open on *one* side, which
will expose its contents; these are to be removed, together with the
lining membrane, which easily peels off, beginning at the cut edge.
Then take away the gall-bladder from the liver, after which it may be
separated from its attachments, but leaving the heart with it: the
two forming the appendages of the one wing, as the gizzard does of

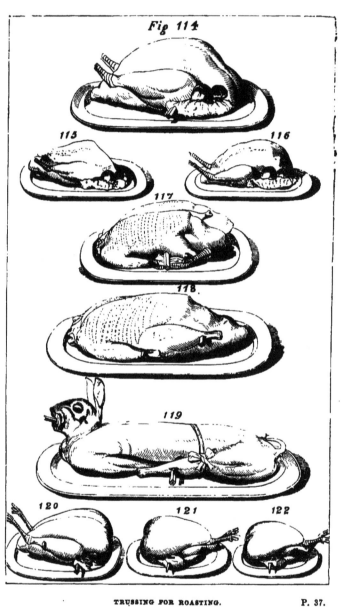

Fig 114.

115   116

117

118

119

120   121   122

TRUSSING FOR ROASTING.   P. 37.

Fig. 114.—Turkey.   *Figs.* 115, 116.—Fowl.   *Fig.* 117.—Duck.
    118.—Goose.   ,,   119.—Hare,   ,, 120.—Pheasant.
    1.—Grouse.   ,,   122.—Partridge.

the other. The lungs are left closely attached to the back-bone, being small and perfectly innocent. No water should, on any account, be used to wash out poultry, unless any of the hollow organs have been broken, in which case water must be freely applied; but otherwise it is injurious, both from its causing loss of flavour, and a tendency to putrefaction. In geese, ducks, and often in fowls, there is a quantity of internal fat with the intestines, which should be preserved. In the two last kinds it serves to baste them, when melted, and *goose-grease* is useful for many purposes.

TRUSSING FOR ROASTING.

59. Trussing for Roasting is managed in a different way from that for boiling, described under the chapter on that process. The following list of the methods adopted for roasting include the various kinds of poultry and game. It should be carefully remarked, that all skewers and strings should be removed after roasting, except the fine thread used in sewing up the belly of the hare or rabbit.

To TRUSS TURKEYS, FOWLS, AND PIGEONS.

60. Turkeys, Fowls, and Pigeons are trussed alike, with very slight variations. The legs are first broken half-way between the feet and the next joint, then fixing the feet in a door-joint, or a table-drawer, or in a screw-press, the sinews are torn out. Next place a doubled-up cloth on the breast, and press or beat the bone till it gives way. After this the wings have a slit cut in their thin expansion of skin, and through this the gizzard and liver are passed, one on each side; next to which the pinions are turned over the back, and a wooden skewer is passed through the flesh of each wing close to the bone, transfixing the body, and also each thigh. The head is cut off close to the body, first drawing the skin well back so as to leave a long covering for the end. This piece of skin is then passed under the ends of the pinions, or if in a stuffed turkey it is tied with a piece of coarse string, which is removed after roasting. In stuffing be careful not to fill the skin too full, or it will burst in roasting. All is now described but the legs, which should have been pushed up under the skin of the breast, and secured there by the skewer transfixing them and the wings through the body, and passing through them close to the joints. The horny skin is scalded and peeled, after which a piece of string or a small skewer, at the small end of the legs, completes the operation. If the skewer is used, it transfixes the side-bones (see *figs.* 114 and 115).

To Truss Geese and Ducks.

61. Geese and Ducks have their heads cut off in the same way as described at (a); but the legs are cut off at the first joint above the feet, and the wings are also removed at the first joint. Sometimes, however, the legs of ducks are left on as in fowls. Next introduce the stuffing, and tie the skin as described at (a). After this the wings are transfixed by a skewer through the body, and the legs the same, keeping them down by the side of the side-bones. The giblets, including the pinions, legs, liver, heart, gizzard, head, and neck, are separately cooked (see *figs*. 117 and 118).

To Truss Wild-fowls.

62. Wild-fowl are trussed as described at (b), except that their legs are left on, and twisted each at the knuckle, so as to rest the claws on each side the back, where they are secured by transfixing them with a skewer, which also tacks the end of the pinion. The legs are scalded to get off the outside skin (see *fig*. 124).

To Truss Guinea-fowl, Pheasants, and Partridges.

63. Guinea-fowl and Feathered Game are trussed like the turkey, except that the heads are left on and turned under the left wing. The feet of partridges and grouse are also left on, having removed the toes, and generally those of pheasants and guinea-fowl. But sometimes they are now removed (see *figs*. 120, 121, and 122).

To Truss Hare and Rabbit.

64. Hares and Rabbits, for roasting, are first filled with stuffing; after which they are sewn up with a needle and thread. The head is then bent back upon the shoulders, and fixed there by a skewer passed through the mouth and into the body. The fore-legs are extended straight along the sides, and skewered there through the body; after which the hind-legs are also brought straight forward, sometimes requiring a slight notch behind the joint to allow of this, and they are secured with a skewer. A string is then crossed under the belly, so as to catch the four points of the skewers, after which the ends are brought up over the back and tied (see *fig*. 119).

To Truss Fowls and Partridges with the Legs concealed.

65. Fowls and Partridges are now often trussed so as to conceal the legs under the skin, and to dispense with skewers altogether. This is done by first rolling the skin backwards and forwards over the roots

of the thighs, and then pushing these joints completely under the skin of the breast. Next take a long straight trussing needle, and pass it through the end of the first pinion across the body, and into that of the opposite side, bringing it back through the joint of the thigh *while thus under the skin*, then carry it across and transfix the opposite thigh in the same way, and tie it to the other end of the string tight enough to maintain the proper shape. After this, the legs only require to be tied to complete the trussing. There is, however, no advantage in this plan over the skewers, and the string is more difficult to withdraw (see *fig.* 116).

DIRECTIONS FOR BONING.

66. Boning is rather a difficult process, and should scarcely be attempted without an actual demonstration by a skilful and practised hand. After the feet and head are cut off and drawn as above, the skin is divided along the back, and then, with a very sharp knife, it, with the flesh, is gradually turned down on each side from the ribs, breast, side-bones, and merry-thought, which are left as bare as possible. In doing this it is necessary to take the legs and wings out at their sockets, and carry them with the rest of the flesh; but when all this is removed, their bones, *as far as they are covered with flesh*, are made to project, with the one hand from the cut surface, while with the other the knife is carried round close to the bone, until, by continued repetition of this cutting, there is nothing left but the pinions covered with skin, and the lower half of the drumsticks, which are left to keep up the original appearance. When all this is done the skin is turned outwards, and with the aid of skewers, needles and thread, and stuffing, the bird is made to assume its natural shape, or as near an approach to it as possible.

DIRECTIONS FOR JOINTING.

67. Joints of Meat which are to be divided in carving should be carefully jointed by the butcher, but it is the duty of the cook to see that this has been done, as without it the carver has a most troublesome task. Jointing is particularly necessary in loins of mutton or veal, and in the fore-quarter of lamb, or in neck of veal; the joints require to be well separated with the chopper, which should be made to pass deeply between the bones.

SECT. 4.—GENERAL MANAGEMENT OF THE FIRE.

68. During the Preparation of the Articles to be Roasted, the fire should be gradually getting into a proper condition for the process;

but in order to this it must have been made up previously, with enough coal to carry it well through, unless the joint to be roasted is a very large one. Thus, a haunch of mutton or venison, or sirloin of beef, require a large fire to be made up an hour before they are put down, without which they cannot possibly be properly roasted; while for smaller joints half an hour is long enough. It is not desirable that the fire should be at its best when the meat is first put down, but it must be burning up briskly, and throwing out a good heat. For small joints, or for poultry, &c., a small brisk fire will suffice, and, in fact, will roast better than a very large one. In every case, the fire should be made up to the top-bar with lumps, and as soon as these are burning pretty strongly they should be somewhat damped, by heaping up some wetted small coal or cinders upon them, so that a very slight stirring at intervals will keep the fire at a strong but steady heat without flame. Just before the joint is put down a stir should be given, which should be forcible enough to last for some time. Unlike boiling, the temperature of the open fire varies greatly, according to its size and kind of coal used. Some of these throw out a scorching heat, such as the Brooch coal of Staffordshire, and yet their temperature in the mass itself is said to be really lower than that of the Newcastle coals. It is difficult to measure the heat in roasting, without a thermometer of a description different to the ordinary ones, as it is far above the boiling point of water, as evidenced by the charring effect on the fat, which is not altered at that temperature from its natural state as to colour. In Dr. Kitchener's justly celebrated *Cook's Oracle*, at page 125, the calculations for roasting are said to be " for a temperature of about 50 degrees of Fahrenheit;" but this is evidently a mistake, either of his own or of his printer, as that temperature would not even warm the meat, much less roast it. I believe that it ranges from 350 to 600 degrees of Fahrenheit, or even still higher in very fierce fires. This calculation is for the distance of twelve inches from the front of the fire, that being about the average. In small fires there must be a much closer proximity of the joint, say at six or seven inches, while in very large ones fifteen inches will not be too far off.

69. IF THERE IS A SMOKE-JACK, place the dripping-pan under the meat, far enough from the fire to escape the coals dropping out, but near enough to catch all the dripping as it falls from the meat. Then put down the spit in the rack, and bring up the screen, placing it so that it will not only reflect the heat of the fire, but keep off all draughts of

cold air. Where a screen and jack together are used with a dripping-pan attached, the whole are placed before the fire at the same time.

SECT. 5.—GENERAL PRINCIPLES OF ROASTING.

70. According to Liebig, it is essential to the successful and economical management of roasting, to put the joint down first of all *close to the fire*, so as to coagulate the albumen on the surface, and thus to prevent the escape of it in a fluid state. This answers remarkably well in boiling, but not in roasting, because the heat is not applied to the whole surface at once, but only to one half of it, the other half being cooled at that time, so that it is impossible to raise the surface, without scorching it, up to the coagulating point of albumen, until the whole mass is also above 150 degrees. In a Dutch oven the plan is good, both in theory and practice; but with a revolving spit it is totally erroneous, and the old directions, to put down the joint first at a distance, and then gradually bring it nearer to the fire, are the correct ones. In roasting, very little besides water and fat are expelled from the meat, the former by evaporation, and the latter by liquefaction from the increased temperature, and by contraction of the fibrous tissues owing to the same cause. A small quantity of gravy, containing the juice of the flesh (osmazome), is also expressed; but the loss in this way is very trifling, not amounting to more than a few ounces of gravy in a large joint of meat, and never being more than enough to serve as gravy. Indeed, in roasting, there is absolutely no loss whatever of any thing but water, the fat being collected as dripping, and of equal value with the meat, while the osmazome is saved in the form of gravy, or else it is collected about the dripping-pan, from which it is dissolved in the water poured into it, to make the gravy served with the meat. Although, therefore, there is a great difference between the weight of a joint when cooked and that which pertained to it when raw, yet this loss, after allowing for the weight of dripping and gravy, is to be considered as due to the water passing off by evaporation; so that a roast joint of meat, together with its dripping and gravy, contains all the nourishment which pertained to it beforehand. This, we shall presently see, is not the case with boiled meat.

71. Besides this absolute economy in roasting, there is also the advantage that roast meat is more grateful to the stomach than boiled, and can be eaten for a longer time without change. This is probably due to the presence of the saline ingredients; but to whatever cause it may be referred, there is no doubt of the fact, that any one will much

sooner get tired of boiled mutton than roast, or of boiled than roast beef; and also, that invalids can digest roast in preference to boiled mutton, both being fresh.

72. THE WEIGHT thus lost by evaporation and dripping of fat and gravy, varies a good deal according to the quality of the meat, the proportion of bones, and the amount of fat, as described at page 12 of the *Economical Housekeeper*. It is also said that, by roasting with gas, there is less loss by evaporation, with a greater saving of dripping; and this, I am assured upon good private authority, as well as from public experiments recently made. According to an experiment made by M. Soyer, at the Greenwich Hospital (the account of which was published in the *Mechanics' Magazine*), twenty-three legs of mutton, weighing 184 lbs., were roasted by gas at a cost of $10\frac{1}{2}$d.; the gas costing 4s. per 1000 feet.

When cooked they weighed	145 lbs.
Dripping	19 „
Gravy, or osmazome	$2\frac{1}{4}$ „
Water, or loss	$17\frac{3}{4}$ „
	184 lbs.

Twenty-three joints, also weighing 184 lbs., were afterwards cooked in one of Count Rumford's ovens, usually considered more economical than roasting, and consuming 102 lbs. of coke and 30 lbs. of coal, valued at 1s. 8d.,—

They weighed when done	132 lbs.
Dripping	18 „
Gravy	0 „
Water, or loss	34 „
	184 lbs.

The gain by the use of gas was therefore—

	s.	d.
13 lbs. of meat	6	6
1 lb. of dripping	0	5
$2\frac{1}{4}$ lbs. of gravy	3	6
Difference in cost of fuel	0	$9\frac{1}{2}$
Total gain	11	$2\frac{1}{2}$

In this, as in other similar experiments, I cannot help thinking that the saving is more apparent than real, and that it depends upon the more regular application of the heat, and upon *the meat being done in the one case more thoroughly than in the other*. It is an acknowledged fact, that there is no loss in roasting except by evaporation of water; and if so, what became of the thirteen lbs. of meat which were said to be gained by the gas-roasting at Greenwich? It did not fly away as meat, it did not ooze out as dripping, nor as osmazome, for there was less of the former and none of the latter; and therefore I should conclude that it was dissipated as vapour or water, leaving the meat in this case done thoroughly, while that from the gas-roaster must, I should fancy, have been rather under-done. In order to try this experiment properly, it requires the superintendence of a person not interested in the success of either plan, and who has not been previously biassed, so that he would, as far as possible, permit both sets of joints to be cooked to the same degree; and when this is done, I believe, from theoretical principles as well as practical experience, that the result will be as nearly as possible the same. But with regard to the comparative efficiency of gas I have no doubt, as I am persuaded that it is quite equal to the most sanguine expectations of its advocates, and with this great advantage, *that the dripping and gravy are quite clear, and free from cinders or dust.* So that there is, practically, not the slightest loss in this kind of roasting.

73. TABLE showing the LOSS PER CENT. by the various JOINTS in ROASTING and BAKING :—

		100 lbs. loss
Roasting with gas...	(Soyer)	21½ lbs.
Baking in Count Rumford's oven	(do.)	27½ „
Do. in common oven	(Tilloch)	30 „
Roasting beef before fire	(do.)	22 „
Do. shoulders of mutton	(do.)	31½ „
Do. loins	(do.)	35½ „
Do. necks	(do.)	32½ „
Do. sirloins and ribs, beef	(Donovan)	19½ „
Do. legs and shoulders, mutton	(do.)	24½ „
Do. lamb	(do.)	22½ „
Do. poultry ...	(do.)	20 „

The loss, as stated by Tilloch, agrees very closely with experiments made by myself. Under this head are included the dripping and gravy, the calculation being based on the difference in the weight before and after roasting.

74. A KNOWLEDGE OF THE TIME REQUIRED FOR ROASTING is very essential to the cook; and in cooking for parties she should be careful to put her meat down so as to be ready for the *second* course, not for the first, which usually occupies about ten minutes. Nevertheless in such cases it is always better to have the meat done a little too soon, and to keep it hot before the fire, rather than to have to send it up under·done. The precise time occupied in roasting each article will come better under the next section; but, as a general rule, a quar:⸗

of an hour to each pound of meat is the proper allowance, adding a
little for large joints, and taking off in the same way for small ones.
It is better in roasting joints of any size to lay them in the dripping-
pan at a distance from the fire, so as to warm through before beginning
to time them. Many cooks also at this time sprinkle them over with
salt, and I think with great advantage.

To Make Gravy.

75. Gravy is always made after the meat is taken up, except when
what is called "made-gravy" is intended to be used, as for game and
poultry, in which there is no osmazome pressed out in the roasting,
and consequently nothing to make it of in the dripping-pan. With
mutton, beef, and butcher's meat generally, after the meat is taken up,
so as to liberate the dripping-pan, the fat in that vessel is poured off,
and then a small quantity of boiling water is put into it, and thoroughly
washed over its surface by moving it horizontally with a little dexterity,
leaving it in while the spit, skewers, &c., are being removed, after
which the water, now become gravy, is poured into the dish containing the meat, and is often of very excellent quality, depending greatly
upon the manipulations of the cook and the age of the meat.

Basting.

76. Basting is the most important of all the requisites for roasting,
and it is for want of its being properly done that roast joints are so
constantly spoiled. In fat meats, such as beef, mutton, or pork, their
own dripping, after it has run into the well of the pan, is the best
thing for the purpose; but in poultry, veal, and game there is nothing
coming out which will serve, and they must be basted either with
plain *butter* (*good* salt or potted), *mutton or beef dripping, water and salt,
milk, melted-butter,* or sometimes with *cider, ale,* or *wine.*

Dredging.

77. Dredging is another item connected with roasting, and requires
a tin box with a perforated lid, called a dredger, This usually holds
wheat-flour; but for some joints, &c., this is mixed with *grated bread,
or dried herbs, or grated lemon or orange-peel.* The dredger is shaken
over the roast at short intervals, so that its contents remain on the
surface, and form with the fat oozing out a kind of *coating,* which is
sometimes intentionally made very thick, as for hare; but these
coatings are not now so common, or fashionable either, as they

formerly were, when every kind of roast was sent to table covered with a thick brown crust—whereas now a pale brown is the usual colour, clear of all flour.

To Prevent Burning by Paper or Paste.

78. Paper is often wrapped or skewered over the fat to prevent its wasting away, as in the inside of the sirloin of beef, or on both sides of the haunch of mutton or venison. For these last also a paste is often made of flour and water, and applied about half an inch thick, when the joint is first put down. Whether the paper or paste is used, it is only suffered to remain on until within half an hour of the finishing, when it is removed, and the surface allowed to assume a delicate light-brown, without any great loss of substance. In this is the great art of roasting to perfection, according to the fashion of the present day.

79. The directions for roasting the several joints, &c., embrace the exceptional and peculiar modes of dressing each kind. It will be understood that the general principles described in the last section apply to them all; but that superadded to them are also some other points, which differ in each, more or less, and require attention to give to each dish its characteristic appearance and flavour, as is usual in this country.

Larding.

80. Larding consists in the introduction of thin and narrow pieces of ham or bacon into poultry and meats naturally somewhat dry and devoid of flavour. Indeed whatever roast or stewed dish is usually eaten with these additions, is improved by their introduction into its substance by means of the larding-needle. Thus veal, turkeys, fowls, and rabbits may all be larded with advantage, and roasted or stewed at the conclusion of the operation.

81. A Larding-needle is merely a short thick needle, with a spring opening or slit instead of an eye, so that a narrow slip of bacon may be introduced—just as a penholder is inserted in a steel pen. Charged with this larding, the needle is passed through a pinched-up portion of flesh, and having inserted it so that its two ends project, the slit of the needle is opened and liberates its charge. These pieces of bacon are inserted in regular order, and at intervals of about an inch, in the breast of a turkey, a fowl, or in the substance of veal, &c.; after which the article is considered larded, and is ready for being dressed.

SECT. 6.—OVEN-ROASTING.

82. IN COMMON BAKING AND OVEN-ROASTING (by which latter name cooking in ventilated ovens is called), the meat is always prepared as in the last section, except that it is not spitted, but put in a dish supported upon an iron wire frame, which suspends it from the bottom.

The dripping-pan should be fixed upon another pan filled with hot water, from which the steam has the power of escaping; this is very important, as it prevents the peculiar flavour often given to the meats by the iron oven, and the meat requires less basting. In gas-ovens, the space is purposely made large enough to suspend a joint from the top, and, as the jets are all round it, the process is very evenly conducted, and hence arises its economy. M. Soyer has invented a very simple open frame-work of wire, which lies upon a deep tin or earthenware dish, in two stages, and supports a joint *together with a dish of potatoes*, so that these may be baked upon it, while a Yorkshire pudding is also baked in the dish beneath. As the meat is raised above the potatoes, and these again are above the pudding, dripping falls upon both. It is a very useful addition to the poor man's means of comfort. When these joints are sent to the public bakehouse, the baker knows how long they will take; but if baked at home the time will be as nearly as possible the same as for roasting, depending, however, partly upon the heat of the oven. Sucking pig, leg of pork, and perhaps beef or veal, are nearly as good baked as roasted; but baked mutton, lamb, game, and poultry, are not to be compared with these articles when properly roasted.

CHAP. V.—THE BOILING, STEAMING, AND STEWING OF ANIMAL FOOD.

SECT. 1.—GENERAL OBSERVATIONS.

83. In comparing roasting with boiling at page 32, I have observed that though the latter appears to be a more simple process, it is not so in reality, because it requires a greater advance in the mechanical arts to procure the saucepan or pot in which the water must be contained. But, in the present day, in comparing roasting and boiling, there is no question that the former requires much more art and experience than the latter; and every one's experience will recall to his

memory more instances of spoiled roasted articles than of boiled meats injured in the same way.

SECT. 2.—UTENSILS.

84. The utensils for boiling meat and poultry are very simple, consisting only of round or oval saucepans of various sizes, which are better lined with enamel, though it is by no means necessary. Where a large oval pot is adopted for the purpose of boiling a number of things together, a net of twine is very useful to keep each separate; and, for boiling white meats, in that case a cloth must be wrapped round them. A trivet placed at the bottom of the pot will also be useful for large joints, in order to prevent them from burning. Stew-pans and steamers will be described under the sections devoted to stewing and steaming. Large iron spoons and skimmers complete the list.

SECT. 3.—GENERAL PRINCIPLES OF BOILING.

85. As in roasting, so in the process now under discussion, the principal effect is the coagulation of the albumen, and the rendering tender of the fibrous membranes. This makes the whole much more digestible; and if it were not for the dissolving out into the water of the saline matters, as well as the soluble gelatine and albumen, there would be a superiority in boiling over roasting in every respect. But from their occurrence it follows that unless the liquor is used with the meat, there is a want of these essential ingredients; so that a person fed upon boiled meat alone, with bread and potatoes, and none of the broth, would speedily lose health and strength. The plan recommended by Liebig, for the purpose of keeping in the juices by rapidly coagulating the albumen on the surface, answers well in point of economy, the saving being fully two or three per cent.; but I do not believe that the meat so treated is *quite* so tender. His plan is to immerse the meat in boiling water, and boil for five minutes. After this, lower the temperature down to that which will not scald the hand, either by the simple addition of cold water, or by first abstract-ing sufficient boiling water to allow of its being poured in. After this, the boiling is carried on at a slow simmer until the meat is done. It is easy to understand how water boiled rapidly acts more energetically upon the meat than when boiled more slowly; for though it never rises above 212 degrees, yet it gives out a much greater quantity of heat in a given time, and consequently, raises the temperature of the

meat much more quickly. Water is kept at a certain temperature in boiling, because whatever articles are raised above that temperature are converted into steam and escape; but meat in it is not capable of being converted into steam, and in water thus rapidly boiled it is capable of being raised above the boiling degree, or 212 degrees, and if not thus raised, it is much more quickly heated, because it receives the superfluous temperature of a greater mass of steam given off in the bubbles accompanying the "galloping" process. It has been observed, under the head of Roasting, at page 41, that, independently of the watery particles flying off by steam, the loss in that process is solely from the fat and gravy which drop into the dripping-pan, and which ought to be collected and saved; but in boiling there is nearly as much dissolved in the liquor in which the boiling takes place, as we shall presently see. According to Mr. Tilloch, whose experiments are corroborated by my own on the large as well as the small scale, the loss by boiling is as follows:—

Beef in boiling loses	...	...	...	...	...	...	In 100 lb. 26½ lb.
Legs of mutton	...	...	...	...	...	...	„ 21½ „
Boiling salt beef (Donovan)	...	...	...	...	...	„ 15 „
„ Legs of mutton (do.)	...	...	...	...	...	„ 10 „
„ Hams (do.)	...	...	...	...	...	„ 12½ „
„ Salt pork (do.)	...	...	...	...	...	„ 13½ „
„ Bacon (do.)	...	...	...	...	...	„ 6½ „
„ Turkeys (do.)	...	...	...	...	...	„ 16 „
„ Chicken (do.)	...	...	...	...	...	„ 13½ „

Donovan's estimate is here pretty correct, except in reference to the legs of mutton, which certainly lose more than 10 per cent.; and, I believe, fully what is stated on Tilloch's authority, namely, 21½ per cent.

86. In comparing Boiling, therefore, with roasting, there is an *apparent* gain, according to Tilloch's experiments, of about 10 per cent. in favour of boiling mutton, and, according to Donovan's, of 14¾ per cent in legs of mutton, and about 14 per cent. in poultry. But then it must be recollected, that 100 lbs. of roasted meat will produce about ten lbs. of good dripping, and also a pound or two of good gravy, neither of which can be obtained from the boiling process when the liquor is not used; consequently it is imperative that this should be saved, and employed in some way, if this kind of cookery is to be considered more economical than roasting, for otherwise the loss in dripping will counterbalance the saving in other respects. If the boilings are wasted, there is an absolute loss of at least 20 per cent. of good useful matter in the shape of the fat (which, by the way, is

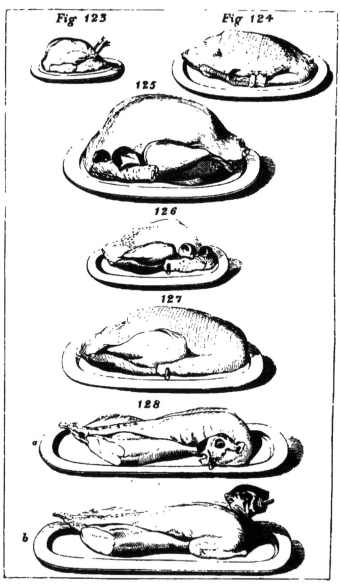

Fig 123   Fig 124

125

126

127

128

TRUSSING FOR ROASTING AND BOILING.   P. 49.

123.—Pigeon (roast).   *Fig.* 124.—Wild Duck (roast).
25.—Turkey (boiled).   ,, 126.—Fowl (boiled).
27.—Goose (boiled).   ,, 128.—Rabbit, (*a*, trussed or
        boiling in the London mode : *b*, in the country mode)

always to a certain extent mixed up with scum in boiling, and therefore comparatively useless), and of the dissolved gelatine, albumen, and
salts. The gelatine and saline matter may be saved in solution, and
when not too salt, as in boiling salt meats, it may be made into good
soup; but the albumen and fat are skimmed off during the boiling, and
they are not easily cooked up into any useful article of food. Here,
as in all kinds of cookery, the chief art in point of economy consists
in making use of every part of the food which is fitted to support life;
by imparting proper and wholesome nourishment, and a variety in the
regular routine, the boiling process is quite capable of effecting all the
purposes of the cook, when conducted with the provisions here mentioned and insisted upon.

SECT. 4.—DIRECTIONS AND MODES OF TRUSSING FOR BOILING.

87. Turkeys, Guinea-fowls, and Fowls, are all trussed in the
same way for boiling, the heads being removed as for roasting. The
legs are pulled off also in a similar way, but very close to the joint,
and the breast-bone depressed. The legs are then gradually insinuated under the skin, and when there the wings are secured through the
legs to the body (see *figs.* 125 and 126). Lastly, a sufficient quantity
of stuffing is introduced into the neck of turkeys and guinea-fowls, but
not in common fowls. They should all be boiled according to Liebig's
method, by putting them in boiling water and then cooling it down
(see par. 85). The allowance of a quarter of an hour to each pound,
reckoning from the time the water boils, is about that required. The
boiling should be very slow, and the water should be constantly skimmed. Bacon, ham, or tongue, always accompany these articles; and
oyster or bread sauce, with good gravy.

To BOIL AND TRUSS GEESE AND DUCKS.

88. Geese and Ducks are sometimes boiled. They are then
trussed as for roasting, and boiled in the same manner as turkeys,
with or without a stuffing of sage and onions, and served with onion
sauce and gravy. (*Fig.* 127.)

To TRUSS AND BOIL RABBITS.

89. Rabbits should be well washed for boiling, and, if very bloody
at the shoulder, they should be treated as described for hare at (*k*),
par. 79. Truss them with the heads brought back against the right
side (see *fig.* 128), then boil. They are best when dropped into boil-

E

ing water, which should be kept gently boiling and well skimmed for half an hour, or rather better. They are generally covered with onion sauce, or with white sauce. Sometimes a sauce is made with the livers chopped and mixed with fine herbs.

GENERAL DIRECTIONS FOR BOILING JOINTS.

90. In all joints the plan of boiling suggested by Liebig is the most economical, and also the best in point of flavour, though, as I before observed, not quite so well calculated to make it tender. For the mode recommended here, see par. 85. In the directions appended to each joint the time is generally in accordance with the quarter-of-an-hour calculation.

SECT. 5.— THE STEAMING OF MEAT, &c..

91. In this method the meat is placed in a kettle, with a valve to it, and without water. Steam is introduced; and according to the pressure on the valve will be the temperature at which it is steamed. If there is no valve, it will not rise above 212 degrees; but with a very slight weight upon a common metal plug it soon rises to 240 degrees, or even higher. There is much less waste in this way, both of heat and of the juices of the meat; and in point of economy, therefore, the plan is a very good one. In the London eating-houses, dinners for a hundred people, or even more, are cooked at one fire by the aid of ovens and steam-boilers, and at an expense of not more than a third or half a ton of coals weekly. The steam-kettles may be placed at any moderate distance from the fire (see *fig.* 68, F F F); and the pipes being furnished with stop-cocks, the steam is either admitted at the full or partially, and under pressure or not, a waste-pipe being also fitted. Vegetables steamed in this way are particularly tender, but not of quite so good a colour as in boiling.

92. When it is desirable to boil water by steam for the purpose of cooking, as for some vegetables, soups, &c., it is only necessary to fill any of the above steam-kettles with water, and then turn on the steam as usual. The water is soon heated to the boiling-point, and then acts exactly as if placed upon an ordinary fire.

93. IN THE OLD-FASHIONED STEAMER a vessel is placed upon another, fitting tightly into it. The bottom of the upper vessel being perforated with holes, the steam passes through and acts in the same way as if admitted by a pipe; but the objection is that the condensed steam, and the other juices of the vegetables, &c., cooked in the steamer, are

very apt to return into the lower vessel, and injure the flavour of its contents. It has been chiefly used for potatoes, which are thought by many people to be better when steamed than when boiled in water.

SECT. 6.—THE PRINCIPLES OF STEWING.

94. Under this head is comprised slowly-boiled or stewed meats, served with their gravy, and generally flavoured with vegetables of some kind. The chief art here is to keep down the temperature, so as to avoid the hardening of the fibres, and too rapid coagulation of the albumen by heat. For this purpose the meat is put into *cold* water, and it is very gradually raised to a very low boiling point—what is called a "gallop" never being permitted.

95. THE UTENSILS are merely stewpans of suitable sizes, which may or may not be heated by steam-pipes. Stewpans are now almost always rather shallow vessels, or saucepans of enamelled iron, or sometimes of block-tin or tinned copper; and they are either heated on a hot-plate, or kept a proper distance from an ordinary fire, or placed in a water-bath.

96. The various receipts hereafter given, will be found exceedingly nourishing and of good flavour, and in point of economy will go further than any other dishes whatever. It will be seen that in a great many cases, in order to improve the flavour, the meat is either roasted or fried before it is stewed.

CHAP. VI.—FRYING OR *SAUTEING*, BROILING, TOASTING, AND BRAISING OF ANIMAL FOOD.

SECT. 1.—FRYING OR SAUTEING.

97. THIS method of cooking is universally adopted among all classes, and in all nations where iron vessels are to be obtained. The French *sauté* is nothing more than their method of frying, but carried out with rather more care than usual. Whether in French or English cookery, however, frying is *boiling in oil or fat;* the chief difference being, that in our country only a little of this material is put into a shallow pan, while in France they half fill a somewhat deep iron vessel with oil or lard, and when this is hot enough they immerse the article to be fried in the oil till sufficiently brown. In French kitchens a vessel is set apart to receive this oil from day to day, and the same quantity serves for months together by straining it through a sieve—so that

none is lost excepting that which is absorbed by the food in the process. In point of economy, therefore, the French beat us here, as in our method the fat left in the pan is seldom preserved till the next time, but it goes into a wash-tub or some other waste receptacle. Besides this loss, there is a still greater one occasioned by the way in which the frying is conducted. In the French plan the fat or oil is first heated to such a temperature that it will convert water into steam directly a drop falls upon it, making it " spit," as the cooks say. At this stage the meat, or other article, is immersed, by which a coating of coagulated albumen is immediately made, soon to be partially carbonized or browned, but so rapidly formed that scarcely any juice is allowed to escape, and therefore the nourishing particles are not wasted; and, as the whole is immersed, the action is simultaneous on all sides. Contrast this with the English method, and it will be found that here, as soon as the lard is melted, the steak or other article is put into the pan, which is soon raised to a very high temperature, and contracts the fibrinous matter on the lower side, *squeezing the gravy out on the upper*, from which it may be seen to ooze in a full stream; and it is not until it is turned downwards that this is at all checked. The consequence of this is, that not only is there a great waste of nutritious matter, but the lard is mixed with a great quantity of good gravy, which is so rich that it is generally mixed with a little flour and spice, and eaten with the steaks. It is from this custom that the French do not understand dressing a beefsteak in the English fashion; but when frying it they do it to perfection in every respect but the gravy, which being deficient from the nature of the process, is supplied by some sauce or other poured over it. A broiled steak they can accomplish *if they can get the meat;* but beef in Paris fit for such a process is rather rare. Hence it is that for steaks, when they are to be fried, the English method is really to be preferred; while for every other operation done in the frying-pan, the French plan will be found vastly superior, especially for fish, missolles, fritters, and every dish which required to be served *dry*, as this cannot be accomplished unless they are completely immersed in boiling butter, lard, or oil.

98. The FRYING-PAN should be, in some measure, proportioned the size of the article to be fried, especially on the English plan; for the French method, one large enough for a full-sized sole will equally serve for a sprat or a single cutlet. The English frying-pan is generally round and shallow, that is, about two inches deep. On the other hand, the French pan should be six or eight inches deep, and

Fig. 129

130

131

132

133

135

134

136

fitted with a lining of open wire-work; so that, when sufficiently done, the article or articles may be raised out of the fat, and suffered to drain for a few seconds, without which they will be oily and gross, while with it they become crisp, and so free from grease that they do not even soil a napkin when in contact with it. The metal is iron, and the bottom should be tolerably thick (see *figs*. 131 and 132).

99. FAT of some kind is essential to frying, and it may be either *olive-oil*, or *lard*, or *bacon-fat*, or *clarified dripping*, or *suet*, or *butter*, or even the *skimmings of the stock-pot*. OLIVE-OIL requires great care in its use, being very apt to burn, and not answering the purposes of English frying: but for the more delicate kinds of fish, or indeed for any kind of *sautés* (see par. 97), oil is capable of being made use of in the frying-pan to great advantage. LARD and BUTTER answer well for any purpose, as do suet and dripping, or even the skimmings when clarified; the proper mode of doing which will be given in the next paragraph.

To CLARIFY DRIPPING, LARD, AND SUET.

100. To Clarify Dripping or Skimmings, put either into a clean saucepan over a stove, hot plate, or small fire. Melt it very slowly, and skim till quite clear at the upper part; let it just boil for a second, then strain it through a sieve, and let it get cold. There will always be more or less watery gravy at the bottom; but the upper part will be clear fat, free from admixture with any other matter, and quite good enough for any ordinary fryings, or for basting meat.

101. To CLARIFY LARD OR SUET.—The kidney-fat of either animal must be cut into small pieces, and must then be put into a water-bath, or in a cool oven, or on a very cool hot-plate or stove; the slightest increase of temperature more than sufficient to liquefy the fat gives a taste of burning, which is not pleasant. If there is no water-bath at hand, an earthenware jar immersed in a saucepan of water, and covered over with a saucepan-lid, answers all the purpose. Whichever plan is adopted, the process must be very slow, as the cells in which the fat lies take a long time to empty themselves. When the lumps have shrunk almost to nothing, strain the whole through a sieve, and increase the heat a little for the remaining portion; the water-bath not being sufficient to extract all the fat. Keep this last part separate, as it is only fit for frying, and not for pastry. Tie down the jar when cold, and either suet or lard will then keep a long time.

MANAGEMENT OF THE FIRE.

102. The fire for frying should be clear of black coals, and consequently of blaze, but only just burnt up; and there should be a good light above, for the cook to judge by the eye of the progress of her cookery. Care must, of course, be taken not to set fire to the fat.

DIRECTIONS FOR FRYING.

103. In Frying, first heat the pan and the fat in it (whether on the English or French plan) till it has ceased to hiss or "spit," and will immediately turn brown a small piece of bread. Then either put the article in on the bottom, and turn it as soon as the under-side is brown, turning it back again to complete the process. Many articles are put into the frying-pan without any preparation beyond reducing them to a proper thickness; but others are coated with bread-crumb, which is made to adhere by white of egg. In the French plan there is little or no necessity for turning, and after introducing the wire-lining, and properly heating the fat, the article to be fried is smoothly dropped in, and suffered to remain quietly until it is quite brown enough, when it is removed by the wire-lining, and drained over the pan for about half a minute. In any case where bread-crumb is used, and especially in frying fish, the oil or fat remaining should be imbibed either by blotting-paper or a clean white cloth, changing these until they are not stained; but if the oil or fat is hot enough, it runs off so completely while in the wire that nothing is left behind.

SECT. 2.—BROILING.

104. Broiling differs from frying, in the fact that there is no addition of oil or fat; and that the effect is produced by the direct radiation of heat from a clear fire, the broiling articles being supported over it by a gridiron. As a necessary consequence, the gravy *will* ooze out from the upper side, and is generally lost by falling into the fire. This may partially be avoided by the use of a particular gridiron, which will presently be described.

THE ORDINARY GRIDIRON.

105. The ordinary gridiron is merely a square frame of iron, with cross bars of the same. An improvement upon this consists in making the upper surface of these bars concave or grooved, and all terminating in a hollow in the handle, so as to save a little of that rich

gravy which would otherwise fall into the fire. In theory this is very pretty, but in practice there is not much gain, as the bars do not bear a very large relative proportion to the open spaces between, and consequently they do not catch a great deal of the gravy. Before using a gridiron, it should be clean, and the upper surface should be well greased with lard or dripping, to prevent its sticking; and it should be set slanting downwards towards the hand of the cook. A PAIR OF STEAK-TONGS are required for really-artistic broiling, but most ordinary cooks are content with the common fork.

106. THE FIRE FOR BROILING must be very clear, and free from smoke or flame. Charcoal, coke, or wood is the best; but good coals, at a certain stage, answer every purpose. A little salt thrown on the fire makes it burn much more clearly, and frees it from smoke.

DIRECTIONS FOR BROILING.

107. In broiling, after heating and larding the gridiron, put on the steak, chop, or other article, and continually turn it every half-minute, moving it gently all the time, to avoid the marks left by the bars if suffered to remain still. It is rather difficult to judge of the time when it is sufficiently done, especially as different people have such very different ideas of the proper degree of dressing. Nothing but experience, and ascertaining whether they are liked well-done or underdone, will ensure satisfaction. When the concave enamelled gridiron is used, a little gravy of good flavour may be served; but, otherwise, either the steak or chop must be eaten plain, or a made-gravy must be prepared beforehand. It is usual to dredge broiled articles with salt and pepper mixed, and sometimes having a little mushroom powder added to them.

SECT. 3.—TOASTING MEATS, &c.

108. Chops, kidneys, pigeons, &c., may be done very effectually and nicely before the fire in a small Dutch oven or hanging oven. (See par. 52, and *fig.* 112.) They require occasional turning and basting; and the process is certainly more like roasting than frying or broiling.

SECT. 4.—BRAISING.

109. Braising is only a very elaborate method of baking or broiling, which has been introduced from France into this country of late years. It is, in fact, an air-tight oven, placed on a stove, with a braising-iron

on the top, so that the heat descends as well as ascends, and yet it is so graduated that it does not cause much of the steam to escape. Although considered a French novelty, it differs in no respect from the old English "jugging," in which a hare is placed in a jar, covered over closely, and then deposited in an oven, by which the same kind of heat is communicated; and I fully believe there is no cook who could tell a braised turkey done in the most artistic way, from another deposited in a braising-pan and then placed in an oven at the required temperature. All the old receipts for stewing in covered pans in the oven depend upon the same principle; that is, that the article to be stewed should nearly fill the dish or jar, and should in that state, with very little but its own juice, be submitted to a low dry heat, with closed doors, to obviate the loss by evaporation. A braising-pan is certainly a most convenient mode of carrying out the process, either with or without the oven, but it is by no means essential to it.

CHAP. VII.—ON THE COOKING OF FISH BY BOILING, FRYING, &c.

SECT. 1.—GENERAL REMARKS.

110. THE VARIOUS KINDS OF FISH, with their seasons, and the best modes of procuring them, as well as their ordinary prices, will be found given at length in the *Economical Housekeeper*.

TO CLEAN FISH.

111. In cleaning fish, it is only necessary to remove the gills, and slit open the belly to take out the intestines, liver, &c., using plenty of fresh water; but if the fishmonger does not perform his duty, fish is seldom very nicely cleaned; but in great towns it is washed beyond what is necessary for cleaning, and by perpetual watering diminishes in flavour. When quite clean, if to be boiled, a table-spoonful of salt and two of vinegar should be put into the water to give firmness. Turbot, cod, whiting, and haddock, are far better if rubbed over with salt, and kept a day; and, if it is not very hot weather, they will be good for two days. Fresh water fish has often a muddy smell and taste, to take off which soak it in strong salt and water after it is nicely cleaned; or, if of a size to bear it, scald it in the same; then dry, and dress it.

UTENSILS.

112. For Boiling Small Fish, saucepans or fish-kettles of various sizes are required; and for large and long fish, like salmon and turbot, a full-sized kettle called a turbot-kettle, of tin, is the proper article, containing a false bottom perforated with holes to lift the fish out with in order to avoid breaking it (see *figs*. 133 and 134). For frying or broiling fish, nothing more is wanted than the ordinary frying-pans and gridirons. (See pars. 98 and 105.)

To Boil Fish.

113. After cleaning and adding salt and vinegar (see par. 111), the fish must be put into the water while cold, and set to boil very gently, or the outside will break before the inner part is done. The water should also be carefully skimmed, or the fish will look dirty, from the scum setting on it as it is taken out. Crimped fish should be put into boiling water; and when it boils up, pour a little cold water in to check extreme heat, on the principles advocated by Liebig, and explained at par. 85; after which simmer the fish for the proper number of minutes. If the fish is large, the fish-plate on which it is to be done may be drawn up to see if it is ready, when it will leave the bone. It should then be immediately taken out of the water on the plate, or it will soon be woolly. The fish-plate should be set crosswise over the kettle, to keep hot for serving; and a clean cloth should cover the fish to prevent it losing its colour.

To Fry Fish.

114. For frying fish, it ought to be wrapped in a nice soft cloth, after it is well cleaned and washed. When perfectly dry, wet with an egg, and sprinkle the finest crumbs of bread over it; if done a second time with the egg and bread, at an interval of five minutes, the fish will look much better. Then, having a thick-bottomed and deep frying-pan on the fire, with a large quantity of lard or dripping boiling-hot, plunge the fish into it, and let it fry rather quickly, till the colour is of a fine brown yellow, and it is judged ready. If it is done enough before it has obtained a proper degree of colour, the cook should draw the pan to the side of the fire, carefully take it up, and either place it on a large sieve turned upwards, and to be kept for that purpose only, or on the under side of a dish, to drain; and if wanted to look very well, a sheet of cap-paper must be put to receive the fish, which should

have a beautiful colour, and all the crumbs should appear distinct; the fish being free from all grease. The same dripping, with a little fresh, will serve a second, third, and fourth time (see par. 97). Butter gives a bad colour; oil fries of the finest colour for those who will allow the expense. It is customary to garnish with a fringe or curled raw parsley, or parsley fried, which must be thus done:— When washed and picked, throw it again into clean water; when the lard or dripping boils, throw the parsley into it immediately from the water, and instantly it will be green and crisp, and must be taken up with a slice; this may be done after the fish is fried.

To Broil Fish.

115. If fish is to be broiled, it must be seasoned with pepper and salt, floured, and put on a gridiron that is very clean; which, when hot, should be rubbed with a bit of suet to prevent the fish from sticking. It must be broiled on a very clear fire, that it may not taste smoky; and not too near, that it may not be scorched.

Time Required to Dress Fish.

116. The time required to dress fish will be appended to each kind; but this must be considered only as a slight guide to enable the cook to calculate when to put her fish on the fire, as the reliable test is to be found only in the exact state of the fish itself, and the readiness of the flesh to leave the bone.

Cutlets of Fish.

117. Cut fish either cooked or uncooked into well-shaped cutlets; put plenty of chopped sweet herbs and a little butter into a stewpan, just to melt the butter; flavour this with essence of anchovies or Reading sauce; when cold, lay it with a knife upon both sides of the fish, and strew over it plentifully fine bread crumbs; fry dry in hot lard, or cook in a Dutch oven; have ready a sauce made of any vegetables, and flavoured with a little onion or shallot, all of which must be stewed in a little broth, and chopped or rubbed through a cullender. Heap this in the centre of a dish and lay the cutlets round, garnishing with pickle or lemon sliced.

If the fish is cooked, and is not large enough for cutlets, pull it fine and mix it with egg and crumbs, and the other ingredients; then form into cutlets, and dip into yolk of egg and strew crumbs before frying.

FISH CAKES OR BALLS FRIED.

118. Mash a few potatoes in butter or cream; then take double the quantity of any dressed fish, after clearing off all bones and skin. Mix it well with the potatoes, season with pepper and salt, and mace, if approved, and make it into cakes or round balls, or put in scallop-shells. Fry them a light brown, and serve in a napkin; or, if in scallops, brown in a Dutch oven.

TO WARM UP FISH THE SECOND DAY.

119. Salmon may be put into boiling water, and just heated through, taking care to add vinegar as at first. Turbot, brill, and codfish are best picked from the bones, and warmed up with cream or white sauce; then mash some potatoes, and form a wall round a dish (which may or may not be egged and browned), in which the fish is to be placed and served.

A REMARKABLY FINE FISH PIE.

120. Boil two pounds of small eels; then having cut the fins quite close, pick the flesh off, and throw the bones into the liquor, with a little mace, pepper, salt, and a slice of onion; boil till quite rich, and strain it. Make forcemeat of the flesh, an anchovy, parsley, lemon-peel, salt, pepper, and crumbs, and four ounces of butter warmed, and lay it at the bottom of the dish. Take the flesh of soles, small cod or dressed turbot, and lay on the forcemeat, having rubbed it with salt and pepper. Pour the gravy over, cover with paste, and bake. Observe to take off the skin and fins, if cod or soles are used.

PULLED FISH.

121. One pound of meat pulled from the bones of any fish, two tea-spoonfuls essence of anchovies, two ounces of butter, one table-spoonful of mustard, quarter of a pint of cream, crumbs of bread as for scalloped oysters, pepper and salt to taste, brown before the fire.

BREAKFAST DISH OF FISH.

122. Take any white fish that has been dressed, break it up small, put it in a stewpan with a large lump of butter, add a large break-fast cup full of boiled rice, a little cream, four hard boiled eggs, minced, a little cayenne and salt; mix all well together, make it quite hot, pile it in a dish, and send it to table.

GENERAL DIRECTIONS TO PICKLE FISH.

123. Wash and clean well the fish inside and out; take out the ribs and cut off the heads; dry them *well* with a cloth; rub a little saltpetre on the backbone of each fish; season well inside and out with black pepper, Jamaica pepper, and salt; lay them one by one in a pipkin, with alternate layers of sliced onion and bay leaves; pour over them some vinegar with water, according to taste, cover close, and bake them in a bread oven, after the extreme heat has subsided.

SECT. 2.—SPECIAL DIRECTIONS FOR DRESSING RIVER FISH.

TO FRY TROUT AND GRAYLING.

124. Scale, gut, and well wash; then dry them, and lay them separately on a board before the fire, after dusting some flour over them: or they may be egged and crumbed according to the directions given at par. 114. Fry them of a fine colour, with fresh dripping. Serve with crimped parsley and plain butter. Time, from five to eight minutes.

TROUT A-LA-GENEVOISE.

125. Clean the fish very well; put it into a stew-pan, adding half Champagne and half Moselle, or Rhenish, or sherry wine. Season it with pepper, salt, an onion, a few cloves stuck in it, and a small bunch of parsley and thyme; put in it a crust of French bread; set it on a quick fire. When the fish is done, take the bread out, bruise it, and then thicken the sauce with it; add flour and a little butter, and let it boil up. See that the sauce is of a proper thickness. Lay the fish on a dish, and pour the sauce over it. Serve it with sliced lemon and fried bread.

PERCH, DACE, ROACH, AND GUDGEON.

126. These may be dressed in either of the above modes. (See pars. 124 or 125.)

PERCH, TENCH, AND CARP.

127. To Boil.—Put them into cold water, boil them carefully, and serve with melted butter and soy. Perch are most delicate fish. They may be also stewed; but in stewing they do not preserve so good a flavour. Time, five to fifteen minutes.

128. To STEW.—Scald and clean, take care of the roe, &c., lay the fish in a stew-pan with a rich beef-gravy, an onion, eight cloves, a dessert-spoonful of Jamaica pepper, the same of black, add port-wine to the extent of a fourth part of the quantity of gravy (cider may do), simmer closely covered. When nearly done, add two anchovies chopped fine, a dessert-spoonful of made mustard, and some fine walnut ketchup, a bit of butter rolled in flour; shake it, and let the gravy boil a few minutes. Serve with sippets of fried bread, the roe fried, and a good deal of horseradish and lemon.

129. To BAKE.—Clean a large carp; put in a stuffing as for veal (see Forcemeat): sew it up, brush it all over with yolk of egg, and add plenty of crumbs; then drop on the top some oiled butter to baste it; place the carp in a deep earthen dish, with a pint of stock, a few sliced onions, some bay-leaves, a fagot of herbs (such as basil, thyme, parsley, and both sorts of marjoram), half a pint of port-wine, and six anchovies; cover over the pan, and bake it an hour. Let it be done before it is wanted. Pour the liquor from it, and keep the fish hot while you heat up the liquor with a good piece of butter rolled in flour, a tea-spoonful of mustard, a little Cayenne, and a spoonful of soy. Serve the fish on the dish, garnish with lemon, parsley, and horseradish, and put the gravy into the sauce-tureen.

EELS.

130. To SPITCHCOCK.—Take one or two large eels, leave the skin on, open them on the belly side, cut them into pieces of three inches long, clean nicely and wipe them dry, and then wet them with beaten egg, and strew over on both sides chopped parsley, pepper, salt, a very little sage, and a bit of mace pounded fine and mixed with the season-ing; rub the gridiron with a bit of suet, and broil the fish of a fine colour. Serve with anchovy and butter for sauce.

131. To FRY.—If small, should be curled round and fried, being first dipped into egg and crumbs of bread. If large, they should be *skinned* and cut into lengths, after which they are treated like the small ones.

132. To BOIL.—The small ones are best. Do them in a small quan-tity of water, with a good deal of parsley, which should be served up with them and the liquor. Serve chopped parsley and butter for sauce. Time required, from ten to fifteen minutes.

133. To COLLAR.—Bone a large eel, but do not skin it; mix pepper, salt, mace, allspice, and a clove or two, in the finest powder, and rub over the whole inside; roll it tight and bind with a coarse tape; boil

in salt and water till done, then add vinegar, and when cold keep the collar in pickle. Serve it either whole or in slices. Chopped sage, parsley, and a little thyme, knotted marjoram, and savoury, mixed with the spices, greatly improve the taste.

134. To Stew.—Cut them in short pieces; fry them a little, then put them in a stew-pan and season with salt, pepper, and nutmeg; just cover with gravy, then put in one onion stuck with eight cloves, some mace, lemon-peel, and a little horseradish; when half done add a handful of parsley cut small, a quarter of a pint of port-wine, and a quarter of a pound of fresh butter.

135. Eel Pie.—Cut the eels in lengths of two or three inches, season with pepper and salt, and place in the dish with some bits of butter and a little water, and cover it with puff paste.

LAMPREYS AND LAMPERNS.

136. To Stew Lampreys.—Mix spice enough in the following proportions, to rub in every part of the fish: one-fourth of mace, three-fourths of cloves pounded, as much pepper as the two, and nearly as much salt as the whole, adding a little cayenne; stew down one calf's foot (or other good stock) as stiff as possible, taking the fat from it when cold; add to this jelly equal quantities of rough cider, walnut ketchup, and mushroom ketchup, making in the whole sufficient to cover the fish, which must be pinned up round to the size of the earthen pot intended to contain it: keep it in the stew-pan for an hour, letting it stew as slowly as possible, adding to it a glass of port-wine ten minutes before taking it up. It will do if the above are put into an earthen pot and set in the roaster or oven; an anchovy, a little lemon pickle, and mushroom essence will be an improvement.

137. To Pot.—The above seasoning, without the gravy, is right for potting lampreys, merely letting the fish stew for an hour in its own gravy, then putting it into pots, and pouring melted butter over it when cold.

138. To Stew Lamperns.—The lamperns should be well cleaned in salt and boiling water with a whisk; put them to stew gently in a small quantity of good cider for about half an hour, then add some strong gravy and a sufficient quantity of spice, mixed as above, to make the dish palatable; after stewing till they are tender, add some port-wine and a little walnut ketchup, with flour to thicken the gravy. Garnish the dish with horseradish.

To Bake Pike (otherwise Jack) or Bream.

139. Scale the fish, and open as near the throat as possible, then clean and stuff it with the following:—grated bread, herbs, anchovies, oysters, suet, salt, pepper, mace, half a pint of cream, four yolks of eggs: mix all over the fire till it thickens, then put into the fish and sew it up; put butter over it in little bits, and bake it. Serve sauce of gravy, butter, and anchovy. *Or*, make a stuffing with bread crumbs, herbs, salt, pepper, a chopped anchovy, and a little *butter;* put it in, place a buttered paper under and over the fish; one from three to four lbs. will require an hour's baking in rather a slow oven. Serve with a good gravy nicely flavoured.

Flounders.

140. To Fry.—Let them be rubbed with salt inside and out, and lie two hours to give them some firmness. Dip them into egg; cover with crumbs and fry them.

141. Water Souchy.—Stew two or three flounders, some parsley leaves and roots, thirty peppercorns, and a quart of water, till the fish are boiled to pieces; pulp them through a sieve. Set over the fire the pulped fish, the liquor that boiled them, some perch, tench, or flounders, and some fresh leaves and roots of parsley; simmer all till done enough, then serve in a deep dish. Slices of bread and butter are to be sent to table, to eat with the souchy.

Salmon and Salmon Trout.

142. To Boil.—Clean it carefully, boil it gently, putting it in cold water, and take it out of the water as soon as done. Let the water be boiling if the fish is crimped or split in slices. If under-done it is very unwholesome. Serve with shrimp or anchovy sauce. Salmon takes nearly as long as meat, and for a large fish a quarter of an hour per pound will not be too much to allow.

143. Salmon Cutlets are excellent, the fish being divided with a knife into slices across it, each being about three-fourths of an inch thick. They are then boiled in the same way as other fish, requiring about ten minutes more or less, according to the thickness of the slices.

144. To Broil.—Cut slices an inch thick, and season with pepper and salt; lay each slice in half a sheet of white paper well buttered, twist the ends of the paper, and broil the slices over a slow fire six or eight minutes. Serve with raw pickles and anchovy sauce.

145. To Pot.—Take a large piece, scale and wipe, but do not wash it; salt very well, let it lie till the salt is melted and drained from it, then season with beaten mace, cloves, and whole pepper; lay in a few bay leaves, put it close into a pan, cover it over with butter, and bake it; when well done, drain it from the gravy, put it into the pots to keep, and when cold cover it with clarified butter.

146. To Curry.—Broil slightly as above; then mix half an ounce of curry-powder to each pound of fish, with a good gravy or stock; stew gently in this for half an hour, and serve with rice as usual (see Curry, under Made-dishes).

147. To Kipper.—Cut the fish down, take out the inside and roe. Rub the whole with common salt after scaling it; let it hang twenty-four hours to drain. Pound three or four ounces of saltpetre, according to the size of the fish, two ounces of bay salt, and two ounces of coarse sugar; rub these, when mixed well, into the salmon, and lay it on a large dish or tray two days, then rub it well with common salt, and in twenty-four hours more it will be fit to dry; wipe it well after draining. Hang it either in a wood chimney or in a dry place, keeping it open with two small sticks, or rub with brown pyroligneous acid. Kippered salmon is eaten broiled in paper, and only just warmed through, with egg sauce and mashed potatoes; or it may be boiled, especially the part next the head.

148. To Pickle.—After the salmon has been boiled as usual, let it drain till quite dry on a fish-drainer or cloth; then put it into some of the following pickle:—Take of the water in which the fish was boiled and vinegar equal quantities, to which add a few peppercorns, a little mace, and a very little allspice; boil for a few minutes, and let it stand till cool. The spice may be varied according to the taste; in twelve hours it is fit to be used; but it will keep for weeks in cool weather, or in the summer by the addition of a little ice occasionally.

149. To Collar.—Split such a part of the fish as may be sufficient to make a handsome roll, wash and wipe it, and having mixed salt, white pepper, pounded mace, and Jamaica pepper in quantity to season it very high, rub it inside and out well. Then roll it tight and tie it up with broad tape, put as much water and one-third vinegar as will cover it, with bay-leaves, salt, and both sorts of pepper. Cover close, and simmer till done enough. Drain and boil the liquor quickly, and put on when cold. Serve with fennel. It is an elegant dish, and extremely palatable.

SALMON PATTIES.

150. Scrape some Salmon very fine with a knife, season it very high with cayenne, nutmeg, salt, &c., rub in some fresh butter, and mix the yolk of an egg with it. It may be enclosed in puff paste, or made alone into cakes.

SECT 3.—SPECIAL DIRECTIONS FOR COOKING SEA FISH.

TURBOT, BRILL, OR PLAICE.

151. To BOIL.—The turbot-kettle must be of a proper size, and in the nicest order. Do not skin the fish, as I have known done by an ignorant cook. Set it in cold water sufficient to cover it completely, throw a handful of salt and a glass of vinegar into it, and let it gradually boil; be careful that no blacks fall; but skim it well, and thereby preserve the beauty of the colour. Sprinkle the belly, or white side, with the roe of the lobster, and turn that side up. Serve it garnished with a complete fringe of curled parsley, lemon, and horseradish. The sauce should be the finest lobster, shrimp, or anchovy, and plain butter, served plentifully in separate tureens. Time, about two minutes per pound.

152. To FRY.—Sprinkle with salt, and keep twenty-four hours; then wash and wipe it dry, wet over with egg, and cover with crumbs of bread; make some lard, or fine dripping, and two large spoonsful of vinegar boiling hot; lay the fish in, and fry it a fine colour, drain it from the fat, and serve with fried parsley round, and anchovy sauce. This mode is particularly adapted for plaice.

SOLES.

153. Soles are skinned, and may be boiled in the same way as turbot. They are served with plain butter, or parsley and butter. Time, about five or six minutes per fish.

154. To FRY.—Skin them, and dry carefully with a cloth; then dip in egg and bread-crumb, and fry as directed in par. 114.

155. As CUTLETS.—Take two or three soles, separate the flesh from the backbone, and take off the heads, fins, and tail. Sprinkle the inside with salt. roll them up tight from the tail end upwards, and fasten with small skewers. If large or of middling size, put half a fish in each roll—small do not answer. Dip them into yolks of eggs, and cover with crumbs. Do the egg over them again, and then put more

F

crumbs, and fry them a beautiful colour in lard, or, for fast-days, in clarified butter.

156. SOLE PIE.—Split some soles from the bones, and cut the fins close; season with a mixture of salt, pepper, a little nutmeg and pounded mace, and put them in layers, with oysters. They eat excellently. A pair of middling-sized ones will do, and half a hundred of oysters. Put in the dish the oyster-liquor, two or three spoonfuls of broth, and some butter; cover with paste. When the pie comes home, pour in a cupful of thick cream.

COD-FISH.

157. To BOIL.—Some people boil the cod whole; but a large head and shoulders contain all the parts that it is proper to dress, the thinner parts being overdone and tasteless before the thick are ready. But as the whole fish may be purchased at times more reasonably, the lower half may be sprinkled with salt, and hung up, when it will be in high perfection in one or two days. Or, it may be made more salt, and served with egg sauce, potatoes, and parsnips, as salt-fish. Cod, when small, is usually very cheap. If boiled quite fresh, it is watery; but eats excellently, if salted and hung up for a day to give it firmness, then stuffed and broiled. Boiled cod's head and shoulders will be firmer, and have a better flavour, if a little salt is rubbed down the bone, and along the thick part, even if it is to be eaten the same day. Tie it up, and put it on the fire in cold water, which will completely cover it; throw a handful of salt into this with a couple of spoonsful of vinegar. Great care must be taken to serve it without the smallest speck of black or scum. Garnish with a large quantity of double parsley, lemon, horseradish, and the milt, roe, and liver, and fried smelts, if approved. If with smelts, be careful that no water hangs about the fish; or the beauty of the smelts will be taken off, as well as their flavour. Serve with plenty of oyster or shrimp sauce, and anchovy and butter. Time, about three minutes per pound.

158. CRIMPED COD, OR SLICES OF COD, must be put into boiling water, and after a space of three minutes, dash in cold water to lower the temperature; then finish as above.

159. To FRY OR BROIL slices of cod-fish, proceed as directed in the general remarks at pars. 114 and 115.

160. CURRY OF COD should be made of sliced cod, that has either been crimped or sprinkled for a day with salt to make it firm. Fry it of a fine brown with onion; and stew it with a good white gravy, a

little curry powder, a bit of butter and flour, three or four spoonsful of rich cream, salt, and add cayenne, if the powder is not hot enough.

161. To DRESS SALT COD.—Soak and clean the piece to be dressed, then lay it all night in water, with a glass of vinegar. Boil it enough, then break it into flakes on the dish; pour over it parsnips boiled, beaten into a mortar, and then boiled up with cream and a large piece of butter, rubbed with a bit of flour. It may be served as above with egg sauce instead of the parsnip, and the latter sent up whole. *Or*, the fish may be boiled and sent up without flaking, and sauces as above. Time, the same as for fresh cod.

· 162. COD PIE.—Take a piece of the middle of a small cod, and salt it well one night. Next day wash it, and season with pepper, salt, and a very little nutmeg, mixed; place in a dish, put some butter on it, and a little good broth of any kind into the dish. Cover it with a crust; and when done add a sauce of a spoonful of broth, a quarter of a pint of cream, a little flour and butter, a grate of lemon and nutmeg, and give it one boil. Oysters may be added.

163. SALT FISH, which is too strong to be eaten dressed in this way, will be much improved by boiling it, and then mashing it up with potatoes in equal quantities, and browning before the fire in a Dutch oven.

COD SOUNDS BOILED.

164. Soak them in warm water half an hour, then scrape and clean; and if to be dressed white, boil them in milk and water; when tender, serve them in a napkin with egg sauce. The salt must not be much soaked out, unless for fricassee.

165. To LOOK LIKE SMALL CHICKENS.—Wash three large sounds nicely, and boil in milk and water, but not too tender; when cold put a forcemeat of chopped oysters, crumbs of bread, a bit of butter, nutmeg, pepper, salt, and the yolks of two eggs; spread it over the sounds, and roll up each in the form of a chicken, skewering it; then lard them as you would chickens, dust a little flour over, and roast them in a tin oven slowly. When done enough, pour over them a fine oyster sauce. Serve for side or corner dish.

166. To BROIL.—Scald in hot water, rub well with salt, pull off the dirty skin, and put them to simmer till tender; take them out, flour, and broil. While this is being done, season a little brown gravy with pepper, salt, a tea-spoonful of soy, and a little mustard; give it a boil with a bit of flour and butter, and pour it over the sounds.

167. En Ragout.—Prepare as above; then stew them in white gravy, seasoned, cream, butter, and a little bit of flour added before you serve, gently boiling up. A bit of lemon peel, nutmeg, and the least pinch of pounded mace should give the flavour.

HADDOCKS AND WHITING.

168. To Boil.—Treat like cod-fish, the allowance for time being very nearly the same, unless very small, when it may be reduced one-third.

169. To Dry.—Choose them of two or three pounds' weight; take out the gills, eyes, and entrails, and remove the blood from the back-bone; wipe them dry, and put some salt into the bodies and eyes; lay them on a board for a night, then hang them up in a dry place, and after three or four days they will be fit to dress; skin and rub them with egg, and strew crumbs over them; lay them before the fire, and baste with butter until brown enough. Serve with egg sauce.

170. Whitings, if large, are excellent in this way; and it will prove an accommodation in the country where there is no regular supply of fish.

SKATE.

171. Skate, Thornback, and Maids (all usually sold as *skate*), should be hung one day at least before dressing. They may be boiled in slices (called crimped), or fried in crumbs with egg, or in butter.

MACKEREL.

172. Boil till the tail splits, and serve with butter and fennel. The time is usually about ten, fifteen, or twenty minutes, according to size.

173. To Broil them, split them and sprinkle with herbs, pepper, and salt; or stuff with the same, crumbs, and chopped fennel.

174. Collared, as eel (page 61).

175. Potted.—Clean, season, and bake them in a pan with mixed spice, bay-leaves, and some butter; when cold, lay them in a potting-pot, and cover with butter.

176. Pickled.—Boil them, then boil some of the liquor with a few peppercorns, bay-leaves, and a third part of the quantity of vinegar; when cold, pour it over them.

177. *Another Method of Pickling.*—Clean and divide them, then cut each side into three, or, leaving them undivided, cut each fish into five or six pieces; to six large mackerel take nearly an ounce of pepper,

two nutmegs, a little mace, four cloves, and a handful of salt, all in the finest powder; mix and, making holes in each bit of fish, thrust the seasoning into them, and rub each piece with some of it; then fry them in brown oil; let them stand till cold, then put them into a stone jar, and cover with vinegar; if to keep long, pour oil on the top. Thus done, they may be preserved for months.

178. MACKEREL PIE will do well, the fish being treated in the same way as described for cod at page 65, but do not salt them till used. Parsley, picked and put in, may be used instead of oysters.

RED MULLET.

179. Clean from the gills and small intestines, but leave the rest in the inside, fold in oiled paper, and gently bake in a small dish; make a sauce of the liquor that comes from the fish, with a piece of butter, a little flour, a little essence of anchovy, and a glass of sherry; give it a boil, and serve in a boat, and the fish in the paper cases.

To DRESS PIPERS.

180. BOIL OR BAKE them with a pudding, well-seasoned, like pike. If baked, put a large cup of rich broth into the dish, and when done, take that, some essence of anchovy, and a squeeze of lemon, and boil them up together for a sauce.

To FRY SMELTS.

181. They should not be washed more than is necessary to clean them; dry them in a cloth, then lightly flour them, but shake it off; dip them into plenty of egg, then into bread-crumbs grated fine, and plunge them into a good pan of *boiling* lard; continue gently boiling, and a few minutes will make them a bright yellow brown; take care not to take off the light roughness of the crumbs, or their beauty will be lost, and for this purpose use the wire frame (see *fig.* 132).

HERRINGS AND SPRATS.

182. To FRY.—Do them of a light brown, with onions sliced, and serve them very hot.

183. To BROIL.—Flour them first, and do of a good colour; plain butter for sauce.

184. To POT.—Do them as for mackerel (which see).

185. To CURE AS BLOATERS.—Clean, and lay them in salt and a little saltpetre one night; then hang them on a stick, through the

eyes, in a row; have ready an old cask, in which put some sawdust, and in the midst of it a heater red-hot; fix the stick over the smoke, and let them remain twenty-four hours.

186. To DRESS RED HERRINGS.—Choose those that are large and moist, cut them open, pour some boiling small-beer over them, and let them soak half an hour; drain them dry, and make them just hot through before the fire, then rub some cold butter over them and serve. Egg-sauce, or buttered eggs and mashed potatoes, should be sent up with them.

187. To BAKE.—Wash and drain, without wiping them; season with allspice in fine powder, salt, and a few old cloves. Lay them in a pan with plenty of black pepper, an onion, and a few bay-leaves; add half vinegar and half small-beer enough to cover them. Tie paper over the pan, and bake in a slow oven. If approved, throw saltpetre over them the night before, to make them look red. Gut through the vent, but do not open them.

SECT. 4.—SPECIAL DIRECTIONS FOR DRESSING SHELL FISH.

LOBSTERS, CRAYFISH, PRAWNS, AND SHRIMPS.

188. To BOIL.—Put them into a pot of boiling water; the lobsters must not remain any longer than fifteen or twenty minutes, unless very large indeed. From the shells and small claws bruised will be extracted a juice that will much improve the sauce. When cold, split the tail down the middle, and crack the claws, for which purpose nothing serves so well as the chink at the hinge of a back-kitchen door. Place the body in the middle, half a tail on each side, and the large claws top and bottom.

189. To ROAST.—After boiling the lobster, take it out of the shell, and while hot rub it with butter, and lay it before the fire. Continue basting it with butter till it has a fine froth; then serve.

190. To STEW.—Pick the lobster, put the berries into a pan in a warm bath, and rub them down with a bit of butter, two spoonsful of any sort of gravy, one of soy, or walnut ketchup, a little salt and cayenne, and a spoonful of port; stew the lobster cut into bits with the gravy as above.

191. To POT.—Half boil them, pick out the meat, cut into small bits, season with mace, white pepper, nutmeg, and salt, press close into a pot and cover with butter, bake half an hour; put the spawn in. When cold, take the lobster out, and put it into the pots with a little

of the butter. Beat the other butter in a mortar with some of the spawn; then mix that coloured butter with as much as will be sufficient to cover the pots, and strain it. Cayenne may be added, if approved.

Another Receipt.—Boil them till half done, take out all the meat, &c. (the tail and claws whole). Skin the tail, season it with pepper and salt, mace, and the least possible of nutmeg; bake an hour and half, with butter enough to cover them, having tied them over very closely. When cool, press closely in pots, mixing as much of the liquor they were baked in as will colour it highly; cover the pots when cold with clarified butter.

192. TO POT PRAWNS AND SHRIMPS.—They should be selected as large as possible. When boiled take them out of the skins, and season them with salt, white pepper, and a very little mace and cloves. Press them into a pot, set it in the oven ten minutes, and when cold cover them with a layer of clarified butter.

193. SHRIMP PIE (*Excellent*).—Pick a quart of shrimps; if they are very salt, season them with only mace and a clove or two. Mince two or three anchovies: mix these with the spice, and then season the shrimps. Put some butter at the bottom of the dish, and cover the shrimps with a glass of sharp white wine. The paste must be light and thin. They do not take long baking.

194. CURRY OF LOBSTERS OR PRAWNS.—Take them from the shells, and lay in a pan, with a small piece of mace, three or four spoonsful of veal gravy, and four of cream; rub smooth one or two tea-spoonsful of curry-powder, a tea-spoonful of flour, and an ounce of butter; simmer an hour; squeeze half a lemon in, and add salt.

195. LOBSTER RISSOLES.—Extract the meat of a boiled lobster, mince it fine as possible, and mix with it the coral pounded smooth, and some yolks of hard-boiled eggs pounded also. Season it with cayenne pepper, powdered mace, and a very little salt. Make a batter of beaten egg, milk, and flour. To each egg allow two large table-spoonsful of milk, and a large tea-spoonful of flour. Beat the batter well, and then mix the lobster with it gradually, till it is stiff enough to make into oval balls, about the size of a large plum. Fry them in the best salad oil, and serve them up either warm or cold.

196. LOBSTER PIE.—Boil two lobsters (or three small), take out the tails, cut them in two, take out the gut, cut each in four pieces, and lay in a small dish, then put in the meat of the claws and that picked out of the body; pick off the furry parts from the latter, and

take out the lady; beat the spawn and all the shells in a mortar, and set them on to stew with some water, two or three spoonsful of vinegar, pepper, salt, and some pounded mace: a large piece of butter rolled in flour, must be added when the goodness of the shells is brought out. Give a boil or two, and pour into the dish strained. Strew some crumbs, and put a paste over all. Bake slowly, but only till the paste be done.

197. CROQUETTES OF LOBSTER.—Pound or chop fine the fleshy part of a lobster, and add a quarter as much of sifted bread crumbs, season with pepper, salt, anchovy, and a little mace, and add a little vinegar or lemon juice, and a few spoonsful of cream, if no white sauce be at hand. Warm it, and beat in the yolk of an egg. When cool, make it into either round or oval balls, or flat cakes; dip in egg and crumbs, and fry them dry in lard.

198. LOBSTER PATTIES.—Make them with the same seasoning as for oysters, adding a little cream, and the smallest bit of butter.

Another.—Roll out some very light puff paste to a little more than half an inch in thickness. Cut it with a fluted paste-cutter, either in round or oval shapes; then with another cutter a size smaller. Mark them half through; dipping *this* cutter into hot water to prevent the paste from adhering to it. Bake ten minutes or more, according to the state of the oven, and while hot, take out the portions that have been cut through with the small cutter, and scoop out the crumbs—the lid may be laid on again or not. Fill with lobster prepared as for croquettes (par. 197). N.B.—This forms a more dressy patty than those ordinarily made.

199. To FORCE LOBSTERS.—Boil them well, and take out the *bodies*, and the meat from the feelers, and mix with it one or two boiled whitings, and two anchovies chopped fine, two eggs beaten, a piece of butter, some thyme, parsley, shalot, and pepper and salt. Fill the bodies again with this mixture, and bake half-an-hour. Serve cold with the tail cut in half, and with the claws arranged round the bodies.

CRABS.

200. To BOIL.—Proceed as for lobsters.

201. To DRESS HOT.—After picking the meat out of the shell, season it with pepper and salt. Then wash the shell clean, and after making the white meat hot in a saucepan, lay it in the shell with the soft part at top; strew crumbs of bread, and brown it over.

202. To DRESS COLD.—Empty the shells, and mix the flesh with

oil, vinegar, salt, and a little white pepper and cayenne; then put the mixture into the large shell, and serve; very little oil is necessary, and by some people it is altogether disliked.

OYSTERS.

203. To FEED.—Put them into water, and wash them with a birch-besom till quite clean; then lay them round side downwards in a pan; sprinkle with flour or oatmeal and salt, and cover with water; do the same every day, and they will fatten. The water should be pretty salt, and rather more so than sea-water. Bay salt is the best for the purpose when it is at hand.

204. To BOIL.—Open the shells, and clean and drain them into boiling water; then drop the oysters into a saucepan of boiling water, and boil them gently for three or four minutes. Serve in the shells with a little cold butter, vinegar, and pepper.

205. To STEW.—Open and separate the liquor from them, then wash them from the grit; strain the liquor, and put with the oysters a bit of mace or lemon-peel, and a few white peppercorns. Simmer them very gently, and put some cream and a little flour and butter Serve with sippets.

206. To ROAST.—Place the oysters unopened between the bars of a fire or in a charcoal stove. They require about six or eight minutes' time.

207. To SCALLOP.—Put them with crumbs of bread, pepper, salt, into scallop-shells or saucers, and bake before the fire in a Dutch oven. Cream mixed with the bread is a great improvement.

208. To FRY.—Make a batter of flour, milk, and eggs, season it a very little with pepper and salt, dip the oysters into it, and fry them a fine yellow-brown. A little nutmeg should be put into the seasoning, and a few crumbs of bread into the flour.

209. DUTCH OYSTERS.—Roll rock oysters in yolk of egg, then dip them in grated bread crumbs and white pepper, one by one, and fry them in butter: serve with melted butter in a sauce-tureen.

210. As LOAVES.—Open them and save the liquor; wash them in it; then strain it through a sieve, and put a little of it into a tosser with a bit of butter and flour, white pepper, a scrape of nutmeg, and a little cream. Stew them, and cut in dice; put them into rolls sold for the purpose.

211. As SAUSAGES.—Take a quarter of a pound of chicken or veal, three ounces of crumbs of bread, one ounce of beef-suet, thirty oysters chopped, and half the yolk of an egg; to be seasoned with mace,

cayenne, and black pepper, and made either into balls, or of a long form, and fried. To be served with a rich brown gravy.

212. As Toast.—Pour some well-thickened and flavoured oyster-sauce upon a buttered toast. The number of oysters is from two and a half to three score, depending on the size of the corner-dish. This is very good for a top or bottom dish in a second course.

213. To Pickle.—Wash four dozen of the largest oysters you can get in their own liquor, wipe them dry, strain the liquor off, adding to it a dessert-spoonful of pepper, two blades of mace, a table-spoonful of salt, unless the liquor is already very salt, three of white wine, and four of vinegar.

214. Oyster Patties.—Put a fine puff-paste into small patty-pans, and cover with paste, with a bit of bread in each; and against they are baked have ready the following to fill them with, after taking out the bread:—Take off the beards of the oysters, cut the other parts into small bits, put them in a small tosser, with a grate of nutmeg, a very little white pepper and salt, a morsel of lemon-peel cut so small that you can scarcely see it, a very little cream, and a little of the oyster liquor. Simmer for a few minutes before filling; then serve.

CHAP. VIII.—SOUP-MAKING, SOUPS, AND BROTHS.

SECT. 1.—GENERAL REMARKS.

215. Upon the management of this department depends, in great measure, the degree of economy or waste going on in any establishment. It will always happen, and especially in large families, that there are refuse bones and pieces of meat, which are left either in the dish or in the plates. Every scrap of these should be collected together, with any odds and ends of all kinds of animal food, such as heads and necks of poultry, trimmings of meat, &c. If these are not approved of for the house, they will, at all events, afford good useful soup for the poor, who will, many of them, be grateful for the broth or soup produced from them. Besides these, the boilings of all meat and poultry should be saved, and the strength increased by adding bones, scraps, &c. The liquor from salt-meat is too salt, and part only must be mixed with more boilings of water to form the foundation for all sorts of soups, gravies, &c.; the liquid thus furnished being on this account called by the name, "stock."

SECT. 2.—THE UTENSILS.

216. These are—1st, *the digester;* and, 2nd, *the stock pot.*

THE DIGESTER.

217. Usually named after its inventor, Pepin (see *fig.* 129), is a strong iron vessel with a moveable handle, by which it may be suspended over the fire. In the centre of the lid is a metal valve, which should always be attended to, as it might otherwise rust in its socket, and occasion the bursting of the pot. A little grease prevents this, but the greatest preventive is cleanliness. Besides this valve, which allows the steam to escape as soon as it rises with sufficient force to overcome the weight of the piece of metal, there is a peculiar adaptation of the lid, by which it is very securely closed. It is not only placed upon the top of the digester, but, by a twist, it is hooked under three projecting arms (see *fig.* 129), and is consequently kept down closely, its under surface being ground to correspond with the upper edge of the pot. When, therefore, the bones, &c., are placed in the digester with water, and the lid adapted to it properly, the heat is raised considerably above 212 degrees, because the pressure is greater than that of the atmosphere by the weight of the valve. The consequence is, that bones are compelled to give out their gelatine, and are left almost with nothing but their lime. This is the most economical of all cooking utensils, and is the means of saving an immense amount of nutritive matter; but it is of no use whatever unless the lid is securely adapted to the pot.

THE STOCK-POT.

218. This is merely a common saucepan, with a well-fixed lid (*fig.* 130). It is intended for the slow boiling of meat in the liquor which has come out of the digester from the bones. Some people use the digester as a stock-pot, but it is better to put the bones in by themselves with any pieces of gristle, as much more gelatine is dissolved by water than by a strong soup made from meat; besides which, the increased temperature in the digester is unfavourable to the solution of the meat. At all events, the bones should be first boiled, and the meat added afterwards; but the better plan is to boil the bones first, and extract every thing from them; then pour off into the stock pot, and add what meat or other soft bits may be intended to be used, stewing them for some hours very slowly. Most soups will require

from four to six hours' gentle boiling, and almost all should be prepared
the day before they are to be used, by which plan they may be allowed
to become cold, when the fat collected on the top, and become solid,
may easily be separated. If all the fat is not removed, a piece of clean
silver paper passed over the surface will effectually get rid of it.

Sect. 3.—Soup-making.

219. In making the various sorts of soups, three different kinds of
gelatinous solutions are alluded to—1st, *boilings*, which mean the
water in which meat has been boiled; 2nd, *brown stock*, which is soup
made from beef, and cow-heels, or knuckle of veal, with or without
the addition of any boilings; and 3rd, *white stock*, which is made from
veal, or any white meat, as chickens, turkey boilings, &c. ;—besides
these are mentioned *browning* and *glaze*, which will be presently described.

To Make Good Stock.

220. Put whatever bones are at hand in the digester (previously
breaking them in pieces); boil them for three or four hours at least,
then pour off the liquor into the stock-pot, and add to each gallon the
meat off a knuckle of veal, a pound of lean beef, and a pound of the
lean of a gammon of bacon, all sliced, with two or three scraped
carrots, two onions, two turnips, two heads of celery sliced, and two
quarts of water. Stew the meat quite tender, but do not let it burn.
When thus prepared it will serve either for soup, or brown or white
gravy. If for BROWN GRAVY, add colouring, and boil a few minutes.
One knuckle of veal, two pounds of lean beef, or a shin of beef,
a quarter of a pound of ham, with a cow-heel, will make sufficient
soup for a party of eighteen. A little Indian soy, or shalot wine,
is a great improvement in flavouring brown soups. A little sugar
improves almost every soup. When you make any kind of soup—
particularly portable, vermicelli, or brown gravy soup, or any soup
that has roots or herbs in, always observe to lay these last over the
meat, cover it close and set it over a very slow fire; this will draw all
the virtue out of the roots or herbs, and give the soup a very different
flavour to that which it has when water is put to it at first. When
the gravy is almost dried up, fill the pan with water, and as soon as it
begins to boil take off the fat, and follow the directions of the receipt
according to the sort of soup which it is desired to make. When it is
desired to make old peas soup, take soft water; but for green peas

hard is the best : it keeps the peas a better colour. To make a white soup do not put in the cream till you take it off the fire. Always dish up soups the last thing ; if it is peas soup, it often settles and looks thin.

A Good Brown Stock.

221. Cut in pieces a shin of beef and a knuckle of veal. Rub a quarter of a pound of butter on the bottom of a stewpan which will hold two gallons of water, and put in the meat with half a pint of water, a little salt, three or four onions, a turnip, a carrot or two, a head of celery, and one or two leeks—add a few cloves and a little mace ; put the stewpan over a sharp fire (occasionally stirring the whole with a wooden spoon) till it becomes of a brown colour, and the stew-pan is covered with a thickish glaze, then fill up the pan with cold water, and, when on the point of boiling, draw it off the fire and simmer very gently for three or four hours. Skim it frequently, strain through a hair sieve and it is ready for use. From this may be made any brown soup, as clear gravy soup, ox tail, Julienne soup, &c.

To Make Stock for Brown or White Fish Soups.

222. Take a pound of skate, four or five flounders, and two pounds of eels ; clean them well, and cut them into pieces ; cover them with water, and season them with mace, pepper, salt, an onion stuck with cloves, a head of celery, two parsley roots sliced, and a bunch of sweet herbs. Simmer an hour and a half closely covered, and then strain it off for use. If for brown soup, first fry the fish brown in butter, and then do as above. It will not keep more than two or three days.

Glaze.

223. Glaze is a boiled-down animal jelly, made from the stock as above ; but avoiding the use of salt, as when boiled down sufficiently it would be too strong of that saline material. It only requires care not to burn it, and should be properly strained. A quart of stock will only make about a spoonful of glaze ; and as it consists almost entirely of gelatine, the portable soups sold in the shops answer all the purpose at much less trouble and cost ; indeed, glaze itself may be bought there cheaper than it can be made at home.

To Clarify Stock.

224. To Clarify Stock, which process is now often wanted, as it is the fashion to use it clear in mock-turtle and many other soups, which

were formerly thickened, the following method must be adopted:—
Put the stock over a good fire, and when boiling add the white of one
egg to each quart of stock, proceeding as follows:—Beat the eggs up
in a little water, then add a little hot stock, beat to a froth, and pour
gradually into the pot, when the whole is to be whisked. Boil up, and
immediately remove and strain through a fine sieve or cloth.

BROWNING FOR SOUPS AND GRAVIES.

225. Put four ounces of lump sugar, a gill of water, and half an
ounce of the finest butter into a small tosser, and set it over a gentle
fire. Stir it with a wooden spoon till of a bright brown; then add half
a pint of water; boil, skim, and when cold bottle and cork it close.
Add to soup or gravy as much of this as will give a proper colour.

Another.—Put four ounces of pounded loaf sugar into a frying-pan,
with one ounce of butter; set it over a clear fire and stir it; when it is
frothy, and the sugar is dissolving, hold it higher till it becomes a deep
brown, pour in by degrees a third of a pint of port-wine, add a little
lemon-peel, salt, three spoonfuls of mushroom ketchup, a little mace,
six cloves, an onion, and some allspice, boil all slowly for ten minutes,
skim it, pour it into a basin, and when cold bottle for use.

BROWNED FLOUR FOR COLOURING AND THICKENING SOUPS AND GRAVIES.

226. Browned Flour for Colouring and Thickening Soups and
Gravies, may be made by spreading some flour upon tins in a cool
oven, and carefully watching and turning it lest the edges should
become too dark. Keep it in a dry place, and mix with butter when
used.

SECT. 4.—RECEIPTS FOR SOUPS.

MUTTON BROTH WITH THE MEAT IN.

227. Cut a neck of mutton into chops, taking off *every bit* of fat four
hours before dinner; put it in the stewpan, and pour it nearly full of
boiling water; cut in slices four carrots and six small turnips, and put
in the pan at the same time; let it simmer and boil till dinner-time;
flavour with salt, and skim off the fat. Some people add an ounce or
two of rice with the vegetables.

TO MAKE MUTTON OR VEAL BROTH.

228. Take one pound of meat, free from the bone, and put it on the
fire with a quart of water; when it boils skim it as clear as possible,

then add a little more cold water, which will make the scum rise afresh; then take it off, and season with parsley root about the size of two fingers, a small carrot, an onion or two, a blade of mace (and about two ounces of clean bacon if you like this addition); boil it an hour and a half at least, till the meat is tender; then strain it. It may be made with mutton, beef, or veal, or the three combined.

To Make Gravy Soup.

229. Fry three or four pounds of meat, then fry half a dozen carrots and turnips, after which fry three or four onions, taking care not to let them burn; stew altogether with a little pepper, salt, a clove or two, and a stick of celery; strain it; when cold skim off the fat, and boil it up again with the white of three or four eggs to clear it; strain it through a cloth; it is then fit for use. Soak half a rasped roll in a little gravy, and stick it with almonds, to put in the soup when in the tureen; or, as is generally preferred, add some vermicelli, or macaroni made in small shapes for the purpose, or the piped macaroni cut in short lengths. (It forms a pleasing variety to add, instead of the above, some pieces of carrot cut long and thin, or in their season a few heads of asparagus cut in short lengths and made tender, but not to break. These make it like Julienne soup.)

To Make Clear Gravy Soup.

230. Take a slice of beef, a piece of knuckle of veal, a small slice of lean ham or bacon, two or three carrots *according to size*, one large or two small turnips, six onions, a little parsley, two heads of celery and a small bunch of sweet herbs; cut the meat into small slices, and put it into a stewpan that will hold about six quarts, with about two ounces of butter, and the vegetables and herbs; cut the vegetables into moderate-sized pieces, and slice the onions; add half an ounce of black peppercorns, half an ounce of allspice, a blade or two of mace, about six cloves, and as much salt as you think necessary; put the stewpan over a brisk fire, and let it fry all together, keeping it frequently stirred to prevent its burning; as soon as it becomes of a light-brown colour fill up the stewpan with cold water, and just before it boils pull it off the fire and let it just simmer four or five hours; skim it frequently, strain through a sieve, and when cold take off every particle of grease, and it is fit for use; add a little pepper and salt if required: it is seldom served without something being put into it, either Italian paste, which you may buy at any Italian warehouse, and at

some grocers, or a little macaroni, having previously boiled it in water till it is soft, and then it is usual to hand grated Parmesan cheese, and sometimes semolina is served with it: the meat may be boiled a second time; it will make stock for some other kind of inferior soup.

MEAT SOUP FOR FAMILY USE OR VILLAGE DISTRIBUTION.

231. To make 120 quarts, use fifteen or twenty pounds of beef, half a bushel of turnips, a quarter of a peck of carrots, a quarter of a peck of onions, one peck of peas (or, instead of peas, three pounds of rice), one large spoonful of bruised celery-seed, three quarters of a peck of flour, or rather more; one ounce and a quarter of pepper, and the third of a peck of salt. The bones should be broken in pieces and separately boiled in a digester in half the water, and the liquor added to the remainder in which the meat and vegetables are boiled.

VEAL BROTH.

232. Stew a small knuckle in about three quarts of water, with two ounces of well-washed rice, or, what is still better, the same quantity of sago thoroughly washed, a little salt, and a blade of mace, till the liquor is half wasted away.

OX-TAIL SOUP.

233. Boil an ox-tail, divided at the joints, slowly in a pint of water with a small lump of butter or good beef-dripping, for three hours, till the water is reduced one-half; then add half a carrot and turnip, an onion, and a small head of celery, a little lemon, and common thyme and parsley. Five or six peppercorns and a pinch of cayenne should be added, and also a tea-spoonful of salt. When the vegetables are quite tender, take them out and pulp them through a coarse sieve, after which mix with them two table-spoonsful of flour, and rub all up with the gravy in the stewpan; then add three pints of boiling water, stirring it in. Finally, boil up for a few minutes, and add a little browning, or good brown gravy. It may be made clear by omitting the flour.

234. For CLEAR OX-TAIL SOUP, nothing farther than the stock, for which a receipt is given at par. 221, will be required, except ox-tails cut through at each joint, and boiled tender in a stewpan. Add a little more salt and pepper.

235. For THICK OX-TAIL SOUP, thicken the same with flour and

butter, and if approved put a glass of sherry or madeira wine into the tureen before pouring in the soup.

Ox-cheek Soup.

236. Ox-tail Soup is merely the stewed ox-cheek (which see), with the soup somewhat reduced, and, if approved of, thickened like the ox-tail soup.

Pot-au-Feu.

237. The celebrated French Pot-au-Feu, according to the recognised authority of M. Soyer, consists of six pounds of beef, four quarts of water set near the fire, and skimmed; when nearly boiling, add a spoonful and a half of salt, half a pound of liver, two carrots, four turnips, eight young or two old leeks, one head of celery, two onions (one of them burnt), with a clove in each, and a piece of parsnip. Skim again, and simmer four or five hours, adding a little cold water now and then; take off part of the fat, put slices of bread into the tureen, lay half of the vegetables over, and half the broth, and serve the meat (*bouilli*) separately with the other half of the vegetables.

French Soup (very Good and Cheap).

238. A sheep's head and pluck boiled gently in a gallon of water till reduced to half the quantity, a small teacupful of pearl-barley, six large onions, one turnip, one carrot, a bunch of sweet herbs, and a few cloves and peppercorns. Add a little mushroom ketchup, and thicken with some flour rolled in a lump of butter. It is better to boil it the day before it is wanted. Cut the meat off the head in slices as for hashed calf's head (taking it out for this purpose as soon as it is sufficiently tender), and then into small squares, which must be put into the soup again when it is warmed up for use. Finish it up with forcemeat and little egg-balls, and a teacupful of white wine, which, with the addition of a *little* sugar, makes it nearly equal to mock-turtle.

Mulligatawny Soup.

239. Take a knuckle of veal five pounds weight; put it on with enough water to cover it. When it is about half done take it off; cut the meat in slices, put it in a cool place till the next day, then take the fat off and fry the veal in a little butter, and put it in the soup

G

with four dessert-spoonsful of curry-powder, a little salt, and four onions sliced and fried in butter. Let all simmer together for two hours; if too thin, thicken it with flour and butter. Serve it up with rice in another dish.

Another.—Take four pounds of beef, one and a half of scrag of mutton, two of ham, and a knuckle of veal; cut in small pieces, and put in a gallon of water; reduce to two quarts; add two onions, four turnips, and plenty of carrots. Strain it off, let it cool, take off the fat, and warm it up with two or three sticks of celery, and rub it through a sieve; put it back in the sauce-pan, and add walnut or mushroom ketchup, a table-spoonful of curry-powder, a little cayenne pepper, and the juice of a lemon. Prepare rice as for curry to hand round with it.

MOCK-TURTLE SOUP

240. Halve a calf's head, take out the brains, and put as much water as you wish to make soup, with sweet herbs, parsley, a few onions, and some lemon peel. Stew it gently until the meat is tender; then take it out and let it get cold; thicken the soup with a little flour and butter, and strain it through a sieve. Add sherry wine, a little walnut and mushroom ketchup, pounded mace, and cayenne. Take the brains and beat them up with a little flour and two eggs into a light batter, adding pepper and salt, and some parsley chopped very fine; then take the yolks of two eggs and beat them up; make them into as many portions as you please, tying each in a bit of muslin, and boil them in little round balls; the batter made with the brains is to be fried into cakes a light brown. When the head is cold it must be cut into small pieces and laid in the gravy, the cakes and eggs, with some forcemeat balls, to be laid on the top of the soup just before it is sent to table. Every particle of fat must be removed from the surface before warming the soup for the table.

Another Receipt.—Cut one neat's foot and two calf's feet in thin slices; if you like ox palates, six will do, and in that case only one calf's foot will be required. Boil these till tender enough for a fricassee. Put them into a full quart of good mutton-gravy, entirely free from fat; cover it down close, and let it stew gently rather more than three-quarters of an hour with the following—one large onion, one dozen of bearded oysters and their liquor, and some lemon peel, a large bunch of sweet-herbs, a good-sized anchovy, some salt, nutmeg, and cayenne. The onion, oysters, herbs, anchovy, and lemon peel must be chopped very fine, and half a pint of madeira or sherry wine added just before it is sent to table; squeeze in half a lemon, and put in egg and forcemeat-balls, if approved of, the balls being well-seasoned. About three-quarters of a pound of scrag of mutton will make the gravy.

Another and Plainer Receipt.—Scald the hair off a calf's head, but leave the skin on. Make three pints of stock with three pounds of mutton or veal, flavour with whole pepper, mace, onion and sweet herbs. Cut the outside of the head (the clear part till you come to the flesh) in pieces two or three inches square, stew it in the soup two or three hours till tender, add cayenne, the rind of half a lemon, and madeira wine; serve with the meat and egg balls. The remainder of the head will boil.

241. MOCK-TURTLE SOUP (*Clear*).—Either of the above receipts may be made clear by thickening them with arrowroot instead of flour, and clarifying them (see par. 224). When this mode is preferred, the soup is served without forcemeat or egg-balls.

HARE SOUP.

242. Cut a large old hare in small pieces, and put it in a jug with a little lean ham, some celery, two onions sliced, a bunch of sweet herbs, quarter of a pint of red wine, and three quarts of water. Stew it, closely covered, for two or three hours, till the meat is done to rags. Strain off the soup and take the meat from the bones, pound the meat in a mortar, add it to the soup till it is of a proper thickness, give it a boil up, and add two teaspoonsful of soy and one of ketchup, with cayenne pepper and salt, and a *little* moist sugar. The brains may be made with the stewed and pounded liver into forcemeat balls, or the liver may be pounded with the meat for thickening the soup. Some prefer to add the port-wine before serving, in which case a good glass would be sufficient; a small quantity of excellent soup may be made from the *remains* of a roast hare; in this case a little thickening of flour and butter also may be required. A clear soup may be made by stewing the hare in some veal or other light stock, and extracting the goodness of the meat by stewing for two or three hours without adding pounded meat to the soup. More wine in this case must be added, and a little of the meat may be served in squares in the soup.

Another.—Take a hare, and after skinning it don't soak it in water in the usual way, but cut it up into pieces, put it into a stewpan, also **three** or four heads of *moderate sized celery*, and the same of onions, and

a very small bunch of sweet herbs, pepper and salt to taste, and about
four or eight cloves; add a gallon of water, and let it stew one and
half hour; then take out the back or any other part, and cut off meat
enough to serve with it when done, put back the bones into the stewpan, and let it stew four or five hours longer. Next strain it through
a sieve, and pound in a mortar the whole of the meat off the bones,
add celery and onions, cut as fine as you can, *and then rub through a
sieve* (of course not the pieces which you have previously cut off to
serve with the soup), put it back to the soup and let it stew another
hour, and serve with the pieces of *meat in it, and if you like a few
forcemeat balls;* should it not be thick enough add a little thickening.

Another.— Cut a hare in pieces, stew it in any broth or boilings of
meat that happen to be in the house till it is tender, then cut off,
pound, and rub through a sieve the best part of the meat, with a little
of the stock. When that is done return all the bones, &c., to the
stock-pot (if the hare is small and the stock not good, add some gravy,
beef, and a little lean ham)—one onion, some sweet herbs, a little
flour and butter mixed, mushroom ketchup and cayenne, and simmer
for three or four hours; then strain it, and add the pounded hare, a
little currant jelly, and port-wine: half a teacupful of cream is an improvement before it is served.

To Make Hare Soup with Hare that has been Cooked.

243. First cut off some nice pieces of meat to serve in the soup,
then chop up the remainder and put into a stewpan, with any *bones* or
odd pieces of meat you may have, or else some good stock; put as
much stock or water as will make the soup required. Add celery,
onions, cloves, pepper, and salt, but not sweet herbs, as the stuffing
will suffice; let it stew four or five hours, and then strain it off;
pound and rub it through a sieve, then add it to the soup again, and
let it stew another hour, when serve with the meat and forcemeat
balls. Add a little thickening if required.

Partridge or Grouse Soup.

244. Take a knuckle of veal, a piece of lean ham, three good-sized
carrots, three large onions, two blades of mace, some white peppercorns, and five quarts of water, and make a good stock; then add four
partridges or three grouse, stew till they are quite tender, take the
best parts off, beat them fine, and rub them through a sieve with a
little of the stock; stew the bones, &c., in the stock, strain, and add

the whole to the pounded meat; when served, season with some good cream, a spoonful of sugar, and one or two glasses of port-wine.

GIBLET SOUP.

245. Scald and clean three or four sets of goose or duck giblets; set them to stew, with a pound or two of gravy-beef, scrag of mutton, or the bone of a knuckle of veal, an ox-tail, or some shanks of mutton, with three onions, a large bunch of sweet herbs, a tea-spoonful of white pepper, and a large spoonful of salt. Put five pints of water, and simmer till the gizzards (which must be each in four pieces) are quite tender; skim nicely, and add a quarter of a pint of cream, two tea-spoonsful of mushroom-powder, and an ounce of butter mixed with a dessert-spoonful of flour. Let it boil a few minutes, and serve with the giblets. It may be seasoned, instead of cream, with two glasses of sherry or madeira, a large spoonful of ketchup, and some cayenne. When in the tureen, add salt to the taste.

PORTABLE SOUP FOR TRAVELLERS.

246. Take three large legs of veal, one of beef, and the lean half of a ham; cut them in pieces, put a quarter of a pound of butter at the bottom of a large stock-pot, then lay in the meat and the bones, with two ounces of mace, pepper and salt to taste; add three carrots, and four or five sticks of celery cut small. Cover the pot close, and set it over a moderate fire; keep taking out the gravy with a spoon as it is drawn out, till you have taken the whole. Then cover the meat with water, and set it on the fire again. Boil slowly for more than four hours; then strain the liquor through a sieve into a pan, and allow it to boil till reduced to one quarter of the original quantity. Next strain the gravy which was taken from the meat, and add it to the soup, with some cayenne and ketchup, and a little Indian soy. Boil again slowly, skimming off the fat as it rises, till it looks like a thick glue. Pour it into earthen dishes, and cut it out with round tins a little larger than a crown-piece, dry them on dishes in the sun, carefully turning them, and store them in tins, with writing-paper between each layer. This is useful in families: one cake with a pint of boiling water will make good broth, or with less water a good gravy. It will keep long.

CRAYFISH SOUP.

247. Take fifty crayfish, pull out the tails, and then pound the rest

in a mortar with the shells and spawn. Have ready the meat and
spawn of a lobster, two quarts of good veal and ham broth, and put
the pounded crayfish into it, with the crumbs of two French rolls, and
half a pint of good cream. Let it have one boil, and then press it
through a sieve. Put in the tails of the crayfish, and serve with the
crust of French rolls.

LOBSTER SOUP.

248. Take the meat from the claws, bodies, and tails of six small
lobsters; take away the brown fur, and the bag in the head; beat the
fins, chine, and small claws in a mortar. Boil very gently in two
quarts of water, with the crumb of a French roll, some white pepper,
salt, two anchovies, a large onion, sweet herbs, and a bit of lemon-
peel, till you have extracted the goodness of them all. Strain it off.
Beat the spawn in a mortar, with a bit of butter, a quarter of a nutmeg,
and a tea-spoonful of flour; mix it with a quart of cream. Cut the
tails into pieces, and give them a boil up with the cream and soup.
Serve with forcemeat-balls made of the remainder of the lobsters.
mace, pepper, salt, a few crumbs, and an egg or two. Let the balls be
made up with a bit of flour, and heated in the soup.

OYSTER SOUP.

249. Take two quarts of fish stock, as directed in par. 222; beat the
yolks of ten hard-boiled eggs and the solid part of two quarts of oysters
in a mortar, and add this to the stock. Simmer it all for half an hour;
then strain it off, and put it and the oysters (cleared of the beards, and
nicely washed) into the soup. Simmer five minutes; have ready the
yolks of six raw eggs, well beaten, and add them to the soup. Stir it
all well one way on the side of the fire till it is thick and smooth, but
do not let it boil. Serve altogether.

250. OYSTER SOUP WITH CREAM—EXCELLENT FOR SUPPER.—Strain
the liquor from the oysters, and rinse them well in the liquor. Then
take a portion of the pale veal stock of which the soup is to be made,
and simmer the beards in it for nearly half an hour. Flavour the
stock with mace and pepper, and add to it that portion in which the
beards have been simmered, first straining the latter. Then put the
oysters and their liquor into a saucepan, and simmer them till the
oysters are plumped up, after which take out the oysters, and add
the liquor to the stock. Thicken with arrow-root (mixed with a little
cold milk), or flour and butter, and add, just before serving, from three-

quarters to a pint of boiling cream, and a little ketchup. The oysters (also hot) must be put into the tureen before the soup is poured into it. Threescore of oysters will make two quarts of soup.

EEL SOUP.

251. Take three pounds of small eels; put to them two quarts of water, a crust of bread, three blades of mace, some whole pepper, an onion, and a bunch of sweet herbs; cover them close, and stew till the fish is quite broken, then strain it off. Toast some bread, cut it into dice, and pour the soup on it boiling. A piece of carrot may be put in it at first. This soup will be as rich as if made of meat. A quarter of a pint of rich cream, with a tea-spoonful of flour rubbed smooth in it, is a great improvement.

CARROT SOUP.

252. CARROT SOUP (WITHOUT MEAT). Take four or five large carrots, one turnip, three onions, and three heads of celery shred fine; put into a stew-pan with a quarter of a pound of butter, three cloves, some peppercorns, and a blade of mace; stir till it is a pulp; add half a pint of peas boiled to a pulp, two anchovies, and three quarts of water; let it simmer two hours, and rub through a hair sieve. If not thick enough, add a little flour and butter.

Another.—Slice two good-sized carrots, two large onions, one large turnip, and one stick of celery; dredge flour over them and fry till tender, with just butter enough to keep them from burning; put them in a stewpan, and pour enough boiling water to cover them. Stew them about four hours, and when half done add boiling water to make the proper thickness. Mash and strain through a sieve, and season with pepper and salt. If approved of, add a little cream.

Another Carrot Soup.—Take one turnip, two or three onions, and twelve carrots; boil them in some stock till *quite* tender, then rub them through a hair-sieve. Season with peppercorns and salt, if necessary, and thicken with a little flour and butter.

253. CARROT SOUP (WITH MEAT).—Put some beef-bones with four quarts of the liquor in which a leg of mutton or beef has been boiled, two large onions, a turnip, pepper, and salt, into a saucepan, and stew for three hours. Have ready six large carrots scraped and cut thin, strain the soup on them, and stew till soft enough to pulp through a hair-sieve or coarse cloth, then boil the pulp with the soup, which is to be as thick as pea-soup. Use two wooden spoons to rub the carrots

through the sieve, and pulp only the red part of the carrot, not the
yellow. Make the soup the day before, and add cayenne to the
palate.

254. Carrot Soup (with Cream).—To the liquor that a knuckle
of veal has been boiled in, add twelve large carrots; boil till the carrots
will mash through a sieve, put them through, and then let them boil
in the broth till quite smooth; add half a pint of cream and a little
salt. It should be boiled till smooth, and of the consistence of pea-soup.
Or, the stock may be made of one pound and a half of scrag of mutton,
stewed in three quarts of water.

Asparagus Soup.

255. Make rather a weak stock, and boil with it some fresh mint,
a stick of celery, a turnip, carrot, and one onion; boil it about three
hours; strain it, and boil with it a handful of mint till it is flavoured;
take two bunches of asparagus, and cut all the tender part, about the
size of peas, into cold water; take these out, and boil in half a pint
of cold water till tender; pour them into the stock and thicken with
flour and butter: add salt and a handful of mint chopped very fine
when it is nearly thickened, and at the same time put in half a tea-
cupful of spinach-juice (made by tying spinach leaves in a muslin
after they have been washed, and pounding them, then squeezing the
juice); pea-leaf would do better if it could be had.

Julienne Soup.

256. Take some carrots, turnips, a few heads of celery, and a very
few leeks and onions, cut them in fillets an inch long, and the size of a
wooden skewer; then take two ounces of butter, and a little brown
sugar, and lay it at the bottom of the stewpan, with the roots over; fry
them over a slow fire, stirring gently; moisten them with veal broth
or a quart of water: let them boil on the corner of a stove; skim all
the fat off, and add a quart or two of clear soup. In summer add green
peas, asparagus-tops, French-beans, some lettuce or sorrel.

Turnip Soup.

257. Take off a knuckle of veal all the meat that can be made into
cutlets, &c., and set the remainder on to stew with an onion, a bunch
of herbs, a blade of mace, and five pints of water; cover it close, and
let it stew on a slow fire four or five hours. Strain and set it up till
next day, then take the fat and sediment from it, and simmer it with

turnips cut into small dice till tender, seasoning it with salt and pepper. Before serving, rub down half a spoonful of flour with half a pint of good cream, and the size of a walnut of butter. Let a small roll simmer in the soup till soaked through, and serve this with it. It should be as thick as middling cream.

GREEN-PEA SOUP.

258. Take the insides of six cos-lettuces and three cucumbers, pare and slice them, and cut the lettuces in pieces; add half a pint of young peas, an onion both top and bottom, and a very little parsley; put them into a stewpan, with half a pound of butter and a little salt and black pepper; cover them close, and stew gently two hours; shake the pan frequently, but do not open the lid; boil some younger peas till tender, rub them through a colander, and add the pulp to the stew; the next day add another half-pint of young peas, and as much of the pea-water as will reduce the soup to the thickness you wish to have it. By way of variety, all the vegetables may be rubbed through the colander, and it will make a nice smooth soup.

Another Green-pea Soup.—To a gallon of water add half a peck of large green peas and a French roll; let them boil till the peas are broken; strain them through a colander, put to them some whole pepper and mace, half a peck of young peas, and let them boil; take a handful of spinach, two or three cabbage-lettuces, a few green onions; cut them in pieces not too small, put them in a stew-pan with half or a quarter of a pound of butter; let them stew till very tender; when the peas are enough boiled put in a few marigold leaves, and let them boil together; cut a quantity of bread in little squares, and fry them very dry to eat with the soup.

WINTER PEAS SOUP.

259. Slice four carrots, four onions, three turnips, some outside stalks of celery, and brown them in a buttered stewpan. Stew them for four or five hours with some parsley and herbs in four or five pints of good stock or broth, with a quart or more of peas, soaked over night. Add a spoonful of walnut and mushroom ketchup, and a little brown sugar, and slice a little fresh celery into the tureen before pouring in the soup, and serve with fried toast and powdered mint. If the pen-powder is used the soup can be made more quickly.

Another Receipt.—Save the water of boiled pork or beef; and if too salt, put as much fresh water to it, or use fresh water entirely with roast beef bones, a ham or gammon bone, and an anchovy or two. Simmer these with some good whole or split peas; these should always be put in water to soak the night before; the smaller the quantity of water at first, the better. Simmer till the peas will pulp through a colander; then pulp them, and boil the pulp in the liquor that boiled the peas, with two carrots, a turnip, a leek, a little parsley, and a stick of celery cut into bits, or use the tincture of celery or celery seed; stew till all are quite tender, then season with pepper and salt; strain, and serve with bread toasted, and cut in dice, or fried in the same shape. Dried mint is to be finely powdered and served with it. This soup is much improved by adding a little cream; if not thick enough, add a little flour and butter.

260. PEA-SOUP (WITHOUT MEAT).—Boil one pint of split peas four or five hours, till quite tender, in two quarts of water. Add two large carrots and two turnips, a stick of celery, and some potatoes cut all in pieces, and boiled till they will pulp through a sieve. Cut one *large* onion in slices, and fry it in flour and butter, with pepper and salt enough for the whole soup. Add this to the above with a little soy and ketchup, and it will scarcely be distinguished from the soup made with meat.

261. PEA-SOUP FOR LENT.—Put three pints of boiling peas into five quarts of soft cold water, three anchovies, three red herrings, two large onions, two or three cloves, a carrot and parsnip sliced in, a few Jerusalem artichokes, and a bunch of sweet herbs, boil all together till the soup is thick, strain it, and add a sliced stick of celery, one ounce of butter, a little brown sugar and ketchup, or Indian soy. Serve with fried squares of bread, and dried mint if liked.

SOUP MAIGRE.

262. Melt half a pound of butter into a stewpan, shake it round, and throw in six middling onions sliced. Shake the pan well for two or three minutes, then put to it five heads of celery, two handsful of spinach, two cabbage lettuces cut small, and some parsley. Shake the pan well for ten minutes, then put in two quarts of water, some crusts of bread, a tea-spoonful of beaten pepper, three or four blades of mace, and if you have any white beet leaves add a large handful of them cut small. Boil gently an hour. Just before serving, beat in two yolks of eggs and a large spoonful of vinegar.

Another Soup Maigre.—Cut two onions into very small slices, and put them into a stewpan with two ounces of butter; fry them a little, taking care not to discolour them. Have ready three or four handsful of sorrel well washed and cut into ribbons, and add them to the onions with a table-spoonful of flour, then mix well, adding one pint of milk and one quart of water; boil altogether for two minutes, keeping it well stirred; then take it off the fire, and stir in quickly the yolks of two eggs, mixed with half a pint of cream. Do not boil it after the eggs are in.

Another.—Flour and fry a quart of green peas, four onions sliced, the coarse stalks of celery, a carrot, a turnip, and a parsnip, then pour on them three quarts of water. Let it simmer till the whole will pulp through a sieve, then boil in it the best of the celery cut thin.

Spinach Soup.

263. Shred two handsful of spinach, a turnip, two onions, one head of celery, two carrots, and a little thyme and parsley. Put all into a stewpot with a bit of butter the size of a walnut, and a pint of broth, or the water in which meat has been boiled; stew till the vegetables are quite tender; work them through a coarse cloth or sieve with a spoon, then to the pulp of the vegetables and liquor put a quart of fresh water, pepper and salt, and boil altogether. Have ready some suet dumplings the size of a walnut, and, before pouring the soup into the tureen, put them into it. The suet must not be shred too fine, and take care that it is quite fresh.

Onion Soup.

264. Take about two pounds of mutton or veal, put it on to stew with twelve large onions, sliced. When the onions are very soft, put them through a fine sieve, or put a cloth into the colander, and mash the onions in it, pouring the gravy over them till they are nearly all run through. This quantity will make three pints of soup; add one pint of new milk, with two table-spoonsful of flour mixed with it, one table-spoonful of essence of anchovy; mace, pepper, and salt to the taste.

265. Brown Onion Soup.—Peel and slice eight or ten large Spanish onions, fry them in butter a nice brown; when tender, lay them on a sieve to drain. Boil them an hour in five quarts of boiling water, and stir them after adding pepper and salt, and the crumbs of a penny loaf rubbed fine, then boil two hours more, stirring often, or it will be lumpy. Before serving, add the yolks of two eggs, with two spoonsful of vinegar and a little sugar, to a small portion of the

soup; pour this in gently, and stir it ten minutes: flavour with a tea-spoonful of Indian soy and some ketchup.

266. GREEN ONION SOUP.—To be prepared as brown onion soup, (265), but with fresh drawn onions, of which the *green* part should be added to the roots, and some of them cut in very narrow strips an inch long, and put into the soup later, so as to remain in shape when it is served; at the same time that they must be boiled quite tender.

RICE SOUP.

267. Boil about two teacupsful of rice in a quart of water with two onions and two sticks of celery, till the rice is quite soft. Put one or two ounces of butter and about two table-spoonsful of flour into a stewpan, and when melted add the above with some stock (which is best made of some veal bones or boilings), and stir till of a proper thickness. Flavour with a little salt and pepper, and just before serving add a tea-spoonful of cream.

WHITE SOUP.

268. Take the bony part of a knuckle of veal, break the bones quite small, cover it close down in a pan, with a little mace, a few black and a few white peppercorns, just broken, a little turnip, carrot, onion, and celery; put in a quart of water, and let it simmer gently for three hours. Stir them together, and put in as much water as will make the quantity; put it through a sieve. When wanted to be used, put it into a pan with half a pint of good cream, and thicken with flour and butter. Boil a roll in the soup till quite soft; just before taking it up, have the roll rubbed through a sieve with a little of the soup, and just give it a boil in the soup to add to the thickness of it. If a French roll cannot be got, cut the crust from a common one, or it will discolour the whole.

Another.—Take a shoulder or knuckle of veal, a piece of lean ham, a little mace, and an onion; boil them to a strong gravy; during the time put in a small bunch of pot-herbs for ten minutes; strain it, and let it get cold; boil a pint of good cream, and pour it upon the crumb of a penny loaf; let it stand some time and strain; blanch one ounce of sweet almonds, and beat them in a mortar with the yolks of four eggs boiled hard; mix them well together, and add them to the gravy; stir all over a slow fire, taking care it does not boil. Two ounces of vermicelli cut small is a great improvement.

269. A WHITE SOUP OF JERUSALEM ARTICHOKES.—The stock of

veal, to which add three pounds of artichokes, to be pulped through a sieve; season with salt and a small quantity of cayenne pepper, and before it is poured into the tureen stir in some good thick cream; it must on no account be permitted to *boil* after the cream has been added, but care must be taken that it is not chilled by it.

270. To MAKE SOUP FOR SUPPER.—Take a quart of good new milk, and add a pint of cream, a bit of lemon-peel, a laurel-leaf or two, a stick of cinnamon, a few coriander-seeds, and a small piece of sugar; boil a few minutes, and set it to cool; then beat the yolks of ten eggs, and blanch and pound two ounces of sweet almonds, and two or three bitter almonds, with a little water in a mortar till very fine; then put them with the cream; mix the eggs smoothly with it in the stewpan, having previously run the mixture through a coarse sieve; stir it over a gentle fire till it begins to thicken like a custard; then pour it into the tureen with some slices of French roll as thick as biscuits.

271. JENNY LIND'S SOUP.—Make three quarts of stock, which strain through a fine sieve into a stewpan; add to it three ounces of sago, and let it boil gently for twenty minutes, then skim it. The stock, being previously seasoned, will only require half a tea-spoonful of sugar, a little salt, pepper, and nutmeg; a little thyme, parsley, and a bay leaf will vary the flavour. Just before serving, put into a basin the well-beaten yolks of four eggs, and add to them half a pint of cream; then take the stewpan off the fire, pour it in, stir quickly for one minute, and serve immediately. If it boil again it will be spoiled.

VEGETABLE SOUP.

272. Put a lump of butter into a stewpan, let it boil; have ready a small quantity of cabbage, red and white, beet, sorrel, onions, carrots, potatoes, peas, French beans, cauliflowers, parsley leaves and root, lettuces, cucumbers, artichoke bottoms, Jerusalem artichokes, and asparagus chopped very fine; let them stew in the butter till quite tender, stirring to prevent their burning. Season with cayenne, salt, pepper, and ketchup, and celery seed, add some good meat broth, and boil it all together, and serve hot. Any of the vegetables may be omitted, but the greater variety the better, and care must be taken that the flavour of any one vegetable does not predominate over the rest.

Another.—Put into two quarts of cold water two pounds of Jerusalem artichokes pared and halved, one pound of turnips pared and sliced, two or three onions, and a stick of celery. Boil all together slowly for two and a half hours, with a stock made of veal or rabbits; then add two table-spoonsful of flour, one ounce of butter, and pepper and salt to the taste. Let it simmer half an hour longer, skimming it carefully, then serve.

273. A TRANSPARENT WHITE SOUP.—Take a large knuckle or small leg of veal, and cut off all the meat as thin as possible, and break the bone in pieces. Put the meat in a large jug or stock-pot, the bones at the top, with a bunch of sweet herbs, a quarter of an ounce of mace, and a quarter of a pound of Jordan almonds beaten fine. Pour on it four quarts of boiling water; let it stand by the fire all night covered close; the next day put it in a well-tinned or enamelled saucepan; let it boil gently till reduced one half; remove the scum and fat as it rises while it is boiling; strain it into an earthen pan to settle, and in two or three hours' time pour it again with a spoonful of sugar into a clean saucepan, clear from all sediment. Add, before serving, vermicelli or carrot, or French beans cut in long thin narrow strips, or asparagus in short lengths, previously boiled, and serve the whole very hot; a little white wine may be added if approved.

CHAP. IX.—GRAVIES, SAVOURY SAUCES, FORCEMEATS, AND SAUSAGES.

SECT. 1.—GENERAL REMARKS.

274. Gravies, Sauces, and Stuffings, are savoury compounds, intended to give flavour and zest to the more insipid and solid joints, such as roast veal or poultry. The sauces here described differ from the permanent sauces given with vinegar pickles, in the *Economical Housekeeper;* inasmuch as though the former are, by good housekeepers, always kept in the house, yet it is only for a short time, and the great art consists in using them up before they become spoiled. Thus, the proper course in these matters is so to arrange the principal and side dishes for to-morrow, that they shall use up the sauces concocted to-day, or yesterday, or perhaps even the day before that.

SECT. 2.—GRAVIES AND SAVOURY JELLIES.

275. Gravies are distinguished from sauces, in their predominating element being the osmazome of meat, commonly called gravy, however it may be disguised. Gravy may be made quite as good of the skirts, or any other coarse part, of beef, and even from the liver or the

kidney, as of any other meat prepared in the same way; so also it may be procured from the shank-end of legs of mutton that have been dressed, if much is not wanted. The raw shank-bones of mutton are a great improvement to the richness of gravy; but first it is necessary to soak them well, and scour them clean. Sheep's heads also make excellent gravy.

BROWNING FOR GRAVY.

276. This is pretty nearly the same as for soup (see page 78); but the following is, perhaps, still better adapted for the purpose:—

Put two ounces of moist sugar into an iron saucepan and boil till brown, then add half a pint of water, some pepper, salt, and mace, and about half a tea-spoonful of the gravy settled at the bottom of the dripping-pot. Boil for two or three minutes till it is of a good brown, and bottle it. Put half a tea-cupful of hot water, with a tea-spoonful of browning dissolved in it, into the dish with the meat, and put a tea-spoonful into the hashes.

Another.—Put into a stewpan one lb. of good sugar, one oz. of butter, six cloves, twelve allspice, and boil it three minutes; then add a quart of boiling water, and keep stirring it for five minutes; pour it into a basin, and when cold clear away the scum, bottle, and keep it tightly corked.

GLAZE.

277. Glaze for Gravy is also pretty nearly the same as for soups (see page 77), or as follows:—

Break the bones of several joints of cooked meat as small as possible; put them to boil in two quarts of water for two hours; then strain the bones out and boil about an hour, till reduced to rather more than a teacupful; flavour it with black pepper and salt, and add a little browning (par. 276). It should be dried in saucers till of the consistence nearly of India-rubber, and will in this state keep for three months or more.

To Make Brown Thickening for Soups, Gravies, &c.

278. Put into a stewpan a lump of butter, according to the quantity of thickening required. Melt it gently, then put flour enough to make a paste. Fry it on a slow fire until it becomes of a light brown colour, then pour it into an earthen pan for use. It will keep for some time.

A good thickening for hashes and gravies may be made by melting very *slowly* half a pound of butter, and after skimming it, and allowing the sediment to settle, pour it clear off into a stew or frying pan, over a clear but gentle fire, and dredge very gradually into it nearly half a pound of well-dried flour—shaking the pan the while. Stir well and carefully till the whole is well mixed, and is fried a light brown colour. It must on no account be burnt in the slightest degree. This will keep in a jar for some little time, and may be added as required to soups or gravies while boiling. If to be used for white soups or sauces, the thickening must not acquire the least tinge of brown in the frying.

To Preserve Beef Liver for Gravy.

279. Take a clear liver, and rub it well all over with four ounces of coarse sugar or treacle; let it lie twenty-four hours, then rub it well all over with two ounces of saltpetre, four ounces of bay salt, and one ounce of common salt. Let it lie in the pickle for three weeks, turning and rubbing it every day. Hang it near the fire to dry, and when used cut slices off and boil them in as much water as is required for the gravy. Add herbs, or an onion, if approved.

Plain Joint Gravy.

280. The ordinary kind is described under the head of Roasting, at page 44.

Or, put a small piece of glazing into a teacup, and fill the cup with boiling water; when quite dissolved, pour it over the joint and serve.

Made Gravy.

281. Made Gravy, fit for ordinary purposes, such as roast poultry or game, as served in everyday dinners, may be made so that it will keep a week in moderately cool weather as follows:—Cut lean beef thin, put it into a frying-pan without any butter, and set it on a fire covered, but take care it does not burn; let it stay till all the gravy that comes out of the meat is dried up into it again; put as much water as will cover the meat, and let that stew away. Then put to meat a small quantity of water, herbs, onions, spice, and a bit of lean ham; simmer till it is rich, and keep it in a cool place. Do not take off the fat till going to be used.

Another.—Take any bones or meat in the house, and put in a stew-pan with onions, parsley, and sweet herbs. Let it stew well, and thicken it with flour and butter, mixed up; then pass it through a sieve, and add soy, ketchup, Reading or Worcestershire sauce, port-wine, a little pounded mace, and cayenne, to the taste, with a little browning, to colour it if necessary. Put it in a basin, and, when cold, melt some suet and pour over it to preserve it. Sheep's melts for gravy very cheap, one penny each, and enough for twice, stewed like other meats.

282. CULLIS OR BROWN GRAVY.—Lay over the bottom of a stewpan as much lean veal as will cover it an inch thick; then cover the veal with thin slices of undressed gammon, two or three onions, two or three bay-leaves, some sweet-herbs, two blades of mace, and three cloves; cover the stewpan, and set it over a slow fire; but when the juices come out let the fire be a little quicker; when the meat is of a fine brown, fill the pan with good beef-broth; boil and skim it, then simmer an hour, and add a little water, mixed with as much flour as will make it properly thick; boil it half an hour, and strain it. This will keep for a week.

283. VEAL GRAVY is made as directed under par. 282, but without the spice, herbs, and flour.

284. CLEAR GRAVY.—Slice beef thin; broil a part of it over a very clear quick fire, just enough to give colour to the gravy, but not to dress it; put that and the raw part into a very nicely tinned stewpan, with two onions, a clove or two, whole black peppers, berries of allspice, and a bunch of sweet herbs; cover it with hot water, give it one boil, and skim it well two or three times; then cover it, and simmer till quite strong.

A RICH GRAVY.

285. Cut the beef into thin slices, according to the quantity wanted; slice onions thin, and flour both; fry them of a light-pale brown, but do not on any account suffer them to get black; put them into a stew-pan, pour boiling water on the browning in the frying-pan, boil it up, and pour on the meat; put to it a bunch of parsley, thyme, and savory, a small bit of knotted marjoram, the same of tarragon, some mace, berries of allspice, whole black peppers, a clove or two, and a bit of ham or gammon of bacon; simmer till you have extracted all the juices of the meat, and be sure to skim the moment it boils, and often after; if for a hare or stewed fish, anchovy should be added.

VENISON GRAVY FOR MUTTON.

286. One wine-glass of sherry, one table-spoonful of vinegar, one dessert-spoonful of catsup. Add as much good stock or plain joint gravy as these ingredients put together; and also from six to eight

H

lumps of sugar, and a little thickening; the whole should not boil more than a minute, when serve.

ECONOMICAL GRAVY FOR POULTRY.

287. Wash the feet nicely, and cut them and the neck small; simmer them with a little bread browned, a slice of onion, a bit of parsley and thyme, some pepper and salt, and the liver and gizzard in a quarter of a pint of water, till half-wasted; take out the liver, bruise it, and strain the liquor to it; then thicken it with flour and butter, and add a tea-spoonful of mushroom ketchup, and it will be very good.

HAM GRAVY SAUCE.

288. When a ham is almost done with, pick all the meat clean from the bone, leaving out any rusty part; beat the meat and the bone to a mash with a chopper and rolling-pin; put it in a saucepan with three spoonsful of gravy; set it over a slow fire, and stir it all the time, or it will stick to the bottom. When it has been on some time, put to it a small bundle of sweet-herbs, some pepper, and half a pint of beef-gravy; cover it up, and let it stew over a gentle fire. When it has a good flavour of the herbs, strain off the gravy. A little of this is an improvement to all gravies.

GRAVY FOR WILD-FOWL.

289 To one wine-glassful of port-wine add a table-spoonful each of walnut ketchup, mushroom ketchup, and lemon-juice, one shalot sliced (or a little of the essence), a small piece of lemon-peel, and a blade of mace. These should all be scalded, strained, and added to the mere gravy that comes from the fowl in roasting. The breast of the fowl should be scored in three or four places, and the gravy poured *boiling hot over it* before it is sent to table.

Another.—Simmer a tea-spoonful of made mustard, the same of anchovies and cayenne, a tablespoonful of ketchup, one onion, a tea-cupful of good gravy, a lump or two of white sugar, a little salt, nutmeg, and mace, and the juice of half a lemon, for ten minutes—then add a tea-cupful of port-wine and give it one boil;—it may be bottled, and warmed and served in a boat when required.

IMITATION BROWN GRAVY (WITHOUT MEAT).

290. Take of water and ale that is not too bitter one pint of each; of walnut pickle, mushroom pickle, and ketchup, two table-spoonsful

of each; two anchovies, two onions sliced, some salt, two or three blades of mace, and some whole pepper. To the above ingredients add a little butter, with a small portion of flour, having previously made it brown by stirring it till the froth sinks. Boil the whole together for twenty minutes.

WINE GRAVY OR SAUCE.

291. Make a strong rich gravy by either of the receipts given at pars. 281 or 282. The second of those, given at par. 282, is the best for the purpose. Take about one-third of a sauce tureen of this, heat it, and when ready for use add from two to three table-spoonsful of rich and new port-wine.

SWEET SAUCE FOR SAVOURY JOINTS.

292. This is served with mutton and venison, and often with hare also. It is made by dissolving two or three table-spoonsful of red currant jelly in a small enamelled saucepan, and when hot adding one or two table-spoonsful of port-wine.

STRONG FISH GRAVY.

293. Skin two or three eels or some flounders; gut and wash them very clean; cut them into small pieces, and put into a saucepan. Cover them with water, and add a little crust of bread toasted brown, two blades of mace, some whole pepper, sweet herbs, a piece of lemon-peel, an anchovy or two, and a tea-spoonful of horseradish. Cover close, and simmer; add a bit of butter and flour, and boil with the above.

SAVOURY JELLY, TO PUT OVER COLD PIES.

294. Make it of a small bare knuckle of leg or shoulder of veal, or a piece of scrag of that or mutton; or, if the pie be of fowl or rabbit, the carcasses, necks, and heads added to any piece of meat will be sufficient, observing to give consistence by cow-heel or shanks of mutton. Put the meat, a slice of lean ham or bacon, a fagot of different herbs, two blades of mace, an onion or two, a small bit of lemon-peel, and a tea-spoonful of Jamaica pepper bruised, and the same of whole pepper, and three pints of water, in a stew-pot that shuts very close. As soon as it boils, skim it well, and let it simmer very slowly till quite strong; strain it, and when cold take off the fat with a spoon first, and then, to remove every particle

of grease, lay a clean piece of cap or blotting-paper on it. Wher
cold, if not clear, warm it, and, after letting it stand for a few
minutes, pour the clearer part off the sediment, and then boil the
former for a few minutes with the whites of two eggs, after which it
must be strained through a fine cloth in a strainer, and put by to cool,
then it must be skimmed.

JELLY TO COVER COLD FISH.

295. Clean a small skate and put it into three quarts of water,
with a calf's foot or cow-heel, a stick of horseradish, an onion,
three blades of mace, some white pepper, a piece of lemon-peel,
and a good slice of lean gammon; stew till it becomes jelly; strain
it off, and when cold remove every bit of fat; take it up from the
sediment and boil it, omitting the fat, with a glass of sherry, the
whites of four or five eggs, and a piece of lemon; boil without
stirring, and after a few minutes set it by to stand half an hour,
and strain it through a bag or sieve with a cloth in it; cover the fish
with it when cold.

SECT. 3.—SAVOURY SAUCES.

296. These are distinguished from gravies by their foundation being
composed of gelatine, milk, cream, butter, or some other mild material
variously flavoured.

WHITE SAUCE FOR FRICASSEE OF FOWLS, RABBITS, WHITE MEAT, FISH, OR VEGETABLES.

297. It is seldom necessary to buy meat for this favourite sauce, as
the proportion of that flavour is but small; the water that has boiled
fowls, veal, or rabbit, or a little broth that may be in the house,
or the feet and necks of chickens, for raw or dressed veal, will suffice. Stew with a little water any of these with a bit of lemon-peel,
some sliced onion, some white peppercorns, a little pounded mace or
nutmeg, and a bunch of sweet herbs, until the flavour is good; then
strain it, and add a little good cream, a piece of butter, and a little
flour; salt to the taste. A squeeze of lemon may be added after the
sauce is taken off the fire, shaking it well. Yolk of egg is often used
for fricassees, but cream is better, as the former is apt to curdle.

Another, cheaper, but very good.—Add to a little boiling milk a blade
of mace, and thicken with flour and butter, and flavour with pepper,
salt, and a little Worcestershire sauce, or cucumber or mushroom

ketchup. If it is desired richer, a little cream should be put, instead of all milk. This will do for fish sauce, with the addition of a little anchovy; and if oyster, shrimp, or lobster sauce is required, leave out the anchovy.

An Excellent Sauce for Carp or Boiled Turkey.

298. Rub two ounces of butter with a tea-spoonful of flour, put to it a little water, melt it, and add nearly a quarter of a pint of thick cream and half an anchovy chopped fine, not washed; set it over the fire, and as it boils up add a large spoonful of real India soy; if that does not give it a fine colour put a little more; turn it into the sauce tureen, and put some salt and half a lemon; stir it well to hinder it from curdling.

Onion Sauce.

299. Boil the onions gently in milk and water till they are quite soft, then rub them through a colander with a wooden spoon, and boil them up with cream or the yolk of an egg, beaten up with milk or with melted butter.

Mushroom Sauce.

300. Wash and pick a pint of young mushrooms, and rub them with salt to take off the tender skin; put them into a saucepan with a little salt, some nutmeg, a blade of mace, a pint of cream, and a good piece of butter rubbed in flour. Boil them up and stir them till done; then pour the sauce round the chickens, &c. Garnish with lemon. If you cannot get fresh mushrooms, use pickled ones done white, with a little mushroom powder added to the cream, &c.

Lemon White Sauce for Boiled Fowls.

301. Put the peel of a small lemon, cut very thin, into a pint of sweet rich cream, with a sprig of lemon thyme, and ten white pepper-corns. Simmer gently till it tastes well of the lemon; then strain it; and thicken it with a quarter of a pound of butter, and a dessert-spoonful of flour rubbed in it. Boil it up; then pour the juice of the lemon strained into it, stirring it well. Dish the chickens, and then mix a little white gravy, quite hot, with the cream, but do not boil them together; add salt to the taste.

Liver Sauce.

302. Chop boiled liver of rabbits or fowls, and put it in melted butter

with a very little pepper and salt, and some parsley; give it one boil and it is ready. Or, cut the livers and slices of lemon in dice, with scalded parsley and hard eggs; add salt, and mix them with butter, boil them up, and pour over fowls; also over roast-rabbits.

LIVER SAUCE FOR ROAST HARE OR RABBIT.

303. The liver should be well stewed in brown stock if for hare, or white if for rabbit; when quite done pound it with a few herbs, a clove of shalot, and afterwards add to the gravy in which it has stewed a little vinegar or lemon-juice, a glass of white wine if for rabbit, if for hare a glass of port-wine, with, if approved, half a glass of currant jelly. Simmer the whole, and flavour with salt and pepper.

Another Liver Sauce for a Hare.—Bruise the liver of a hare raw with a spoon, melt a little butter, with some milk and flour, and put the liver into it hot; add a little salt and good cream, with some of the gravy from the hare. Simmer it altogether over the fire, stirring it all the time.

EGG SAUCE.

304. Boil the eggs hard, and chop them into small pieces; then put them to melted butter, and boil up.

Another Egg Sauce.—Boil three or four eggs for full a quarter of an hour, and when quite cold cut all the yolks into small dice, and chop two-thirds of the whites into small pieces; mix them in the sauce-boat and sprinkle salt over them, pour upon them some white sauce; and serve hot.

SAUCE FOR SUCKING PIG.

305. Boil the inside of a French roll with an onion and salt, then take a quarter pint of the gravy from the roasting pig, and having chopped the brains and a sage leaf or two, beat them and the roll up with the gravy; add a little butter, lemon-juice, mushroom ketchup, and half a glass of port or white wine. For currant sauce, if preferred (see par. 312).

MINT SAUCE.

306. Chop mint leaves with a sharp knife, and quickly, to preserve the colour; put them into a sauce-tureen with sufficient sugar to take off the extreme acidity of the vinegar, which must be added in such quantity as to make the leaves float in a liquid.

CURRANT SAUCE. 103

SORREL SAUCE.

307. Mix a quarter of a pint of sorrel juice, a glass of white wine, and half a pint of gooseberries scalded. Add an ounce or two of sugar, and a bit of butter. Boil them up.

GOOSEBERRY SAUCE.

308. Boil a pint of green gooseberries in sufficient water to cover them until they are tender. Then pass them through a colander or strainer; add ten grains of ginger and a few lumps of sugar, with a small piece of butter. Mix all together, and boil up.

BREAD SAUCE.

309. Boil a large onion (cut in four) with some black pepper and milk, till the onion is quite a pap. Pour the milk, after straining it, on grated white stale bread, and cover it. In an hour put it in a saucepan, with a good piece of butter mixed with a little flour; boil up together, and serve—a little cream added is a very great improvement.

A BREAD SAUCE FOR ROAST HARE.

310. Steep the crumb of a penny loaf in port-wine, put it in a saucepan with some butter, beat it well while warming till quite smooth; add pepper, salt, and currant jelly, with three large spoonsful of cream, or, instead of the cream, substitute the same quantity of vinegar. Serve very hot.

APPLE SAUCE FOR GOOSE AND ROAST PORK.

311. Pare, core, and slice some apples; put them in a stone jar, then into a saucepan of water, or on a hot hearth. If on a hearth, let a spoonful or two of water be put in to hinder them from burning. When they are done, bruise them to a mash, and put to them a bit of butter the size of a nutmeg, and a little brown sugar. Serve it in a sauce-tureen.

CURRANT SAUCE.

312. Boil an ounce of dried currants in half a pint of water for a few minutes; then add a small tea-cupful of bread crumbs, six cloves, a glass of port-wine, and a bit of butter. Stir it till the whole is smooth.

LEMON SAUCE.

313. Cut thin slices of lemon into very small dice, and put them in melted butter; give it one boil, and pour it over boiled fowls.

CARRIER SAUCE FOR MUTTON.

314. Chop six shalots fine, and boil them up with a gill of gravy, a spoonful of vinegar, some pepper and salt.

HORSERADISH SAUCE FOR COLD MEAT OR GAME.

315. Mix well together one ounce of grated horseradish, half an ounce of salt, a table-spoonful of made mustard, and three dessert-spoonsful of moist sugar, the same quantity of vinegar, and milk or cream, to make it of the consistence of good cream, or thicker, if preferred.

SAUCE FOR COLD FOWL OR PARTRIDGE.

316. Rub down in a mortar the yolks of two eggs boiled hard, an anchovy, two dessert-spoonsful of oil, three of vinegar, a shalot, cayenne if approved, and a tea-spoonful of mustard. All the spice and herbs should be pounded before adding them.

DUTCH SAUCE FOR MEAT OR FISH.

317. Put six spoonsful of water and four of vinegar into a sauce-pan, warm and thicken it with the yolks of two eggs. Make it quite hot, but do not boil it; squeeze in the juice of half a lemon, and strain it through a sieve.

SAUCE ROBART FOR RUMPS OR STEAKS.

318. Put a piece of butter the size of an egg into a saucepan, set it over the fire, and when browning throw in a handful of sliced onions cut small; fry them brown, but do not let them burn; add half a spoonful of flour, shake the onions in it and give it another fry; then put four spoonsful of gravy, and some pepper and salt, and boil it gently ten minutes; skim off the fat, and add a tea-spoonful of made mustard, a spoonful of vinegar, and the juice of half a lemon; boil it all, and pour it round the steaks. They should be of a fine yellow brown, and garnished with fried parsley and lemon.

SAUCE A-LA-MAITRE D'HOTEL.

319. Put a piece of butter into a saucepan with some curled parsley,

some tarragon leaves, a shalot, two leaves of balm, a little salt, lemon, or a glass of verjuice, and mix the whole with a spoon until they are well incorporated, and simmer them for a few minutes.

To Melt Butter.

320. Mix in the proportion of a tea-spoonful of flour and a good pinch of salt to four ounces of the best butter, on a trencher. Put it into a small saucepan with about half a pint of hot water, boil quick a minute, shaking it all the time, and turning it always in one direction. Milk used instead of water requires rather less butter, and looks whiter.

Another Method of Melting Butter.—Mix very smoothly a large tea-spoonful of flour with a tea-cup of cold water, and add a pinch of salt. Put to these, in your saucepan, two or three ounces of good fresh butter, cut in small pieces, and shake the saucepan round one way and almost without intermission till the ingredients are perfectly mixed, and it has simmered for two or three minutes.

A plainer sauce may be made by adding one-and-a-half ounce of butter to the above flour and water. And for an inexperienced person it is easier to add the butter after the flour and water have *boiled* for a couple of minutes, and then boil the whole for one minute more, stirring or shaking all the time.

To Clarify Butter.

321. Simmer it gently over a clear fire, and when melted take it off, skim it, and let the sediment settle. Pour the butter off clear into jars for use, keep them in a cool place. Some persons make a supply in the autumn, to serve when butter rises in price.

Fennel Sauce.

322. This is made like parsley and butter (see 324).

Caper Sauce.

323. Add whole capers to melted butter with a portion of the vinegar they are found in. Cream is a great improvement to the butter. A substitute for capers may be found in the nasturtium seed pickled, (see *Economical Housekeeper*).

Another Substitute for Caper Sauce, inferior to Nasturtiums.—Boil parsley slowly, to let it become a bad colour, cut, but do not chop it fine; put it to melted butter, with a tea-spoonful of salt, and a dessert-spoonful of vinegar. Boil up and serve.

PARSLEY AND BUTTER.

324. Boil parsley-leaves and chop very fine; then mix with melted butter, and boil.

Another.—When no parsley leaves are to be had, tie up a little parsley seed in a bit of clean muslin, and boil it a few minutes in some water. Use this water to melt the butter; and throw into it a little boiled spinach minced, to look like parsley.

LOBSTER SAUCE.

325. Take a large fresh lobster, carefully pick out the berries and all the inside: cut it small; make a sauce with a lump of flour and butter, a little milk or cream, a *very* small quantity of essence of anchovy, a very little mace, beat fine, and cayenne; then pull the rest of the lobster to pieces with two forks; add the sauce, by degrees, to the berries, and put in the lobster. Give it a boil, stirring all the time, and it is ready to serve.

To MAKE OYSTER SAUCE.

326. Take the oysters, open the bodies, and remove the beards; put the former into a saucepan with the liquor and a little water; put the beards into a piece of muslin, and boil them with the oysters to extract the juice and flavour; thicken with flour and butter; and after removing the beards, add some cream, a little mace, pepper, and salt. Cockles or mussels for sauce, taking care to remove the dark spot in the body of the mussel, as it is considered poisonous, and to clean the cockles thoroughly from all particles of sand.

SHRIMP SAUCE.

327. If the shrimps are not picked at home, pour a little water over them to wash them; put them to butter melted thick and smooth, give them one boil, and add the juice of a lemon. If the shells are boiled in a little water and strained off, and that used to make the sauce, fewer shrimps are necessary.

BROWN SAUCE FOR FISH.

328. Melt some butter in cream (instead of flour and water) with as much walnut ketchup boiled in it as will make it of a nice light brown.

WHITE SAUCE FOR FISH.

329. Boil some cream, thicken it with flour and butter, then let it

simmer till smooth; add a tea-spoonful of essence of anchovy to a tureenful, and, if it is liked, a little walnut or mushroom ketchup. For cod sauce, omit the ketchup, and add a little soy. If cream is scarce, use milk and the yolk of an egg.

FISH SAUCE WITHOUT BUTTER.

330. Simmer very gently a quarter of a pint of vinegar, and half a pint of water (which must not be hard), and then add an onion, half a handful of horseradish, and the following spices lightly bruised: four cloves, two blades of mace, and a half tea-spoonful of black pepper. When the onion is quite tender, chop it small with two anchovies, and set the whole on the fire to boil for a few minutes, with a spoonful of ketchup. In the mean time, have ready and well beaten the yolks of three fresh eggs; strain them, mix the liquor by degrees with them, and when well mixed set the saucepan over a gentle fire, keeping a basin in one hand, into which toss the sauce to and fro, and shake the saucepan over the fire that the eggs may not curdle. Do not boil them, only let the sauce be hot enough to give it the thickness of melted butter.

SECT. 4.—STUFFINGS, FORCEMEATS, &c.

331. These articles, whether in the form of stuffing, forcemeat, or balls, make a considerable part of good cooking by the flavour they impart to whatsoever dish they are added to, if properly compounded. Exact rules for the quantities of which they are composed cannot easily be given; but the following observations may be useful, and habit will soon give knowledge in mixing them to the taste. According to what it is wanted for, should be the selection from the following list, observing that of the most pungent articles least must be used. No one flavour should predominate greatly; and if several dishes are served on the same day, there should be a marked variety in the taste of the forcemeat, as well as the gravies. It should be consistent enough to cut with a knife, but not dry and heavy.

FORCEMEAT INGREDIENTS.

ESSENTIAL.	ACCESSORY.
Cold fowl or veal.	Oysters.
Scraped ham.	Anchovy.
Fat bacon.	Tarragon.
Beef-suet.	Savoury herb.
Crumbs of bread.	Pennyroyal.
Parsley.	Knotted marjoram.
White pepper.	Thyme.

ESSENTIAL.	ACCESSORY.
Salt.	Basil.
Nutmeg.	Yolks of hard eggs.
Yolk and white of egg well beaten	Cayenne.
to bind the mixture.	Garlic.
	Shalot.
	Chives.
	Jamaica pepper, in fine powder, or
	two or three cloves.

The first column contains the articles of which the forcemeat may be made without any striking flavour; and to those may be added some of the different ingredients of the second column to vary the taste.

COMMON STUFFING, OR FORCEMEAT.

332. Take three or four ounces of suet, with an equal quantity of veal (or if for turkeys, chopped oysters), two ounces of finely-grated bread, chop these up with parsley already minced very finely, and flavour with a little lemon-peel, nutmeg, or mace, white pepper and salt (lemon-thyme or sweet marjoram are thought an improvement by some). Then blend all with the yolks of two or three eggs well beaten.

STUFFING OR FORCEMEAT FOR FOWL OR VEAL.

333. Shred a little ham or gammon, some cold veal or fowl, some beef-suet, a small quantity of onion, some parsley, a little lemon-peel, salt, nutmeg, or pounded mace, and either white pepper or cayenne, and bread crumbs. Pound in a mortar, and bind it with one or two eggs beaten and strained, adding thyme or marjoram, or both together, according to fancy. For forcemeat patties, the mixture as above.

STUFFING FOR HARE.

334. To make this, chop up the liver with an anchovy, some fat bacon, two ounces of suet, herbs as for veal, pepper, salt, nutmeg, a little onion, two ounces of crumbs of bread, and an egg to bind it all.

FORCEMEAT BALLS.

335. Beat half a pound of lean veal or pork and half a pound of suet well in a mortar, put in three eggs, and some grated bread; season it with pepper, salt, nutmeg, and lemon-peel, two cloves, and a blade or two of mace. Make it into small balls, and fry them a light brown.

Another Receipt.—A pound of fresh suet, one ounce of ready-dressed veal or chicken chopped fine, bread crumbs, a little shalot or onion, salt, white pepper, nutmeg, mace, pennyroyal, parsley, and lemon thyme finely shred ; beat as many fresh eggs, yolks and whites separately, as will make the above ingredients into a moist paste; roll into small balls, and fry them in fresh lard, putting them in just as it boils up. When of a light brown, take them out and drain before the fire. If the suet is moist or stale, a great many more eggs will be necessary. Forcemeat balls made in this way are remarkably light; but being somewhat greasy, some people prefer them with less suet and eggs.

FORCEMEAT BALLS FOR FISH SOUPS OR STEWS.

336. Beat the flesh and soft parts of a middling lobster, half an anchovy, a large piece of boiled celery, the yolk of a hard egg, a little cayenne, mace, salt, and white pepper, with two table-spoonsful of bread crumbs, and one of oyster liquor, two ounces of butter warmed, and two eggs long beaten ; make into balls, and fry of a fine brown in butter.

LITTLE EGG BALLS FOR STEWS OR SOUPS.

337. Beat three hard yolks of eggs in a mortar, and make into a paste with the yolk of a raw one, roll it into small balls, and throw them into boiling water for two minutes to harden.

Another.—Boil three eggs hard, remove the whites, and pound the yolks in a mortar; when reduced to a powder, add the size of three walnuts of butter and a table-spoonful of fine flour; make them into balls the size of marbles.

STUFFING FOR GEESE AND DUCKS.

338. Geese and Ducks, before being spitted for roasting, are usually stuffed with sage and onions, boiled, chopped fine, and then mixed with an equal quantity of potatoes.

STUFFING FOR SUCKING PIGS.

339. The pig is always stuffed with some kind of stuffing containing sage, a *good receipt* for which is, to take a quarter of a pound of crumbs of bread, one onion, a small handful of sage, a raw egg, and a small piece of butter; these should be well mixed together with a little pepper and salt. Then fill the belly of the pig, and sew up with a common needle and thread. *Another plan* is to cut a round of bread thick, as for toast, brown it very lightly, and butter it, then soak it in

some water in which a handful of sage and an onion have been boiled, cut it into long pieces, and lay it in the belly, with alternate layers or the boiled sage leaves, but no onion, after which it is to be closed as above.

STUFFING FOR ROAST PORK.

340. This is the same as for Geese and Ducks (see par. 338.)

FRIED BREAD TO SERVE WITH SOUP.

341. Cut slices of stale bread nearly half an inch in thickness, and again into squares or diamonds, or with a cutter into shapes, put a slice of butter into the frying-pan, and when melted put in the bread. Turn it constantly while frying till it is all of a nice light brown. Drain the butter from it, and dry it on a cloth before the fire, or on paper in a sieve. It will take nearly an ounce of butter to fry a quarter of a pound of bread.

SIPPETS OF BREAD TO GARNISH HASHES.

342. May be made by simply toasting slices of bread an inch in thickness; paring off the crusts, and cutting the slices into angular pieces. *Or*, by cutting the bread in the shape of common sippets, soaking them for three quarters of an hour with a spoonful of cream gently dropped upon each, and then frying them in butter of a light brown; after which they must be drained on a cloth by the fire, and served hot and dry. If as an ornamental garnish, they may be cut in shapes with a paste-cutter.

FRIED BREAD CRUMBS AN ACCOMPANIMENT TO ROAST PHEASANTS, PARTRIDGES, AND GROUSE.

343. Grate some stale bread, and if not very fine *shake* the crumbs through a colander so as to lie lightly in the dish. Melt a slice of butter in a frying-pan, and fry the crumbs till all are well and equally colour-ed, stirring them to prevent burning, then well drain and dry them on paper, or a cloth spread upon a sieve. If preferred, the crumbs may be browned very gently in a cool or a Dutch oven, without butter. They are easily removed with a slice.

SECT. 5.—SAUSAGES, BLACK PUDDINGS, &c.

344. THESE SAVOURY COMPOUNDS are made with various materials chopped and mixed together, either by the hand or with the aid of a

common chopper and board, or with a sausage-making machine, which last acts remarkably well, but is not required often enough in private houses to warrant its purchase. They are afterwards put into properly cleaned lengths of the entrails of the ox, sheep, calf, or pig, and tied at short intervals with common fine string. In cleaning the entrails they are turned inside out, stretched on a smooth stick, and well scraped and washed in several waters.

PORK SAUSAGES.

345. Chop fat and lean of pork together; season it with sage, pepper, and salt, and add two or three berries of allspice; (*or*, chop pork meat, rather more lean than fat, flavour with pepper, salt and cayenne, and a little lemon-peel if approved; six ounces of bread crumbs to about two pounds of meat to be chopped with the meat;) *half fill* hogs' entrails that have been soaked and made extremely clean; or, the meat may be kept in a very small pan closely covered, and rolled and dusted with a very little flour before it is fried; serve on mashed potatoes put in a form, plain, or browned with the salamander, or before the fire; the sausages must be pricked with a fork before they are dressed or they will burst, unless they are very carefully fried. (See *Frying*, page 54.)

BOLOGNA SAUSAGES.

346. Chop very fine a quarter of a pound veal, a quarter of a pound of salted beef, and a quarter of a pound of salt pork; mince not too fine half a pound of bacon; mix these together, and season with one tea-spoonful of sage, three tea-spoonsful of mixed herbs, half a tea-spoonful of ground pepper, three tea-spoonsful of mixed spice, fill the skin (a large one), and boil quickly for nearly an hour, prick it, lay it on straw until cold, then hang it up to dry.

LARGE SMOKED SAUSAGES OR POLONIES.

347. Season fat and lean pork with some salt, saltpetre, black pepper, and allspice, all in fine powder, and rub into the meat; the sixth day cut it small, and mix with it some shred shalot or garlic, as fine as possible; have ready an ox-gut that has been scoured, salted, and soaked well, and fill it with the above stuffing; tie up the ends, and hang it to smoke as you would hams, but first wrap it in a fold or two of old muslin; it must be high-dried. Some eat it without boiling, but others like it boiled first. The skin should be

tied in different places, so as to make each link about eight or nine inches long.

Oxford Sausages.

348. Chop a pound and a half of pork, and the same of veal, cleared of skin and sinews; add three-quarters of a pound of beef-suet; mince and mix them; steep the crumb of a penny-loaf in water, and mix it with the meat, with also a little dried sage, pepper, and salt.

Beef and Veal Sausages.

349. These are made with beef or veal in the same way as for pork (345), but there is generally a larger proportion of spice; the herbs added are marjoram, thyme, and parsley instead of sage.

To Make Black Puddings.

350. The blood must be stirred with salt till cold. Put a quart of it, or rather more, to a quart of whole grits, to soak one night; and soak the crumb of a quartern loaf in rather more than two quarts of new milk made hot. In the mean time prepare the entrails by washing, turning, and scraping with salt and water, and changing the water several times. Chop fine a little winter-savoury and thyme, a good quantity of penny-royal, pepper and salt, a few cloves, some allspice, ginger and nutmeg; mix these with three pounds of beef-suet and six eggs well beaten and strained; and then beat the bread, grits, &c., all up with the seasoning; when well mixed, have ready some hog's fat cut into large bits, and as you fill the skins put it in at proper distances. Tie in links only half filled, and boil in a large kettle, pricking them as they swell, or they will burst. When boiled, lay them between clean cloths till cold, and hang them up in the kitchen. When to be used, scald them a few minutes in water; wipe, and put them into a Dutch oven. If there are not skins enough, put the stuffing into basins, and boil it covered with floured cloths; and slice and fry it when to be used.

Another Receipt.—Soak all night a quart of bruised grits in as much boiling hot milk as will swell them and leave half a pint of liquid. Chop a good quantity of pennyroyal, some savoury and thyme; then add salt, pepper, and allspice, finely powdered. Mix the above with a quart of the blood, prepare as before directed; then half fill the skins after they have been cleaned thoroughly, and put as much of the leaf (that is, the inward fat) of the pig as will make it pretty rich.

Boil as before directed. A small quantity of leeks finely shred and well mixed is a great improvement.

WHITE HOG'S PUDDINGS.

351. When the skins have been soaked and cleaned as before directed, rinse and soak them all night in rose-water, and put into them the following filling :—Mix half a pound of blanched almonds cut into seven or eight bits, with a pound of grated bread, two pounds of marrow or suet, a pound of currants, some beaten cinnamon, cloves, mace, and nutmeg, a quart of cream, the yolks of six and whites of two eggs, a little orange-flower water, a little fine Lisbon sugar, and some lemon-peel and citron sliced, and half fill the skins. To know whether properly flavoured, warm a little in a pannikin. In boiling, much care must be taken to prevent the puddings from bursting. Prick them with a small fork as they rise, and boil them in milk and water. Lay them in a table-cloth till cold.

Another White Hog's Pudding.—Two quarts of groats steeped in one and a half pint of water, then add five pints of milk. Boil the skin of the leaf, and any bits of fat or pork dripping with the groats; when thoroughly done, add twelve cloves pounded, a good handful of pennyroyal, two onions (previously boiled to make them less strong), seven or eight leeks, a little marjoram and nutmeg plant, with pepper and salt. When the skins are stuffed and tied, put them into *boiling water*, and boil for twenty minutes, lay them on straw to drain and cool.

SAVELOYS.

352. These are made of *salt* pork, of which the fat and lean are mixed together and chopped with a fourth part of bread, a little pepper and allspice, and a rather liberal use of sage leaves. They are put in skins as for pork sausages, and boiled slowly for half an hour, then put by and eaten cold.

CHAP. X.—THE COOKING OF RAW BUTCHER'S MEAT.

SECT. 1.—REMARKS.

353. The general directions for roasting, baking, boiling, frying, and broiling, will be found under their respective Chapters, at pages 41 *et seq.*, while the preparations of sauces, &c., are described at pages 94 *et seq.*

I

354. For REMARKS on the quality of meat, quantity of bone in the various joints, price, choosing, description of joints, &c., see the *Economical Housekeeper*, page 10 *et seq.*

SECT. 2.—BEEF.

355. For the most economical joints see *Economical Housekeeper*, pages 19, 20.

356. ROAST BEEF being generally thick in substance, and the joint of large size, the fire must be made of plenty of coals. The sirloin requires the fat to be prepared on the inside, as well as that on the ribs. Constant basting is necessary at first with strong salt and water, and afterwards with its own dripping. Gravy may always be made for beef according to the plan given at page 96. Horseradish scraped is generally served round the dish; and also for sauce (see Horseradish Sauce). Time for roasting, from a quarter of an hour per pound, to twenty minutes, according to the size of the joint and the taste of those who intend to partake of it, some liking meat half done, while others require it entirely free from a red colour.

357. A BEEF HEART, or as it is sometimes called BULLOCK'S HEART, should be well washed (not soaked) in water, and stuffed with the same as for veal (see pars. 332, 333). Tie up all the openings with strong cotton, and then roast according to weight (fifteen to twenty minutes per pound, the latter for most tastes).

IMITATION HARE.

358. A thick piece of steak may be covered with the same stuffing as for heart (see last par.), then roll it, tie with fine string, and roast according to weight (fifteen to twenty minutes per pound).

TO BOIL MARROW-BONES.

359. The large ends of the marrow bones should be sawn, so that they will stand upright both when boiling and when served, and the cut ends first be covered with a paste of flour and water, and then with a cloth tightly tied over each to prevent the escape of the marrow. Boil them from one and a half to two hours, according to the size. Remove the paste and serve hot on a napkin, with pieces of toasted bread arranged round. The marrow-bones should be more than half-boiled if required to be kept before using.

BOILED BEEF (SALTED).

360. Requires, like all boiled meats, vigilant skimming. The addi-

tion of vegetables to the pot in the same water appears to prevent much of the juice being extracted, and is, therefore, economical, as well as improving the flavour. Carrots, parsnips, greens, turnip-tops, and peas-pudding are eaten in different families with it; also a plain suet-pudding. The liquor from salt-beef is generally too full of salt to make soup without any addition of other stock or water; but mixed with from two-thirds to three-quarters of either it serves very well, and contains a large quantity of nutritive matter, highly valued by the poor who are at all imbued with economical principles; and therefore, when not wanted at home, it should be saved for any poor and deserving neighbours. Many people stuff boiled parsley into holes cut in boiled beef. The time must be reckoned from the moment that the water boils, after being dashed with cold; and here, as in the case of roasting, it may vary from a quarter of an hour per pound, to twenty minutes, according to taste.

A Wholesome Method of Cooking Beef.

361. Put the beef in a saucepan (with a lid), at the side of the fire. Put *very little* or *no* water, and let it simmer for three or four hours, according to the size of the piece of beef.

To Stew a Rump of Beef.

362. Wash it well, and season high with salt, allspice, pepper, cayenne, three cloves, and a blade of mace, all in fine powder. Bind it up tight, and lay it in a pot that will just hold it. Fry three large onions sliced, and put them to it, with three carrots, two turnips, a shalot, four cloves, a blade of mace, and some celery. Cover the meat with good beef broth or weak gravy. Simmer it as gently as possible for several hours, till quite tender. Clear off the fat; add to the gravy half a pint of port-wine, a glass of vinegar, and a large spoonful of ketchup; simmer half an hour, and serve in a deep dish. Half a pint of table-beer may be added. The herbs to be used should be parsley, thyme, basil, marjoram, or knotted marjoram, and some chives if at hand, but observe to proportion the quantities to the pungency of the several sorts; let there be a good handful all together. Garnish with carrots, turnips, mushrooms, or pickles of different colours, cut small, and laid in little heaps separately; chopped parsley, chives, beet-root, &c. If, when done, the gravy is too much to fill the dish, take only a part to season for serving, but the less water the better; and to increase the richness, add a few beef-bones and shanks of mutton in stewing.

A spoonful or two of made mustard is a great improvement to the gravy.

SHIN OF BEEF.

363. Take off the skin and cut long pieces off; stew them gently in a little water till tender, then add tomata sauce (or, if fresh tomatas, boil and rub through a sieve), and boil. Season with pepper and salt.

Or—Dip it in vinegar; stew gently till tender, with one or two onions, and serve.

STEWED BEEF STEAK.

364. Fry a tender steak in the usual way, but lightly, with the onions, turnips, and carrots; then stew as above, and it will be better flavoured than when in a large mass. It may be done with or without the carrots and turnips. If without them, the gravy must be flavoured with Worcestershire sauce and anchovy, and thickened with a little flour or arrowroot.

TO STEW BRISKET OF BEEF.

365. Put the part with the hard fat into a stew-pot with a small quantity of water; let it boil up, and skim it thoroughly; then add carrots, turnips, onions, celery, and a few peppercorns. Stew till extremely tender; then take out the flat bones, and remove all the fat from the soup. Serve that and the meat in a tureen; or the soup alone, and the meat on a dish, garnished with some vegetables. The following sauce is much admired, served with the beef:—Take half a pint of the soup, and mix it with a spoonful of ketchup, a glass of port-wine, a teaspoonful of made mustard, a little flour, a bit of butter, and salt; boil all together a few minutes, then pour it round the meat.

A PLAIN BEEF STEW.

366. Cut steaks from a sirloin or tender round of beef without fat or bone, season, and put them in a pot with one quart of water to every three pounds of meat. When the whole has simmered one hour and been well skimmed, mix with it twelve potatoes, and six turnips pared and quartered; and, if liked, two onions sliced thin. If the stew appears dry, add a little boiling water; let it stew slowly till the whole is tender; serve with vegetables round. Beef stewed with parsnips only is very good.

BEEF-BOUILLI.

367. Beef-bouilli is *fresh beef* boiled very slowly in a small quantity of water; the liquor being in this way preserved for stock, and not being salt, there is no loss. To an English palate, fresh beef boiled to rags is not pleasant, but when served with vegetables it is by no means to be despised; and, as a regular article of diet, is the only one which preserves all the goodness without waste. It is true that the same may be done with the liquor of boiled mutton; but here more water is used, and consequently the liquor is not so good, neither will the meat bear so much boiling. The economist is, therefore, strongly advised to try this plan once a week for a family, and in a very short time it will be relished here as much as in France. When boiled with winter peas, or green peas (old), or greens, the flavour of the meat is improved, and the soup the next day is more easily made. (See the *Pot-au-feu,* among the soups.)

To Boil a Tongue.

368. If a smoked or dried tongue it should be soaked overnight, but if fresh from the pickle three or four hours will be long enough. Put it on the fire in cold water, and let it take an hour or two in coming to a boil; then draw it back, and let it simmer for three or four hours longer, till tender quite through. A few carrots and turnips sliced and boiled in the water improve the flavour. Trim the root, peel and glaze the tongue, and garnish with a paper frill around the root end, and a rose, or some one or two flowers cut in turnip, and stuck upon small branches of Portugal laurel on the top, over the windpipe.

To Stew a Tongue.

369. Salt a tongue with saltpetre and common salt for six or seven days, rubbing and turning it every day. Boil it till tender enough to peel; then stew it in a pretty good gravy, seasoned with ketchup, cayenne, and a little mace, adding salt if needed. The tongue should be served with truffles, morels, and mushrooms stewed in gravy, and little heaps of mashed turnips round the dish, or portions of brocoli.

A ROLLED TONGUE TO EAT COLD.

370. After being well seasoned and salted, the tongue should be removed from the pickle, and either boiled or laid in a small pan with

some butter over it, and covered with a flour-and-water-crust, then baked very slowly till extremely tender; peel, and press it into a tin mould with as much fat as possible (or roll it round into a smaller tin than is used for a brawn); lay a weight upon it, and when perfectly cold it is ready for use. Fold writing-paper round, with a frill at the top, if the latter shape be used.

Another Mode.—A tin is also necessary for the purpose, the same as that used for mock-brawn, or a white preserve-jar, with a large hole knocked in the bottom, will answer very well. When the tongue is boiled and skinned, lay it in the jar or tin, coiled up, with the tip outside the root, and upon the top a garden saucer, fitting the tin or pot, and containing at least a weight of ten pounds, then set it by till cold. To turn it out, loosen the sides with a knife, then turn it upside down, and push it out through the hole in the bottom. The slices being cut horizontally all round, the fat and the lean must go together.

FILLET OF BEEF STEWED.

371. Take the inside of a sirloin of beef, stuffed or plain, rolled up with the fat in the centre. Put a little good stock into the stewpan with a few slices of lean ham, and then the meat, which must be covered with carrots and celery cut in dice, or the former in shapes, a few small onions, savoury herbs, and a little chopped pickle; flavour with salt, pepper, mace, and a little ketchup, simmer till tender, and brown the beef before the fire; skim and season the sauce, remove the herbs, and serve the whole hot.

BEEF STEWED A-LA-MODE.

372. Choose a piece of thick flank of a fine heifer or ox. Cut into long slices some fat bacon, but quite free from rancidity; let each bit be near an inch thick; dip them into vinegar, and then into a seasoning ready prepared of salt, black pepper, allspice, and a clove, all in fine powder, with parsley, chives, thyme, savoury, and knotted marjoram, shred as small as possible, and well mixed. With a sharp knife make holes deep enough to let in the larding; then rub the beef over with a seasoning, and bind it up tight with tape. Set it in a well-tinned pot over a fire or rather stove; three or four onions must be fried brown and put to the beef, with two or three carrots, one turnip, a head or two of celery, and a small quantity of water; let it simmer gently ten or twelve hours, or till extremely tender, turning the meat

twice. Put the gravy into a pan, remove the fat, keep the beef covered, then put them together, and add a glass of port-wine. Take of the tape, and serve with the vegetables; or you may strain them off, and send them up cut into dice for garnish. Onions roasted, and then stewed with the gravy, are a great improvement. A tea-cupful of vinegar should be stewed with the beef.

A FRICANDEAU OF BEEF.

373. Take a nice piece of lean beef; lard it with bacon seasoned with pepper, salt, cloves, mace, and allspice. Put it into a stewpan with a pint of broth, a glass of white wine, a bundle of parsley, all sorts of sweet herbs, a clove of garlic, a shalot or two, four cloves, pepper, and salt. When the meat is become tender, cover it close; skim the sauce well, and strain it; set it on the fire, and let it boil till it is reduced to a glaze. Glaze the larded side with this, and serve the meat on sorrel sauce.

BEEF COLLOPS.

374. Take some beef that is tender and free from skin, cut it into small thin pieces, hack it with a knife; then butter a stewpan, and put in as much beef as will cover the pan, with a little onion, some cucumber cut small, and salt and pepper. Put it over a quick fire, and give two or three tosses about; two or three minutes will do them. Add a little flour, butter, and water to the stewpan after taking the collops out, to make your gravy. Garnish, if approved, with pickles.

BEEF ROBART.

375. Take the inside of a sirloin of beef, cut it very thin, then fry it in butter just to change the colour; put it in a pan with some gravy, to stew with shalots, anchovy-essence, mushrooms, and oysters. Thicken the gravy, and serve with fried sippets of bread.

ROLLED BEEF.

376. Take nearly two pounds of the inside of a sirloin or other tender beef, with three quarters of a pound of bacon; chop them finely, and mix well together, with nearly a spoonful of black pepper, and a little cayenne, salt, mace, and the grated rind of a lemon. Roll it up together, in a paper well buttered, and cover the whole with a thin paste of flour and water. Bake it two hours, and, after removing the coverings, serve it in a rich brown gravy. Veal may be substituted

for the beef, in which case mushrooms or curry powder would be an improvement.

BEEF PALATES, STEWED.

377. Simmer them for several hours till they will peel; then cut the palates into slices, or leave them whole, as preferred; and stew them in a rich gravy till as tender as possible. Before serving them up, season with cayenne, salt, and ketchup. If the gravy was drawn clear, add also some butter and flour. If to be served white, boil them in milk, and stew them in a fricassee-sauce, adding cream, butter, flour, and mushroom powder, and a little pounded mace.

To ROLL BEEF PALATES.

378. Boil five or six palates gently, till you can peel and trim them; what you cut away should be stewed with a little of the liquor, seasoned with a glass of white wine, and thickened with flour and butter till the gravy is *good*. Cover the outside of the palates with yolk of egg, and then with a well-seasoned forcemeat. Roll the palates up, and tie them tightly with a string or tape; lay them in a stewpan, with a little butter, and a quarter of a pint of milk or cream, and simmer gently for two hours. Lay the stewed trimmings upon a dish, squeeze the juice of half a lemon over it, and then lay on the rolled palates; pour over it the mixed gravy from both stewpans, and garnish with mushroom pickle, forcemeat, and egg balls.

To FRY PALATES.

379. Boil them till half done, split them in halves, spread some forcemeat, and roll up the halves; make a batter of yolk of eggs, flour, a little butter, and a few spoonsful of white wine, the batter must be added by degrees, and should be as thick as *good* cream; fry them a light brown, and serve on a napkin, or with a good gravy, or they may be dipped simply in egg and crumbs.

To STEW AN OX-TONGUE.

380. Salt a tongue with saltpetre and common salt for a week, turning it every day. Boil it tender enough to peel; when done, stew it in a moderately strong gravy; season with soy, mushroom ketchup, cayenne, pounded cloves, and salt, if necessary. Serve with truffles, morels, or mushrooms. In this receipt the roots must be taken off the tongues before salting, but some fat left.

STEWED OX-CHEEK (PLAIN).

381. Soak and cleanse a fine cheek the day before it is to be eaten; put it into a stewpot that will cover close, with three quarts of water; simmer it after it has first boiled up and been well skimmed. In two hours put plenty of carrots and leeks, two or three turnips, a bunch of sweet herbs, some whole pepper, and four ounces of allspice. Skim it often; when the meat is tender, take it out; let the soup get cold, take off the cake of fat, and serve the soup separate or with the meat. The colour should be a fine brown, which may be effected by adding burnt sugar, or by frying some onions quite brown with flour, and simmering them with it. This last way improves the flavour of all soups and gravies of the brown kind. If vegetables are not approved in the soup, they may be taken out, and a small roll be toasted, or bread fried and added. Celery is a great addition, and should always be served. Where it is not to be got, the seed gives quite as good a flavour boiled in, and strained off.

To FRY OR BROIL RUMP OR BEEF STEAKS.

382. Let the steaks be cut from the rump in rather thin layers, and the chops be as usual. Then fry in lard or dripping in the English manner (see pars. 97 and 103), turning them repeatedly until done. When ready, keep them hot in a dish by the fire, while making the gravy, which is done as follows:—Pour off as much of the fat as possible, but leaving behind all the gravy or coloured part (there must be, at least, altogether two table-spoonsful of gravy, or gravy and fat). Thicken this with a table-spoonful of flour, stirred into it dry; put the pan on the fire, and brown it slightly, then add a table-spoonful of ketchup (mushroom or walnut), a table-spoonful of Worcestershire sauce, or a little of mixed pickle chopped up; pepper and salt slightly, and reduce to a proper degree of thickness by adding hot water by degrees. Large onions sliced are sometimes fried with beef-steaks, or pickled mushrooms, and served with them, in which case they are taken out with the steaks, and the sauce made afterwards in the same way as above. If onions or mushrooms are not liked, it is usual to garnish with scraped horseradish, or pickles.

(For directions to fry, see page 54.)

383. BROILED STEAKS should be cut from a well-kept rump, and they are generally liked about three-quarters of an inch thick. Most cooks beat them well with a rolling-pin for ten minutes; but if the

meat is of good quality, and the rump has been well kept, there will be no necessity for this. Just before finishing, rub a lump of butter over, and lightly dredge with pepper and salt, adding the mushroom powder at discretion. Pickles and scraped horseradish make a good garnish, and for sauce, (see Meat Sauces.)

(For directions to broil, see page 54.)

To Fry Beef Kidney.

384. Cut in slices, and soak for an hour in cold water. Then fry it in the same way as for steaks, (par. 382.)

Fillets of Beef.

385. Cut the inside of a sirloin of beef into slices half an inch in thickness, trim them, and season with pepper and salt, and fry them, and serve with tomata or sorrel sauce.

Tripe.

386. Tripe should always be bought ready prepared by the tripe-seller, in which state it merely requires boiling for an hour.

To Boil Tripe.

387. Put it into milk and water mixed in equal quantities, with two or three onions previously boiled in several waters. Serve the whole together, and with it melted butter or oyster sauce, or by some people onion sauce is preferred.

To Fry Tripe.

388. Dip each piece in butter, and fry in the usual way with sliced onions.

Cow Heels.

389. Cow heels, like tripe, are best prepared by the tripe-seller, or they require careful soaking and cleansing. They then merely require warming up in boiling water, or milk and water, after which they should be served with cuttle sauce, or with parsley and butter, or simple melted butter. They are sometimes eaten cold with vinegar and salad.

Sect. 3.—Mutton.

390. For the most economical joints, &c., see *Economical Housekeeper*, page 24.

To Roast Mutton.

391. Mutton, except the haunch, is not of sufficient size to require quite so large a fire as beef; still it cannot be roasted without a brisk and full fire. It should be papered wherever there is fat to be saved for eating, as in the inside and outside of the haunch or the loin ; but necks and shoulders are none the better for this care. For ordinary purposes the gravy made as in par. 75, is sufficient, but for haunches, and sometimes for legs and saddles, a wine gravy is made (which see) and served with currant jelly ; with shoulders some prefer onion sauce. Mutton is not improved by basting with water and salt, but should be well basted in its own fat; and towards the last plentifully dredged with flour. The time required is, on the average, as for beef—viz., one quarter of an hour per pound; but, whatever the weight, the time for *long and thin joints*, like necks and loins, will be nearly the same. Legs or saddles of ten pounds will take two and a half hours. The shoulder, being more flat, will take a quarter of an hour less than the usual allowance—say, for nine pounds, two hours. The loin and neck, also, will require rather less than that calculation.

To Boil Mutton.

392. A leg or shoulder of Mutton may be boiled, but the former is the most frequently dressed in this way. Turnips or greens are the ordinary concomitants, and caper sauce, or nasturtium sauce, without any other gravy than that coming out of the meat when cut. The time taken will be in accordance with the regular rule, or rather more —say, for large legs, half an hour in addition. The liquor makes good stock.

Neck of Mutton

393. Is boiled and served like the leg, but it will not take more time than the regular allowance.

Shoulder of Mutton with Bread-crumbs

394. Is first boiled, and then slightly browned before the fire in a Dutch oven, being first dredged with bread-crumbs. In this way the flavour is much improved.

A Loin or Neck of Mutton

395. Is rendered less gross, by being partly roasted and partly boi'·

—either may be done first—according as it is to appear as a roast or a boiled joint at table; but it looks best if sent as a roast joint.

Stewed Mutton—(Irish Stew).

396. Take some mutton-chops and cut off part of the fat, lay them in the bottom of a stewpan, slice some onions very thin, and strew them over with pepper and salt, cut a quantity of potatoes in halves and lay on the top, put water sufficient to keep it from burning, and to make gravy when it is turned out; let it stew gently for about three hours before adding the potatoes, and three-quarters of an hour after.

Haricot of Mutton.

397. Take a loin or neck of mutton, cut it in thin steaks, and take away part of the fat. Then butter a stewpan; flour the meat, dredge a little pepper and salt over it, lay the best pieces into the pan, and set it over the fire to brown; turn them one at a time; then put in some onions and celery, some sliced carrots and turnips (first boiled and then fried), and lay them on the mutton with just water enough to cover the meat. Put a layer of mutton, and then carrots. This will take three hours to stew. Add a little ketchup, or anchovy, or Worcestershire sauce to the gravy before serving.

Another Receipt.—Take the middle of a neck or loin of mutton, cut it into thin steaks, season them with pepper and salt, and brown them in a pan with butter; when brown, pour off the butter, and put in three pints of boiling water, one anchovy, one onion, a few turnips and carrots, cut into shapes. Stew it gently for two hours, or more. Thicken with flour and butter just as you send it up. The haricot is richer if the carrots and turnips are browned in the pan after the steaks are taken out, before being stewed.

Stewed Mutton Cutlets (French).

398. Skin a loin of mutton, and cut it into steaks. Make a force-meat with lean of veal, beef suet, thyme, sweet marjoram, and one onion, all cut small; essence of anchovy, nutmeg, pepper and salt, and the yolks of two eggs, with some grated bread. Insert some of the forcemeat in the lean of the steaks, and cover all thickly with it. Stew till tender in a little gravy. Then put each steak in a buttered piece of writing-paper; turn in the corners of the paper to keep in the moisture, and finish them on the gridiron; or they may be baked from the first in the oven. Serve in the papers.

Hot-Pot.

399. Take some fine chops from a neck of mutton, and trim them nicely, taking off most of the fat. Lay them at the bottom of a deep and rather wide dish, and season them with pepper and salt. Lay a few slices of an onion in the middle at the bottom of the dish, if the flavour is approved, and pour a quarter of a pint of cold water upon the whole. Then cover it with a layer of sliced potatoes, on the top of which lay a few more small chops, well-seasoned, and cover all with another layer of sliced potatoes. Bake from an hour to an hour and a half, or more, according to the size of the dish; in a very moderate oven.

Mock Venison Stewed.

400. Take a fat loin of mutton, the outer skin must be stripped off, and the bones cut out. Put the bones into a stewpan with a good-sized onion stuck with cloves, one anchovy, some peppercorns, and a bunch of sweet herbs. Stew for three hours in a small quantity of water, then strain. The mutton should be beaten with a rolling-pin, and nutmeg grated over the inside the previous night. Before it is put in the stewpan it must be rolled up tight, beginning at the tail end, and tied with a strong string. Add half a pint of port-wine to the gravy, and let it all stew together for three hours at least. A large loin or saddle will require four hours. When done the fat must be skimmed off, and the gravy thickened with a little flour and butter, and a small quantity of ketchup added.

Stewed Mutton Cutlets (American).

401. Remove the fat and bone, beat the cutlets, and season with pepper and salt, and nutmeg. Put them in a circular tin kettle, with bits of butter rolled in flour. Set the kettle closely covered upon a trivet inside a flat-bottomed pot. Pour boiling water round; set the pot on a slow fire, and let the stew simmer two hours; then lift up the meat, and put under it a lettuce cut in four, three cucumbers cut up, two onions sliced, mace, salt, and a little more butter rolled in flour; set again in boiling water, always taking care that the water should not be above the top of the inner kettle; let it simmer two hours more and serve; place the meat on the vegetables, and laying a ridge of boiled peas round. The bone may be left in each cutlet if preferred

ROLLED LOIN OF MUTTON.

402. Bone a loin of mutton, stuff it with veal stuffing. Roll it round, roast it, and serve with gravy and sweet sauce.

STEWED FILLET OF MUTTON (AMERICAN).

403. Cut a fillet from a leg of mutton, remove the fat from the outside, and take out the bone. Beat it well with a rolling-pin, and rub it with pepper and salt; fill the place of the bone with a stuffing of firmly mixed onions, bread crumbs, butter, salt, pepper, and nutmeg, well mixed. Make deep cuts all over the surface of the meat, and fill them with the stuffing. Bind a tape round the meat, put it in a stew-pan with sufficient water to cover it, and let it stew slowly four, five, or six hours according to its size, skimming frequently. Serve with its own gravy. A thick round of fresh beef is very good stuffed and stewed in the same manner; it will take longer stewing than the mutton.

TO STEW A LOIN OF MUTTON.

404. Remove the bones from a loin of tender mutton; take off the skin, and remove the fat from the inside; brown it with butter in a stew-pan or Dutch oven, then add broth to cover it; carrots and turnips cut in shapes, celery, and a very little onion; stew till very tender, and flavour with ketchup, and a glass of port-wine. After placing the meat on the dish, keep it hot, while carefully scumming the fat from the gravy before pouring it over the meat.

TO STEW A SHEEP'S HEAD.

405. Split a sheep's head open, and after browning it in a Dutch oven, stew it for two hours or more in a gallon of water, with a quarter of a pound of Scotch barley or rice, three onions, three turnips, a little parsley; then mix a quarter of a pound of oatmeal in a pint of water, pour it in, and let it all boil up together.

HODGE-PODGE.

406. Take a scrag of mutton, and half a pound of green split peas, and two pints of water, and let it boil two hours; strain the soup through a cloth, then add carrots, turnips, lettuce, onions, mutton chops (without any fat), a table-spoonful of sugar, and salt to your taste; half a pound of dried green peas; or, in their season, peas from the garden. If the dried peas are used, they must be put into

soft water, and gently simmered till they are tender, and added to the soup half an hour before dinner.

Another (A Genuine Scotch Receipt).—Put on as much water in a good-sized goblet as will make two days' soup to serve six or eight of a family; three hours before dinner-hour add two pounds of hough (*Anglicè*, leg of beef), half a dish of old peas, one dozen of middling-sized carrots cut down in small pieces, and four onions cut down; let this boil an hour and a half, then add the other half-dish of peas, and two pounds of mutton chops. When it has all boiled for three hours, take out the hough and serve it up with the mutton chops in it. It is considered best the second day; it should be as thick as porridge nearly. A few beans and turnips can be added, but the turnips are apt to sour it; yet, when peas are scarce and young, it is necessary to put turnips to make it thick enough.

Mutton Chops.

407. Mutton chops when fried are done exactly like steaks, see par. 382, except that from their bones they will not bear beating. They are served in their own sauce, or with the appropriate sauce (see Sauces).

408. To Broil Mutton Chops proceed as for beefsteaks, (par. 382.)

Mutton Cutlets.

409. Mutton Cutlets are fried with the bread-crumb, just like the veal cutlets; and, if fried in the English fashion, they generally give out enough gravy to serve without any thing extra; but the articles described under the next paragraph may be added.

French Cutlets (*Côtelettes de Mouton*).

410. Skin a loin of mutton, and cut it into steaks. Then make a forcemeat with an equal weight of lean veal and beef suet, and two anchovies, all pounded; parsley, thyme (and a little onion previously boiled till mild), chopped fine; add grated bread crumbs, and the yolks of two eggs. Make holes in the steaks and fill them with the forcemeat, with which also they must be well covered. Place each carefully in a buttered paper, so that no moisture shall escape, and broil them. Serve in a gravy, with a few of the herbs shred fine, and a little lemon-juice or vinegar to flavour it.

—either may be done first—according as it is to appear as a roast or a boiled joint at table; but it looks best if sent as a roast joint.

STEWED MUTTON—(IRISH STEW).

396. Take some mutton-chops and cut off part of the fat, lay them in the bottom of a stewpan, slice some onions very thin, and strew them over with pepper and salt, cut a quantity of potatoes in halves and lay on the top, put water sufficient to keep it from burning, and to make gravy when it is turned out; let it stew gently for about three hours before adding the potatoes, and three-quarters of an hour after.

HARICOT OF MUTTON.

397. Take a loin or neck of mutton, cut it in thin steaks, and take away part of the fat. Then butter a stewpan; flour the meat, dredge a little pepper and salt over it, lay the best pieces into the pan, and set it over the fire to brown; turn them one at a time; then put in some onions and celery, some sliced carrots and turnips (first boiled and then fried), and lay them on the mutton with just water enough to cover the meat. Put a layer of mutton, and then carrots. This will take three hours to stew. Add a little ketchup, or anchovy, or Worcestershire sauce to the gravy before serving.

Another Receipt.—Take the middle of a neck or loin of mutton, cut it into thin steaks, season them with pepper and salt, and brown them in a pan with butter; when brown, pour off the butter, and put in three pints of boiling water, one anchovy, one onion, a few turnips and carrots, cut into shapes. Stew it gently for two hours, or more. Thicken with flour and butter just as you send it up. The haricot is richer if the carrots and turnips are browned in the pan after the steaks are taken out, before being stewed.

STEWED MUTTON CUTLETS (FRENCH).

398. Skin a loin of mutton, and cut it into steaks. Make a force-meat with lean of veal, beef suet, thyme, sweet marjoram, and one onion, all cut small; essence of anchovy, nutmeg, pepper and salt, and the yolks of two eggs, with some grated bread. Insert some of the forcemeat in the lean of the steaks, and cover all thickly with it. Stew till tender in a little gravy. Then put each steak in a buttered piece of writing-paper; turn in the corners of the paper to keep in the moisture, and finish them on the gridiron; or they may be baked from the first in the oven. Serve in the papers.

STEWED MUTTON CUTLETS (AMERICAN).   125

Hot-Pot.

399. Take some fine chops from a neck of mutton, and trim them nicely, taking off most of the fat. Lay them at the bottom of a deep and rather wide dish, and season them with pepper and salt. Lay a few slices of an onion in the middle at the bottom of the dish, if the flavour is approved, and pour a quarter of a pint of cold water upon the whole. Then cover it with a layer of sliced potatoes, on the top of which lay a few more small chops, well-seasoned, and cover all with another layer of sliced potatoes. Bake from an hour to an hour and a half, or more, according to the size of the dish; in a very moderate oven.

Mock Venison Stewed.

400. Take a fat loin of mutton, the outer skin must be stripped off, and the bones cut out. Put the bones into a stewpan with a good-sized onion stuck with cloves, one anchovy, some peppercorns, and a bunch of sweet herbs. Stew for three hours in a small quantity of water, then strain. The mutton should be beaten with a rolling-pin, and nutmeg grated over the inside the previous night. Before it is put in the stewpan it must be rolled up tight, beginning at the tail end, and tied with a strong string. Add half a pint of port-wine to the gravy, and let it all stew together for three hours at least. A large loin or saddle will require four hours. When done the fat must be skimmed off, and the gravy thickened with a little flour and butter, and a small quantity of ketchup added.

Stewed Mutton Cutlets (American).

401. Remove the fat and bone, beat the cutlets, and season with pepper and salt, and nutmeg. Put them in a circular tin kettle, with bits of butter rolled in flour. Set the kettle closely covered upon a trivet inside a flat-bottomed pot. Pour boiling water round; set the pot on a slow fire, and let the stew simmer two hours; then lift up the meat, and put under it a lettuce cut in four, three cucumbers cut up, two onions sliced, mace, salt, and a little more butter rolled in flour; set again in boiling water, always taking care that the water should not be above the top of the inner kettle; let it simmer two hours more and serve; place the meat on the vegetables, and laying a ridge of boiled peas round. The bone may be left in each cutlet if preferred.

To Stew Lamb's Head.

423. Boil the head three-quarters of an hour, the liver a quarter of an hour, and the lights an hour, or rather more. Rub the head with the yolk of an egg; add some parsley, lemon-peel, a very small quantity of thyme, pepper, salt, nutmeg, and some bread-crumb. Grill it, make brain-cakes the same as for calf's head or forcemeat, and serve in some very rich gravy; and, if it is not thick enough, add a little flour and butter just before taking it off the fire.

Lamb's Sweetbreads.

424. Wash and parboil them, stew as the calf's sweetbreads, with the addition of a few very young peas or French beans.

Sect. 5.—Veal.

425. For the choice of veal and its most economical joints, see *the Economical Housekeeper*, pages 25, 26, and 27.

Roast Veal.

426. Veal, in order to look and eat well, should be thoroughly done at a strong fire, and browned very evenly, with a certain amount of coating caused by the dredging with flour, or with flour and bread-crumb mixed. It must be constantly basted with lard, dripping, or butter, as its own fat is not sufficient for the purpose. It is usual to stuff the fillet with forcemeat (par. 333), either filling with it the place where the bone was taken out, or else the flap where the fat lies, or by many it is preferred in both situations. For gravy, either make it from the dripping-pan (see par. 44), or else use any gravy at hand made from other sources, and mix with melted butter. It is served with slices of lemon. The time for roasting is as follows:—A fillet, stuffed, weighing nine pounds, two hours and a half; a shoulder of eight pounds, an hour and three-quarters; a breast of six pounds, one hour and a quarter; loin, an hour and a quarter to two hours, according to size; and for these joints, when either larger or smaller, add or subtract a quarter of an hour per lb.

To Boil Veal.

427. Veal must be put in plenty of boiling water, and be most carefully skimmed, or it will look dirty and brown. Some cooks use a fourth part of milk, and this has an advantage in avoiding the extrac-

tion of the juices. The time is in accordance with the general rule. The parts boiled are usually the *knuckle*, the *fillet* stuffed as for roasting, and the breast with its sweetbread. Bacon or ham are eaten with it; and for sauce, either parsley and butter, or white sauce; or, by some people, onion sauce. The water in which veal is boiled makes good stock, with additions; but if milk is used it soon turns sour.

VEAL CUTLETS.

428. Cutlets are cut from a leg of veal, about a third of an inch thick, and of such a size as may be preferred. Fry them in plenty of *hot* lard or dripping on the French plan, or, if the English is used, turn them quickly. Before putting them into the pan they are to be coated evenly with white of egg well beaten, using an egg-brush, and then dipping them in finely-powdered stale bread-crumb. They should be fried a delicate brown, and carefully drained from the fat. For gravy, some other meat must be had recourse to, as there is too little from veal in the frying-pan to make it of.

DUTCH CUTLETS OF VEAL.

429. Cut a thick slice from a leg of veal, beat it, and shape it into cutlets, and, dip them in yolk of egg. Mix a well-seasoned forcemeat, to which the addition of oysters is a great improvement, and spread it over the cutlets. They should be rolled up and finished with egg and crumbs in the usual way of veal cutlets; then roast them in the oven or before the fire, and serve with balls of the forcemeat described at par. 335, and which is improved by the addition of some lean ham. Serve with a good gravy flavoured with lemon-juice, mushroom ketchup, and a glass of sherry, or they may be served in a white sauce.

ITALIAN CUTLETS.

430. Cut some well-shaped veal cutlets, and prepare some parsley and other sweet herbs, by chopping fine, and simmering them in a little butter melted in the pan. Dip the cutlets in yolk of egg, then spread on them the herbs and butter, upon which lay, plentifully, fine bread crumbs; again put on egg, herbs, and crumbs, and nicely fry them, drain the fat from them, and glaze or not. They must be served in a rich and well-flavoured gravy.

CUTLETS OF VEAL, WITH OYSTERS.

431. Take two pounds of veal cutlets, cut them into thin pieces.

put them in a frying-pan with boiling lard, and let them fry till the veal is half done; then add a quart of large oysters, their liquor thickened with grated bread-crumbs, and seasoned with mace and nutmegs. Continue frying till veal and oysters are thoroughly done; serve in a covered dish.

VEAL CUTLETS, WITH TOMATO SAUCE.

432. Season the bread-crumbs with a little salt, and a very little India seasoning and pepper, then fry as usual. Make the gravy of the prepared tomato sauce and a little stock, thicken, put the cutlets in a dish, and pour the gravy *round* the dish.

FRENCH WAY OF DRESSING A SHOULDER OF VEAL.

433. Cut the veal into squares and parboil them, then put the meat in the dish in which it is to go to table; season with salt, cayenne, nutmeg, powdered mace, and grated lemon rind, adding some butter or veal dripping rolled in flour. Make a gravy of the bones and trimmings, strain, and pour it in. Set it in a hot Dutch oven, and bake till brown; when nearly done add two glasses of white wine, and serve hot.

TO STEW A KNUCKLE OF VEAL.

434. Break the bone in two or three places; put to it five pints of water, eight shalots, a bunch of sweet-herbs, some whole black pepper, a little salt and mace; boil it together till half the water is consumed, then take out the meat, herbs, and spice, thicken with two spoonsful of flour, and boil it till the flour is sufficiently done; then put back the best of the meat, add two glasses of Madeira wine, lemon-juice, and cayenne. Two calf's feet improve it much. It should be stewed over a slow fire.

A FILLET OF VEAL STEWED WHITE.

435. Add to one pint of water or gravy a little lemon-peel, mace, nutmeg, white pepper, and salt; put a fillet in, stuffed as for roasting, and when it has stewed one hour and a half take it out, strain the gravy, add two dozen oysters, half a pint of white wine, and butter rubbed in flour; put the veal in again, and stew it half an hour; just before serving, stir in half a pint of cream. The gravy should be rather thick, and poured over the veal.

SCOTCH COLLOPS (WHITE).

436. Cut them off the thick part of a leg of veal, the size and thick-ness of a crown-piece; put a lump of butter in a stewpan, and set it over a slow fire, or it will discolour the collops; lay some of them in before the pan is hot, and turn them over till the butter becomes of the consistence of a thick white gravy; put all together in a pot, and set them on the hearth to keep warm; repeat this till all are fried, then pour the gravy into the pan again, with a tea-spoonful of lemon-pickle, ketchup, caper-liquor, mace, cayenne-pepper, and salt; thicken it with flour and butter; when it has boiled gently five minutes, put in the yolks of two eggs with a teacupful of thick cream; keep shaking the pan over the fire till the gravy looks thick, then put in the collops and shake them till they are quite hot; put them in the dish with balls and pickled mushrooms.

SCOTCH COLLOPS (BROWN).

437. Take a leg of veal, and cut some thin collops; fry them, and season with salt and nutmeg. Boil some gravy, and when they are done pour it into the pan, with ketchup, walnut-pickle, and port-wine, to the taste.

TO COLLAR BREAST OF VEAL TO EAT HOT.

438. Bone the veal, take some thyme, marjoram, pepper, salt, and nutmeg, a little pounded mace, shred suet, crumbs of bread, and a score of oysters; beat all these in a mortar to mix them together, strew the mixture thickly over the veal, then roll it up into a collar, sew it tightly in a cloth, and boil it three hours. Serve with white sauce; forcemeat-balls can be added, if liked.

TO STEW A BREAST OF VEAL.

439. Cut it in pieces and put it into a pot with a bunch of sweet herbs, a small piece of bacon, a little mace, and a few black pepper-corns, salt, and one or two onions, and as much water as will cover it. Let it stew well over a slow fire. Boil some peas and lettuce by themselves, and, when the veal is stewed enough, strain the liquor from it, and put it into a stewpan with part of the liquor, the peas, lettuce, and a piece of butter, and let them stew again. Thicken with the yolks of two or three eggs and a little flour.

Another Receipt.—Cut it in the middle, bone it, and lay one part on

the other, with half a pint of white wine and gravy made from the
bones sufficient to cover it; add mace, cloves, whole pepper, salt, and
two anchovies; when sufficiently stewed, put some oysters in, and
thicken with flour and butter, after which keep stirring it until it is
taken off the fire.

FILLET OR BREAST OF VEAL, TO STEW WHITE.

440. Let the veal be two or three hours in milk, or clean cold
water, lay it in a stewpan and cover with water, allowing for its boiling away. Add twenty white peppercorns, and a little mace; before
serving, add a glass of white wine, a little mushroom powder, lemon-
pickle, or lemon juice, and a small piece of the peel. Put in as much
cream as will make it quite white, and thicken it with the yolks of two
eggs. If that is not sufficient, add a little butter and flour well mixed
together. Serve with boiled forcemeat balls, and garnish with lemon;
a little good veal stock would be a great addition to this stew.

FRICANDEAU OF VEAL.

441. Cut a large piece from the fat side of the leg, about nine inches
long, and half as thick and broad; beat it with the rolling-pin; take
off the skin, and trim off the rough edges. Lard the top and sides,
and cover it with fat bacon, and then with white paper. Lay it in the
stewpan with pieces of undressed veal or mutton, four onions, a carrot
sliced, a fagot of sweet herbs, four blades of mace, four bay-leaves, a
pint of good veal or mutton broth, and four or five ounces of lean ham
or gammon. Cover the pan close, and let it stew slowly three hours;
then take up the meat, remove all the fat from the gravy, and boil it
quick to a glaze. Keep the fricandeau quite hot, and then glaze it;
and serve with the remainder of the glaze in the dish, and sorrel sauce
in a sauce-tureen.

A Cheaper, but equally good Fricandeau of Veal.—With a sharp knife
cut the lean part off a large neck from the best end, scooping it from
the bones in lengths about that of the hand, and prepare it the same
way as in the last receipt; three or four bones only will be necessary,
and they will make the gravy; but if the prime part of the leg is cut
off, it spoils the whole.

RAGOUT BREAST OF VEAL.

442. Take a breast of veal, cut off the two ends, and fry the centre
in butter till a good brown; then put it into a stewpan with some

good gravy and a few small bits of bacon; cover close, and stew till nearly done enough. Take it out, and strain the gravy through a sieve; skim off all the fat, and take as much of the liquor as is required, and thicken it with flour and butter, and flavour with lemon pickle or juice, walnut and mushroom ketchup, or Worcestershire sauce.

Another.—Break the ribs of a breast of veal in two places, lard it with bacon, and roast till nearly done. Season some strong broth with mace, nutmeg, salt and pepper, and anchovy. Strain it, then put the veal in a stewpan and cover with the broth; boil some forcemeat balls a little in salt and water, then add them to the stew with some sweetbreads cut and fried, the bottoms of artichokes, truffles and morels, (or, in place of the latter, dried champignons, which are found in our English pastures). Thicken the gravy, if preferred, with flour and butter, lay the slices of sweetbread with rolled bacon on the veal, and fry some of the forcemeat in puff paste to lay round the dish—a little lemon juice and white wine may be added with ketchup.

HARICOT OF VEAL.

443. Take the best end of a small neck; cut the bones short, but leave it whole; put it into a stewpan, and just cover with brown gravy When it is nearly done, have ready a pint of boiled peas, six cucumbers pared and sliced, and two cabbage-lettuces cut into quarters, all stewed in a little good broth; put them to the veal, and let them simmer ten minutes. When the veal is in the dish, pour the sauce and vegetables over it, and lay the lettuce with forcemeat balls around it.

Another.—Take a portion of the breast of veal, or, still better, the best end of a neck, in which case the bones must be a little shortened if required. Brown in a Dutch oven, and then stew it in a good brown stock. When half done add some peas, vegetable marrows, lettuce, cucumbers, carrots, and turnips cut in squares. The vegetables must be previously fried in butter and stewed in a weak broth, or fried and put to stew at first with the meat. Thicken the gravy if required, and flavour with pepper and salt.

TO STEW A KNUCKLE OF VEAL.

444. Fry it with sliced onions and a little butter till it is well browned; put to it some good broth if you have it, otherwise water, and stew till tender. Then add lettuce, onion, cucumber, peas, parsley,

and celery, previously cut up and stewed. Season with pepper and salt, and serve.

Stewed Knuckle of Veal, or Veal à la Bourgeoise.

445. Take a good-sized stewpan, put in a little butter, a few turnips, carrots, onions, spices, a little lean bacon, pepper, salt, and thyme, moisten with two spoonsful of broth, and let the whole stew for two hours on a very slow fire; cut the turnips and carrots in small shapes or squares.

To Roll a Breast of Veal.

446. After removing the larger bones, beat the veal well on all sides, to make it tender and pliable. Lay the underside uppermost, and cover it with yolk of egg, pounded lean of cooked ham, and chopped parsley and thyme (more of parsley than of thyme), seasoned with pepper, salt, and a little mace or nutmeg. Make a light batter of cream or milk and eggs, well stiffened with soaked bread-crumbs, which lay thickly on, and again strew with herbs and ham. Roll up the veal, and secure it tightly with a cloth and tapes. Stew till quite tender for full six hours. Press it for a day with a heavy weight, if to be eaten cold. If hot, serve with a rich gravy, made from the bones flavoured with lemon-juice and ketchup, and, if liked, a glass of white wine. In either case glaze it before sending to table.

To Stew a Calf's Head.

447. Boil the head, if convenient, the day before it is wanted, till the bones will come out easily. The following day brown it before the fire, then put it in a stewpan, with a quart of *good* and *well-flavoured* gravy, a bunch of sweet herbs, and a little onion; let it simmer for an hour, take it out and add to the gravy a glass of white wine, and the juice of half a lemon with a little of the peel grated. Dish it up nicely; and garnish with brain cakes and egg balls, and a few slices of rolled bacon. When the bones are taken out, the head may be larded with bacon by way of variety.

For a corner dish half a head would be sufficient. The remains may be served a second day in slices as hashed calves' head, and afterwards laid while hot into a mould, with the garnish and gravy intermixed, and served cold at breakfast or luncheon.

Ox-cheek may be stewed in the same way.

To Boil a Calf's Head.

448. A calf's head is first cut in two, down the middle, leaving the tongue whole. The brains are then taken out. Next soak the head for an hour in cold water, to get out the blood which collects in the inside, and spoils the appearance. The head is either dressed with the skin on or off; if the former, it is a much better dish. Put plenty of water in the pot, and boil very gently about two hours, if the skin is off, more or less according to size. With the skin on, it will take nearly another hour. The tongue will not take more than an hour to boil, if put in by itself, which is the best plan; and it is served with some of the brains on a separate dish. While the head is boiling, well wash the brains, and soak afterwards in salt and water. Then boil for fifteen minutes, putting them into cold water and reckoning from the time when the water begins to boil. About a dozen sage leaves should be boiled separately, and chopped up finely. These, mixed with the brains, and a *slight flavour* of onion (not more than a quarter of a small one), boiled with a little melted butter, make the sauce. Egg-sauce is sometimes used in addition. Ham, bacon, or tongue is generally eaten with this dish.

Hashed Calf's Head.

449. Half boil a calf's head in two quarts of water, very gently lay a cloth over it to keep it a good colour, turn it over when half done. When cold cut it in slices with the tongue, make a good stock of veal with a little lemon thyme, winter savory, a little parsley, pepper, salt, and mace; thicken it with a little butter and flour, half a tea-cupful of white wine, and a little nutmeg. It is very good if basted in its own liquor, wholly or in part, instead of gravy. Skin the brains and beat them up (without boiling) with an egg, a little flour, salt, and nutmeg. Fry them in cakes with forced-meat and egg balls, and rolled bacon, garnish with slices of lemon.

450. Calf's Head Hashed White.—Let the head be well washed, and then boil it in soft water. Take the meat from the bones and cut it into thin collops, then take of the water it was boiled in enough to stew it till the meat is thoroughly hot. Work two ounces of butter well with some flour, and mix with it a little essence of anchovies, three blades of mace, a little nutmeg, with pepper and salt. Put this to the collops, and mix it well together. Take the yolk of an egg well beaten, stir it up with half a pint of milk, or omit the egg and milk.

and use half a pint of cream, add it to the hash. When done, squeeze in the juice of a lemon, and garnish with balls of forcemeat and egg balls.

451. To Hash Calf's Head Brown.—From a head half boiled cut off the meat in slices, half an inch thick, and two or three inches long. Brown some butter, flour, and sliced onions, and throw in the slices with some good gravy, truffles, and morels; give it one boil, skim it well, and set it in a moderate heat to simmer till very tender. Season with pepper, salt, and cayenne, at first; and ten minutes before serving throw in some shred parsley, and a very small bit of tarragon and knotted marjoram, cut as fine as possible. Just before serving add the squeeze of a lemon, and a table-spoonful of ketchup, and if liked a glass of white wine with brain cakes. Forcemeat balls and bits of bacon rolled round.

To Make Brain Cakes.

452. Blanch the brains of a calf or sheep, and beat them up with yolk of egg, a spoonful of cream, some pepper, salt, a little butter and some chopped parsley. Lay them in your frying-pan in cakes of a nice size and fry a light brown. Drain, before serving them, on paper or a cloth. They may be used alone or as an accompaniment to calves' head hash, &c.; or for croquettes, the brains may be blanched and beaten up with a little parsley and sage, some bread crumbs, moistened with cream, salt and pepper to taste, and a beaten egg to bind them; form into round or oval balls, and fry a light brown. Serve in a napkin.

To Roll a Calf's Head.

453. When sufficiently tender by boiling, remove the bones, roll it, tie it tightly with a cloth and tape, or put it in a mould. Finish boiling, and serve it with a good white sauce.

Or, if stewed brown the cloth must be omitted, and it must be stewed in a good gravy, and garnished as hashed or stewed calf's head.

Or, Scald the skin of a calf's head, and take out the brains, boil it till the bones will come out easily. Then proceed as " to roll a breast of veal " (446). Skin and beat the brains with the egg and milk, to form the light batter, adding a few bread-crumbs, and serve it hot with a well seasoned brown gravy. It must be very neatly rolled.

To Stew a Calf's Foot.

454. After thoroughly cleaning, cut the foot into well-shaped pieces,

and stew them with veal or beef, of the same weight; should the meat not
have hung some days it must be beaten. Pepper and salt the above
on each side, and lay it in a stew pan with cold water, stew till quite
tender, probably for three or four hours. Strain the gravy from the
meat, and, when perfectly cold, remove every particle of fat, add
cayenne and lemon juice; if a brown gravy is desired flavour with
some browning, walnut ketchup, and (if approved) a little white wine;
but should veal be used it will be better to substitute cucumber
ketchup, thickened cream or milk, with a little lemon peel. The feet
must be thoroughly warmed up in the gravy, but not boiled. Garnish
with crisp parsley, or lemon in slices. Calves' feet may be boiled till
tender, and served with parsley and butter, and a little lemon pickle
served on the dish as a garnish.

To Fry Calves' Feet.

455. Remove while warm the bones, two feet previously boiled till
tender. When cold and firm cut them into pieces of a suitable size
and shape. Strew them with pepper and salt, and dip them in egg
and crumbs; then fry them of a nice brown, or instead of the egg and
crumbs cover them with a nice light batter like a small fritter, each
one the size of a poached egg. Serve on a napkin, or garnish with
pickles.

Fried Calves' Feet.

456. Take four calves' feet; boil till tender, take out the bones, and
then fry the meat in butter. The bones and liquid make a nice stock.

To Stew Sweetbreads.

457. Take two large round sweetbreads, and stew them as you
would veal (see page 133); then make a rich gravy with truffles,
morels, mushrooms, or artichoke-bottoms, and serve it round.

458. SWEETBREADS, STEWED WHITE.—Carefully wash some sweetbreads, and stew them from half an hour to three-quarters in a white
gravy; to which add cream, flour, butter, mace, salt, and white pepper,
and a little cucumber ketchup.

459. SWEETBREADS, STEWED BROWN.—Stew as above in a brown
gravy, after thoroughly scalding the sweetbreads.

Another Way.—Lard some sweetbreads, and after parboiling, cover
them with egg-crumbs mixed with a little chopped parsley and marjoram, pepper and salt. Brown them in a Dutch oven, and stew them
twenty minutes in a rich gravy, and flavour with ketchup.

SWEETBREADS ROASTED.

460. Parboil two large ones; when cold, lard them with bacon, and roast them in a Dutch oven. For sauce, plain butter and mushroom ketchup.

SWEETBREAD RAGOUT.

461. Cut them about the size of a walnut, wash and dry them, then fry of a fine brown; pour on them a good gravy seasoned with salt, pepper, allspice, and either mushrooms or mushroom ketchup; strain, and thicken with butter and a little flour. You may add truffles, morels, and mushrooms.

SWEETBREADS FRICASSEED.

462. Cut up the remnants of a cooked sweetbread in small portions, and prepare a sauce or gravy as in stewing either white or brown; lay the sweetbread in the pan with the gravy, and give one boil up. Garnish with slices of lemon or sippets of bread.

MOCK SWEETBREADS.

463. Beat three-quarters of a pound of veal well in a mortar, then put to it a little suet or bacon, and the yolks of two eggs, with a few breadcrumbs. Season it with pepper, mace, and salt; add a spoonful of cream. Make it in the shape of sweetbreads. and brown before the fire in a Dutch oven. Serve them up with a good gravy.

CUTLETS OF SWEETBREADS.

464. Boil some sweetbreads for five-and-twenty minutes, and when cold, cut them in slices; dip them in yolk of egg, and bread-crumbs, with pepper, mace, salt, parsley, and thyme, or lemon. Fry them a light brown, and place them separately on some slices of cooked tongue pared, and similarly seasoned and fried. Serve them with a little rich gravy at the bottom of the dish. The tongues may be omitted though an improvement.

VEAL CUTLETS.

465. Cutlets are cut from a leg of veal, about a third of an inch thick, and of such a size as may be preferred. Fry them in plenty of *hot* lard or dripping, on the French plan, or if the English is used, turn them quickly. Before putting them into the pan, they are to be coated

evenly with white of egg well beaten, using an egg-brush, and then dipping them in finely-powdered stale bread-crumb. They should be fried a delicate brown, and carefully drained from the fat. For gravy, some other meat must be had recourse to, as there is too little from veal in the frying-pan to make it of. The bone taken out of the fillet with part of the knuckle will boil down and make good stock, browning it in the usual way (see Gravies), and flavouring with a little mushroom ketchup and Worcestershire sauce; adding also a sprig of lemon thyme and a blade of mace. Some fresh parsley should be fried quite crisp after the cutlets are done, and laid on the top; and it is usual to fry with them some thin slices of ham or bacon rolled, which are put round the dish, the gravy being poured into it, but not over the cutlets.

SECTION 6.—PORK.

466. For choice of pork see *Economical Housekeeper*, page 29.
467.—For general directions to roast, boil, &c. see page 32 *et seq.*

TO ROAST PORK.

468. Pork, before being roasted, when the joint has the skin on, must be scored with a knife. This is sometimes done by the butcher, but if not, the cook must be careful not to neglect it, as it is quite impossible to cut slices through the skin after it is roasted. They should always be made through the skin only, and in such directions and at such distances apart as will correspond with the slices in carving the joint. Pork requires to be put at a distance from a brisk and strong fire, and should be thoroughly done, but not scorched. It must be well basted, and when there is no skin, as in what is called "pig-meat," that is, the meat from large bacon-hogs, a strong solution of salt in water should be used at first to baste it. When there is outside skin, a little dripping or lard must be put in the pan to begin with. Leg of pork is generally stuffed with sage and onions, boiled and chopped fine, and if these are mixed with an equal quantity of boiled potatoes the flavour will be improved, with less danger of unpleasant reminiscences. The stuffing is forced into a slit cut in the large end, near the bone. Gravy is made from the dripping-pan (see par. 75); it is usual to serve with apple sauce (which see). The time required is for the leg fully half an hour more than the usual quarter of an hour per pound; for other joints that allowance will suffice.

SUCKING-PIG.

469. Sucking-pig may be either roasted or baked. If roasted, it must be put down at a distance from the fire, and should be basted with oil, dripping, or lard. The pig is always stuffed with some kind of stuffing containing sage. *A good Receipt* for which is to take a quarter of a pound of crumbs of bread, one onion, a small handful of sage, a raw egg, and a small piece of butter; these should be well mixed together with a little pepper and salt. Then fill the belly of the pig, and sew up with a common needle and thread. *Another plan* is to cut a round of bread thick, as for toast, brown it very lightly, and butter it, then soak it in some water in which a handful of sage and an onion have been boiled, cut it into long pieces, and lay it in the belly, with alternate layers of the boiled sage leaves, but no onion, after which it is to be closed as above. A pig about a month old will take from an hour and three quarters to two hours; and if two weeks older, another hour. After taking it from the spit cut the head off, and leave the body in the dripping-pan. Then divide the head longitudinally, and take out the brains for sauce; after which, return it to the dripping-pan. When the sauce is made, divide the body down the middle, and lay the two halves back to back, with half the head at each end. The sauce is made by chopping the brains up very finely with boiled sage, and mixing with some good plain stock, or the gravy made from the dripping-pan. Some made gravy should also be served with it.

TO BOIL PORK, HAMS, AND BACON.

470. Pickled pork is boiled like beef. If very salt, it should be soaked three or four hours before boiling. The time required is nearly double that for beef, or about twenty-five minutes per pound, very slow boiling. The vegetables eaten with it are the same as for beef, but pease-pudding is almost constantly taken with pork. Great care should be exercised that pork is sufficiently boiled, as, when under-done, it is neither wholesome nor well flavoured. The skin is left on.

471. HAM AND BACON, generally, require soaking, the former, from eighteen to twenty-four hours, and the latter for twelve. After soak-ing, the dirty and rough parts should be scraped off, and then the ham or bacon may be boiled in the way detailed at page 47, allowing twenty-five minutes for each pound, and boiling very slowly. When taken up, the skin is peeled off, and the fat is covered with grated toast. The knuckle of a ham is generally guarded with a roll of paper, fringed.

To Boil Pig's Pettitoes.

472. Boil them, the liver, and the heart, in a small quantity of water, very gently; then cut the meat fine and simmer it with a little of the water, and the feet split; thicken with a bit of butter, a little flour, a spoonful of cream, and a little salt and pepper; give it a boil up, pour it over a few sippets of bread, and put the feet on the mince.

To Prepare Pig's Cheek for Boiling.

473. Cut off the snout, and clean the head; divide it, take out the eyes and the brains; sprinkle the head with salt, and let it drain twenty-four hours. Salt it with common salt and saltpetre; let it lie eight or ten days if it is to be dressed without stewing with peas, but less if to be dressed *with* peas; and it must be washed first, and then simmered till all is tender.

To Fry Pork.

474. Pork chops may be dressed like mutton, being either fried or broiled in the usual way, but they are best fried in the French fashion, when, however, they require a made-gravy. When this is not at hand keep back the last spoonful of the lard, and use this as described at 382, adding a chopped onion and a tea-spoonful of mustard to the flour, and a-table-spoonful of Worcestershire sauce or pickle to the water.

To Dress Pig's Fry.

475. Boil the lights first, then chop them up, and put them to stew with a little broth or gravy, seasoning them with pepper and salt. Thicken with gravy; and if not brown, add a little of the gravy from the frying-pan, which, when the liver, &c., have been *fried*, is made by adding some flour and water to the contents of the frying-pan. Fry the liver as for steaks or chops (par. 474), then place it round the dish, with the minced lights in the centre. The heart should be stuffed and roasted, to form a separate dish.

Leg of Pork à la Boisseau.

476. A leg of pork for this purpose should be in salt about four days. Put it in boiling water, take it up and skin it, spit it and put it to the fire to roast, it will take two hours; half an hour before it is taken up, shake on plenty of bread-crumbs until it looks a nice brown colour, take it up and put under it a little sage and onion chopped

very fine and boiled in good thick brown gravy. Apple sauce should be eaten with it.

Sect. 7.—Venison.

477. For choice of venison see *Economical Housekeeper*, page 36.

478. For general directions for roasting, boiling, &c., see the chapters under these headings.

To Roast Venison.

479. Venison takes about the same time as mutton (par. 391), and requires still greater care in papering or in enveloping in paste (par. 78), which latter plan is that usually adopted. It is necessary to proceed as follows. If the venison is kept for any length of time as most people prefer it, the joint should be washed in warm water, but not soaked. If very high, brush over the worst parts a little distilled vinegar, and then wash well off. Dry carefully, and at once put down to the fire as soon as the fat is properly protected. The joint should be constantly basted till done, and should be served with good gravy, and sweet sauce, or currant jelly.

To Stew Venison.

480. Let the meat hang till fit to be dressed: then take out the bone, beat the meat with a rolling-pin, mix with some slices of mutton fat that has lain a few hours in a little port wine, sprinkle a little pepper and allspice over it in a fine powder, roll it up tight, and tie it; set it in a stewpan that will just hold it, with some mutton or beef gravy, not strong, half a pint of port wine, and some pepper and allspice; simmer it close-covered, as slowly as you can for three or four hours; when quite tender take off the tape, set the meat in a dish, strain the gravy over it, and serve with currant-jelly sauce. This is the best way to dress these joints, unless very fat, and then they should be roasted. The bone should be stewed with them.

Venison Steaks.

481. The neck chops are those used, and the gridiron should be placed over a charcoal, or bright coals will do in an ordinary kitchen range.

CHAP. XI.—SAUSAGES, BLACK PUDDINGS, &c.

SECT. 1.—SAUSAGES.

482. These savoury compounds are made with various materials, chopped and mixed together either by the hand or with the aid of a common chopper and board, or with a sausage-making machine, which last acts remarkably well, but is not required often enough in private houses to warrant its purchase. They are afterwards put into properly-cleaned lengths of the entrails of the ox, sheep, calf, or pig, and tied at short intervals with common fine string. In cleaning the entrails they are turned inside out, stretched on a smooth stick, and well scraped and washed in several waters.

PORK SAUSAGES.

483. Chop fat and lean of pork together; season it with sage, pepper, and salt, and add two or three berries of allspice; *half-fill* hogs' entrails that have been soaked and made extremely clean; or the meat may be kept in a very small pan closely covered, and rolled and dusted with a very little flour before it is fried; serve on mashed potatoes put in a form, plain, or browned with the salamander or before the fire; they must be pricked with a fork before they are dressed or they will burst, unless they are very carefully fried.

BEEF AND VEAL SAUSAGES.

484. These are each made in the same way as for pork (483), but there is generally a larger proportion of spice; the herbs added are marjoram, thyme, and parsley instead of sage.

Sausages are dressed either by frying, broiling, or toasting, and are generally served on toast. (See Frying, Broiling, and Toasting.)

LARGE SMOKED SAUSAGES OR POLONIES.

485. Season fat and lean pork with some salt, saltpetre, black pepper, and allspice, all in fine powder, and rub into the meat; the sixth day cut it small, and mix with it some shred shalot or garlic, as fine as possible; have ready an ox-gut that has been scoured, salted, and soaked well, and fill it with the above stuffing; tie up the ends, and hang it to smoke as you would hams, but first wrap it in a fold or two of old muslin; it must be high-dried. Some eat it without boiling, but others like it boiled first. The skin should be tied in different places, so as to make each link about eight or nine inches long.

L

OXFORD SAUSAGES.

486. Chop a pound and a half of pork, and the same of veal, cleared of skin and sinews; add three quarters of a pound of beef-suet; mince and mix them; steep the crumb of a penny-loaf in water, and mix it with the meat, with also a little dried sage, pepper, and salt.

SECT. 2.—BLACK PUDDINGS, AND WHITE PUDDINGS.

TO MAKE BLACK PUDDINGS.

487. The blood must be stirred with salt till cold. Put a quart of it, or rather more, to a quart of whole grits, to soak one night; and soak the crumb of a quartern loaf in rather more than two quarts of new milk made hot. In the meantime prepare the entrails by washing, turning, and scraping with salt and water, and changing the water several times. Chop fine a little winter-savoury and thyme, a good quantity of penny-royal, pepper, and salt, a few cloves, some allspice, ginger, and nutmeg; mix these with three pounds of beef-suet and six eggs well beaten and strained; and then beat the bread, grits, &c., all up with the seasoning; when well mixed, have ready some hog's fat cut into large bits, and as you fill the skins put it in at proper distances. Tie in links, only half filled, and boil in a large kettle, pricking them as they swell, or they will burst. When boiled, lay them between clean cloths till cold, and hang them up in the kitchen. When to be used, scald them a few minutes in water; wipe, and put them into a Dutch oven. If there are not skins enough, put the stuffing into basins, and boil it covered with floured cloths; and slice and fry it when to be used.

Another Receipt.—Soak all night a quart of bruised grits in as much boiling hot milk as will swell them and leave half a pint of liquid. Chop a good quantity of penny-royal, some savoury and thyme; then add salt, pepper, and allspice, finely powdered. Mix the above with a quart of the blood, prepared as before directed; then half fill the skins, after they have been cleaned thoroughly, and put as much of the leaf (that is, the inward fat) of the pig as will make it pretty rich. Boil as before directed. A small quantity of leeks finely shred and well mixed is a great improvement.

WHITE HOG'S PUDDINGS.

488. When the skins have been soaked and cleaned as before directed, rinse and soak them all night in rose-water, and put into

them the following filling:—Mix half a pound of blanched almonds cut into seven or eight bits, with a pound of grated bread, two pounds of marrow or suet, a pound of currants, some beaten cinnamon, cloves, mace, and nutmeg, a quart of cream, the yolks of six and whites of two eggs, a little orange-flower water, a little fine Lisbon sugar, and some lemon-peel and citron sliced, and half fill the skins. To know whether properly flavoured, warm a little in a pannikin. In boiling, much care must be taken to prevent the puddings from bursting. Prick them with a small fork as they rise, and boil them in milk and water. Lay them in a table-cloth till cold.

Sect. 3.—Saveloys.

489. These are made of *salt* pork, of which the fat and lean are mixed together and chopped with a fourth part of bread, a little pepper and allspice, and a rather liberal use of sage leaves. They are put in skins as for pork sausages, and boiled slowly for half an hour, then put by and eaten cold.

CHAP. XII.—THE COOKING OF POULTRY.

490. The best mode of purchasing and the choice of poultry are alluded to in the *Economical Housekeeper*.

To Roast Poultry.

491. The general directions for roasting are given under the chapter on that head at page 35, and to truss poultry for roasting, see pages 37, 38, and for boiling, see page 49.

To Roast Turkeys, Guinea Fowl, and Chickens.

492. Those kinds of poultry which have white meat all require the same management in roasting. They are first trussed according to the mode described at page 35, *et seq.*, and then either put in a cradle-spit, or on a small common spit, or suspended from a bottle-jack. All of these require lard, dripping, or butter, to baste them with, the last being the best, but either answering the purpose well enough, pro- vided they are used almost constantly. They should be well floured at first, and kept at a distance from the fire for about half the time, after which they may be put nearer, and when the thin skin rises in little bladders they are generally done enough. Turkeys, and

sometimes large fowls, have their necks stuffed with forcemeat (which see), and require a made-gravy for them, which can generally be obtained from odds and ends, including their heads, necks, and legs cut off. Bread sauce and sometimes sausages are served in addition, and the invariable concomitants, ham or tongue, must not be forgotten. Time required, as near as may be, one quarter of an hour per pound.

To Boil Chickens or Turkey.

493. Wrap the chickens in a cloth and throw them into boiling water. *Boil* gently for about three quarters of an hour, (a turkey would require an hour and three quarters.) They eat much better if a slice of fat bacon is skewered on the breast of each fowl, or of a turkey. Serve with celery, parsley, mushroom, or oyster sauce, or simple white sauce, and garnish with lemon.

Fowl Dressed with Mushroom Sauce.

494. Put the fowl in a stew-pan with a bit of bacon under and over, and a spoonful or two of good gravy. Cover it closely with a lid, and put it in rather a slow oven, and let it stew gently for an hour and a half, turning it often ; pour the gravy from it, take off the fat, and put some pickled mushrooms with some of the vinegar to it, and a little more good gravy if you require it; make it quite hot, and pour it over.

Chicken and Tomatoe.

495. Cut up a young fowl. Put in a stew-pan one ounce of butter, a tea-spoonful of flour, and an onion chopped small. Brown them over the fire; and the pieces of chicken, with eight or ten tomatoes, and a salt-spoon of salt. Cover the pan and stew till the tomatoes are dissolved, and the fowl thoroughly done. If it is a very young chicken, do not put it in at first, as half an hour will do it. Cold fowl will answer the purpose.

To Stew a Turkey or Fowl.

496. Pick the fowl very clean, put it into a saucepan, with cabbage, turnips, celery, and onions, all cut very small; add salt and pepper, with a bunch of sweet-herbs, then just cover with water, and let it stew as slowly as possible till quite tender. This mode of cooking is chiefly adapted for an old fowl.

CHICKENS STEWED WHOLE.

497. Fill the insides of a couple of fowls with large oysters and mushrooms, and fasten a tape round the body to keep them in. Put them in a tin kettle with a cover; set them in a large saucepan, with boiling water, which must not reach quite to the top of the kettle; keep it boiling till the fowls are well done, which they should be an hour after they begin to simmer; take off the lid occasionally to remove the scum, but cover again directly; as the water in the kettle boils away, replenish it with boiling water; take from them all the gravy, and put it into a small saucepan, covering the kettle close to keep the fowls warm, meantime. Thicken the gravy with butter and flour, and add two table-spoonfuls of chopped oysters or mushrooms, the yolks of three eggs boiled hard and minced fine, some seasoning, and a little cream. Boil five minutes, and dish the fowls.

CHICKEN CUTLETS.

498. Cut, in as large pieces as possible, the fleshy parts of a couple of chickens, either cooked or uncooked. Season well with a mixture of pepper, mace, cayenne, and salt, then cover them with egg and bread-crumbs, and fry them a light brown. They should be served in a thickened and well-seasoned gravy, made from the bones, with the heads and legs of the chickens.

A STEWED HOWTOWDIE WITH DRAPPIT EGGS. (*Meg Dods.*)

499. Prepare and stuff with forcemeat a young, plump fowl. Put it into a *yetling* concave-bottomed small pot, with a close-fitting lid, with button-onions, spices, and at least a quarter of a pound of butter. Add herbs if approved. When the fowl has hardened and been turned, add half a pint, or rather more, of boiling water, or broth. Fit on the lid very close, and set the pot over embers. An hour will do a small fowl, and so in proportion. Have a little seasoned gravy, in which parboil the liver.

TO STEW FOWL WITH RICE.

500. Stew the fowl very slowly in some clear mutton broth, well-skimmed, and seasoned with onion, mace, pepper, and salt. About half an hour before it is ready, put in a quarter of a pound of rice, well washed and soaked. Simmer till tender; then strain it from the broth, and put the rice on a sieve before the fire. Keep the fowl hot,

lay it in the middle of the dish, and the rice around it, without the broth. The broth will be very nice to eat as such ; but the less liquor the fowl is done with the better. Gravy, white sauce, or parsley and butter, for sauce. *Or*, boil a pint of rice, and while warm, mix with it one ounce of fresh butter. Beat four eggs, and mix with it gradually ; line a deep dish with the rice, and place on it a parboiled fowl cut in pieces, with a little of the liquor seasoned. Add butter, flour, and a little cream. Cover with the rice, set it in the oven and bake brown. Ham or tongue is an improvement.

Fowl with Spinach.

501. Poach nicely in the gravy, five or six small eggs. Dress them on flattened balls of spinach round the dish, and serve the fowl in the centre, rubbing down the liver to thicken the gravy and liquor in which the fowl has been stewed, which pour over it for sauce, skimming it nicely, and serving all hot. Mushrooms, oysters, and forcemeat balls may be put to the sauce. The spinach may be, and often is, replaced by greens or turnip-tops.

To Roast Geese and Ducks.

502. Geese and ducks are trussed and spitted as shewn at page 38, after which they are put down at a distance from a good fire ; previously, however, stuffing their whole bodies with sage and onions, boiled, chopped fine, and then mixed with an equal quantity of potatoes. They require plenty of dredging and basting with lard or dripping, and a made-gravy must be served with them ; also apple sauce (which see). Time required, strictly according to the regular rule.

To Stew a Duck or Goose.

503. Half-roast a duck or goose : put it into a stew-pan with a pint of beef gravy, a few leaves of sage and mint cut small, pepper and salt, and a small bit of onion, shred as fine as possible. Simmer a quarter of an hour, and skim clean ; then add near a quart of green peas. Cover close and simmer near half an hour longer. Put in a piece of butter and a little flour, and give it one boil ; then serve in one dish.

To Stew a Duck (*an Entrée*).

504. Put an onion scalded, a few chopped sage leaves, and some pep-

per, inside the duck, then half cook it in the Dutch or common oven. Dredge it with flour, pepper, and salt, and cover it with water in a stewpan, in which put some sprigs of mint and parsley. When nearly done, strain off the gravy, and return it to the pan, adding either a glass of port wine, *or*, a good pint of young peas, and a little sugar, and stew again.

A Rich Stew of Duck (*for an Entrée*).

505. Cut a fine young duck into joints, and lay it in a large shallow tin pan. Pour over it a pint of strong beef broth or gravy. Scum it when it begins to boil. Season *well* with cayenne, sage, and lemon-peel, and simmer from three quarters of an hour to an hour. Thicken the gravy with a table-spoonful of flour, and flavour it with a glass of port-wine, and some lemon-juice. Serve it hot.

To Stew Giblets.

506. After very nicely cleaning goose or duck giblets, stew them for several hours with a small quantity of water, onion, black pepper, and a bunch of sweet herbs, till nearly done; season them with salt and pepper, and a very small piece of mace. Before serving, give them one boil with a cup of cream, and a piece of butter rubbed in a tea-spoonful of the flour.

Fricassee of Ducks.

507. Half roast and cut up a couple of ducks, put them in a stewpan and season. Cover them with a mixture of onion, sage, and sweet marjoram chopped, tomatoes scalded, peeled, and quartered; ket-chup, one ounce of butter rolled in bread-crumbs, one glass of port-wine, and a little powdered mace. Add a little water to keep from burning, cover closely, and stew till done thoroughly. Venison, lamb, pigeons, hares, and rabbits, may be stewed in this way.

To Roast Wild-fowl.

508. Wild-duck, widgeon, and teal are all roasted like common ducks, but *without stuffing*, and with rather a less allowance of time, though it is not now the fashion to send them to table almost raw, as was formerly the case. Before carving, the knife is drawn along the breast in the situation of the slices; and upon these a lemon is squeezed, and a little cayenne pepper sprinkled. They all require a made-gravy, with port-wine (which see).

To Stew a Wild Duck.

509. Chop some sage and sweet-herbs very fine, into some good stock, add half a glass of port-wine, some lemon-juice, pepper and salt, and stew the herbs for more than ten minutes; meantime, the duck should be roasting in a Dutch oven, and when rather more than half-roasted, should be added, with the gravy from it, to the stew; the gravy should be allowed to cool a little, that the fat may be carefully excluded; and the whole simmered gently till done. *Or*, the duck may be cut up in joints when put into the stew. In any case, care must be taken that the gravy shall well moisten both the *exterior* and interior of the duck.

Roast Hare.

510. Hare should not be roasted unless moderately young, and well kept, or it will be tough and devoid of flavour. The hare should be paunched as soon as possible, and its inside kept dry by wiping it, at the same time rubbing it with a little pepper-dust. Most cooks, after skinning the hare, soak it for two or three hours to get the blood out from the shoulders; but this is a great mistake, for it does not effect this object until it has completely robbed the muscles of the back and legs of their juice and flavour. The proper plan is to carry a knife between the joints of the shoulders and the breast, as if about to divide them, and then, after wrapping up the whole of the rest of the body in a thick cloth, pump water into these slits for ten minutes; or, better still, turn a cock of water upon them, to wash the blood from the insides of the shoulders where it lodges, without touching the back and loins. Next fill the body with stuffing (par. 334), and truss according to the directions given at page 38. Proceed to roast it before a quick fire, not too fierce, and baste it perpetually for the first half-hour with hot milk; afterwards use dripping, and towards the last give it plenty of flour with the dredger, alternately basting *with great care*, and dredging, until a fine frothy coat is raised, in which the art of a good cook is shown. The time required is about an hour and a quarter to an hour and a half, according to size. Made-gravy is necessary, and currant-jelly.

To Stew a Hare.

511. Prepare a hare as for roasting, cut it into joints, some of which may if too large be divided. Brown them slightly in the Dutch oven

or stewpan, basting them well with butter, and adding a little lean ham, cut in thin slices; stew in a full pint of gravy, and while stewing season with mace, salt, cayenne, and lemon-peel; and before serving, thicken the gravy with flour and butter, or arrowroot, and add two table-spoonfuls of ketchup, or one with some Reading or Worcestershire sauce, and the juice of half a lemon. If wished *rich* add half a teacup of port-wine, and serve garnished with forcemeat balls browned and simmered in the stew. Currant jelly should be handed round with the above.

Or, Skin the hare, and cut it in small pieces, but do not wash it; stew it in butter till the blood is set, then put to it some gravy, with a bunch of sweet-herbs, two onions, a few cloves, a little mace, and black pepper; when it is stewed enough, strain off the butter, and put to it two or three spoonfuls of port-wine, and a little lemon juice; then thicken it with butter and flour, and season with salt to the taste. Oysters, mushrooms, and eggs boiled hard, with a little anchovy, are an agreeable addition.

To Jug a Hare.

512. Skin the hare and clean it, cut it up scientifically, and put it in a pan with a bouquet of sweet-herbs and parsley, also an onion adorned with cloves, a blade of mace, a glass of port-wine, and rather more water than will cover it. Put it on the stove and let it stew very gently till the meat is done, then take it off and thicken the gravy; when sufficiently boiled pass it through a sieve, then add a little ketchup soy, and cayenne to the taste, and pour it over the hare. Take care to have it dished up hot; and some add to it a few forcemeat balls.

To Roast Rabbits.

513. Rabbits are roasted exactly like hare, but, being smaller, they require less time. They also ought not to be soaked in water, but washed as directed for hare. From thirty to forty minutes will roast any wild rabbit. Large tame rabbits will take as long as a hare.

To Boil Rabbits.

514. For a couple of rabbits make a stuffing with a little grated bread, the yolks of three eggs boiled hard and pounded, and one unboiled yolk; add a little butter, and season with pepper and salt; stuff the rabbits well with this, and when done a sauce may be made by

mixing a little stuffing taken from the rabbits, in melted butter, or they may be covered with onion sauce, or simple white sauce.

STEWED RABBITS.

515. Wash a couple of rabbits well in warm water, cut them up in joints, and put them into a saucepan with enough of water, or broth if you have it, to cover them. Put in a bunch of parsley and thyme, and a fine large onion peeled. Stew gently for three hours, with a little mace, and pepper and salt. When ready to dish up put the meat into your tureen, and thicken the broth with flour and milk, before pouring it over the meat. The bunch of herbs should be taken out, but any particles which have broken off may be left in.

FRENCH STEW OF RABBITS (AMERICAN.)

516. Having cut up the rabbits, lay the pieces in cold water to soak out the blood, then wash in another water; season, put them in a jar, adding chopped celery, sweet marjoram, and tarragon leaves; mix in a little ham or tongue, and add a teacup of water and two glasses of sherry. Cover the jar closely, set it over the fire in a kettle of cold water, and let it stew slowly two hours; thicken with butter and flour. Hare and venison may be stewed in the same way. You may substitute rich cream for the wine.

TO FRICASSEE RABBITS.

517. WHITE.—Blanch your rabbits by putting them into boiling water and boiling them for six or seven minutes; when cold cut them up as for eating, and put them into a stewpan, with a pint of veal or other light-coloured stock; flavour with cucumber, ketchup, or lemon pickle.

518. BROWN.—Cut your rabbits into joints, fry them of a light brown in butter, and then put them in a stewpan with a pint of water, a large spoonful of mushroom ketchup, the same of browning, a tea-spoonful of lemon juice or pickle, a little essence of anchovy, a little lemon peel, and cayenne and salt to taste. Thicken and strain the gravy, and pour it over the rabbits before serving.

TO FRY RABBITS.

519. First wash, soak, and prepare the rabbit for cooking, and then boil it (in *boiling* water) for six or seven minutes; drain it, and when nearly cold take off the legs and shoulders, and cut the back into joints. Dip each piece into yolk of egg and crumbs, the latter

having been seasoned with pepper and salt, and (if approved) a little finely chopped parsley and lemon peel. Boil the liver, and when cold rub it down fine, and add it to some thickened and well-seasoned gravy, to which also put a little cream, lemon juice, and ketchup. Serve the rabbit with the gravy under it, taking care it is sent to table hot.

If wanted plain, omit the egg and crumbs, and make a gravy by adding water to the contents of the fryingpan, when the meat has been taken out; adding flour and butter to thicken it, and any flavouring which may be approved.

To Roast Winged Game.

520. These are dressed in the following modes : winged game, consisting of pheasants, black-cock, grouse, and partridges, are all dressed and served alike, the time only varying. Pheasants and black-cock will take from thirty to fifty minutes, according to size, at a brisk, but not strong fire. Grouse and partridges from twenty-five to thirty minutes. They require constant basting, but no dredging, as they ought not to be more browned than necessary, according to present fashion. Pheasants and black-cock are served with bread sauce and made-gravy only, but partridge and grouse usually have fried breadcrumbs also.

To Broil Partridge.

521. Split the partridge and wipe, but do not wash it, and broil it to a pale brown. *Sprinkle with pepper and salt*, rub a little butter over it as soon as it is taken from the fire. Make a sauce of meat stock, or water thickened with flour and butter, and flavoured with salt, pepper, ketchup, and a squeeze of lemon. If preferred, the bird may be dipped more than once into clarified butter and bread-crumbs before being broiled. ·

Pigeons, Thrushes, Larks, Ortolans,

522. And other small birds, are trussed and dressed like partridges, and served with the same crumbs, sauce, and gravy. They are sometimes dipped in egg and crumbs before roasting. From ten to fifteen minutes will roast any of them, except the pigeon, which will take from eighteen to twenty minutes. All should be well basted with butter or dripping.

Pigeons to Boil.

523. Should be trussed in the same manner as boiled fowls, put into boiling water, and after boiling for a quarter of an hour, should be served with parsley and butter, some of which should be poured over them.

To Stew Pigeons.

524. Take six pigeons, cut the flesh from one, and with the livers from all and a good slice of fat bacon, beat all together well in a mortar. Then take a few sweet-herbs and a little shalot and mix with the above to stuff the pigeons. Cut off their legs and pinions; stew the bones and trimmings to make gravy (and add a little mutton if required;) then put the pigeons into the gravy, when cleared of all bones and meat, with their breasts downwards, turning them carefully till they are done. Add a little port-wine, thickened with flour and butter, and put in a little walnut pickle.

Wood Pigeons.

525. Are generally dressed like tame pigeons, but if dressed like wild duck they are far superior in flavour.

Woodcock and Snipe.

526. Are dressed with the whole inside left in. They should not be spitted on any account, but suspended, legs downwards, over a toast of bread, which is eaten as a great relish. Twenty or thirty minutes will roast a "cock" and fifteen a snipe. Serve with gravy and bread sauce.

CHAP. XIII.—WARMED-UP MEATS AND MADE-UP DISHES OR ENTRÉES.

Sect. 1.—General Remarks.

527. This chapter contains the receipts for warming up cold meats in the shape of hashes, minced-meats, &c., by which they are rendered much more palatable to most people, and not much more expensive. No one who has tried the experiment can contend that they are as economical as the cold meat would be, if eaten in its plain unadorned state, but as few people like cold beef or cold mutton for three or four consecutive days, it is well to be able to vary the bill of fare, even if it is

done at a trifling increase in the weekly bills. The very circumstance, that warmed-up dishes are more generally liked than cold meats, proves that more will be eaten, and, consequently, that they are more costly, for the difference in consumption is a main item affecting all systems of housekeeping. To the rigid economist, therefore, I cannot advise these improved editions of cold meats, but to those who can afford the slight difference in the cost, they are unobjectionable, especially as they may be made even more wholesome than the plain cold meat, which, moreover, few will eat without the addition of indigestible cold pickles, or a large proportion of salad. Besides these warmed-up dishes, some few side-dishes, entrées, &c., are given, which are serviceable for more than ordinary occasions, or for those who habitually indulge in such luxurious fare.

Sect. 2.—Utensils.

528. The Utensils required are chiefly the various sized stewpans; but for browning over certain dishes a salamander is almost imperatively necessary. This is a long iron in the form shown at *fig.* 136, and when heated in the fire and held over a dish, already at a boiling heat, it browns the surface, and makes it much more pleasing to the eye.

529. The Bain-marie is merely a water-bath (see *fig.* 135), capable of holding several stewpans or small saucepans. It is chiefly used for making such dishes as will be injured by a high rate of boiling, and also for keeping them warm without injury.

530. Many Entrées are now sent to table heated with a spirit-lamp under them, and certainly it is the only way of ensuring a proper temperature. Silver and plated dishes are made and sold expressly for the purpose, and therefore it is not necessary to describe them here, especially as their construction is exceedingly simple.

Sect. 3.—Dressed Meats and Poultry Warmed up.

Minced Beef or Mutton.

531. Make a gravy according to par. 282; thicken it with flour or arrowroot, which is still better), then add to it the minced-up beef and warm it. In warming up any meats in this way, they should be done in a stewpan on a hot-plate, or in a water-bath, commonly called a *bain-marie*, as it is owing to *boiling* hashes or minces that they get hard. All sorts of stews, or meat dressed a second time, should be only gently simmered, and that for a short time only, so as

to be just warmed through. After mincing the beef with some of the fat, season it and add boiled carrots, with a little onion or shalot chopped fine. Have a small hot dish with sippets of bread ready, and pour the mince into it, but first mix a large spoonful of vinegar with it; if shalot vinegar is used as a seasoning, there will be no need or the onion or the raw shalot.

Minced Mutton or Beef Browned.

532. Cut some lean meat from a roast leg of mutton, chop it fine, season it with pepper and salt, chopped parsley, and a little onion; mix altogether with a quarter of a pound of grated bread, moisten with a table-spoonful of vinegar and a cup of good gravy; when put into the dish lay an ounce of butter in small bits on the top, grate bread over it, and add a little more butter; brown before the fire.

To Hash Beef or Mutton.

533. Do it the same as in the last receipt, except that the meat is to be in slices, and add a spoonful of walnut liquor or ketchup.

Another Way.—Cut the meat into small thin slices, put two table-spoonfuls of flour into a dish, with a tea-spoonful of salt, and a salt-spoonful of pepper; mix them together, and rub the slices of meat with it; place in a large and shallow stewpan a piece of butter the size of a walnut (and if liked, three small onions cut in small pieces); put it on the fire till the onion is browned, then add the meat, which warm on one side, and turn over. When warmed through, pour over it a pint of hot water, and two pickled gherkins cut in slices, and a table-spoonful of the vinegar from the pickle, also a table-spoonful of walnut ketchup; boil up and serve with sippets of toasted bread.

Another Way.—Cut thin slices of mutton or beef, and put into half a pint of broth, let it simmer a quarter of an hour and *skim all the fat from it;* then season it with pepper, salt, and mushroom ketchup, with a squeeze of lemon or a spoonful of vinegar; after which thicken with flour and butter. The hash eats less greasy in this way, as the flour absorbs the fat when added at first.

Another Way.—Slice the mutton, lay it in the saucepan with a little water, and simmer for a quarter of an hour, then carefully skim off all the fat and add a little mushroom ketchup, pepper, and salt, and thicken with flour and butter. *Give one boil up,* and dish it up with sippets of toasted bread.

BEEF EN MIROTON.

534. Cut thin slices of cold roast beef, and put them into a frying-pan with some butter and six onions, turn the pan frequently, then mix a little broth, add pepper and salt, and after a few boils serve up hot. This dish is excellent and economical.

TO DRESS THE INSIDE OF A COLD SIRLOIN OF BEEF.

535. Cut out all the meat, and a little fat, in pieces as thick as the finger, and two inches long; dredge it with flour, and fry in butter of a nice brown; drain the butter from the meat, and toss it up in a rich gravy, seasoned with pepper, salt, anchovy, and shalot. Do not let it boil on any account. Before serving, add two spoonfuls of vinegar. Garnish with crimped parsley.

A FRICASSEE OF COLD ROAST BEEF.

536. Prepare some very thin slices of cold roast beef (not too much cooked). Put to fry in a stewpan, an onion, some celery, and a good bunch of chopped parsley, with a little flour and butter, then add some strong broth, season with pepper and salt. It must simmer gently for nearly twenty minutes; then stir into it a glass of port-wine, a little lemon-juice or vinegar, and two yolks of eggs. Put in the beef, after which it must simmer, *not* boil, or the beef would become hard.

BEEF OLIVES.

537. Cut slices half an inch thick, and four inches square; lay on them a forcemeat of crumbs of bread, shalot, a little suet or fat, pepper and salt. Roll them, and fasten with a small skewer; put them into a stewpan with some gravy made of the beef bones, or the gravy of the meat, and a spoonful or two of water, and stew them till tender. Fresh meat will do.

BEEF CAKES, FOR A SIDE DISH OF DRESSED MEAT.

538. Pound some beef that is under-done with a little fat bacon or ham; season with pepper, salt, and a little shalot or garlic; mix them well, and make into small cakes three inches long and half as wide and thick; fry them a light brown, and serve them in a good thick gravy.

TO DRESS THE SAME CALLED SANDERS.

539. Mince beef, or mutton, small, with onion, pepper, and salt; add

a little gravy; put it into scallop-shells or saucers, making them three parts full, and fill them up with potatoes, mashed with a little cream; put a bit of butter on the top, and brown them in an oven, or before the fire, or with a salamander.

To Dress the Same, called Cecils.

540. Mince any kind of meat, crumbs of bread, a good deal of onion, some anchovies, lemon-peel, salt, nutmeg, chopped parsley, pepper, and a bit of butter warm, and mix these over a fire for a few minutes; when cool enough, make them up into balls of the size and shape of a turkey's egg, with an egg; sprinkle them with fine crumbs, and then fry them of a yellow brown, and serve with gravy as before directed for beef-olives.

A Corner Dish of Minced Meat.

541. Take a piece of the crumb of bread, cut it into rounds about three inches high; take out the centre; fry them in butter, and fill them with mincemeat.

Cooked Beef or Ham on Toast.

542. A buttered toast, with cooked ham or beef scraped upon it and fried or browned before the fire, is excellent for breakfast or supper, especially if made with ham.

Or, Take a cold smoked tongue or ham and grate or mince it fine. Mix it with cream and beaten yolk of egg, and give it a simmer of the fire. Toast and slightly butter some bread, lay them on a flat warm dish, and cover thickly with the tongue mixture. Serve very hot.

Bubble and Squeak.

543. Boil and strain, then chop and fry, some cabbage, with a little butter or dripping, pepper and salt, and lay on it slices of under-done beef, lightly fried, and seasoned with pepper and salt.

Meat Balls.

544. Chop the meat as fine as for sausages; then mix a small quantity of crumbs of bread, mace, pepper, cloves, and salt, all pounded well, and mix them with one egg, making them up into balls the size of a goose's egg. They should be rolled in crumbs of bread and egg, and fried; dish them up with gravy, flavoured with walnut ketchup.

MUTTON EN MASQUERADE.

545. Take a shoulder of mutton, and let it be half roasted, then cut the skin off and mince the meat with a good gravy. Season it, and put it back upon the bone. Cover with crumbs of bread, and brown it over. Oysters, or any other flavouring material may be added; and the mince may be made of the underside of the shoulder, if the joint has been roasted and sent to table previously.

BEEF OR MUTTON SCALLOPED.

546. Chop some mutton or beef very fine, adding some good broth or gravy, with some walnut ketchup and a little Worcestershire sauce poured upon it, and pepper, salt, and chopped pickle, mixed with the meat. Put it in scallop-shells; then grate some bread, and strew thickly over it; brown it nicely, and serve quite hot. Mutton is the best meat for the purpose, and must be *well moistened* with the broth.

COLD BEEF OR MUTTON STEWED WITH PEAS.

547. The directions are as follows:—Shell three quarters of a peck of green peas, not very young, and put them in a stewpan with the heart of a lettuce cut in pieces and an onion sliced. Simmer in half a pint of broth for an hour and a half; cut the beef in slices, sprinkle each side with pepper and salt, and put them in the stewpan. Simmer another hour and a half, then stir in a little Worcestershire sauce, and add flour and butter, with a little flour of mustard, to thicken it. Give one boil up and serve. This would be even better with uncooked meat, in which case it must be put on with the vegetables. A turnip previously boiled in the broth would improve the flavour.

MIROTON OF VEAL.

548. Mince some cold boiled or roasted veal with a third part of ham, bacon, or tongue; add to these a fifth part of bread-crumb soaked in milk, and an egg or two well beaten; season with pepper and salt, and a chopped onion browned in the frying-pan; stew all these together, then butter a mould adapted to the quantity made, put it in while hot, and bake in an oven till the surface is brown; then turn out of the mould, and serve with the gravy (see par. 282).

MINCED VEAL.

549. Cut cold veal as fine as possible, but do not chop it; put to it

M

a very little lemon-peel shred, two grates of nutmeg, some salt, and four or five spoonfuls of either weak broth, milk, or water; simmer these gently with the meat, but take care not to let it boil, and add a bit of butter rubbed in flour. Put sippets of thin toasted bread, cut into a three-cornered shape round the dish. *Or*, mince as above, and serve with rolled bacon toasted before the fire, and one or two poached eggs arranged on the surface.

MARSDEN, OR VEAL CAKE.

550. Take a pie dish and butter it; cut hard-boiled eggs into slices, and lay them round the sides of the dish and at the bottom, then slices of cold veal, ham, and pickles; season it well, and pour over it all some good rich gravy; then place layer after layer as at the beginning, filling it up with good gravy; when quite full, bake twenty minutes. Turn out when cold.

Or, Take the best end of a neck of veal, bone it and cut it into small pieces; boil six eggs hard, divide the yolks, and cut the whites into pieces; take two anchovies, some parsley chopped fine, ham rather lean cut in thin slices, season these well with cayenne, black pepper, salt, and nutmeg; put a layer of veal, parsley, ham, &c., till the deep dish is full; pour a cup of water over it and the bones at the top; cover it close down, and bake it in a slow oven for four hours; take the bones off when it comes out, and turn it out when cold.

Another.—Take the thick part of a leg of veal, free from skin and sinews, some good fresh suet or marrow, with a little bit of clear fat bacon. Beat it in a marble mortar till it comes to a paste. Season with white pepper, cayenne, salt, nutmeg, and mace, and, if it is liked, with a little lemon-peel. Make it up in cakes about the size of a biscuit; fry them in clear dripping till they become of a nice light brown. Serve them up with white sauce, which must not be put over them. This makes a pretty corner dish, or for first or second course for a small party.

VEAL BALLS.

551. Two ounces of beef suet, two ounces of veal, the yolks of one raw and one boiled egg, one small onion, pepper, salt, mace, nutmeg, and lemon-peel to the taste. Beat them all well together, fry, and serve in gravy.

VEAL OLIVES.

552. Take eight or ten cutlets; wash them over with batter of eggs;

then season, and lay over them a little forcemeat, roll them up, and tie them with thread, which is to be removed before serving, and fry them; then put them in a stewpan with some good gravy, an anchovy, pepper, and mace; make some balls, boil them a little, and put them in : thicken with flour and butter.

Another.—Cut some cold veal and cold ham in thin square slices of the same size; lay a slice of veal on every slice of ham, and spread yolk of egg over the veal; lay on it a forcemeat of bread-crumbs, sweet marjoram rubbed fine, butter, grated lemon-peel, nutmeg, and cayenne; then roll up each slice tightly with the ham, tie them round with coarse thread; run a bird spit through them, and roast well. Serve with sauce made of gravy (282), a spoonful of cream, and mushroom ketchup.

MINCED VEAL IN SHAPE OF A FILLET.

553. Mince the lean of a cold fillet of veal as fine as possible, mix with it a quarter of a pound of fat cold ham chopped small, add a teacupful of grated bread-crumbs, a grated nutmeg, some powdered mace, grated rind of a lemon, and two beaten eggs. Season with salt and cayenne, mix well together, and make it the shape of a small fillet; then glaze over with yolk of egg, and strew the surface over with bread raspings, set it in a Dutch oven, and bake till hot through, adding a veal gravy made from the trimmings, and thickened after the meat is taken out with beaten yolk of egg. Serve with the gravy poured round. Fillet of chicken or turkey may be made in the same manner.

A WARMED-UP FILLET.

554. A cold roast fillet of veal may have the outside pared off, and be warmed up, re-browned, and served with white sauce over and around it.

A COLD HASH OF VEAL OR CHICKEN.

555. Mince very small some cold veal or the white meat of fowls with some anchovies, and pickled oysters, and a little pickled lemon or cucumber. Garnish with pickles and eat it with oil and vinegar.

TERRAPINS.

556. Cut some cold roast veal in small squares, put it in a stewpan, pour over it a dressing made of six hard-boiled eggs minced fin

tea-spoonful of made mustard, do. of salt and cayenne, half a pint of cream and two glasses of sherry thoroughly mixed; stir in well and stew it over the fire ten minutes. Serve hot in a deep dish. Cold duck, fowl, or venison, may be dressed as above.

QUENELLES OF VEAL.

557. Take half a pound of good veal without sinews; take also half a pound of beef suet or *calf's udder boiled.* Chop it fine and pound it in a mortar; take half a pound of bread-crumbs; soak in white stock or milk, when soaked squeeze them through a tammy sieve or clean cloth; add it to the veal and suet, season with pepper, salt, and spices; add two eggs (white and yolks), pound it all together till quite smooth. Cut it with a spoon in the shape of an egg and poach in water, or put it in any small shapes and steam. Serve with good white sauce. The same may be done with chicken, game, or any white fish.

VEAL RISSOLES.

558. Slice a pound of crumb of bread and soak it in milk a quarter of an hour, lay it in a sieve and press it dry; mince finely a pound of veal cutlets, with six ounces of veal suet, mix in gradually the bread, season and add grated lemon, moisten with two beaten eggs, then roll into oval balls rather smaller than an egg. Strew over them dry bread-crumbs, fry them in lard or butter; drain well and send to table hot. Serve veal gravy thickened with butter and flour, yolk of egg and lemon juice in a boat to eat with the rissoles. Minced chickens or turkey may be dressed as above.

VEAL CUTLETS WITH RICE.

559. Pound some cold veal or chicken, and separately, an equal quantity of lean cooked ham, or tongue, then pound a teacupful of rice which has been previously boiled in milk until *quite* tender; mix the whole with yolk of egg, and make them into small cutlets. Before frying these cutlets they must be rubbed over with yolk of egg. Serve with a good well-flavoured brown gravy, and pickled lemons or mushrooms.

HASHED VENISON.

560. Cut neatly some slices of venison, and lay them in a stewpan with three quarters of a pint of good gravy or broth. Simmer for

about fifteen minutes, then carefully skim off the fat, and flavour the gravy with salt and pepper, walnut and mushroom ketchup, and half a teacupful of port-wine. Thicken with flour and butter, and just boil it up before serving. *Send it to table very hot.*

Another.—Cut the venison in small slices, and lay them in a saucepan, pour on them some good gravy or stock, flavoured with Worcestershire or Christopher North's sauce, and let them stand a quarter of an hour, then place the saucepan on the fire, and very gradually bring it *nearly* to a boil, serve immediately.

A plainer Hash of Venison.—Stew the bones and trimmings with mutton or other bones, a slice or two of carrot, a few savoury herbs, and a quart of water or meat boilings, till reduced to one-half. Strain, and when cool, clear it of *all* the fat, thicken with flour and butter, or the brown roux (par. 278), or with arrowroot; flavour with mushroom and walnut ketchup, salt, and pepper.

RISSOLES.

561. Take out the inside of small rolls; take mutton or chicken—if the former, moisten with gravy or stock; if the latter, with white sauce. The meat must be cut as for patties; season to the taste; fill the inside with the meat, then put the little bit you cut off the top of the roll on again; tie it round with thread. Beat up an egg with a little cream, and dip them in; strew with fine bread-crumbs, and salamander them all over, or else fry them in butter; garnish with a little fried parsley.

CALF'S HEAD HASHED WHITE.

562. Let the head be well washed, and then boil it in soft water. Take the meat from the bones and cut it into thin collops, then take of the water it was boiled in enough to stew it till the meat is thoroughly hot. Work half a pound of butter well with some flour, and mix with it a little essence of anchovies, three blades of mace, a little nutmeg, with pepper and salt. Put this to the collops, and mix it well together. Take the yolk of an egg, well beaten, and stir it up with half a pint of cream, then add it to the hash. When done, squeeze in the juice of a lemon, and garnish with balls of forcemeat and egg balls.

TO HASH CALF'S HEAD BROWN.

563. From a head half boiled cut off the meat in slices, half an inch

thick, and two or three inches long. Brown some butter, flour, and sliced onions, and throw in the slices with some good gravy, truffles, and morels; give it one boil, skim it well, and set it in a moderate heat to simmer till very tender. Season with pepper, salt, and cayenne, at first; and ten minutes before serving throw in some shred parsley, and a very small bit of tarragon and knotted marjoram cut as fine as possible. Just before serving add the squeeze of a lemon, and a table-spoonful of ketchup, and if liked a glass of white wine. Forcemeat balls and bits of bacon rolled round.

CALF'S HEAD JELLY, OR CHICKEN, OR VEAL.

564. Put to a head, nicely soaked, as much water as will cover it, with salt, herbs, vegetables, horseradish, celery, and black peppercorns, sufficient to make it savoury. Let it simmer until quite tender, take out the head, remove the bones, and return them to the stewpan, with any part you like to cut off. Let the jelly boil until stiff. Strain, and let it stand till next day. Take off the fat and sediment, and melt the clear part, adding a glass of sherry. Cut the meat in small pieces, with some ham or tongue. Season with powdered mace, cayenne pepper, and salt. Place slices of hard-boiled eggs round a pie-dish or mould, lay in the meat as lightly as possible, adding the jelly, a little warm, by degrees, until the dish is full. Let it stand until set, then turn it out, and garnish with lemon.

SCALLOP OF COLD VEAL OR CHICKEN.

565. Mince the meat extremely small; and set it over the fire with a scrape of nutmeg, a little pepper and salt, and a little cream, for a few minutes; then put it into the scallop-shells, and fill them with crumbs of bread, over which put some bits of butter, and brown them before the fire. Either veal or chicken looks and eats well prepared in this way, and lightly covered with crumbs of bread fried; or these may be put on in little heaps.

TO WARM UP COLD POULTRY WHOLE.

566. Poultry or game if not over roasted may be warmed whole by being wrapped in a well-buttered paper, and put down before the fire till warmed through.

MINCED TURKEY OR CHICKEN.

567. Take the meat off the bones, remove the skin, and mince finely

with two or three slices of cold smoked tongue or ham, and some button mushrooms or oysters; add nutmeg and mace, and put the whole in a stewpan, thicken with flour and butter, and add sufficient cream, to moisten it well, let it stew ten minutes then serve in a deep dish or with a wall of potatoes.

To Fricassee Chickens.

568. Mix together a cupful of cream, some mace beat fine, essence of anchovy, lemon-peel and juice or pickle, and salt to the taste. Let these simmer on the fire for an hour, then thicken it with flour and butter; have ready the chickens nearly done enough to eat, skin them, leave out the drum-sticks, liver, and gizzard, then put the chicken into the sauce, and make it thoroughly hot. To garnish the fricassee, make very small forcemeat balls of veal or pork, a little grated bread, chopped parsley, suet, nutmeg, pepper, salt, and lemon-peel, mixed up with an egg, and boiled half an hour in milk and water. For family use, milk may be in part, or wholly, substituted for the cream; and chicken which has previously appeared at table is excellent cooked in this way.

Veal Cutlets from Dressed Meat.

569. These are much better when made from a cooked fillet of veal than from raw meat.

Pie from Cold Chickens.

570. Cold boiled or roast chicken may be skinned and made into a pie, adding plenty of good stock or gravy, with eggs and flour.

To Devil Chicken.

571. Take the pinions, rump, thighs, and gizzard; strew over them half a tea-spoonful of cayenne pepper, and a spoonful of salt; put a lump of butter in a saucepan, add a small tea-spoonful of mustard, a dessert-spoonful of mushroom ketchup, or soy, and the same quantity of walnut liquor. Make this sauce hot, well broil the chicken, and lay it in. Squeeze some lemon juice over it.

Another Devil (hotter).—Mix together lemon juice, grated lemon peel, salt, mustard, cayenne pepper, port-wine, Harvey's sauce, King of Oude's sauce (or indeed any other except anchovy), at discretion. Cut slices of cold meat or fowl, butter them well, and put them to soak in the mixture. If any sauce or gravy is left from the meat employed, it will improve the devil.   When required, warm it altogether in a saucepan, and serve it up exceedingly hot.

COLD ROAST OR BOILED PORK, FRIED WITH CABBAGE.

572. This cold meat is very good warmed up with fried cabbage, like bubble and squeak (par. 543).

HASHED PORK.

573. Cut into thin slices, and season with pepper and salt; then flour over all, and put into a stewpan, with a gravy composed of a little broth, or even water will do seasoned with a spoonful of vinegar, a chopped onion, a leaf or two of sage, and a blade of mace; boil the vinegar, onion, broth, and spices together, then strain, and add the slices for a few minutes; and when warm through, serve.   Or, prepare as above, and serve with a margin of pease-pudding warmed up and laid round the dish.

COLD PORK, DEVILLED.

574. Cold Pork may be devilled according to the receipt given for chicken at par. 571, of course dispensing with the liver and gizzard.

COLD PORK, BROILED.

575. Slices of cold Pork are also very good sprinkled over with powdered sage leaves, and broiled.

PORK OLIVES.

576. Cut slices from a fillet or leg of cold pork, cover them with a common forcemeat, with sage leaves instead of sweet herbs.   Roll and tie them; stew them slowly in cold pork gravy or lard.   Drain well before serving on a bed of mashed turnips, or potatoes, or pease-pudding.

A STEW OF VEGETABLES AND COLD MEAT.

577. Put a few slices of beet, a little onion, one lettuce, and a cucumber sliced, into a stewpan with a little water and a proper quantity of butter, pepper, and salt: set the pan in the oven, and when the vegetables have been stewed some time, put some boiled peas and meat into the pan, and let the whole stew till the meat is ready to serve up; lay the vegetables on the dish round the meat.   Mutton, lamb, and veal are excellent dressed in this manner, and it is a good way of using up cold meat.

SECT. 4.—VARIOUS ENTRIES, OR CORNER DISHES.

BIRD'S NEST.

578. Eggs boiled hard, and each surrounded with forcemeat; after which it is fried or browned in some way, and nicely cut in half and laid in the dish with gravy.

BEEF, PORK, OR VEAL RAISED PIES.

579. These made about the size of a teacup, make pretty side-dishes.

POTATO PIE.

580. Mashed potatoes raised to a pie, scalloped at the top, brushed over with yolk of egg and browned, filled with veal minced or cut in small slices and done white; or small potatoes scooped out of old ones and dressed with cream; or fish; or fricasseed chickens may be put in, and it will serve as a top dish.

POACHED EGGS AND SPINACH.

581. Spinach, with fried toast in three-cornered pieces stuck over it, and poached eggs laid upon them.

CUTLETS AND STEAKS.

582. Mutton Steaks, with the bones shortened and the fat taken off, may be arranged over a mould of mashed potatoes, or placed round the dish with tomato sauce in the centre.

583. PORK STEAKS, with apple sauce in the centre; or arranged round a mould of spinach, well boiled and mashed with a little butter and salt.

584. VEAL CUTLETS, dressed with egg and crumbs.

STEWED BEEF TONGUE.

585. Tongue, after it has been boiled, cut into thick slices, and stewed in a rich brown gravy.

TO FRICASSEE TONGUE.

586. When boiled till tender, or previously cooked, pare off the outside, and cut it into thin slices, fry them, then put them into good gravy with a few sweet herbs, pepper, mace, and salt. Stew it half an hour. Strain the gravy and thicken it with flour and butter, and the yolks of two eggs.

GIBLETS FRIED IN BUTTER.

587. Giblets, fried with butter a light brown, and a little sliced onion with them, then stewed.

STEWED OX PALATES.

588. Ox Palate, stewed, will make, if the whole, a nice top-dish; or if the half, a corner-dish.

STEWED CALF'S HEAD.

589. Calf's Head, stewed or hashed, forms a good top or corner dish. In hashing calf's head it is an improvement to dye some of the egg balls green with spinach juice.

SWEETBREAD OMELET.

590. For an omelet of six or seven eggs, take two sweetbreads, split and soak them well, then boil ten minutes, take them out and set them to cool; mince them small and season. Beat the eggs with four of the whites, till very light, then mix in the chopped sweetbreads; put three or four ounces of butter in a small frying-pan, and place it over the fire; stir the butter with a spoon till it melts, and when it boils, put in the mixture, stirring it for a time. Fry it a rich brown. An omelet should never be turned; while frying, the top may be well browned with a salamander, or red hot shovel. While frying the omelet, lift the edge occasionally, by slipping a knife blade under it, that the butter may get beneath. If cooked too much they become tough. Serve with gravy.

SWEETBREAD CROQUETTES.

591. Mince your sweetbreads very fine, add grated bread and a little salt, pepper, mace, and nutmeg, and grated lemon-peel. Moisten with cream, and make them up into small cones forming and smoothing them nicely; dip each into a mixture of egg and bread-crumbs, and fry them slowly in butter. Similar croquettes may be made of chicken, veal, or raw oysters.

RICE CROQUETTES.

592. Boil half a pound of rice till soft and dry, mix it with a little grated cheese and butter and powdered mace. Mince fine some cold chicken or turkey, six oysters, nutmeg, and lemon-peel, mix and moisten

with cream. Take of the rice a piece about the size of an egg, flatten it and put in the centre a spoonful of the mixture, close the rice round it, like a dumpling, and form it in the shape of an egg. Brush it over with yolk of egg, and powder with bread-crumbs, or pounded biscuit. Make up the whole, and throw into a saucepan of boiling lard two at a time to brown them, take out with a perforated skimmer, drain them, and serve hot.

CROQUETTES OF VEAL, &c.

593. One pound of cooked meat without sinews, a slice of ham, tongue, or lean bacon; chop very fine, season with pepper, salt, and spices. Put into a stew-pan one ounce of butter, one spoonful of flour; let it boil five minutes, add three or four spoonfuls of good white stock, two spoonfuls of cream. Let it stand all together, till it becomes of the consistence of thick cream; add the chopped meat, and let it boil, and mix it well; then spread it on a dish to cool. When quite cold, roll it into round balls, or any other shape, and fry in boiling lard or dripping till they come to a light brown. Serve with fried parsley.

CROQUETTE OF CHICKENS.

594. Shred and chop very fine the breast of a cold chicken or fowl; have ready some good, thick white sauce, with a little glaze in it, mix it with the fowl, and put it aside to cool; when quite cold, roll it up into balls the size and shape of a walnut. Beat up one or two eggs, and have ready some very fine bread-crumbs, dip the balls into the egg, then into the crumbs three or four times, lay them on paper to dry, and just before dinner, fry them of a *light brown* in a little boiling lard; take them up and lay them on a sheet of paper on a sieve to drain; dish then up on a napkin, with fried parsley round. Care must be taken that they do not look greasy. Cold veal or game does as well.

RISSOLES.

595. Prepare the forcemeat as for croquettes. Make a little puff paste, roll it very thin, cut it in square pieces; put a little forcemeat on; wet round the edges of the paste, turn it over, unite the paste well together to keep in the meat. Cut it in any shape you like with cutters. It is pretty in small round balls the size of a *small* apple. Fry the same as rissoles, and serve on a napkin.

596. Rissoles of Turkey or Chicken.—Pick the meat from the bones, and take off the skin; add some lean ham or tongue, with a quarter of the weight of the meat in finely grated stale bread-crumbs, a little butter, an onion boiled in two waters, and rendered as mild as possible, and finely chopped, with pepper and salt, and bind the forcemeat with two eggs beaten; roll out some puff-paste, very thin, cut it in square pieces, and lay a teaspoonful of the forcemeat in the centre; fold the paste up, taking care to unite the edges, which should be smooth and moistened with water. Dip each rissole in crumbs, and fry them *dry* in lard. Crisp parsley is a good garnish for this dish.

Puree of Fowl.

597. After chopping fine and pounding the white meat of turkey or fowl, add enough of white sauce to pass it through a sieve, flavoured with lemon-peel and juice, or lemon pickle, and a little cucumber ketchup. This may be heaped in the middle of a dish and garnished with the broiled legs, or it may be served in a wall of mashed potatoes, or rice egged over and browned; if rice, strew upon the egg some fine bread-crumbs before browning.

Sausages and Potatoes.

598. Potatoes nicely mashed and shaped in a basin, or deep pie-dish, turned out and covered with sausages; all the ties crossing at the top.

Potato Balls Ragout

599. Are made by adding to one pound of potatoes a quarter of a pound of grated ham, some sweet herbs, chopped parsley, an onion or shalot, salt, pepper, a little grated nutmeg or other spice, with the yolk of a couple of eggs; fry them in clear dripping, or brown them in a Dutch oven.

A Pretty Corner Dish of Forcemeat.

600. Take four large eggs, boil and peel them; make a rich forcemeat, covering them well with it moderately thick; fry them of a fine brown, and serve them up with a rich brown gravy.

To Boil Rice for Curry.

601. Take one pound of Patna rice, well washed and picked; put it

in a saucepan, and pour over it boiling water, cover it close, and let it stand by the fire for a quarter of an hour; pour the water off, and set it over the fire for two minutes to dry the rice, stirring it well with a fork, great care should be taken not to *harden* the rice with the heat.

CHICKEN CURRY.

602. Cut up the chicken raw, slice onions, and fry both in butter with great care, of a fine light brown; or, if you use chickens that have been dressed, fry only the onions. Lay the joints, cut into two or three pieces each, into a stewpan, with a veal or mutton gravy, and a clove or two of garlic. Simmer till the chicken is quite tender. Half an hour before serving it, rub smooth a spoonful or two of curry-powder, a spoonful of flour, and an ounce of butter; and add this, with four large spoonfuls of cream, to the stew. Salt to the taste. When serving, squeeze in a little lemon. Slices of under-done veal, or rabbit, turkey, &c., make excellent curry. Rice boiled dry must be served round the curry. For directions to do this, see following par.

Another Chicken Curry, more easily made.—Cut up a chicken or young rabbit; if chicken, take off the skin. Roll each piece in a mixture of a large spoonful of flour, and half an ounce of curry-powder. Slice two or three onions, and fry them in butter, of a light brown; then add the meat, and fry all together till the meat begins to brown. Put it all into a stewpan, and pour boiling water enough just to cover it. Simmer very gently two or three hours. If too thick, put more water half an hour before serving. If the meat has been dressed before, a little broth will be better than water; but the curry is richer when made of fresh meat.

Another.—Take two large spoonfuls of curry-powder, mix it with a teacupful of water, half a teacupful of vinegar, and a dessert-spoonful of salt. Stew slowly for an hour, and when it becomes too thick add a little more vinegar and water. About three-quarters of an hour before dinner, put in the fowl, veal, mutton, or fish, cut into square-sized pieces, and previously fried of a pale-brown, with six large onions sliced thin. Then stew the whole together till it becomes quite tender.

RABBIT CURRY.

603. Cut up two rabbits into small pieces, roll each bit in flour, and fry in dripping a nice brown; fry four or five middle-sized onions cut in shreds, then put all together into a stewpan, with enough gravy to

cover it; mix four dessert-spoonfuls of curry-powder, a little salt, and
half a tea-spoonful of chutnee in four table-spoonfuls of mushroom
ketchup, and the same quantity of vinegar, add it to the rabbit, then
let it stew slowly three or four hours, and just before dishing add the
juice of one and a half lemon.   If the gravy is thin, mix a little flour
with cold gravy, and add to it.

EAST INDIA CURRY.

604. Cut up the rabbit or other meat and sprinkle it with flour.
Fry it in butter with two middling-sized onions cut small, then put it
into a stewpan with one pint of good beef gravy, one large table-
spoonful of curry-powder, one table-spoonful of mushroom ketchup,
one tea-spoonful of salt, two ounces of butter, the juice of a small
lemon, one large potato and one large apple chopped, and stew for
twenty minutes.   Serve with rice.

A MADRAS CURRY.

605. Take three large onions, slice and fry them in butter; then fry
the fowl, meat, or lobster in the same pan, first taking out the onions;
stir into it one pint of good gravy, well seasoned, two large spoonfuls
of curry-powder and a little salt, add it to the meat, and stew gently
an hour and a half; when nearly done add the juice of a lemon, and
serve it up with boiled rice.

PILLAU.

606. Boil a large fowl in three pints of water until it is done; wash
one pound of rice three or four times, strain it till quite dry, then fry
it in half a pound of butter till almost brown; throw in the fowl, add
one table-spoonful of cloves whole, a little salt, two or three bay-
leaves, and some mace; let them all boil together till the water is dried
up; take out the fowl and rice, and when dished fry some onions
brown, and stew over the pillau.   Garnish with hard-boiled eggs.

LOBSTER RISSOLES.

607. Extract the meat of a boiled lobster, mince it fine as possible,
and mix with it the coral pounded smooth, and some yolks of hard-
boiled eggs pounded also.   Season it with cayenne pepper, powdered
mace, and a very little salt.   Make a batter of beaten egg, milk, and
flour.   To each egg allow two large tea-spoonfuls of milk, and a large
tea-spoonful of flour.   Beat the batter well, and then mix the lobster

with it gradually, till it is stiff enough to make into oval balls, about the size of a large plum. Fry them in the best salad oil, and serve them up either warm or cold.

MACARONI.

608. If for a corner, take a quarter of a pound of macaroni, scald it till tender, but not to break or stick together. When scalded, cut it in pieces one-third of an inch in length, and a perfect pipe; then make a brown mince of every kind of meat, game, and poultry you happen to have cooked, with a little fat and lean of ham or bacon. Add a small piece of onion, finely chopped, pepper, salt, a little cayenne, or ketchup and Worcestershire sauce about a tea-spoonful of each, and a small quantity of gravy to moisten it. Butter the basin thickly, and stick the macaroni closely into it, so as to give the appearance of a honeycomb when turned out, and fill up with the mince-meat, laying the rest of the macaroni at the top. Boil an hour, if a large basin, having tied a pudding-cloth tightly over it, and take it out of the water five minutes before turning it out of the basin. Serve with a tureen of gravy, putting a very little in the dish.

Another.—Boil it about an hour and a half till tender, strain the water from it, and put it back into the saucepan. Add a little pepper, salt, and a very little cayenne, a small bit of butter, and a little cream; put it on a dish with some cheese cut thin, leave it before the fire a few minutes; or, when you have made the macaroni quite ready and hot, stir some grated cheese into it, and send it to table.

VEAL AND HAM MACARONI, OR RICHLIEU.

609. Boil three ounces of macaroni tender, beat up two eggs, then fill up a pint basin, or melon-shaped mound, with nicely-flavoured minced veal and ham, a little grated lemon peel; mix well, and boil five minutes. Serve with good gravy in the dish.

TIMBALLS MACARONI.

610. Boil the macaroni in water, and an ounce of butter. When it has boiled a few moments, strain it off and return it into the pan. Add half a pint of stock; boil it slowly on a stove, till reduced; then prepare a fricassee of chicken, put the macaroni to it, with a little grated parmesan, make all hot, then set it to cool. Butter a mould well, sprinkle it with bread-crumbs, and line it with half puff paste;

put in the chicken quite cold; cover and bake it in a slow oven. When done, turn it out of the mould; cut off the top, and pour over some white sauce, and some in the dish.

Tête à la Mode.

611. Take an ox-cheek nicely washed, season it well with pepper, salt, mace, and cloves, and some chopped onion rubbed well over it; put it in a stewpan, with as much water as will cover it; stew it two hours, and when cold skim the fat off. Have ready a cow-heel, well cleaned and boiled tender; cut the head and foot in square bits the size of sugar-lumps, place them in layers in an earthen pan; season between each layer with pepper, salt, and mace; fill the pan with gravy, cover it with a plate, and bake it two hours in a slow oven. It is to be eaten cold.

Carrole of Rice.

612. Take some well-picked rice, wash it well, and boil it five minutes in water, strain it, and put it into a stewpan, with a bit of butter, a good slice of ham, and an onion. Stew it over a very gentle fire till tender, have ready a mould lined with very thin slices of bacon, mix the yolks of two or three eggs with the rice, and then line the bacon with it about half an inch thick. Put into it a ragout of chicken, rabbit, veal, or of any thing else. Fill up the mould, and cover it close with rice. Bake it in a quick oven an hour, turn it over, and send it to table in a good gravy or curry sauce.

Salmagundy.

613. This is a beautiful small dish, if in nice shape, and if the colours of the ingredients are varied. For this purpose chop separately the white parts of cold chicken or veal, yolks of eggs boiled hard, the whites of eggs, parsley, half a dozen anchovies, beet-root, red pickled cabbage, ham and grated tongues, or any thing well flavoured, and of a good colour. Some people like a small proportion of onion, but it may be better left out. A saucer, large teacup, or any other base, must be put into a small dish; then make rows round it wide at bottom, and growing smaller towards the top, choosing such of the ingredients for each row as will most vary the colours. At the top a little sprig of curled parsley may be stuck in. Or, without any thing on the dish, the salmagundy may be laid in rows, or put into

the half-whites of eggs, which may be made to stand upright by cutting off a bit at the round end. In the latter case, each half egg has but one ingredient. Curled parsley and butter may be put as garnish between.

SAVOURY OMELET.

614. Make a batter of eggs and milk and a very little flour; put to it chopped parsley, green onions, or chives (the latter are best), or a very small quantity of shalot, a little pepper, salt, and a scrape or two of nutmeg. Make some butter, boil in a small frying-pan, and pour the above batter into it; when one side is of a fine yellow-brown, turn it and do the other. Double it when served. Some scraped lean ham, or grated tongue, put in at first, is a very pleasant addition. Four eggs will make a pretty-sized omelet; but many cooks will use eight or ten. A small proportion of flour should be used. If the taste be approved, a *little* tarragon gives a fine flavour. A good deal of parsley should be used.

Another.—Let eight eggs be well beaten, leaving out two whites; add half a pint of cream, half a pound of melted butter, with some parsley and onions shred fine, a little pepper and salt; this mixture is to be fried in a pan, first browning a good piece of butter in it. Pour some gravy over it.

RAMAKINS.

615. Scrape a quarter of a pound each of Cheshire and Gloucester cheese, and good fresh butter; beat all in a mortar with the yolks of four eggs, and the inside of a small French roll boiled in cream till soft; mix the paste with the whites of the eggs previously beaten, and put into small paper pans made rather long than square, and bake in a Dutch oven till of a fine brown. They should be eaten quite hot. Some like the addition of a glass of white wine. The batter for ramakins is equally good over macaroni when boiled tender; or on stewed brocoli, celery, or cauliflower; a little of the gravy they have been stewed in being put in the dish.

FONDU OF CHEESE.

616. Grate half a pound of parmesan or any mild cheese, put in a stewpan, with two ounces of butter, set it over the stove, and keep stirring till quite melted, then take it off the stove, and mix it thoroughly with six yolks of eggs and a little cream, after which fill some small papers half full, and then bake them.

N

Another.—To a pint of cream put half a pound of grated cheese, and the yolks of four eggs; mix and beat all well together. Then whip the whites of the eggs to a strong froth, and mix them well with the cream, &c.; put the mixture in small paper trays, for a silver dish, and bake it in a slow oven.

GERMAN PATTIES (REMOVE FOR SECOND COURSE).

617. Cut some very thin slices of bread with a round cutter, and soak them in clarified butter, then make a mince of any cold meat, season with salt, pepper, and a table-spoonful of grated cheese, a little curry powder, some good gravy, and a little cream; thicken with flour and butter, then put as much mince as you can between two pieces of the prepared bread, press them together at the edge, egg and crumb them, fry them of a light brown, dish them on a napkin and send them to table very hot.

COLUMBUS EGGS.

618. Cut in half, twelve hard boiled eggs, and cut off a little at each end to make them stand like cups; chop the yolks, and mix with ham, cream, and nutmeg; fill with it the cups, press it smooth, arrange on the dish the two halves together like whole eggs.

FRENCH BATTER.

619. Pour half a teacupful of boiling water on an ounce and a quarter of butter, and when melted add three times as much of cold water so that the chill will be just off. Mix the above by degrees and very smoothly, with five ounces of well dried flour, a very little pinch of salt, if for fruit, but double the quantity if the batter is to be served with meat or vegetables; and at the moment it is wanted mix in the white of one egg beaten to a fine froth. This is excellent for fruit fritters or frying with meat or vegetables.

SECT. 5.—POTTED MEATS AND SANDWICHES.

TO POT MEATS.

620. Take any tender and well-done meat, free from fat, bone, skin, and gristle. Pound it thoroughly in a mortar till it is reduced to a paste, putting in a part at a time. When all is thoroughly reduced, add the spice and some butter, according to the nature of the meat; ham requiring less than veal, and veal again less than beef. After mixing them together in the most thorough manner, press the

potted meat into jars with force enough to expel all the air, then pour over the top a layer of clarified butter about a third of an inch thick, which is removed before using the meat. The butter that has covered potted things will serve for basting, or for paste for meat pies.

To Clarify Butter for Potted Things.

621. Put it into a sauce-boat, and set that over the fire in a stew-pan that has a little water in. When melted, take care not to pour the milky part over the potted things, as it will sink to the bottom.

To Pot Beef or Mutton.

622. Take two pounds of lean beef, rub it with saltpetre, and let it lie one night; then salt with common salt, and cover it with water four days in a small pan. Dry it with a cloth, and season with black pepper; lay it in as small a pan as will hold it, cover it with coarse paste, and bake it five hours in a very cool oven. Put no liquor in. When cold, pick out the strings and fat; beat the meat very fine, with a quarter of a pound of fine butter, just warm but not oiled, and as much of the gravy as will make it into a paste. Put into very small pots, and cover with melted butter.

Another.—Take beef that has been dressed, either boiled or roasted; beat it in a mortar, with some pepper, salt, one blade of mace to each pot, some grated nutmeg, and a little fine butter, just warm. The flavour of this is equal to the above, but the colour is not so fine. It is a good way for using the remains of a large joint.

Another.—Pound three or four pounds of lean beef, with half an ounce of saltpetre, the same of sugar, and a large handful of common salt, lay it in a pan for two or three days, turning it occasionally. Wash and put it in a jar with half a pound of butter. Cover close and stew in a water bath till quite tender. Take it out of the liquor, and, while hot, add powdered pepper and mace, and as much of the liquor as is required to make it mix, pound very fine and pot it; and when cold cover with clarified butter.

To Pot Veal.

623. Cold fillet makes the finest potted veal; or it may be done as follows:—Season a large slice of the fillet, before it is dressed, with some mace, pepper-corns, and two or three cloves; lay it close into a potting-pan that will but just hold it, fill it up with water, and bake it three hours; then pound it quite small in a mortar, and

add salt to taste; put a little gravy that was baked to it in pounding, if to be eaten soon; otherwise only a little butter just melted. When done, cover it over with butter.

To Pot Veal or Chicken with Ham.

624. Pound some cold veal or white of chicken, season as directed in the last article, and put layers of it with layers of ham pounded, or rather shred; press each down, and cover with butter.

Another—(A good supper dish.) Make a sauce of thin veal gravy, a quarter of a pound of butter, and a little flour. Pound or dress very fine sufficient cold veal and ham to fill your mould. Mix it with the sauce, and pour it hot into a mould, which must be previously lined with two or three hard-boiled eggs cut in slices. Turn out when cold.

To Pot Uncooked Veal.

625. Stew the veal in the oven with a very little water till tender, then chop it, and to two pounds of meat put half a pound of butter, the rind of half a lemon grated, a little mace, two ounces fat bacon, and pepper and salt to your taste. Pound it very fine in a mortar, and just warm it through in the oven before putting it into the pots; a little butter melted, or clarified suet, must then be poured over it. It *looks* and *tastes* well if alternate layers of potted lean of ham are laid in the pots with the veal.

Potted Ham.

626. Slice some cold ham and mince it small, fat and lean together. Then pound it in a mortar, seasoning with cayenne, and powdered mace and nutmeg. Fill with it a large deep pan, and set it in the oven for half an hour; afterwards pack it hard in a stone jar, and fill up with lard. If sufficiently seasoned it will keep well in the winter, and is convenient for travelling.

Potted Tongue.

627. Tongue is potted exactly like beef.

Potted Hare.

628. Hare is potted also in the same way as beef, removing the meat from the bones after roasting it, and mixing up the forcemeat with it.

To Pot Pigeons.

629. Let them be quite fresh, clean them carefully, and season with

salt and pepper; lay them close in a small deep pan, for the smaller the surface and the closer they are packed the less butter will be wanted; cover them with butter, then with very thick paper tied down, and bake them; when cold, put them dry into pots that will hold two or three in each, and pour butter over them, using that which was baked as part. Observe that the butter should be pretty thick if they are to be kept. If pigeons are boned, and then put in an oval form into the pot, they will lie closer, and require less butter. They may be stuffed with a fine forcemeat made with veal and bacon.

Another Way.—Bone and season them with pepper and salt, put them in a pot with as much butter as will cover them; bake till very tender; drain them from the gravy, and wipe them *dry* with a cloth, season again with salt, pepper, mace and cloves pounded; put them closely into pots, and when cold melt the butter from the gravy, and pour it an inch thick over the meat.

To Pot Partridge.

630. Clean them nicely, and season with mace, allspice, white pepper, and salt, in fine powder; rub every part well, then lay the breasts downwards in a pan, and pack the birds as close as you possibly can; put a good deal of butter on them, then cover the pan with a coarse flour paste, and a paper over, tie it close, and bake. When cold, put the birds into pots, and cover them with butter.

Another (a very cheap way of potting birds).—Prepare them as directed in the last receipt; and when baked and grown cold, cut them into proper pieces for helping, pack them close in a large potting-pot, and, if possible, leave no spaces to receive the butter. Cover them with butter, and one-third part less will be wanted than when the birds are done whole.

To Pot Woodcocks.

631. The same as the pigeons, excepting that the trail must be left in.

To Pot Ox Cheek.

632. When you stew an ox cheek take some of the fleshy part, season well with pepper and salt, and beat it in a mortar, with a little clear fat skimmed off the gravy. Put it close into pots and cover with clarified butter; or, cut it in slices and lay them into an earthenware mould with some of the gravy; when cold, turn it out as a breakfast or supper dish. Calf's head stewed may be treated as above.

To Cut Sandwiches.

633. Butter a two pound loaf, not too stale, and divided smoothly, then cut a thin slice, and lay on it either thin slices of meat, or some of the potted meat just given. If beef or ham is used, a little mustard is usually added. After this, place on the top another slice of bread, similarly buttered, cut off the crust all round, so as to make an oblong square, and divide this into five or six sandwiches, which should be kept moist between two plates, or in a proper sandwich-box. Any number may be cut and added, by placing one layer above the other. *Or*, use potted meat, such as beef, veal, chicken, ham, or tongue, spread on the bread cut as above. This method is far better than the slices, as there is less difficulty in dividing them with the teeth.

Anchovy Butter.

634. Bone three or four anchovies, chop them small, boil some parsley quite green, lay the anchovies and parsley with about two ounces of *good* fresh butter on a sieve, mix all well together through the sieve, and make it into little pats like butter.

CHAP. XIV.—VEGETABLES.

Sect. 1.—General Observations in Dressing Vegetables.

635. Vegetables should be carefully cleaned from insects, by putting them with the stalk or root end upwards into water, or salt and water, and nicely washed. Boil them in plenty of water, and drain them the moment they are done enough. If overboiled they will lose their beauty and crispness. Bad cooks sometimes dress them with meat, which is wrong, except carrots or cabbage with boiling beef.

To Boil Vegetables of a good Green Colour,

636. Take care that the water boils when they are put in. Make them boil very fast. Do not cover, but watch them, and if the water has not slackened you may be sure they are done when they begin to sink. Then take them out immediately, or the colour will change. Hard water, especially if chalybeate, spoils the colour of such vegetables as should be green; a little salt should always be put in the water. To boil them green in hard water, put a tea-spoonful of

carbonate of soda or potash into the water when it boils, before the vegetables are put in.

SECT. 2.—SPECIAL DIRECTIONS FOR DRESSING VEGETABLES.

POTATOES.

637. To BOIL.—*An excellent Receipt.*—Pare or merely wash them, as preferred, and put them in a covered saucepan of cold water, with a tea-spoonful of salt; boil them till they are done (which can be ascertained by running a fork into them) and begin to break a little; then pour the water from them, and hold the saucepan, with the lid off, over the fire for two or three minutes, shaking well at the end of the time; put the lid loosely on so as to allow the steam to escape, and sprinkle a very little salt over them; let them stand till wanted (the sooner the better), but they may remain in this way, if necessary, half an hour or more. Time, twenty to thirty minutes, or longer if very large.

Another way.—Set them on a fire, without paring them, in cold water; let them half boil, then throw some salt in and a pint of cold water, and let them boil again till almost done. Pour off the water, and put a clean cloth over them, and then the saucepan cover, and set them by the fire to steam till ready. Many persons prefer steamers. Potatoes look best when the skin is peeled, not cut. Do new potatoes the same; but be careful they are taken off in time, or they will be watery. Before dressing, rub off the skin with a cloth and salt, and then wash.

638. To BROIL.—Parboil, then slice and broil them. Or, parboil, and then set them whole on the gridiron over a very slow fire, and when thoroughly done send them up with their skins on. This last way is practised in many Irish families.

639. To ROAST.—Half boil, take. off the thin peel, and roast them of a beautiful brown. Or, put them with the peel on in the ashes of a wood fire.

640. To FRY.—Take the skin off raw potatoes, slice them, soak in cold water, and fry them, either in butter or thin batter. Or, as,

641. POTATOE CHIPS.—Wash and peel some potatoes, then pare them, ribbon-like, into long lengths; put them into cold water to remove the strong potatoe flavour; drain them, and throw them into a pan with a little butter, and fry them a light brown. Take them out of the pan, and place them close to the fire on a sieve lined with clean writing paper to dry, before they are served up. A little salt may be sprinkled over them.

642. To BAKE.—Wash and put them whole and unpeeled into a slow oven, and let them remain from an hour and a half to two hours.

643. To MASH.—Boil the potatoes, peel them, and break them to paste; then to two pounds of them add a quarter of a pint of hot milk, a little salt, and two ounces of butter, and stir it all well over the fire. Either serve them in this manner, or place them on the dish in a form, and then brown the top with a salamander, or in scallops before the fire.

644. NEW POTATOES.—TO BOIL.—Procure them of equal size, and if very young, wash them only; if older, rub off the skins with a scrubbing-brush or coarse cloth. Put them into boiling water till tender, and sprinkle a little salt over them, and put a lump of butter in; shake up and serve. Time, fifteen to twenty minutes. If very early potatoes are half boiled the day before, and finished when wanted, they will not be watery—if served in cream sauce they are very nice, especially for supper.

645. COOKED POTATOES.—TO FRY.—Heat some dripping or lard in a fryingpan, then drop in some slices of boiled potatoes, or broken fragments will do quite as well, stir them with a spoon, and in about ten minutes they will be browned enough, then drain off any super-fluous fat, add a little pepper and salt, and serve.

646. OLD POTATOES IN A NEW DRESS.—Wash and pare some large old potatoes, then, with an iron scoop, make them into small balls the size of young ones; steam them, and serve with white sauce poured over them.

647. POTATO BALLS.—Mash very smooth some well-boiled potatoes with a little cream (or butter and milk) and salt, then form them into balls the size of a peach, and indented like one, or into the shape of a pear; warm through, and brown slightly on one side in a Dutch oven. The pears should be served on a napkin with the broad end downwards, and a bit of stalk stuck in the other end. They may also, as a variety, be placed in a well-thickened brown gravy, poured round but not over them.

648. RISSOLES DE POMMES DE TERRE.—Mix with potatoes mashed with milk some fine chopped herbs; roll into long rissoles, fry them a light brown, and send them as hot as possible to table. Or, brush them over with yolk of egg, and dip them in bread-crumbs; then having melted a little butter in a saucepan, put in the rissoles, and shake them gently over the fire till they are a light brown.

CARROTS AND PARSNIPS.

649. These vegetables require a good deal of boiling. When young wipe off the skin after they are boiled; when old, boil them with the salt meat, and scrape them first. (Parsnips should always be scraped.) Average time, from twenty to forty-five minutes.

650. To STEW CARROTS WHITE.—Half boil, then nicely scrape, and slice them into a stewpan. Put to them half a teacupful of any weak broth, some pepper and salt, and half a cupful of cream; simmer them till they are very tender, but not broken. Before serving, rub a very little flour with a bit of butter, and warm up with them. If approved, chopped parsley may be added ten minutes before served.

651. To STEW CARROTS BROWN.—Take six large carrots, wash and scrape them well, put them into boiling water, and let them boil for half an hour; then take them out, drain, and cut each carrot into as many round balls as it will make; put them into the stewpan with a pint of gravy, flavoured with a little pepper, salt, mushroom ketchup, and Worcestershire sauce; let them simmer for twenty minutes, then take them out, pile them in the centre of the dish, thicken the gravy with a little flour and butter, pour it over the carrots and serve.

652. PARSNIPS would be very good cooked in this way.

653. To MASH PARSNIPS OR CARROTS.—Boil them till tender, pare, and then mash them and warm in a stewpan with a little cream, a good piece of butter, and pepper and salt.

654. FRICASSEE OF PARSNIPS.—Boil in milk till they are soft, then cut them lengthways into bits two or three inches long, and simmer in a white sauce made of two spoonfuls of broth, a bit of mace, half a cupful of cream, a bit of butter, and some flour, pepper and salt.

BEET-ROOT.

655. Beet-roots make a very pleasant addition to winter-salad, of which they may agreeably form a full half, instead of being only used to ornament it. These roots are cooling and very wholesome. They should be carefully washed, but not scraped (or the colour will escape), and boiled till tender, after which they should be pared. As a vegetable they may be sent in hot, as carrots.

656. STEWED BEET-ROOT is extremely good boiled and sliced with a small quantity of onion; or stewed with whole onions, large or small, as follows—boil the beet with the skin on, slice it into a stewpan with a little broth, and a spoonful of vinegar; simmer till the gravy is

tinged with the colour, then put it into a small dish, and make a circle round of the button onions, first boiled till tender. Time, one hour and a half to two hours.

Another Mode.—Cut in dice two middling sized onions, put in a pan with two ounces of butter, fry white, stirring continually with a spoon, add a spoonful of flour and milk, enough to make a thinnish sauce, then add to it three salt-spoonfuls of salt, four of sugar, one of pepper, a spoonful of good vinegar; boil a few minutes, then put in the slices of beet-root (already boiled as for salad), and simmer for a quarter of an hour. A little cream may be added to make it richer.

TURNIPS.

657. To BOIL.—Pare them, and if large, split them; if small, leave them whole. Put them in boiling water with a little salt, and keep them well covered until they are tender. They require from fifteen to thirty minutes.

658. To MASH.—Boil them as above till very tender, then press the water from them between two plates, after which mash them, and pass them through a colander. Then put them into a saucepan, add a little salt, and some milk or cream; keep stirring till quite hot, then serve.

ONIONS.

659. To STEW.—Peel six large onions; fry gently of a fine brown, but do not blacken them; then put them into a small stewpan with a little weak gravy, pepper, and salt; cover and stew gently for two hours. They should be lightly floured at first.

660. To ROAST.—They should be done with all the skins on; they eat well alone, with only salt and cold butter, or with roast potatoes or beet-roots.

661. SPANISH ONIONS.—To STEW.—Boil four onions, and when done scoop out the middle, and fill them with forcemeat; fry them a light brown, and make a rich gravy and pour over them. This makes a good corner dish.

662. To FRY ONIONS FOR STEAKS, HERRINGS, &c.—Peel the onions, cut them in slices, fry them in the fat from the steak, &c., which ought to be fried first and kept hot the while. They are usually served in the same dish with the steak or fish.

CELERY.

663. To STEW.—Wash six heads, and strip off the outer leaves;

either halve or leave them whole, according to their size; cut into lengths of four inches; put them into a stewpan with a cup of broth or weak white gravy; stew till tender; then add two spoonfuls of cream, and a little flour and butter, seasoned with pepper, salt, and nutmeg, and simmer all together.

ASPARAGUS.

664. To Boil.—Clean the asparagus, and cut all of a length, then boil till the tops are quite tender; have ready a toast to place them on, and serve while hot. A little mint boiled with asparagus is a great improvement to its flavour. Time, about twenty minutes.

665. ASPARAGUS SERVED AS PEAS.—A variety may be made in the mode of serving asparagus, by cutting up the tender parts into small pieces, and when boiled with a sprig or two of mint till nearly done (half the usual time); they should be dried in a cloth, and finished up as young peas, adding a very little sugar, butter, and a little flour dredged over them.

VEGETABLE-MARROW.

666. To Boil or Stew.—This excellent vegetable may be boiled till tender; then divide it lengthways into two, and serve it up on toast, accompanied by melted butter; or when nearly boiled, divide it as above, and stew gently in gravy like cucumbers. Care should be taken to choose young ones not exceeding six inches in length. Time, from half an hour to one hour.

667. To Mash.—When too old and large to send to table as above, they should be cut in quarters, the seeds taken out, and boiled till tender; then drain the water from them through a colander, mash them with a little pepper, butter, and salt, and serve on a buttered toast.

SEA KALE.

668. This must be boiled very white, and served on toast like asparagus and vegetable-marrow. White sauce may be poured over it. Time for boiling, from half an hour to three-quarters.

669. To Stew Brown.—Boil the kale, as above; then drain it, and simmer slowly in a stewpan, with from half a pint to one pint of rich and well-seasoned clear gravy, for twenty minutes, and serve.

LAVER.

670. This is a plant that grows on the rocks near the sea in the west

of England, and is sent in pots prepared for eating. Set it in a dish over a lamp, with a bit of butter, and the squeeze of a Seville orange; stir it till hot. It is eaten with roast meat, and is supposed to be a great sweetener of the blood. It is seldom liked at first, but people become extremely fond of it by habit.

ARTICHOKES.

671. To DRESS.—Trim a few of the outside leaves off, and cut the stalk even; if young, half an hour will boil them; they are better for being gathered two or three days first. Serve them with melted butter, in as many small cups as there are artichokes. Time nearly an hour.

672. ARTICHOKE BOTTOMS.—If dried, they must be soaked, then stewed in weak gravy, and served with or without forcemeat in each. *Or*, they may be boiled in milk, and served with cream sauce; or added to ragouts, French pies, &c.

JERUSALEM ARTICHOKES.

673. Jerusalem Artichokes must be taken up the moment they are done, or they will be too soft. They usually take about twenty to twenty-five minutes. They must be boiled plain, or served with white fricassee-sauce, or mashed like turnips, seasoning with pepper and salt, and adding a little butter. If the cook points the Jerusalem artichokes when paring them, and sets them upon the dish at the wide end, pouring white sauce over them, they form a pretty dish.

674. To FRY.—First pare, then boil, the artichokes for about ten minutes, and drain them on a sieve. When nearly cold, dip them into egg and bread-crumbs, and fry them of a light brown; drain them from the fat, but do not allow them to cool before serving.

SPINACH.

675. Spinach requires great care in washing and picking it. When that is done, throw it into a saucepan that will just hold it, sprinkle it with a little salt, and cover close. The pan must be set on the fire, and well shaken. When done, beat the spinach well with a small bit of butter; it must come to table pretty dry, and looks well if pressed into a tin mould in the form of a large leaf, which is sold at the tin shops. A spoonful of cream is an improvement; or a few spoonfuls of good gravy, which must be absorbed by again boiling quickly. Plain sippets, or bread cut in shapes and fried, may be added as a garnish.

To Stew Spinach.

676. Wash your spinach in several waters, put it in a colander, and throw it into a large pan of boiling water, with a handful of salt; boil it two minutes to take off the earthy taste, squeeze it well in a sieve, put about a quarter of a pound of butter into a tossing-pan, put in your spinach, keep turning and chopping it with a knife till quite dry and green; lay it upon a plate, press it with another, cut it in the shape of diamonds, and pour round it some good melted butter. It will eat exceedingly mild, far better than when cooked in the common way.

Cauliflowers.

677. To Boil.—Choose those that are close and white, cut off the green leaves, and look carefully that there are no caterpillars about the stalk. Soak an hour in cold water, then boil them in milk and water, and take care to skim the saucepan, that not the least foulness may fall on the flower. They must be served very white, and *rather* crisp, but still sufficiently done. Time, twenty-five minutes or more.

678. In White Sauce.—Half boil it, then cut it into handsome pieces, and lay them in a stewpan with a little broth, a bit of mace. a little salt, and a dust of white pepper; simmer half an hour, then put a little cream, butter, and flour; shake and simmer a few minutes, and serve.

679. Cauliflower Omelet (American).—Take the white part of a boiled cauliflower after it is cold, and chop it very small, and mix with it a sufficient quantity of well-beaten egg, to make a very thick batter, then fry it in fresh butter in a small pan, and send it to table hot.

680. Fried (American).—Having laid a fine cauliflower in cold water for an hour, put it into a pot of hot water that has been slightly salted (milk and water will be still better), and boil it twenty-five minutes, or till the large stalk is perfectly tender, then divide it equally into small tuffs, and spread it on a dish to cool. Prepare a sufficient quantity of batter, made in the proportion of a table-spoonful of flour, and two table-spoonsful of milk to each egg; beat the eggs very light, then stir into them the flour and milk alternately, a spoonful of flour and two spoonsful of milk at a time. When the cauliflower is cold, have ready some fresh butter in a frying-pan over a clear fire. When it has come to a boil, and has done bubbling, dip each tuft of cauliflower twice into the batter, and fry them a light

brown; send them to table hot.   Brocoli may be fried in this manner.

BROCOLI.

651. Cut the heads with short stalks, and pare the tough skin off them. Tie the small shoots into bunches, and boil them a shorter time than the heads. Some salt must be put into the water. Serve with or without toast.

AN EXCELLENT WAY OF BOILING CABBAGE.

682. Having trimmed the cabbage, and washed it well in cold water (examine the leaves to see that no insects are lurking among them), cut it almost into quarters, but do not divide it entirely down at the stem, which should be cut off just below the termination of the leaves. Let it lie an hour in a pan of cold water. Have ready a potful of boiling water, seasoned with a small tea-spoonful of salt. Put the cabbage into it, and let it boil for an hour and a half, skimming it occasionally. Then take it out; put it into a colander to drain, and when all the hot water has drained off, set it under the hydrant. Let the hydrant run on it till the cabbage has become perfectly cold all through. If you have no hydrant, set it under a pump, or keep pouring cold water on it from a pitcher. Then, having thrown out all the first water, and washed the pot, fill it again, and let the second water boil. During this time the cabbage under the hydrant will be growing cold. Then put it on again in the second water, and boil it two hours, or two and a half. Even the thickest part of the stalk must be perfectly tender all through. When thoroughly done, take up the cabbage, drain it well through the colander, pressing it down with a broad ladle to squeeze out all the moisture; lay it in a deep dish, and cut it entirely apart, dividing it into quarters. Lay some bits of fresh butter among the leaves, add a little pepper, cover the dish, and send it to table hot.—(*Miss Leslie*—a great improvement.)

BEANS.

683. TO BOIL BROAD BEANS.—Boil tender with a bunch of parsley, which must be chopped to serve with them. Bacon or pickled pork must be served to eat with, but not boiled with them. Time, twenty to twenty-five minutes.

684. BROAD BEANS MASHED.—Take *old* broad beans, boil them for one hour, mash them through a coarse sieve, and mix with them a

little butter, pepper, and salt. Put the mash into a hot basin or mould, and turn it out before serving.

685. WINDSOR BEANS, FRICASSEED.—When grown large, but not mealy, boil, blanch, and lay them in a white sauce ready hot; just heat them through in it, and serve. If any are not of a fine green, do not use them for this dish.

686. FRENCH BEANS.—To BOIL.—String, and cut them into four or eight; the last looks best. Lay them in salt and water, and when the saucepan boils put them in with some salt. As soon as they are done serve them immediately, to preserve the green colour. Or when half-done drain the water off, and put them into two spoonsful of broth strained; and add a little cream, butter, and flour, to finish doing them.

687. To STEW FRENCH BEANS.—Boil the French beans (as at par. 686). Make a rich clear gravy, well flavoured; drain the beans perfectly dry, and put both into a stewpan, and simmer for a quarter of an hour or twenty minutes; serve hot. Peas may also be stewed in this way.

688. HARICOTS BLANCS.—These beans, so much used in France, are dressed exactly like the old peas (691); but the flavour is not generally liked in this country.

PEAS.

689. To BOIL.—Should be young and of a good sort. They must not be overdone, nor in much water. Boil some mint with them, and chop it to garnish them, and stir a piece of butter in with them. If either too young or too old, a little sugar boiled with them is an improvement. Time, about fifteen minutes.

690. To STEW GREEN PEAS.—Take a quart of peas, three cabbage lettuces cut small, put them into a stewpan with a piece of butter the size of an egg (and a slice of raw ham, if you like), an onion stuck with cloves; let them stew gently till the peas are half-done, then add a pint of good gravy; when stewed, thicken with flour and butter, the yolks of two eggs, and a teacupful of cream. Keep stirring after the eggs are in, or it will curdle. Some think a tea-spoonful of white powdered sugar is an improvement. Gravy may be added, but then there will be less of the flavour of the peas. Chop a bit of mint, and stew in them.

691. To STEW OLD PEAS.—Steep them in water all night, if not fine boilers; otherwise half an hour would do; put them into water, just enough to cover them, with a good bit of butter, or a piece of beef or pork. Stew them very gently till the peas are soft, and the meat is

tender; if it is not salt meat, add salt and a little pepper. Serve them round the meat.

MUSHROOMS.

692. To STEW BROWN.—Peel the mushrooms, and cut off the end of the stalk, then cut them into four or six, according to their size, add a good deal of pepper and salt, with a very small quantity of water; stew them in an earthen pipkin three or four hours as slow as possible; put sippets in the dish. They will keep several days, but should be done as soon as gathered.

693. To STEW BUTTONS WHITE.—Peel some mushrooms, and cut off the end of the stalk, put them in a stewpan with some milk, a little cayenne pepper, and salt; let them stew gently, and thicken with flour and butter.

Another and better Receipt.—Peel some mushrooms, sprinkle them with a little pepper and salt, and lay them in a stewpan; set them on a stove or by the side of the fire to draw the liquor from them, then add cream sufficient to cover them, or a little milk thickened with butter and flour; give them a boil up. Serve with or without sippets round the dish.

694. MUSHROOM POWDER.—Take the thickest, largest buttons you can get, peel them, cut off the decayed end, but do not wash them; spread them separately on pewter dishes, and set them in a slow oven to dry; let the liquor dry up into the mushrooms; it makes the powder stronger, and let them continue in the oven till they will powder. Then pound them in a marble mortar, and sift them through a fine sieve, with a little cayenne pepper and pounded mace. Bottle and keep it in a dry place.

695. BUTTERED MUSHROOMS.—Rub some large button mushrooms with a piece of flannel dipped in salt, and dry them carefully with a cloth: with two teacupsful of buttons thus cleansed, put three quarters of an ounce of fresh butter into a strong saucepan, shake it over the fire till thoroughly melted, and continue to shake the saucepan, to prevent burning, for five minutes; then throw in some salt and pepper, and, if liked, a little mace pounded fine. Stew them till tender, and serve.

696. MUSHROOMS TO BROIL.—The largest and most open mushrooms are the best for this purpose, and the stalks should be cut short, then peel them and lay them on the heated bars of a gridiron (having rubbed the bars previously with suet). Sprinkle them with salt and pepper, and when done rub a little cold butter under and over them,

and serve on a hot dish. They will begin to steam when done enough. If preferred on a toast, prepare them as above, and set them on a buttered toast in the Dutch oven, spreading butter on the top of them before serving.

697. A PURÉE OF MUSHROOMS.—Peel the mushrooms and cut off the stems. Squeeze the juice of half a large lemon into a stewpan with a little water; put in the heads and stew them till tender; drain out the mushrooms and mince them to a pulp; add a piece of butter and the minced mushrooms to the stew; stir on the fire till the butter is melted, and then add half a teacup of good gravy, and the same of cream; when the purée is of a proper thickness, add pepper and serve.

698. MUSHROOMS TO POT.—Rub either small flapped mushrooms or buttons with a new flannel and salt, and if moistened with the salt wipe them dry with a soft cloth. Put into a stewpan one and a quarter ounce of fresh butter, and a pint of mushrooms, a small tea-spoonful of salt, a salt-spoonful of mace and a little cayenne; stew them till tender. When done drain them on a sloping dish, and when cold lay them (pressed down) in small pots. Pour clarified butter over them, and if intended to keep more than a week or two, it would be well to lay a paper over the butter when cold, and then pour over it a thick layer of melted suet. They should be stored in a cool but dry place.

N.B.—The skins and stalks cut away from mushrooms should be carefully collected, and strewn over with salt in a jar or cup, then set by the fire to draw out the liquor, which should be flavoured with spice for present use as ketchup.

CUCUMBERS TO STEW.

699. Pare, and then slice some cucumbers not too thin, put them into a stewpan with some onions and a little salt. Let them stew in their own liquor a little while, then drain all that away, and put to them one anchovy, a little spice, some good gravy, and a little red wine or ketchup. When the anchovy is dissolved, thicken with flour and butter.

Another.—Peel and cut cucumbers in quarters, take out the seeds, and lay them on a cloth to drain off the water. When they are dry, flour and fry them in fresh butter, let the butter be quite hot before putting in the cucumbers; fry them brown, then with an egg-slice lay them on a sieve to drain the fat from them. If the taste is approved of, fry a few small or sliced onions to put with them. When drained, put them into a stewpan with as much gravy as will cover them.

O

ENDIVE.

710. Endive is used in the same way as lettuce; as also is mustard and cress, mixed with sliced radish and water-cress.

ANOTHER SALAD.

711. Add to the lettuce two beet-roots as at 655, a stick of celery cut small, radishes if in season, mustard and cress, and the white of a hard-boiled egg, of which the yolk has been used in the salad dressing. Sorrel is sometimes added.

LOBSTER SALAD.

712. Mix with some ordinary salad mixture (par. 718) the boiled eggs of a lobster; then put in a salad-bowl a layer of salad herbs, lettuce being the best; upon these strew pieces of the flesh and interior of the lobster itself, with some of the eggs; then another layer of herbs, upon which place more lobster and eggs, and upon this pour the salad dressing, taking care to run it gradually over the whole; lastly, on the top of all place a few of the best leaves of the salad, shred very fine, and round the edge place some ornamental cuttings of cucumber, radishes, &c.

713. CRABS, PRAWNS, SHRIMPS, SALMON, or any cold fish may be used in the same way as lobster (see 712).

SECT. 2.—FRENCH SALADS.

714. French salads are mixed with less care than is used by the English, inasmuch as the flavour of raw oil is not objected to by their consumers. The lettuce, endive, dandelion-leaves, or other salad-herbs, are merely chopped up and incorporated with a little tarragon, chervil, and garlic or shalot; after which a mixture of half a tea-spoonful of pepper, a whole one of salt, two table-spoonsful of vinegar, and four of oil, are simply stirred together with a fork and poured over the salad.

715. COLD MEAT, FOWL, FISH, AND GAME, mixed up with the above salad in fine shreds or slices, and flavoured in the same way, are extensively used in France.

ANOTHER FRENCH SALAD.

716. Chop three anchovies, a shalot, and some parsley small; put them into a bowl with two table-spoonsful of vinegar, one of oil, a little mustard and salt; when well mixed, add by degrees some cold

roast or boiled meat in *very thin* slices; put in a few at a time, not exceeding two or three inches long; shake them in the dressing, and then add more; but cover the bowl close, and let the salad be prepared three hours before it is to be eaten. Garnish with parsley, and a few slices of the fat of the meat.

SALAD MAYONAISE.

717. Beat up well the yolks of two eggs, mix and pour in salad oil and a few drops of vinegar until there is sufficient sauce, and it is the consistency of thick cream. Cut slices of cold meat or fowl, and divide in pieces with cold boiled eggs and the hearts of fine lettuces laid in the dish. Then pour over it all the sauce.

SECT. 3.—RECEIPTS FOR SALAD MIXTURES.

ENGLISH SALAD MIXTURE.

718. Beat a raw egg with a salt-spoonful of salt until it is thoroughly smooth, then incorporate with it a tea-spoonful of mustard, made rather thicker than usual. When these are quite smooth, add by degrees one, two, or three table-spoonsful, or even more, of good salad oil, taking care to blend each portion of it with the egg before adding more. This ought to make any quantity, up to a tea-cupful, of a tenacious mass, so thick that a tea-spoon will stand up in it, and as smooth as honey. Dilute it with vinegar till it assumes the consistence of thick cream. No salad mixture is so smooth and rich as this, and at the same time the original oily flavour is completely lost, from the *raw egg* converting the oil into an emulsion. A little anchovy may be added if desired.

Another.—Boil an egg hard, take the yolk after it is cold, and mix it up smoothly with a litttle cream, vinegar, mustard, and salt.

Another.—Take the yolk of a hard boiled egg, rub it down with a spoonful of dry mustard, a little salt, and a floury potato well washed and boiled. Then add a spoonful of good oil, another of cream, and, when thoroughly and smoothly incorporated, add about a spoonful of vinegar.

Another.—The yolk of a raw egg, two and a half table-spoonsful of salad oil, one *flat* tea-spoonful of flour of mustard, one *flat* tea-spoonful of salt, half a tea-spoonful of brown sugar, a little cayenne pepper, one and a half table-spoonful of vinegar. The should be gradually and thoroughly mixed with the yolk o

ENDIVE.

710. Endive is used in the same way as lettuce; as also is mustard and cress, mixed with sliced radish and water-cress.

ANOTHER SALAD.

711. Add to the lettuce two beet-roots as at 655, a stick of celery cut small, radishes if in season, mustard and cress, and the white of a hard-boiled egg, of which the yolk has been used in the salad dressing. Sorrel is sometimes added.

LOBSTER SALAD.

712. Mix with some ordinary salad mixture (par. 718) the boiled eggs of a lobster; then put in a salad-bowl a layer of salad herbs, lettuce being the best; upon these strew pieces of the flesh and interior of the lobster itself, with some of the eggs; then another layer of herbs, upon which place more lobster and eggs, and upon this pour the salad dressing, taking care to run it gradually over the whole; lastly, on the top of all place a few of the best leaves of the salad, shred very fine, and round the edge place some ornamental cuttings of cucumber, radishes, &c.

713. CRABS, PRAWNS, SHRIMPS, SALMON, or any cold fish may be used in the same way as lobster (see 712).

SECT. 2.—FRENCH SALADS.

714. French salads are mixed with less care than is used by the English, inasmuch as the flavour of raw oil is not objected to by their consumers. The lettuce, endive, dandelion-leaves, or other salad-herbs, are merely chopped up and incorporated with a little tarragon, chervil, and garlic or shalot; after which a mixture of half a tea-spoonful of pepper, a whole one of salt, two table-spoonsful of vinegar, and four of oil, are simply stirred together with a fork and poured over the salad.

715. COLD MEAT, FOWL, FISH, AND GAME, mixed up with the above salad in fine shreds or slices, and flavoured in the same way, are extensively used in France.

ANOTHER FRENCH SALAD.

716. Chop three anchovies, a shalot, and some parsley small; put them into a bowl with two table-spoonsful of vinegar, one of oil, a little mustard and salt; when well mixed, add by degrees some cold

roast or boiled meat in *very thin* slices; put in a few at a time, not exceeding two or three inches long; shake them in the dressing, and then add more; but cover the bowl close, and let the salad be prepared three hours before it is to be eaten. Garnish with parsley, and a few slices of the fat of the meat.

SALAD MAYONAISE.

717. Beat up well the yolks of two eggs, mix and pour in salad oil and a few drops of vinegar until there is sufficient sauce, and it is the consistency of thick cream. Cut slices of cold meat or fowl, and divide in pieces with cold boiled eggs and the hearts of fine lettuces laid in the dish. Then pour over it all the sauce.

SECT. 3.—RECEIPTS FOR SALAD MIXTURES.

ENGLISH SALAD MIXTURE.

718. Beat a raw egg with a salt-spoonful of salt until it is thoroughly smooth, then incorporate with it a tea-spoonful of mustard, made rather thicker than usual. When these are quite smooth, add by degrees one, two, or three table-spoonsful, or even more, of good salad oil, taking care to blend each portion of it with the egg before adding more. This ought to make any quantity, up to a tea-cupful, of a tenacious mass, so thick that a tea-spoon will stand up in it, and as smooth as honey. Dilute it with vinegar till it assumes the consistence of thick cream. No salad mixture is so smooth and rich as this, and at the same time the original oily flavour is completely lost, from the *raw egg* converting the oil into an emulsion. A little anchovy may be added if desired.

Another.—Boil an egg hard, take the yolk after it is cold, and mix it up smoothly with a litttle cream, vinegar, mustard, and salt.

Another.—Take the yolk of a hard boiled egg, rub it down with a spoonful of dry mustard, a little salt, and a floury potato well washed and boiled. Then add a spoonful of good oil, another of cream, and, when thoroughly and smoothly incorporated, add about a spoonful of vinegar.

Another.—The yolk of a raw egg, two and a half table-spoonsful of salad oil, one *flat* tea-spoonful of flour of mustard, one *flat* tea-spoonful of salt, half a tea-spoonful of brown sugar, a little cayenne pepper, one and a half table-spoonful of vinegar. The oil should be gradually and thoroughly mixed with the yolk of egg then add the mustard, salt, sugar, and pepper, adding the vinegar *last;* it may be thinned by adding a very little milk.

Or, In the absence of an egg, the oil may be mixed with the mustard and salt only; but it takes a great deal of time to incorporate them properly.

719. For French salad mixture, see (716).

CHAP. XVI.—ON THE MAKING OF PASTRY.

Sect. 1.—General Remarks.

720. Under the term pastry are comprehended all savoury pies, pasties, or patties, together with fruit and other sweet pies and tarts; in fact, every thing which is confined by a paste made with flour and water, mixed also with some kind of fatty matter, such as butter, lard, suet, or dripping. For most purposes it is allowed by all cooks that butter is the best; but as it is far the dearest, it is right, in economical families, to substitute lard or dripping for it, when it is possible to do so without an entire sacrifice of all the benefit afforded by the material for which they are substituted. It will, however, be found that for many purposes they may be used without disadvantage; and as this is the case, receipts in which they are introduced will be found given n the following section; they will be recommended for use where practicable, in the subsequent list of savoury pies, tarts, &c.

721. The Utensils are only a pasteboard, rolling-pin, baking-tins or dishes, and ornamental cutters of various kinds.

Sect. 2.—Receipts for Making Pastry.

Remarks.

722. These receipts are collected together under this head, so that afterwards they may be referred to. Some of them are generally applicable, while others are only suited to one or two kinds of dishes. In all sorts of pastry it must be recollected that the *handling* is of the greatest importance, and that, however completely the proportions may be attended to, if the hand is heavy when it ought to be light, or if rolling is neglected when it is recommended, or *vice versâ*, the cook cannot expect her paste to succeed. Beyond this, the temperature of the oven is next in importance; but this the cook is more likely to

attend to than the precaution relative to the use of her hands, as its effects are more immediately apparent.

BARM CRUST.

723. Of the various kinds of paste, barm crust is the plainest, and the most easily made; but it is not very generally approved of in flavour.

724. *To Make Barm Crust very Plain.*—Mix together one pound of flour, a quarter of a pound of butter or lard, one table-spoonful of barm, and a little salt, with milk enough to make a paste. Let it stand in a moderately warm place till it rises, then roll and use as a crust, baking as quickly after as possible.

Another Barm Crust (sufficient for three Tarts).—Take one pound of flour, three ounces of butter (or an ounce and a half of clarified dripping, and an ounce and a half of lard), the white and yolk of an egg well beaten, and one table-spoonful of yeast. Warm the butter in half a pint of new milk, let it stand till only lukewarm; mix all up together, and let the leaven stand to rise. Then roll the paste, cover the pies, and put them into the oven directly. (If you suspect the barm to be bitter, blow the ashes off a red-hot coal, and put it in.)

SHORT CRUST.

725. Short crust should be made by weighing the proper quantity of flour and putting it into a basin, first taking *from the weight* sufficient to fill the flour-dredge one-third full, then add to it *all* the dripping, lard, or butter which is to be used, and work it very lightly between the thumb and fingers till it is well mixed with the flour, and has the appearance of coarse meal. This mixing must be done very lightly, or the paste will be spoiled; then add water or milk just sufficient to form it into a paste, and with the hands take it out of the basin, first dredging `a little flour on the board, then work it a little with the *fingers*, not the *heels* of the hands; roll it out three times lightly, and put it on the tart.

726. *An Economical Short Crust for Common Purposes.*—Weigh one pound of flour, and half a pound of mixed dripping and lard, or all dripping will do; mix them together with the fingers while dry, as described above, or, if the cook has a hot hand, mix it with a spoon or fork; then add just water enough to wet it and make a paste; roll it out three times. After covering the dish, wet the paste with milk, or the white of an egg, and sift crystallized or "crushed lump" sugar

Stew slowly till they are tender. Take out the cucumbers with a slice, thicken the gravy with flour or butter; give it a boil up, season with pepper and salt, and put in the cucumbers; as soon as warm they are ready to serve. The above, rubbed through a sieve, may be called "cucumber sauce," and is a favourite sauce with lamb or mutton-cutlets, stewed rump-steaks, &c.; for the latter a third part of onions may be added to the cucumbers.

SORREL.—TO STEW, FOR FRICANDEAU AND ROAST MEAT.

700. Wash the sorrel and put it into a silver vessel, or stone jar, with no more water than hangs to the leaves; simmer it as slowly as possible, and when done enough add a bit of butter and beat it well.

TO FRY HERBS, AS IN STAFFORDSHIRE.

701. Clean and dry a good quantity of spinach leaves, two large handfuls of parsley, and a handful of green onions; chop the parsley and onions, and sprinkle them among the spinach; set them all on to stew with some salt, and a bit of butter the size of a walnut; shake the pan when it begins to grow warm, and let it be closely covered over a slow stove till done enough. It is served with slices of broiled calf's liver, small rashers of bacon, and eggs fried; the last on the herbs, the others in a separate dish.

TO BOIL TURNIP TOPS.

702. Gather young turnip tops in the spring, wash and drain well, put them into plenty of boiling water, with a little salt; boil for twenty minutes, or a little longer; then take them out and serve plain after draining them, or chop them fine, and mix them with a little butter, pepper, and salt.

NETTLES AND DANDELIONS.

703. These, gathered before they are in flower, may be dressed like turnip tops, and served on toast like spinach, and are a valuable and wholesome addition to the list of vegetables.

TO DRESS TOMATOES.

704. Boil them in a saucepan of boiling water for ten minutes, drain them, and either serve whole or mashed up, with a little pepper and salt, or roast them in a Dutch oven, taking care to turn them, and serve. A little beef gravy with a shalot is an improvement to the mashed tomatoes.

Hop Tops Served as Asparagus (*excellent*).

705. Break off the young shoots of hops, tie them in bundles, boil them with a little meat in the water for twenty minutes. Serve as asparagus. The shoots of asparagus-kale may be boiled in the same way.

Green Indian Corn (*as a Vegetable*).

706. After removing the sheath and fibres from Indian corn or maize, it should be boiled for half an hour in water, and well salted. Serve as asparagus. *Or*, the corns may be taken out when done, and finished off as green peas, with a little butter in the pan.

To Crisp and Fry Parsley.

707. Wash and drain some sprigs of young parsley, and shake them in a cloth till well dry. Lay them on paper in a Dutch oven, and turn them frequently seven or eight minutes till *crisp*. If to be fried, when *quite* crisp add them to some lard or butter, which is boiling in a frying-pan. The moment they are again crisp, put them to drain on a cloth over a sieve.

Savoury Rice (*a substitute for Vegetables*).

708. Wash a breakfast-cup of rice in cold water, and strain it. Make a good beef gravy, well seasoned with one or two large onions; when properly flavoured, strain off all the grease, add the rice, and let it stew slowly for about an hour, stirring it occasionally. When in season, add two tomatoes and a spoonful of Hervey's sauce. The beef must be fried before making the gravy.

CHAP. XV.—SALADS, AND SALAD MIXTURES.

Sect 1.—Ordinary English Salads.

Lettuce.

709. A bleached lettuce well-washed, and cut up with a few slices of beet-root, is the universal salad in this country; but by some people a few very young onions or chives are added. After being cut up, a mixture variously compounded (see par. 718), is poured over and mixed with the salad-spoon and fork.

ENDIVE.

710. Endive is used in the same way as lettuce; as also is mustard and cress, mixed with sliced radish and water-cress.

ANOTHER SALAD.

711. Add to the lettuce two beet-roots as at 655, a stick of celery cut small, radishes if in season, mustard and cress, and the white of a hard-boiled egg, of which the yolk has been used in the salad dressing. Sorrel is sometimes added.

LOBSTER SALAD.

712. Mix with some ordinary salad mixture (par. 718) the boiled eggs of a lobster; then put in a salad-bowl a layer of salad herbs, lettuce being the best; upon these strew pieces of the flesh and interior of the lobster itself, with some of the eggs; then another layer of herbs, upon which place more lobster and eggs, and upon this pour the salad dressing, taking care to run it gradually over the whole; lastly, on the top of all place a few of the best leaves of the salad, shred very fine, and round the edge place some ornamental cuttings of cucumber, radishes, &c.

713. CRABS, PRAWNS, SHRIMPS, SALMON, or any cold fish may be used in the same way as lobster (see 712).

SECT. 2.—FRENCH SALADS.

714. French salads are mixed with less care than is used by the English, inasmuch as the flavour of raw oil is not objected to by their consumers. The lettuce, endive, dandelion-leaves, or other salad-herbs, are merely chopped up and incorporated with a little tarragon, chervil, and garlic or shalot; after which a mixture of half a tea-spoonful of pepper, a whole one of salt, two table-spoonsful of vinegar, and four of oil, are simply stirred together with a fork and poured over the salad.

715. COLD MEAT, FOWL, FISH, AND GAME, mixed up with the above salad in fine shreds or slices, and flavoured in the same way, are extensively used in France.

ANOTHER FRENCH SALAD.

716. Chop three anchovies, a shalot, and some parsley small; put them into a bowl with two table-spoonsful of vinegar, one of oil, a little mustard and salt; when well mixed, add by degrees some cold

roast or boiled meat in *very thin* slices; put in a few at a time, not exceeding two or three inches long; shake them in the dressing, and then add more; but cover the bowl close, and let the salad be prepared three hours before it is to be eaten. Garnish with parsley, and a few slices of the fat of the meat.

SALAD MAYONAISE.

717. Beat up well the yolks of two eggs, mix and pour in salad oil and a few drops of vinegar until there is sufficient sauce, and it is the consistency of thick cream. Cut slices of cold meat or fowl, and divide in pieces with cold boiled eggs and the hearts of fine lettuces laid in the dish. Then pour over it all the sauce.

SECT. 3.—RECEIPTS FOR SALAD MIXTURES.

ENGLISH SALAD MIXTURE.

718. Beat a raw egg with a salt-spoonful of salt until it is thoroughly smooth, then incorporate with it a tea-spoonful of mustard, made rather thicker than usual. When these are quite smooth, add by degrees one, two, or three table-spoonsful, or even more, of good salad oil, taking care to blend each portion of it with the egg before adding more. This ought to make any quantity, up to a tea-cupful, of a tenacious mass, so thick that a tea-spoon will stand up in it, and as smooth as honey. Dilute it with vinegar till it assumes the consistence of thick cream. No salad mixture is so smooth and rich as this, and at the same time the original oily flavour is completely lost, from the *raw egg* converting the oil into an emulsion. A little anchovy may be added if desired.

Another.—Boil an egg hard, take the yolk after it is cold, and mix it up smoothly with a litttle cream, vinegar, mustard, and salt.

Another.—Take the yolk of a hard boiled egg, rub it down with a spoonful of dry mustard, a little salt, and a floury potato well washed and boiled. Then add a spoonful of good oil, another of cream, and, when thoroughly and smoothly incorporated, add about a spoonful of vinegar.

Another.—The yolk of a raw egg, two and a half table-spoonsful of salad oil, one *flat* tea-spoonful of flour of mustard, one *flat* tea-spoonful of salt, half a tea-spoonful of brown sugar, a little cayenne pepper, one and a half table-spoonful of vinegar. The oil should be gradually and thoroughly mixed with the yolk of e···

of flour into the preparation while boiling; taking care, however, not to put more flour than the liquor can soak up. Stir with a wooden spoon till the paste can easily be detached from the stewpan, and then take it off the fire. Next break an egg into this paste, and mix it well; then break a second, which also mix; do not put more eggs than the paste can absorb, but you must be careful not to make this preparation too liquid. It is almost certain that about five or six eggs will be wanted for the above quantity; then form them *en choux*, by which is meant in the shape of a ball, an inch in circumference. As this paste swells very much, you must dress it accordingly, putting the choux on a baking-sheet, at an inch distant from each other, in order that they may undergo a greater effect in the oven. Brush them over as usual with the dorure or egg-wash, to which has been added a little milk. Put them into an oven moderately hot, but do not open the oven till they are quite baked, otherwise they would flatten, and all attempts to make them rise again would be found to be useless; next dry them. Sometimes they may be glazed; at other times they may be sent up without being glazed. To detach them from the baking-sheet, apply the sharp edge of a knife, and take them off gently. Then make a small opening on the side, into which put, with a teaspoon, such sweetmeats as may be thought proper, and send them up dished *en buisson*.

FRANGIPANE.

743. This is a French paste used for tartlets or entremets. It is made by moistening two ounces of flour with a little milk, and heating the two together in a saucepan; then add three or four eggs, and stir all together till cool enough to make up with the hand.

744. *Frangipane de Pomme-de-Terres.*—Cook some potatoes by steam, take off the skin, beat them well in a mortar, then put them into a basin, add some eggs, a little butter, salt, rasped citron, some bitter macaroons, sugar or not according to taste, and use it as a paste to all sorts of entremets of pastry.

ICING AND GLAZE FOR TARTS OR PUFFS.

745. Beat the white of an egg, mix with it three or four ounces of finely-sifted sugar till it becomes white and glutinous; then when the tarts, &c., are ready, take them out of the oven, brush them over with this glaze, and return them for a few minutes to harden, taking care that it does not become brown.

Or, for common purposes, beat the yolk of an egg and some melted butter well together, wash the tarts with a feather, and sift sugar over as they are put in the oven.

746. To GLAZE savoury pies and pasties, if they are required *to* look well, brush over the crust with the yolk of egg well beaten, before putting them in the oven.

CHAP. XVII.—SAVOURY PIES AND PUDDINGS, PATTIES, AND VOL-AU-VENTS.

SECT. 1.—GENERAL REMARKS.

747. There are few articles of cookery more generally liked than savoury pies, if properly made; and they may be made so of a great variety of things. Some are best eaten when cold, and in that case there should be no suet put into any forcemeat that is used with them. If the pie is either made of meat that will take more dressing, to make it extremely tender, than the baking of the crust will allow, or if it is to be served in an earthen pie-dish, the meat, if beef, must be pre-viously stewed. The crusts used will be specified in each case, refer-ence being made to the paragraph in the last chapter.

SECT. 2.—MEAT, GAME, AND FISH PIES.

BEEF, MUTTON, OR LAMB PIE.

748. Take three pounds of the veiny piece of beef that has fat and lean, or of the chops from a loin or neck of mutton; wash it and season it with salt, pepper, mace, and allspice, in fine powder, rubbing them well in, adding a very little onion or shalot, chopped, and, if approved, a few pickled mushrooms. Set it by the side of a slow fire in a stewpot that will just hold it; put to it a piece of butter, about two ounces, and cover it quite close; let it just simmer in its own steam till it commences to shrink. When it is cold, add more seasoning, forcemeat, and boiled eggs; and, if it is in a dish, put some gravy to it before baking; but, if it is only in crust, do not put the gravy till after it is cold and in jelly. Cover with con

short crust, or puff paste (see pars. 725 and 732). Forcemeat may be put both under and over the meat, if preferred to balls.

BEEF-STEAK PIE.

749. Prepare the steaks by cutting into long strips, and when seasoned as above, and rolled with fat in each, put them in a dish with paste round the edges : put a little water or gravy in the dish, and cover it with a good short crust or puff paste (see pars. 725 and 732), which must be pressed down upon that part round the edge. A few oysters mixed with the beef are a great improvement, adding their liquor to the water or gravy.

VEAL PIE.

750. Take some slices of a knuckle of veal ; lay them at the bottom of a pie-dish, with alternate layers of ham or bacon ; season between each layer with pepper, salt, and portions of hard-boiled eggs, cut in slices, between the meat. Fill up the dish in this way, then pour in some gravy made from the bones, with a little mushroom ketchup, and a very small quantity of Worcestershire sauce ; cover with short crust, or good puff paste, and bake.

751. *A Richer Veal Pie.*—Cut steaks from a knuckle of veal ; season them with pepper, salt, nutmeg, and a very little clove in powder. Slice two sweetbreads, and season them in the same manner. Lay a puff paste on the ledge of the dish ; then put the meat, yolks of hard eggs, the sweetbreads, and some oysters, up to the top of the dish. Lay over the whole some very thin slices of ham, and half fill the dish with stock made from the bones ; cover, and when it is taken out of the oven, pour in at the top, through a funnel, a few spoonsful of good veal gravy, and some cream to fill up ; but first boil it up with a tea-spoonful of flour.

VEAL, OR CHICKEN, AND PARSLEY PIE.

752. Cut some slices from the leg or neck of veal ; if the leg, from about the knuckle. Season them with salt ; scald some parsley that is picked from the stems, and squeeze it dry ; cut it a little, and lay it at the bottom of the dish ; then put the meat, and so on, in layers. Fill the dish with good stock, or gravy, seasoned, but not so high as to touch the crust. Cover it with short-crust or puff-paste (pars. 725 and 732), and bake. Chicken may be cut up skinned, and made in the same way.

CHICKEN, ROOK, OR RABBIT PIE.

753. Cut up two young fowls; season with white pepper, salt, a little mace, and nutmeg, all in the finest powder, and also a little cayenne. Put the chicken, slices of ham, or fresh gammon of bacon, forcemeat balls, and hard eggs by turns, in layers. If it is to be baked in a dish, put a little water; but none if in a raised crust. By the time it returns from the oven, have ready a gravy made of the knuckle of veal, or from a bit of the scrag with some shank-bones of mutton, seasoned with herbs, onions, mace, and white pepper; put as much gravy as will fill the pie-dish; but if made with a raised crust the gravy must be put in cold as jelly, clarifying it with the whites of two eggs after taking away the meat, and straining it through a fine lawn sieve. When *rabbits* are used instead of chicken, the legs must be cut short, and the ribs must not go in, but will help to make the gravy. *Rooks* must be skinned and put to soak in milk, taking care to remove the liver and back. They are then treated like the chicken described above. The crust should be of puff-paste (see par. 732).

FRENCH CHICKEN PIE.

754. Parboil a couple of chickens, put the giblets in a small sauce-pan, and stew with water from the chickens or gravy, add sweet herbs and mace; when the chickens are cold, cut them up and lay them in a deep dish, line with puff-paste, pound some ham and tongue with the liver, and the yolks of six hard boiled eggs, make this forcemeat into balls and put among the chickens; add butter rolled in flour. Cover the pie with puff-paste and bake; mushrooms chopped fine are an improvement, also a little cream.

GREEN-GOOSE PIE.

755. Bone two young green-geese of a good size, but first take away every plug, and singe them nicely; wash them clean, and season them high with salt, pepper, mace, and allspice; put one inside the other; and press them as close as you can, drawing the legs inwards; put a good deal of butter over them, and bake them either with or without crust; if the latter, a cover to the dish must fit close to keep in the steam. It will keep long. Put on a short crust or puff paste (see pars. 725 and 732).

GIBLET PIE.

756. After very nicely cleaning geese or duck giblets, stew

with a small quantity of water, onion, black pepper, and a bunch of sweet herbs, till nearly done; let them grow cold, and, if not enough to fill the dish, lay a beef, veal, or two or three mutton steaks at bottom; put the liquor of the stew in the dish with the above, and cover with short crust or puff paste (see pars. 725 and 732). When the pie is baked, pour into it a large tea-cupful of cream. Sliced potatoes added to it eat extremely well, and some people add to it slices of apple.

DUCK PIE.

757. Cut off the wings and neck of a duck, boil it a quarter of an hour, cut it up while hot, save the gravy that runs from it; then take the giblets, add anchovies, a little butter, a blade of mace, six black peppercorns, two onions, a bit of toasted bread, a bunch of herbs, and a little cayenne pepper. Stew them till the butter is melted, then add half a pint of boiling water, and let them stew till the giblets are tender; then strain it, and put the giblets into the pie. Let the gravy stand till cold, skim off the fat, and put it with what runs from the duck at the bottom of the dish; then put in the duck, well seasoned with pepper and salt and a few lumps of butter, and cover with short crust or puff paste (see pars. 725 and 732). If geese are used instead of ducks, they must be boiled half an hour. Cold duck will do as well, if the skin is taken off.

PIGEON PIE.

758. Rub the pigeons with pepper and salt, inside and out; in the former put a bit of butter, and, if approved, some parsley chopped with the livers, and a little of the same seasoning. Lay a beef-steak at the bottom of the dish, and the birds cut in half on it; between every two, a hard egg. Put a cup of water in the dish; and, if there is any ham in the house, lay a bit on each pigeon; it is a great improvement to the flavour. Season the gizzards and two joints of the wings, and put them in the centre of the pie; and over them, in a hole made in the crust, three feet nicely cleaned, to show what pie it is. Cover with puff paste (see par. 732).

PHEASANT, PARTRIDGE, OR GROUSE PIE IN A DISH.

759. Pick and singe two pheasants, or four partridges or grouse; cut off the legs at the knee; season with pepper, salt, chopped parsley, thyme, and mushrooms. Lay a veal-steak and a slice of ham at the

bottom of the dish; put the partridges in, and half a pint of good broth. Put puff paste on the ledge of the dish, and cover with the same; brush it over with egg, and bake an hour; or place them in a raised crust according to the directions given at par. 735.

To Make a Hare Pie.

760. Take the flesh off the bones in as large pieces as you can; fry it over a slow fire in some butter, two shalots, and a bay leaf, for ten minutes. When it is cold, line the bottom of the pie with forcemeat; season the hare with pepper and salt, lay it in the dish as close as possible, and pour over it the butter in which it was fried; cover it with thin slices of fat bacon. When baked, take off the lid and serve with or without jelly. The forcemeat is made of half a pound of lean beef, the same of suet, with shalots, a handful of bread-crumb, and three eggs to bind it, season well with pepper and salt; if the liver of the hare is good, it will add greatly to the thickness of it.

Venison Pasty.

761. A shoulder boned makes a good pasty; but it must be beaten and seasoned, and the want of fat supplied by that of a fine well-hung loin of mutton, steeped twenty-four hours in equal parts of rape, vinegar, and port. The shoulder being sinewy, it will be of advantage to rub it well with sugar for two or three days; and, when to be used, wipe it perfectly clean from it and the wine.

762. *To Prepare Venison for Pasty.*—Take the bones out, then season and beat the meat; lay it into a stone jar in large pieces, pour upon it some plain drawn-beef gravy, but not a strong one; lay the bones on the top, then set the jar in a *bain-marie*, or a saucepan of water over the fire, simmer three or four hours, then leave it in a cold place till next day. Remove the cake of fat, lay the meat in handsome pieces on the dish; if not sufficiently seasoned, add more pepper, salt, or pimento, as necessary. Put some of the gravy, and keep the remainder for the time of serving. If the venison be thus prepared, it will not require so much time to bake, or such a very thick crust as is usual, and by which the under part is seldom done through. A mistake used to prevail, that venison could not be baked too much; but, as above directed, three or four hours in a slow oven will be quite sufficient to make it tender, and the flavour will be preserved. Either in a shoulder or side, the meat must be cut in pieces, and laid with fat between, that it may be proportioned to each person without

P

breaking up the pasty to find it. Lay some pepper and salt at the bottom of the dish, and some butter; then the meat nicely packed, that it may be sufficiently done, but not to lie hollow, or it will harden at the edges. The venison bones should be boiled with some fine old mutton; of this gravy put half a pint cold into the dish, then lay butter on the venison, and cover as well as line the sides of the dish with a thick crust of puff paste, but do not put one under the meat. Keep the remainder of the gravy till the pasty comes from the oven; put it into the middle by a funnel, quite hot, and shake the dish to mix well. It should be seasoned with pepper and salt.

MOCK VENISON PASTY.

763. Stew an ox-cheek for an hour and a half in some good stock; add vegetables and herbs; when quite tender remove the meat from the bones of the cheek, and cut it in slices. Line a dish with puff paste down the sides, and lay the slices in the dish, then strain the gravy and again put it in the stewpan, flavouring it with ketchup and half a tea-cupful of port wine. Pour it over the cheek, cover with paste, and bake. Should the meat be stewed in weak broth or water, some good gravy must be added to it afterwards. If carefully made, it is little inferior to a real venison pasty.

CALF'S HEAD PIE.

764. Well soak half a calf's head, and boil half an hour, the tongue longer; then cut the meat in pieces; stew the bones with a little mace, white pepper, or any thing that will make it good without colouring the liquor; place at the bottom of the dish some parsley, ham, tongue, and pieces of boiled egg; then put some slices of the brains, which should be boiled rather hard; add salt, and about two spoonsful of water, and cover with short crust. The liquor the bones are boiled in should be reduced till it is strong and of a nice flavour; strain it, and while the pie is hot pour as much in as the dish will hold; let it stand all night, and when wanted turn it out upside down, with parsley round.

765. *A Plainer Calf's Head Pie.*—Boil a calf's head one hour; when perfectly cold cut it in slices; have prepared some gravy, made from two pounds of beef; let it stand till cold; well mix some salt, pepper, mace, and Cayenne, then put some at the bottom of the pie-dish, then a layer of calf's head, then the cold gravy, then the spice,

and so fill up the dish with alternate layers, the last at the top being the tongue sliced; then cover with a good paste.

EGG AND BACON PIE TO EAT COLD.

766. Steep a few thin slices of bacon all night in water, lay them in a pie dish; beat eight eggs with a pint of cream, add pepper and salt, and pour it on the bacon; cover it with a crust, and bake in a moderate oven the day before you require it.

POTATO PIE.

767. Skin some potatoes, cut them into slices, and season them; also some mutton, beef, pork, or veal. Put layers of them and of the meat. Cover with short crust.

Another.—Put hashed veal or meat of any kind into a pie-dish with a good gravy, seasoned with pepper and salt; over this add a layer of mashed potatoes, and brown it in the oven.

A HERB PIE.

768. Take lettuce, leeks, spinach, beet, and parsley, of each a handful; give them a boil, chop them small, and have ready boiled one quart of groats with two or three onions in them; put them in a pan with the herbs and a good deal of salt, one quarter to three quarters of a pound of butter, and a few apples sliced thin; stew them a few minutes; fill either a dish or raised crust with the above; one hour will bake it. If to be a cheap dish, dripping in a small quantity must be substituted for the butter.

VEGETABLE PIE.

769. Lay steaks of mutton or lamb *very well* seasoned at the bottom of a deep pie-dish, pile the dish high with cos lettuce cut as for salad, a little onion chopped fine, a good handful of peas, scatter seasoning over the whole, cover with a crust and bake it.

For Fish Pies see the Chapter on Fish.

SECT. 3.—RAISED PIES.

770. DIRECTIONS.—Raise the crust as ordered at page 201, then fill with meat according to the annexed receipts, and cover; serve cold.

EXCELLENT PORK PIES TO EAT COLD.

771. Raise a crust, according to directions given at page 201, into

VEAL PATTIES.

776. Mince some veal that is not quite done with a little parsley, lemon-peel, a scrape of nutmeg, and a bit of salt; add a little cream and gravy, just to moisten the meat; and, if there is any ham, scrape a little and add to it. Do not warm it till the patties are baked.

TURKEY PATTIES.

777. Mince some of the white meat, and with grated lemon, nutmeg, salt, a very little white pepper, cream, and a very little butter warmed, fill the patties.

For lobster and oyster patties, see pages 72-73.

VOL-AU-VENTS.

778. A Vol-au-Vent is a raised pie, made with very light and rich *puff paste* (pars. 733 or 734), instead of that used for the raised pie, or it may be considered as an enlarged and highly-ornamented patty. There is considerable art in making and baking these cases, as they are put into the oven without their contents, and then filled with them afterwards. The paste is made to line a fluted dish or tin, and baked till it is of a fine light brown; but few cooks can understand how to make it without actual demonstration. *Turbot* and *salmon* are employed for this dish, dressed up with cream, and come to table a second time even with more approbation than in their original form.

SECT. 5.—SAVOURY PUDDINGS.

STEAK OR KIDNEY PUDDING.

779. If kidney, split and soak it, and season it with pepper and salt, which last·is all that the steak will require; make a paste of suet, flour, and milk (see par. 738); roll it, and line a basin with some; put the kidney or steaks in, cover with paste, and pinch round the edge; tie it up in a cloth, and boil a considerable time—that is, three or four hours.

BEEF-STEAK PUDDING.

780. Prepare some fine steaks as for beef-steak pie; roll them with fat between, and if shred onion is approved add a very little; lay a paste of suet, flour, and milk in a basin (see par. 738), and put in the rolls of steaks; cover the basin with a paste, and pinch the edges to

keep the gravy in; cover with a cloth tied close, and let the pudding boil slowly, but for a length of time—say for four hours.

BAKED BEEF-STEAK PUDDING (*Toad-in-a-hole*).

781. Make a batter of milk, two eggs, and flour; lay a little of it at the bottom of the dish; then put in the steaks prepared as above, and very well seasoned; pour the remainder of the batter over them, and bake it.

MUTTON PUDDING.

782. Season with pepper, salt, and a bit of onion; lay one layer of steaks at the bottom of the dish, and pour a batter of potatoes boiled and pressed through a colander, and mixed with milk and an egg, over them; then put in the rest of the steaks and batter; and bake it. Batter with flour instead of potatoes eats well, but requires more egg, without which it is not so good.

783. *Another.*—Cut slices off a leg that has been underdone, and put them into a basin lined with a fine suet crust (par. 738); season with pepper, salt, and finely-shred onion or shalot, then cover, and boil.

VENISON PUDDING.

784. Take steaks of fresh venison, season with salt and pepper, put into a pot with a little fresh butter, and stew in scarcely sufficient water to keep them from scorching; when quite tender, cut the meat from the bones, and set it to cool. Save the gravy, and, when cold, carefully remove all the fat; prepare a paste, three-quarters of a pound of beef suet to two pounds of flour. Roll it out thick, put the venison in it, and pour over gravy to moisten it; close over the paste to form a dumpling, tie in a pudding-cloth, and boil an hour, turning several times; when done, dip into cold water, untie the cloth, and turn out the pudding.

Beef-steak pudding may be made as above.

SUET PUDDING.

785. Shred a pound of suet; mix with a pound and a quarter of flour two eggs beaten separately, a little salt, and as little milk as will make it; boil four hours. It eats well next day, cut in slices and broiled. The outward fat of loins or necks of mutton, finely shred, makes a more delicate pudding than suet.

LARK PUDDING.

786. Lark pudding is an old-fashioned delicacy, and made with about six larks mixed with steak (see 780), and covered with paste as there directed.

SPARROW DUMPLING.

787. Mix half a pint of good milk with three eggs, a little salt, and as much flour as will make it a thick batter. Put a lump of butter rolled in pepper and salt into every sparrow, mix them in the batter, and tie them in a basin with a cloth; boil them half an hour. Serve with melted butter poured over.

POTATO PUDDING WITH MEAT.

788. Boil them till fit to mash, rub through a colander, and make into a thick batter with milk and two eggs; lay some seasoned steaks in a dish, then some batter, and over the last layer put the remainder of the batter; bake a fine brown.

YORKSHIRE PUDDING.

789. Mix five spoonsful of flour and a quart of milk and four eggs well beaten; butter a shallow pan, and bake under the meat; when quite brown, turn the other side upwards and brown that. It should be made in a square pan, and cut into pieces to come to table. It is a good plan to set it over a chafing-dish at first, and stir it some minutes.

PEAS PUDDING.

790. Peas-pudding is made as follows:—Soak split peas for twelve hours in soft water, then tie them in a cloth, but not too tightly, or they will not have room to swell; boil them from three hours and a half to four hours, then take them out and rub them through a hair sieve, adding afterwards a little butter and salt; return them to the cloth, boil again for half an hour, and serve.

CHAP. XVIII.—SWEET PASTRY.

SECT. 1.—GENERAL REMARKS.

791. Barm crust, short crust, and puff-paste, are all used for these

articles by some people; the first kind being employed for the sake of the stomach, the second from economical motives when composed of dripping or lard, and the third by those who consult only their palates, without attending to the interests of their bodies or purses. Under the head of sweet pastry are included all kinds of fruits, whether fresh or preserved, which have any kind of baked crust attached to them; whereas those which either have no crust, or when they have it are boiled instead of being baked, are usually denominated either puddings or sweets. The former definition will, therefore, comprehend all the articles included in this section. With regard to the use of lard, dripping, or butter for the paste used with them, there can be no doubt that butter, either fresh or salt, is the best for the purpose; and for puff-paste is not to be superseded, except perhaps by a very small quantity of lard mixed with it; but for short crust, lard or dripping, or a mixture of the two, will answer well enough for many purposes—such as fruit tarts; and the crust so made is quite as wholesome, and very nearly as good, as when made of butter. (For icing these tarts, see page 204).

SECT. 2.—FRUIT TARTS.

792. In using preserved fruits, it should be known that they are injured by the degree of baking required for the crust; those that have been done with their full proportion of sugar need no baking; and the crust should be baked in a tin shape, and the fruit afterwards added; or it may be put into a small dish or tart-pan, and the covers may then be baked on a tin cut out according to taste, and put in the fruit when ready. Bottled fruits must be treated like fresh fruit.

ORDINARY APPLE TART.

793. Pare, quarter, and core the apples, and fill a pie-dish up; put over them a heaped table-spoonful of sugar, with a little grated lemon-peel, or two cloves, or a little nutmeg. If the apples are mellow, add a table-spoonful of water; then put on a short crust of puff-paste, and bake nearly an hour. Or, wipe the outside of the apples, then pare, quarter, and core them, using the peel and the cores to boil with a little water till it tastes well; strain, and add a little sugar, and a bit of bruised cinnamon or cloves, whichever is preferred, and simmer again. In the mean time, place the apples in a dish, a paste being put round the edge; when one layer is in sprinkle on them half the sugar

and some shred lemon-peel, and squeeze in some lemon juice, or a glass of cider if the apples have lost their freshness; then put in the rest of the apples, sugar, and the liquor that has been boiled. Cover with either of the plain pastes (see pages 200-1). Some add quince-marmalade, or orange-paste, to the apples as an improvement. Apples should never be cut smaller than in quarters, or they do not become tender in baking; nor should they be long exposed to the air after peeling, as they put on a dark colour, and the surface becomes hard.

CODLIN TART.

794. Scald the codlins as is directed under that head; when ready, take off the thin skin, and lay them whole in a dish; put a little of the water the apples were boiled in at bottom, strew them over with lump sugar or fine Lisbon; when cold, put any of the previously-described pastes round the edges and over the tart, or bake a crust in an empty tin or dish, and lift the lid; cut it in quarters, without touching the paste on the edge of the dish, and make the points stand up, or remove the lid altogether to introduce the fruit. Pour a good custard over it when cold, and sift sugar over. *Or*, line the bottom of a shallow dish with paste, lay the apples in it, sweeten, and lay little twists of paste over in bars.

MIXED APPLE AND ORANGE TART.

795. Pare two Seville or China oranges thin, boil the peel till tender, and shred it fine; pare, quarter, and core ten apples; put them in a stewpan with as little water as possible; when half done, add half a pound of sugar, the orange-peel, and juice; boil till pretty thick. When cold, put it in a shallow dish with paste round, or patty pans lined with paste, to turn out, and be eaten cold.

RHUBARB TART.

796. Cut the stalks in lengths of one or two inches, having, if old, taken off the thin skin. Lay them in a dish, and put over a table-spoonful of sugar, then cover with short-crust or puff-paste (see pages 200-1), and bake for half-an-hour to three-quarters. Some add a little grated nutmeg.

GREEN GOOSEBERRY, GREEN CURRANT, RIPE CURRANT, RASPBERRY, RASPBERRY AND CURRANT, AND BLACK CURRANT TARTS.

797. These are all made by placing the respective fruits in a pie-dish,

with about two large table-spoonsful of brown sugar to a small pie-dish, and two or three table-spoonsful of water; then cover with any of the pastes described before, and bake.

GREEN APRICOT TART

798. Should be made by stewing the green apricots till tender, either in a jar placed in an oven or in a stewpan, with a little water and sugar, then putting in a pie-dish. Cover with paste, and bake.

RIPE PLUMS OF ALL KINDS,

799. Including greengages, egg-plums, damsons, bullaces, &c., are made into tarts just in the same way as described under par. 797.

RASPBERRY TART WITH CREAM.

800. Roll out some thin puff paste, and lay it in a patty-pan of what size you choose. Put in raspberries, strew over them fine sugar, cover with a thin lid, and then bake. Cut it open, and have ready the following mixture warm:—Half a pint of cream, the yolks of two or three eggs well beaten, and a little sugar; and, when this is added to the tart, return it to the oven for five or six minutes.

ORANGE TART.

801. Squeeze, pulp, and boil two Seville oranges till tender, weigh them, and add double the weight of sugar; beat both together to a paste, and then add the juice and pulp of the fruit, and the size of a walnut of fresh butter, and beat all together. Choose a very shallow dish, line it with paste, fill it with the fruit, and cover or cross with bars, according as it is desired to be an open or closed tart.

Another.—Line a tart-pan with thin puff paste, put into it orange-marmalade that is made with apple-jelly, and lay across it twisted bars of paste. Bake, and serve when cold.

BLACKBERRY AND CRANBERRY TARTS

802. Are made as for currant (see 797); the former is much improved by the addition of half the quantity of apples, and a little cider or lemon-juice.

BARBERRY TART

803. Is excellent when made with fresh fruit, or with its preserve. For the former strip the berries from the stalks, and add half their

weight of sugar, or rather more if not quite ripe, laying the sugar and fruit in alternate layers, and pouring in water, as for currants, adding any crust which may be approved of, either open or closed. When the preserved barberries are used, the crust must be first half-baked in an open form, then add the preserve, and finish the baking.

SECT 3.—TARTLETS, CHEESECAKES, &c.

804. Tartlets of any of the ordinary preserves are made in small patty-pans of any shape, by lining them with puff-paste, and half-baking them, then filling with the preserve, and finishing the baking.

MINCE PIES.

805. Mince pies are made in small patty-pans, which are lined with puff-paste, and, after putting in some mince-meat, covering them over with more paste, and baking.

806. *To Make the Mince-meat.*—Take three pounds of suet finely chopped and sifted, two pounds of currants, three pounds of raisins, and one pound of apples, all chopped very small, three pounds of moist sugar, three-quarters of a pint of red and white wine mixed, a glass of brandy, the peel of two small lemons, the juice of one, two ounces of candied peel, cut; mix all together with a quarter of an ounce of cinnamon, a quarter of an ounce of mace, and one small nutmeg, all finely powdered. Keep it in a close covered jar, and, if kept a twelve-month, it may require the addition of a little more wine.

Another Receipt.—Take two pounds of suet, chopped very fine and sifted, two pounds of currants, one pound of sun raisins, two pounds of apples, half a pound of bread, one pound and a quarter of moist sugar, three-quarters of a pint of red and white wine, mixed, a glass of brandy, the peel of two small lemons and the juice of one, four ounces of candied orange-peel, cut; mix all together with cinnamon, mace, nutmeg, and salt, to the taste. If preferred, leave out two ounces of bread and put in two biscuits.

LEMON MINCE PIES.

807. Squeeze the juice of six lemons, boil the rinds, pulp, and kernels together, in three or four waters, till the bitterness is gone, and they are quite tender; beat it fine in a mortar, and when cold add to it two pounds of currants, one pound of raisins stoned and chopped, two pounds of sugar, and two pounds of suet; mix all together, and

pour in the lemon juice, with a glass of brandy and whatever dried fruits may be liked.

Another.—Take a large lemon, strain out the juice and boil the rind and pulp till tender, beat it smooth in a mortar, and put to it one pound of currants, half a pound of beef suet, half a pound of moist sugar, the juice of the lemon, a glass of wine and one of brandy: if the lemons are not very large, put two to one pound of fruit.

To Make Cheesecakes.

808. Strain the whey from the curd of two quarts of milk; when rather dry, crumble it through a coarse sieve, and mix with six ounces of fresh butter, one ounce of pounded blanched almonds, a little orange-flower water, half a glass of raisin wine, a grated biscuit, four ounces of currants, some nutmeg and cinnamon in fine powder, and beat all the above with three eggs and half a pint of cream till quite light; then line the patty-pans with puff-paste, and fill them three parts full.

Another.—Turn a curd with three quarts of milk, tie it in a strainer, and when dry rub it through a colander with two ounces of butter and a tea-cup of cream; add five ounces of currants, five eggs, the rind of a lemon grated, four spoonsful of brandy, and good moist sugar. A piece of rennet one inch square, soaked in water twelve hours, will be enough; put it warm to the milk, and put that by the fire; if you buy the liquid rennet use one tea-spoonful to each quart.

Another.—Mix the curd of three quarts of milk, a pound of currants, twelve ounces of Lisbon sugar, a quarter of an ounce each of cinnamon and nutmeg, the peel of one lemon chopped so fine that it becomes a paste, the yolks of eight and whites of six eggs, a pint of thin scalded cream, and a glass of brandy; put a light puff-paste in the patty-pans, and three parts fill them.

Lemon Cheesecakes.

809. Mix four ounces of sifted lump sugar with four of butter, and gently melt them; then add the yolks of two and the white of one egg, the rinds of three lemons shred fine, and the juice of one and a half, with one Savoy biscuit, some blanched almonds pounded, and three spoonsful of brandy; mix well; put in puff-paste.

Another will keep Twelve Months.—To every quarter of a pound of butter put a pound of loaf-sugar broken small, six eggs, leaving out two whites, the rind of two lemons grated, and juice of three.

Put all into a pan, simmer till the whole is dissolved, and it is as thick as honey. When cold, put it into a jar and tie it down for use; half a pound of butter makes a good-sized jar. Should it accidentally mould at the top, it will be perfectly good underneath.

ORANGE CHEESECAKES.

810. Blanch half a pound of almonds, beat them very fine with orange-water, and mix with half a pound of fine sugar beaten and sifted, a pound of butter that has been melted carefully without oiling, and which must be nearly cold before it is used; then beat the yolks of ten and whites of four eggs: pound two candied oranges, and a fresh one with the bitterness boiled out, in a mortar till as tender as marmalade, without any lumps; and beat the whole together and put into patty-pans, lined with puff-paste.

Another.—Boil the peel of two Seville oranges in water till they are tender and the bitterness is gone, pound them in a mortar. Then add a quarter of a pound of sponge biscuits grated, a quarter of a pound of butter; pound again and mix well with eight eggs, half the whites, and one pint of cream scalded. Sweeten to your taste.

POTATO CHEESECAKES.

811. Boil six ounces of potatoes, and four ounces of lemon peel; beat the latter in a marble mortar with four ounces of sugar; then add the potatoes, beaten, and four ounces of butter melted in a little cream. When well mixed, let it stand to grow cold. Put puff-paste in patty-pans, and rather more than half fill them. Bake in a quick oven half an hour, sifting some double-refined sugar on them when going to the oven. This quantity will make a dozen.

APPLE CHEESECAKES.

812. Take three-quarters of a pound of apples, scald and pulp them, half a pound of lump sugar, half a pound of butter melted, eight yolks and four whites of eggs, the grated peel and juice of two lemons; bake in patty-pans lined with a good paste.

ALMOND CHEESECAKES.

813. Take two ounces of sweet almonds blanched and pounded, the yolks of four eggs and the whites of two, a quarter of a pound of butter melted, a quarter of a pound of sugar, a little wine and brandy,

and the rind of half a lemon finely pounded. Put in patty-pans, lined with puff-paste.

DEVONSHIRE CHEESECAKES.

814. Boil one large carrot till tender, rub it through a sieve, and mix well with it two *small* table-spoonsful of flour, half a pound of currants, one egg well beaten, a tea-spoonful of milk, a quarter of a pound of sugar, and a little nutmeg. Then line the patty-pans with pastry, fill them with the mixture, and bake.

LITTLE COCKADES GARNISHED.

815. Spread some puff paste, made according to Ude's receipt (par. 742), about a quarter of an inch thick; cut it with a large fluted round cutter, the same as for patties; cut a hole in the middle with a small plain round cutter, then, as quickly as possible, with the finger turn the paste so as to put the inside on the baking dish, and the outside above; put them at a great distance from each other on the baking dish, as the paste spreads sideways instead of rising; bake in a hot oven, and glaze of a good colour. When done, they represent the exact form of a cockade. Garnish with fillets of sweetmeat, to represent the plaits of the cockade.

APRICOT CAKES TRELLISED.

816. Spread some puff paste (see par. 732) (trimmings will do for these cakes); spread it equally on a large buttered baking-sheet with the rolling-pin. Spread some apricot marmalade over the paste equally, then cut some more paste long and narrow, roll it about the size of strong cord, and arrange it crossways like a trellis over the marmalade; put down over the bars lightly; and lastly, bake it in a moderate oven. When done, cut them into small oblong squares, and dress them on the dish, one above the other.

PUFFS.

817. These are usually made with puff paste (par. 732), which is turned over upon the contents, pressed together at the edges, and baked without any tin or shape.

APPLE PUFFS.

818. Pare the fruit, and either stew them in a *bain-marie* or in a stone jar on a hot plate, or bake them; when cold, mix the pulp of

the apple with sugar and lemon-peel shred fine, taking as little of the apple-juice as possible; bake in thin paste, in a quick oven; a quarter of an hour will do when small. Orange or quince marmalade is a great improvement.

LEMON PUFFS.

819. Beat and sift a pound and a quarter of double-refined sugar; grate the rind of two large lemons, and mix it well with the sugar; then beat the whites of three new-laid eggs a great while, add them to the sugar and peel, and beat it for an hour; make it up in any shape you please, and bake it on paper put on tin plates in a moderate oven. Do not remove the paper till cold. Oiling the paper will make it come off with ease.

SECT. 4.—SWEET SANDWICHES, AND CRISP PASTRY.
SWEET SANDWICHES.

820. The weight of two eggs in butter, sugar, and flour; beat the butter to a cream, the eggs should also be well beaten by themselves, mix all together, spread on a flat tin, and bake in a moderate oven. (They should be watched, as they are apt to burn). When taken out of the oven, they must be cut immediately into the shape required; as, when cold, they break into pieces. Before serving them, spread a layer of preserves, such as strawberry, raspberry, or plum; lay on this a second piece of the pastry, as for meat sandwiches, and trim the edges neatly.

CRISP PASTRY.

821. Take five fresh eggs, with their weight in powdered sugar, one table-spoonful of flour, and the juice of half a lemon. *Beat* all, *not whisk*, these ingredients well together in a stewpan with an iron spoon, warm it a little over the fire, taking care not to make it too hot, or the pastry will be too thin. Drop it on buttered tins in small quantities, and bake a fine brown. Turn them in the shape of a sugar-loaf, and dry them in the sun on a wire sieve. They should be kept in a dry place; and, just before being sent to table, fill them with coloured jellies or creams. This pastry should be made as thin as possible. These proportions are enough for several times.

CHAPTER XIX.—PUDDINGS AND PUDDING SAUCES.

SECT. 1.—GENERAL REMARKS.

822. Puddings may be either boiled or baked, and they are made in such a variety of ways as almost to be beyond the reach of definition. When boiled, they are generally tied up in a cloth.· The outside of a boiled pudding often tastes disagreeably, from the cloth not being nicely washed, and kept in a dry place. It should be dipped in boiling water, squeezed dry, and floured when to be used. If the pudding is of bread, it should be tied loosely; if of batter, tightly over the basin. The water should boil quick when the pudding is put in; and it should be moved about for a minute, lest the ingredients should not be mixed at the moment of setting. Batter-pudding should be strained through a coarse sieve when all is mixed; in others, the eggs are strained separately. The pans and basins must be buttered, to prevent the paste sticking to them; which is also avoided by having a pan of cold water ready, and dipping the pudding in as soon as it comes out of the pot. Very good puddings may be made *without* eggs: but they must have as little milk as will mix them, and boil three or four hours. A few spoonsful of any kind of *bottled* malt liquor, or of *fresh* small beer, or one of yeast, will answer instead of eggs. *Or, snow* is a tolerable substitute for eggs, either in puddings or pancakes. Two large spoonsful will supply the place of one egg, and the article it is used in will be nearly equally good. This is a useful piece of information, especially as snow often falls when eggs are dearest. It may be taken up from any clean spot some hours before it is wanted, and will not lose its virtue until it melts, though the sooner it is used the better. In using eggs, the yolks and whites should be beaten separately, by which the articles they are put into are made much lighter.

823. PLAIN FRUIT PUDDINGS are, most of them, made either with the suet crust (par. 738), lining a basin and covering the fruit, which is then tied up in a cloth, or with the same crust, using butter instead of the suet, but not adding more than six ounces to the pound of flour.

SECT. 2.—PUDDING.

APPLE PUDDING.

824. Is made by lining a basin with the above paste, and filling it with pared, quartered, and cored apples, adding two table-spoonsful

of sugar, covering it with the paste, and then boiling it from one to two hours, according to the size of the pudding and the ripeness of the apples. It is a bad plan to cut the apples up into small pieces, as the exposure to the air renders the cut surface hard and tough.

GOOSEBERRY AND CURRANT PUDDINGS, &c.

825. All other fresh fruit puddings, such as gooseberry, currant, raspberry, &c., are made in the same way as that given for apples (see par. 824).

RASPBERRY PUDDING.

826. Half fill a deep dish with ripe raspberries mashed with sugar, beat six eggs light, and mix them with one pint of milk, sugar, and grated nutmeg. Pour this over the raspberries, bake half an hour in a moderate oven, serve as cold as possible.   .

BAKED APPLE PUDDING.

827. Pare and quarter four large apples; boil them tender, with the rind of a lemon, in so little water that, when done, none may remain; beat them quite fine in a mortar, and add the crumb of a small roll, four ounces of butter melted, the yolks of five and whites of three eggs, juice of half a lemon, and sugar to taste; mix all together, and lay it in a dish with paste to turn out, leaving a hole at the bottom of the size of a sixpence, so that the juice may exude through it, and give a rich flavour to the paste. This makes it doubly delicious.

828. THE OTHER FRUITS mentioned at par. 825 may be used as described at par. 827, and baked in the same way.

A LIGHT BREAD AND APPLE PUDDING.

829. Line a basin with slices of bread, then a layer of sugar; fill it with apples pared and quartered, and lay a slice of bread over them. Tie a cloth over the basin, and boil about one hour and a half.

BAKED RIPE GOOSEBERRY PUDDING.

830. Stew one and a half pound of ripe red gooseberries in a jar, put in the oven or a saucepan of water until they will pulp, take a pint of the juice, press it through a coarse sieve, mix it with three eggs well beaten, and one ounce and a half of butter, then sweeten and bake in a dish lined with a thin paste. A few crumbs of roll, or four

ounces of Naples biscuits, should be mixed with the above to make it firm.

DELICIOUS FRUIT PUDDING.

831. Mix two and a half pounds of red currants and raspberries with one and a quarter pound of raw sugar, then fill a pudding-dish with sliced bread (without crust), and layers of the fruit alternately, leaving a thick layer of the fruit at the top. Bake it in the bachelor's oven for nearly an hour before it is served, and serve it in the same dish, which may be improved in appearance by a knitted cover tied over the edges.

RICE AND FRUIT (*baked*).

832. Wash a sufficient quantity of rice; put a little water to it, and set it in the oven till it is absorbed; then put in a little milk, work it well with a spoon, set it in the oven again, and keep working it from time to time till it is sufficiently soft. A little cream worked in it at the last is an improvement. Fill a pie-dish nearly full of fruit, sweeten it, and lay on the rice unevenly by spoonsful. Bake it till the rice is of a light brown colour.

RICE PUDDING WITH FRUIT.

833. Swell the rice with a very little milk over the fire; then mix fruit of any kind with it (currants, gooseberries, scalded, pared, and quartered apples, raisins, or black currants); with one egg in the rice to bind it; boil it well, and serve with sugar.

BATTER PUDDING WITH FRUIT.

834. This is made by mixing green gooseberries or black currants with batter, and boiling as for batter pudding (which see).

OATMEAL PUDDING.

835. Pour a quart of boiling milk over a pint of the best *fine* oatmeal; let it soak all night; next day beat two eggs, and mix a little salt; butter a basin that will just hold it; cover it tight with a floured cloth, and boil it an hour and a half. Eat it with cold butter and salt. When cold, slice and toast it, and eat it as oatcake buttered.

PREPARED BARLEY PUDDING.

836. Mix four table-spoonfuls of barley with sufficient cold milk to

form a paste, pour on it one quart of scalding milk, then add a small slice of butter and four eggs well beaten; flavour with nutmeg, lemon-peel, bitter almonds, and sugar. Be careful to stir the barley well while pouring on it the boiling milk, and not to put in the eggs till the mixture is cold. The eggs must also be well mixed in. Bake one and a half hour in a slow oven.

Another.—Pour boiling water upon two ounces of pearl barley the evening before; next morning put it into a saucepan with a quart of milk, and a small piece of butter, and some moist sugar. Let it simmer over the fire five or six hours, then put it into a pie-dish and brown it before the fire for a quarter of an hour. It should be nearly as thick as custard, but *not solid.*

GOOD BATTER PUDDING.

837. To one pint of new milk add three eggs, four spoonsful of flour, and some slices of candied peel with the sugar on it; serve with wine sauce, and bake in cups, or boil.

A BATTER PUDDING WITHOUT EGGS.

838. One pint of milk. Mix three spoonsful of flour with a little of the milk first, half a teaspoonful of salt, one teaspoonful of powdered ginger, and one teaspoonful of tincture of saffron. Mix all together and boil an hour—fruit may be added.

HASTY PUDDING.

839. Boil a pint of milk, then whilst boiling stir into it as much flour as will thicken it, generally about a table-spoonful. Serve hot, with cold butter and sugar, or, if preferred, the best treacle.

840. HASTY PUDDING BAKED.—Stir half a pound of flour into a pint of cold milk, and boil it, then take five eggs, and three quarters of an ounce of bitter almonds blanched and pounded, and add them to the hasty pudding when cold. Sweeten with sugar. Bake in cups, and serve with wine sauce.

PLAIN RICE PUDDING.

841. Wash and pick some Carolina rice; throw among it some pimento finely pounded, but not much; tie the rice in a cloth, and leave plenty of room for it to swell. Boil it in a quantity of water for an hour or two. When done, eat it with butter and sugar, or milk

Put lemon-peel, if approved. Many people prefer it without spice, and eat it with salt and butter alone. An egg is an improvement.

Another plain but good boiled Rice Pudding.—Two ounces of Carolina rice boiled in one pint of milk, a few bread crumbs and currants, two eggs, and a little nutmeg and brown sugar well mixed together. Boil it in a basin three quarters of an hour. Serve with wine sauce.

COMMON BAKED RICE PUDDING.

842. Put half a teacupful of rice in a dish, with a pint of skim or new milk, a little sugar, and nutmeg or lemon-peel to be added, with, if preferred, a small slice of butter or dripping, or a few pieces of suet put on the top. Bake slowly, and stir it occasionally at first, to prevent the rice from burning to the bottom. If required to turn out, the dish must be buttered. An egg is a great improvement to this pudding; and, if it is liked in a milky condition, less rice must be used.

Another Baked Rice Pudding (richer).—Boil about two table-spoonsful of rice in water till just soft; then pour away the water and add a pint of new milk, a little nutmeg, lemon-peel, and sugar; then boil again, and, when just off the boil, add the yolk and whites of nearly three eggs; bake and serve with sugar sifted over it.

CURRANT RICE PUDDING.

843. Put half a pound of rice in a saucepan with a quart of milk. Dredge half a pound of Zante currants with flour, and stir them gradually in. Add four ounces of lump sugar rubbed on lemon, with the juice, and two ounces of butter in bits. When the rice is well swollen, mix with it gradually six or eight yolks of eggs well beaten; transfer it to a deep china dish, and put it in the oven for half an hour; sift powdered sugar on the top, and brown with a salamander. These quantities make a very large pudding.

A GROUND RICE PUDDING.

844. Add to one pint of milk four eggs well beaten, and one and a half table-spoonful of ground rice; boil these together, stirring them. Pour the mixture while hot over two ounces of butter, sugar to the taste, and add the grated rind with the juice of a middle-sized lemon. Line the dish with puff paste before putting in the mixture, and bake.

845. *A Plain Ground Rice Pudding* may be made with a fourth part of the eggs and butter given above, or any other proportion of them, and without paste or lemon.

TAPIOCA PUDDING.

846. Soak two table-spoonsful of tapioca in a quart of cold milk for four hours, mix with it two eggs well beaten, two ounces of sugar, and a little grated lemon-peel; let it boil, stirring it all the time to prevent the eggs from turning the milk. Bake it in a dish for half an hour; one egg is enough for common purposes.

SAGO PUDDING.

847. Put three ounces of sago to soak in cold water for half an hour, then pour off the water, and stir the sago by degrees into a pint of milk boiling hot in a saucepan; let it boil ten minutes. Stir it till quite cool. Beat an egg well, mix it with a little cold milk, one ounce of sugar, and a little grated lemon-peel. Mix all well together, and bake in a slow oven an hour and a quarter.

848. *Boiled Sago Pudding:* one and a half ounce of sago to a little more than a pint of milk; boil it together with a stick of cinnamon: grate four sponge biscuits or the same quantity of bread crumbs, pour the sago and milk hot upon it, and let it stand covered till cool. Beat five eggs, leaving out half the whites. Beat all together with a little sugar and white wine, and put it in a buttered basin; a little less than an hour will boil it. Serve with wine sauce. This pudding may be baked, if preferred, in a dish lined with puff paste or not, according to fancy.

SEMOLINA PUDDING.

849. Add two ounces of semolina, previously soaked in a little cold milk for half an hour, to a pint of boiling milk, in the same way as for sago pudding, and add the egg and lemon-peel also, as in that pudding (which see at par. 847).

ARROWROOT PUDDING.

850. Mix an ounce and a half of West Indian arrowroot with a little cold water into a thin smooth paste; while doing this, boil a pint of milk gently with a little cinnamon and sugar; when boiling, pour it into a basin through a strainer upon the arrowroot, stirring it carefully; as soon as this becomes cool, beat three eggs and add them, stirring them well in. Then boil in a basin, or bake in a dish with a crust on the edge. From half an hour to three quarters is sufficient. One egg is enough for a plain pudding.

CUSTARD PUDDING.

851. Mix by degrees a pint of good milk with a large spoonful of flour, and some sugar to the taste: boil them together for ten minutes, then add the yolks of five eggs, and a little pounded cinnamon. Butter a basin that will exactly hold it, pour the batter in, and tie a floured cloth over. Put it in boiling-water over the fire, and turn it about for a few minutes, to prevent the eggs going to one side. Half an hour will boil it. Put currant jelly on it, and serve with sweet sauce.

852. *Another plainer Custard Pudding.*—One pint of new milk poured boiling upon three spoonsful of flour; beat them up together, then add three eggs, and boil an hour.

853. *Rich baked Custard Pudding.*—Add four eggs well beaten to a quart of milk, nutmeg and sugar to taste, line the dish partly, and edge it with paste before pouring in the custard.

854. *Little Custard Puddings.*—Three eggs, three spoonsful of flour, a gill of milk, a little salt, sugar, and nutmeg. Bake in teacups, and serve immediately.

BREAD-AND-BUTTER PUDDING.

855. Slice bread thin, spread it with butter, cut it in rather small pieces, and lay it in a dish with currants or any preserve between the layers. Pour over it a slightly-boiled custard made of milk, with one egg, a little sugar, and lemon-peel; let it soak two hours at least before it is to be baked, and lade the custard over to soak the bread. This is very good made without either currants or preserve.

856. *An excellent Bread and Butter Pudding.* Boil four laurel and two bay leaves in half a pint of milk, pour it over three and a half ounces of bread grated fine, three ounces of loaf sugar and three ounces of butter, stir till well mixed; when cold, add two eggs and a glass of white wine, with a grate of nutmeg and a little lemon-peel; beat it before you put it in the oven, and bake half an hour.

BOILED BREAD PUDDING.

857. Grate white bread; pour boiling milk over it, and cover close. When soaked an hour or two, beat it fine, and mix with it two or three eggs well beaten. Put it into a basin that will just hold it; tie a floured cloth over it, and put it into boiling water. Send it up with melted butter poured over. It may be eaten with salt or sugar.

Another and Richer.—On half a pint of crumbs of bread pour half a pint of scalding milk; cover for an hour. Beat up four eggs, and, when strained, add to the bread a tea-spoonful of flour, an ounce of butter, two ounces of sugar, half a pound of currants, an ounce of almonds beaten with orange-flower water, half an ounce of orange peel, and the same of lemon and citron. Butter a basin that will exactly hold it, flour the cloth, tie tight over, and boil one hour.

858. *Brown Bread Pudding.*—Mix half a pound of brown bread, crumbled, with four ounces of suet, four ounces of moist sugar, four eggs, half a pound of currants, half a pint of milk, and a little brandy. It must boil an hour and a half.

BAKED BREAD PUDDING, PLAIN BUT EXCELLENT.

859. Slice the bread, and pour over boiling new milk enough to cover it; let it stand together to soak twenty minutes. Then add three (or two) eggs, well beaten; a little lemon-peel, loaf sugar, and a squeeze of lemon to make it lighter. Beat for twenty minutes, or half an hour if time allows, before baking. Sift loaf sugar over it when turned out to send to table.

LITTLE BREAD PUDDINGS.

860. Steep the crumbs of a penny loaf grated in about a pint of warm milk; when soaked, beat six eggs, whites and yolks, and mix with the bread, and two ounces of butter warmed, sugar, orange-flower water, a spoonful of brandy, a little nutmeg, and a teacupful of cream. Beat all well, and bake in teacups buttered. If currants are chosen, a quarter of a pound is sufficient; if not, they are good without; or you may put orange or lemon candy. Serve up with pudding-sauce.

BREAD AND RICE PUDDING.

861. Steep a quarter of a pound of rice in new milk till quite soft, and cover it over till cold; then soak about two ounces of white bread; drain it from the milk, and add it to the rice; beat it well with two or three eggs, a little sugar and nutmeg, and boil for an hour. *Or*, if you bake it, put a little butter or suet on the top.

MACARONI PUDDING.

862. Boil a teacupful of macaroni in a quart of milk till tender; then beat well two eggs, yolks and whites separately; stir all together, sugar and spice to the taste, and bake.

863. *A Rich Macaroni Pudding.*—A quarter of a pound of ma-

caroni is to be boiled in a pint of milk for half an hour; then turn it into a dish, and mix with it three eggs, two table-spoonsful of loaf sugar, a little nutmeg, and a few pounded almonds or lemon-peel; butter the mould well, and boil or steam it one hour. Serve it up with wine sauce.

864. *Very Rich Macaroni Pudding.*—Boil a quarter of a pound of macaroni in a pint of milk, with some bitter almonds and cinnamon stick, till tender; then remove the flavourings, and stir in, while hot, a quarter of a pound of butter, a quarter of a pound of sifted sugar, and a pint and a half of cream; mix, and beat hard; and stir in gradually four well-beaten eggs; when it has cooled, add nutmeg and brandy, and bake it. Vermicelli and ground rice may be made in the same manner.

ROLLY-POLLY PUDDING.

865. This well-known pudding is made by rolling out a thin layer of suet or butter paste, as for puddings, upon which either a preserve or dried currants are spread evenly, leaving an inch bare at the edges all round, except on that next the cook, and then the whole is rolled up into a long pudding, closed at the ends by pinching the paste, and enveloped in the same way in a cloth, which is tied with a string at each end, and boiled about one hour.

CHILDREN'S PUDDING.

866. Mix three-quarters of a pound of flour, a quarter of a pound of treacle, half a pound of suet, half a pound of currants, and a little milk, and boil three hours.

SUET PUDDING,

867. If intended to be eaten with sugar or preserve, is made in the same way as for savoury dishes (see par. 785).

PLUM PUDDING.

868. Mix together a quarter of a pound of bread-crumbs, the same of treacle, currants, and suet, and a little nutmeg. Put in a basin or shape, and boil three hours.

869. *Common Plum Pudding.*—Soak nine ounces of white bread in milk from six to twelve hours, squeeze very dry, add to it half a pound of raisins when stoned, four ounces of suet chopped fine, three eggs, three ounces of sugar, a little nutmeg; butter a mould, put it in, and boil three hours. Serve with wine sauce.

870. *Plum Pudding without Eggs.*—Mix together half a pound of bread, four ounces of suet, four ounces of treacle or sugar, a dessert-spoonful of honey-water, and half a pound of currants, with a little milk. Boil it three or four hours.

871. *A Plain Plum Pudding.*—Well mix a large breakfast-cupful of bread-crumbs, the same quantity of flour, the same of finely-chopped beef suet, two eggs well beaten, a cupful of sugar, a little ginger, grated nutmeg and candied peel, a quarter of a pound of currants, half a pound of raisins, two spoonsful of treacle made warm in a little milk. Boil it four hours.

Another Plain Plum Pudding.—Mix a pound of grated bread, half a pound of currants when cleaned, half a pound of raisins when stoned, half a pound of suet, two ounces of candied peel, four eggs, some sugar, a glass of wine or brandy, a little nutmeg, and a teacupful of milk ; put it in a basin, and boil it four hours.

872. *A Richer Plum Pudding.*—Mix together one pound each of plums, currants, moist sugar, suet, and bread-crumbs, four ounces of flour, and four eggs well beaten ; add mixed spice and candied peel to the taste, with a spoonful of brandy and sherry. Boil four hours.

873. *A Rich Plum Pudding.*—Mix together half a pound of grated bread, half a pound of beef suet chopped fine, half a pound of currants, half a pound of apples chopped fine, seven yolks of eggs well beaten, two or three spoonsful of brandy and a little sherry ; sugar and salt to the taste. Let it boil four hours at least. The sauce should be red wine, sugar, and butter.

874. *A very Rich and Excellent Plum Pudding.*—Beat eight eggs and mix them with a pint of good cream, half a pound of flour, and half a pound of crumb of bread ; beat them well together, and put to them one pound of beef suet chopped very fine, one pound of currants, one pound of jar raisins stoned and chopped small, one pound of powdered sugar, two ounces of candied orange-peel, and the same of citron. Grate a nutmeg, and mix all well together with half a pint of brandy and wine ; put it in a cloth, and tie it up close. It will take six hours to boil.

875. *Mock Plum Pudding.*—Add to half a pound of flour half a pound of treacle, and half a pound of suet. Mix them together, and boil for six hours.

876. *Baked Plum Pudding.*—Take half a pound of suet chopped fine, eight or ten ounces of plums stoned and cut in halves, half a pound of bread-crumbs scalded with half a pint of boiling milk ; add

two or three well-beaten eggs, a quarter of a pound of moist sugar, and a little lemon peel or nutmeg. Mix, and bake full an hour and a half in a slow oven. Turn it out of the pie-dish, and serve either cold or hot.

Fig Pudding.

877. Add to one quarter of a pound of grated bread crumbs five and a half ounces of finely chopped suet, and about six ounces of moist sugar, then beat two eggs and put them to the above, adding just enough of cold milk to make the pudding of a proper consistency. Boil it full four hours, and, if approved, it may be served with wine sauce.

Swiss Pudding.

878. Butter a pie-dish, and put into it a layer of bread crumbs, then a layer of sliced apples, sprinkle over moist sugar, then a layer of bread-crumbs, next of apples and sugar, and so on till the dish is filled, finishing with a thick layer of crumbs; melt fresh butter and pour over it. Grate in a little nutmeg, and bake an hour: any fresh fruit may be substituted for the apples.

Snowdon Pudding.

879. Mix together a breakfast-cupful each of chopped suet, crumbs of bread, and sifted sugar; add two eggs and a glass of wine, and the juice and rind of a lemon. Line the basin or mould with raisins, and boil it five hours.

880. *A Richer Snowdon Pudding.*—Take half a pound of bread crumbs, two ounces of sago, half a pound of suet chopped very fine, six eggs, half a glass of brandy, six ounces of orange or lemon marmalade, six ounces of moist sugar. Mix all well together, butter a mould, and ornament with swelled raisins; boil for one hour, and serve with marmalade sauce.

Pembroke Pudding.

881. Mix together two ounces of suet shred fine, two ounces of bread crumbs, two eggs, two spoonsful of sugar and a pint of milk, a little flavouring of spice or lemon-peel improves it; bake it half an hour.

Poor Knight's Pudding.

882. Cut a roll into thin slices with the crust on it, mix up two eggs

with a pint of milk; sugar and nutmeg to the taste. Let the slices soak in this custard for an hour, then pour off, and drain another hour; fry them till they are of a nice brown, and serve with wine sauce.

St. Agnes Pudding.

883. Mix together ten ounces of grated bread, half a pound of suet, half a pound of moist sugar, the rind and juice of a large lemon, and one egg. It takes a long time to mix; a little brandy is a great improvement, and a few currants may be added. Boil it nearly an hour.

Lemonade Pudding a cool Summer Dish.

884. Make a sufficient quantity of lemonade in the usual way, adding the juice of a Seville orange to every pint; when cold, soak in it thoroughly a French roll or rolls, but do not break them, then stick in their surface blanched almonds, pour over them liquefied currant jelly, and serve.

White Pot.

885. Mix three pints of milk, half a pint of spring water, five eggs well beaten, three ounces of butter, a French roll sliced, white sugar and nutmeg to the taste. Bake it in a bowl two hours in a quick oven.

Carrot Pudding.

886. Boil some carrots till they are quite soft; when cold, beat half a pound in a mortar with six ounces of butter; when these are well mixed beat in six ounces of sugar, two eggs (do not beat them first), half a nutmeg, a little brandy, and one spoonful of cream; mix these well together in a dish lined with paste, and put it in just before baking. An hour will bake it.

Another Carrot Pudding.—Weigh eight ounces of carrots; when boiled chop very fine, and mix with six ounces of currants, four ounces of flour, two ounces of suet chopped, six ounces of sugar, and half a nutmeg grated. Then stir in two eggs, and a table-spoonful of milk. This sized pudding requires two hours' boiling. To be served up with a sauce made with brandy, sugar, and butter, with the yolk of a raw egg beaten in it.

Another.—Mix half a pound of raw carrots grated finely, half a pound of suet, half a pound of flour, half a pound of currants, a quarter of a pound of raisins, two table-spoonsful of sugar, and a wine-glassful of sherry. Boil the whole in a cloth for three hours: if desired plainer, the currants and suet may be reduced half, and the wine omitted.

VEGETABLE PUDDING.

887. Half a pound of grated carrots, half a pound of cold mashed potatoes, half a pound of flour, half a pound of suet, half a pound of sugar, four ounces of candied lemon-peel, one quarter of a pound of currants, to be boiled slowly four hours.

POTATO PUDDING.

888. Take a pound of fine mealy potatoes, boil them till very dry and floury, and mash them till perfectly smooth, taking care to avoid destroying their light texture by too heavy a pressure; then mix with them, while hot, four ounces of butter, five and a half of sugar, five or six eggs, a very little salt, and a liberal allowance of grated lemon-peel. Pour these ingredients into a well-buttered dish, and bake the pudding in a moderate oven for about forty minutes. It should be turned out, and served with a layer of sifted sugar over it, or preserve round it. *Or*, it may be boiled, omitting the butter. When cold, this pudding eats like cake, and may be served as such.

Another.—Mash together three-quarters of a pound of potatoes when boiled and peeled, two ounces of powdered sugar, a quarter of a pound of suet or butter (if butter, beat it with the potatoes), and stir in two spoonsful of rose water, then stir in the sugar with nine eggs well beaten, one spoonful of flour, a little mace, a pint of cream or good milk, and a little salt. Put a paste round the dish, and, if you like, a thin paste at the bottom; three-quarters of an hour in a quick oven will bake it, or without paste it may be turned out, and served with preserves round, or sifted sugar over it.

Another.—To half a pound of potatoes, when boiled and mashed through a sieve, add six ounces of butter and six ounces of sifted sugar, while hot; when cold, add four eggs and the rind and juice of a lemon. Put a light paste round the dish and bake it.

LEMON PUDDING.

889. Mix together a quarter of a pound each of butter, loaf-sugar, and a quarter of a pint of milk; put altogether into a saucepan till dissolved, but it should not boil; when rather cool add three eggs

well beaten, the rind of a large lemon grated, and a little juice; line the dish with a thin paste, and bake.

A richer Lemon Pudding.—Boil the peel of a lemon in two waters, then beat it fine in a stone mortar; add half a pound of loaf sugar, half a pound of butter, a sponge biscuit or a few bread crumbs, and six eggs well beaten; mix all well together, add two table-spoonsful of brandy and a little lemon juice, and bake it in a dish lined with a puff paste.

LEMON APPLE PUDDING.

890. Take two or four small apples, boil them to a pulp in a little water; add the peel of one lemon cut fine, the juice of half a one, the yolks of four eggs, a large spoonful of brandy, and two ounces of butter melted; sweeten to the taste. Line a dish with puff paste, and fill with the mixture; then bake it. These proportions are for a rich pudding. For a common one omit the brandy, use one or two eggs and one ounce of butter, and add rather more lemon juice.

LEMON BREAD PUDDING.

891. Mix three ounces of bread grated, three ounces of loaf sugar, three ounces of butter, and the rind of a lemon grated; boil three-quarters of a pint of milk, and pour over it; when cold, add three eggs well beaten, and the juice of one lemon; put paste round the dish, pour in the above ingredients, and bake.

BOILED LEMON PUDDING.

892. Take half a pound of bread crumbs, half a pound of sifted sugar, the grated rind and juice of three small lemons, a quarter of a pound of butter, and six beaten eggs; stir the butter with half the sugar till light, then stir in two table-spoonsful of flour: add the butter and sugar by degrees to the bread crumbs, mix the remaining sugar with the lemon juice, and add gradually to the rest; boil in a cloth or in a mould with a hole in the centre, which can be filled with a sauce of beaten butter and sugar flavoured with lemon.

SIX-HOUR PUDDING.

893. Mix together one pound of suet cut large as dice, three-quarters of a pound of raisins when stoned, six ounces each of flour and moist sugar, the rind of a lemon grated, the yolks of four eggs and whites of two; butter the mould and boil six hours; serve with brandy-sauce.

CABINET PUDDING.

894. Stone two dozen of large table raisins, butter a basin and stick them all over it, then fill up the basin with a thick custard made of milk, three or four eggs, about a tea-cupful of finely-grated bread, two table-spoonsful of sugar, a few chopped almonds, and any other flavour that is approved. Boil an hour and a half, and when turned out the raisins will be outside.

LIGHT-BOILED PUDDING.

895. Boil a pint of new milk with two bay and three laurel leaves; take out the leaves, and pour the milk, when cold, over five ounces of bread-crumbs, a quarter of a pound of loaf-sugar, and one ounce of butter; add three eggs well beaten and a glass of sherry; butter a mould, and stick it round with raisins or not. Boil one hour.

APPLE CHARLOTTE.

896. Boil four large apples, beat them to a pulp and sweeten them with loaf sugar, add one egg and the rind of a lemon grated; pour this into a dish which has been well buttered and lined with bread crumbs, cover the top with crumbs, and bake it a light brown.

BISCUIT PUDDING.

897. Pour one pint of boiling milk on three penny Naples biscuits grated, cover it close; when cold, stir in the yolks of four and the whites of two eggs, a little brandy, half a spoonful of flour, and some sugar. Boil this an hour in a basin, and serve it with pudding-sauce; some almonds may be blanched and cut in four, and stuck over the pudding.

Another.—Weigh two eggs, and take equal weight of flour and sugar, and a quarter of a pound of butter beaten to a cream; add the two eggs beaten, and mix well. This is sufficient for six small cups filled three parts full, bake them in a slow oven twenty minutes. Serve with wine sauce.

WAFER PUDDINGS.

898. Two ounces of butter, the yolks of four eggs, two table-spoonsful of flour and a little milk, whisk the whites to a froth, bake them in patty-pans. Serve them piled on a napkin with sifted sugar.

LEAMINGTON PUDDING.

899. Mix of each, two ounces of flour, sugar powdered, and butter

melted, with three eggs, leaving out one white, and half a pint of cream. Bake it half an' hour, and serve with hot wine sauce. It should be baked in three separate oval tins an inch in depth, and placed one upon the other in the dish, the smallest being at the top. The largest tin should be eight and a quarter inches by five and a quarter, and the others, each rather more than the eighth of an inch smaller than the other.

CHELTENHAM PUDDING.

900. Mix three-quarters of a pound of flour, half a pound of suet chopped very fine, half a pound of currants, two or three eggs, two or three ounces of sugar, half a pint of milk, or enough to make the pudding thicker than batter, but thinner than dough; mix the dry ingredients first, beat the eggs and milk together, then mix all. Bake an hour and a quarter, or half.

FRENCH APPLE PUDDING.

901. Bake some apples with sugar until they become a marmalade; put them into a pie-dish already lined with puff-paste, make a custard with half a pint of milk and two eggs flavoured with butter and sweet almonds, and pour it on the apples. Bake in a slow oven.

MANCHESTER PUDDING.

902. A pint of new milk boiled, three ounces of bread crumbs stewed in the boiling milk, and the grated rind of a lemon, are to be sweetened to the taste with lump sugar; then add the yolks and whites of four eggs, and three ounces of butter melted. Line a dish with a puff-paste, cover the bottom with preserve or marmalade, pour the pudding into it, and one hour will bake it.

CHESTER PUDDING.

903. Take a stewpan, and oil two ounces of butter; blanch twelve bitter and twelve sweet almonds, pound them in a mortar; take four ounces of powdered loaf sugar, the yolks of four eggs well beaten, the rind of a large lemon grated, and the juice. Put all these ingredients into the butter in the stewpan, and stir constantly till quite hot. Then put it into a dish lined with pastry, and bake it half an hour. Beat the whites of the eggs till perfectly stiff, put them upon the top of the pudding, and put it in the oven till it is set, and is of a light-brown colour.

FRENCH PUDDING.

904. Take half a pound of flour, half a pound of suet chopped fine, half a pound of currants, a quarter of a pound of treacle, and half a pint of milk; mix well, and boil in a basin three or four hours.

MARLBOROUGH PUDDING.

905. Put two ounces of candied-peel, shred fine, at the bottom of a dish, add six ounces of lump sugar pounded, six ounces of butter melted over the fire, with six yolks of eggs, taking care not to let the eggs boil, or they will curdle. Pour this hot over the peel. Line the dish with paste, and bake half an hour, or more, *till it is solid.* It requires a hot oven just at first, and then a rather slower heat.

SELKIRK PUDDINGS.

906. Weigh three eggs in their shells, add the same weight for each of lump sugar, butter, and fine flour; beat up the eggs, whites and yolks together, for a quarter of an hour; pound the sugar fine and sift it; place the butter before the fire, and, when a little warmed, beat it to a froth with a wooden spoon; then mix the eggs and butter well together, after which add the flour and then the sugar. Bake in a mould, leaving room for its rising. It should be sent to table with melted butter and brandy.

THORPE PUDDING.

907. Put a layer of preserves at the bottom of a pie-dish, and over it grated bread-crumbs three-quarters of an inch thick, pour over them a custard; bake in rather a cool oven twenty-five minutes. One quart of milk and four eggs makes custard enough for a good-sized pudding.

KENDAL PUDDING.

908. Line a dish with puff paste, put into it a layer of preserves an inch thick, consisting of two or three sorts of jam. Cover the top with two eggs well beaten, mixed with milk and sugar; pour over until the dish is full. Strew over lemon-peel chopped fine, and a little sifted sugar. Bake in a slow oven a nice brown.

ESSEX PUDDING.

909. Weigh three eggs, an equal weight of butter, flour, and pounded sugar; melt the butter and beat the eggs to a froth, add the

flour after the other ingredients are mixed. Put alternately a layer of this batter and one of preserves into a mould until full, then bake it for an hour and a half; turn out, and serve with white wine sauce.

BATH PUDDING.

910. Boil four ounces of ground rice in one pint of cream till tender, and set it to cool. Add to it six yolks and two whites of eggs well beaten, with six ounces of pounded sugar, six ounces of butter, thirty sweet almonds blanched and pounded, and one small glass of brandy. Mix all the ingredients well together, and bake a quarter of an hour or more.

BAKEWELL PUDDING.

911. Cover a dish with thin paste. Put a layer of jam of any kind, half an inch thick. Take the yolks of five eggs, and the white of one, rather less than one pound of sugar, and four ounces of butter melted, and a few well-pounded almonds. Beat all together until it is well mixed. Pour it into the dish, and bake it in a moderate oven for an hour. They may be baked in pattypans to eat cold.

Another, less rich.—The yolks of four eggs, whites of two well beaten, a quarter of a pound of melted butter, two ounces of almonds, sugar to taste, two potatoes boiled, dried, and mashed fine. Line a shallow dish with puff paste, put a layer of jam (strawberry is the best), and pour the batter upon it. Bake it well.

ORANGE MARMALADE PUDDING.

912. Take two table-spoonsful of marmalade, three ounces of butter melted, and one ounce of sugar. Beat this well together in a mortar. Add the yolks of five eggs and the whites of two, and put it in a dish, immediately after which place it in the oven. Three-quarters of an hour will bake it.

RATAFIA PUDDING.

913. Soak two sponge-cakes as for trifle, put over them one or two kinds of preserves, beat the yolks of four eggs, and the white of one; add three-quarters of a pint of new milk and a little nutmeg, sweeten and flavour it; pour it upon the cakes in the dish, place two ounces of ratafias on the top, and bake a quarter of an hour.

Another.—Boil a quart of cream with four laurel leaves; take them out, and break in half a pound of Naples biscuits, the same of butter,

R

some sherry and nutmeg, and a little salt. Take it off the fire, cover it up; when it is almost cold, put in two ounces of blanched almonds grated fine, and the yolks of five eggs. Mix all well together, and bake half an hour. Grate a bit of sugar over the pudding.

COLLEGE PUDDINGS.

914. Grate the crumb of a twopenny loaf, shred eight ounces of suet, and mix with eight ounces of currants, one of citron minced fine, one of orange, a handful of sugar, half a nutmeg, three eggs beaten, yolk and white separately, and a glass of brandy. Mix, and make into the size and shape of a goose-egg. Put half a pound of butter into a frying-pan, and, when melted and quite hot, fry them gently in it over a stove; turn them two or three times till of a fine light brown. Serve with pudding sauce.

COLLEGE PUFFS.

915. Take half a pint of thin cream, three eggs, whites and yolks, one tablespoonful of flour, some nutmeg, and the peel of one lemon grated. Sweeten to your taste. Put it in small teacups; bake it three-quarters of an hour. Serve it up with sweet sauce.

A POUND PUDDING.

916. Beat half a pound of fresh butter with the same quantity of loaf-sugar till it is like cream, then add six eggs, all well beaten separately, half a pound of flour, and flavour it with lemon-peel or candied peel. After the ingredients are all mixed, beat the whole for ten minutes; then put them into small tins and bake them.

LITTLE SPONGE-CAKE PUDDINGS.

917. Mix three eggs, leaving out one white, three ounces of powdered lump sugar, three ounces or spoonsful of flour, three ounces of butter beaten. Add the eggs and then the flour, then the sugar, beating each before adding the other. Bake about a quarter of an hour in *little* cups, putting in the oven as soon as beaten; lay a little orange marma-lade on them when baked.

Another.—Beat the whites of two and the yolks of four eggs, and into that beat six ounces of sugar sifted, and four ounces of flour dried for a few minutes, till well mixed. Put a spoonful into a cup buttered (rather more for a pudding), and bake in a quick oven. This quantity will make ten or twelve cakes. Wine sauce with the puddings.

RICH TEACUP PUDDINGS.

918. Scald five ounces of crumbs of bread in milk, and add six ounces of suet chopped very fine, eight ounces of currants, seven eggs, leaving out two whites, three table-spoonsful of brandy, a little nutmeg, salt, lemon, and candied-peel and sugar to the taste. Bake in teacups, and serve with wine sauce.

LITTLE CITRON PUDDINGS.

919. Take half a pint of cream, one spoonful of fine flour, two ounces of sugar, a little nutmeg; mix it well together with the yolks of three eggs, put it in teacups (five are enough), and stick in it two ounces of citron cut very thin. Bake in a pretty quick oven.

MADEIRA PUDDINGS.

920. Take three eggs, weigh against them in their shell sugar, flour, and butter, separately; beat the butter to a cream, beat the eggs well, mix, and beat together, adding the sugar; then put into cups, and bake in a quick oven. Serve with wine sauce poured over them.

PRUSSIA PUFFS.

921. Make a light batter, and put in some candied orange-peel. Bake in cups, and serve with wine sauce.

SPANISH PUFFS.

922. Take a large breakfast-cup of milk with a small piece of butter; let it come to a boil, but, before it boils up, mix in flour with the left hand, while stirring as quickly as possible with the right, till nearly as thick as dough. Take it off the fire, and drop in three yolks of eggs, mixing one thoroughly before adding another. Then turn it out into a plate, and take a small piece off with the end of a spoon. Fry it in lard, of a nice brown. Sprinkle with sugar and serve in a napkin.

LIGHT GERMAN PUFFS OR PUDDINGS.

923. Melt three ounces of butter in one pint of cream, and let it stand till nearly cold; then mix with it two ounces of fine flour, two ounces of sugar, four yolks and two whites of eggs, and a little rose or orange-flower water. Butter some little cups, pour in the ingredients, and bake for half an hour. They should be taken out of the

cups and served the moment they are done, or they will be heavy; serve with white wine and sugar.

OXFORD PUDDINGS.

924. Take half a pound of suet chopped fine, grate two penny loaves and half a pound of currants, the yolks of six eggs, a quarter of a pound of lump sugar, a little nutmeg, one ounce of candied lemon-peel, and a glass of sherry or brandy; mix this all together till it is stiff, divide into seven or eight parts and fry, or in balls, a light brown; serve with wine sauce.

BALLOON PUDDING.

925. Add three table-spoonsful of flour to five eggs, mix them with a pint of new milk, in which put a small lump of butter; warm the milk sufficiently to melt the butter. Butter some teacups, and fill them half full. Bake a quarter of an hour; serve with wine sauce.

CUP RICE PUDDINGS.

926. Steep a teacupful of rice in rather less than a quart of milk, add four eggs beaten, two ounces of butter, a quarter of a pound of currants, sugar to the taste, grated lemon-peel, and nutmeg; a little cream is a great improvement. Bake in cups, and serve with wine sauce.

EVERTON PUDDING (SMALL.)

927. Take three eggs and their weight in sugar, pounded and sifted, the same weight of flour and butter, and half a lemon. Put altogether, excepting the eggs, and beat them twenty minutes. The eggs must also be well beaten, then added to the other ingredients, and the whole well beaten. Bake in cups half an hour in a cool oven.

SOUFFLÉ PUDDING.

928. *Baked.*—Take eight rusks or buns, and soak them thoroughly in a pint of milk. Make a custard of eight beaten eggs and a pint and a half of milk, stir in a quarter of a pound of sifted sugar, and flavour with vanilla or almond, or rub the sugar on lemons before sifting. Beat and stir the rusk to a smooth mass, and add the custard by degrees, stirring well. Bake in a brisk oven rather more than ten minutes, and serve with sifted sugar over it. The yeast in the rusk will cause it to puff up light.

929. *Soufflé Pudding Boiled.*—Three table-spoonfuls of flour, a quarter of a pound of sifted sugar, two ounces of butter, half a pint of milk; stir altogether over the fire till quite thick; then mix the yolks of six eggs with the batter, and, the last thing before boiling, add three of the whites whisked to a strong froth; steam very slowly in a stewpan with very little water one hour, pour apricot jam over when turned out, or flavour it with ginger or any other flavour, and dish with wine sauce. The mould should not be more than three parts full.

Another.—Take a pint of new milk, put half into the stewpan, and mix the other half with five spoonsful of fine flour. Let the milk be scalding hot, then stir in the other milk and flour. Let it all scald five minutes, stirring it all the time. Then take five eggs, stir in the yolks. Beat the whites to a froth, and *when cold* mix them all together. Sweeten to taste, flavour with any thing you like; strain it stick the mould with any dried fruit. Put a buttered paper under the cloth. Boil it an hour and a half, and take it off five minutes before it is wanted.

Another.—Boil half a pint of very thin cream with lemon-peel, cinnamon, and sugar; let it stand till cold, then add four ounces of butter, two handfuls of flour, five yolks of eggs, the whites beat up to a stiff froth, and a little wine or brandy; (first put the butter and flour into a stewpan, and melt them together, then stir in the cream, &c., that has been boiled, then the five yolks of eggs, one at a time.) Mix all together over the fire, take it off, add the whites, and boil for one hour, as above.

DUTCH WAFER PUDDINGS.

930. Set a pint of cream over the fire, and stir in half a pound of butter; then beat into it a quarter of a pound of flour well dried. Take seven eggs, leaving out four whites, beat them well, and mix them with the other ingredients in an earthen pan; set it before the fire for an hour, then put it into small patty-pans or saucers, and bake them in a hot oven till they are brown; turn them out, and serve at once with good wine sauce poured over them.

EVE'S PUDDING.

931. Weigh four eggs in their shells, and add the same weight of flour, sugar, and butter; beat the butter into cream, then mix the flour, beating it with the butter, then the sugar; add a little citron, bitter and sweet almonds, or lemon-peel; break the eggs, beat y⸍⸍

and whites separate, and mix them in separately; then lightly grease some small patty-pans; put a small quantity in each, and let them rise ten minutes before the fire, after which put them into the oven.

Indian Meal Puffs (*American*).

932. Boil a quart of milk, and stir into it, gradually, eight large table-spoonfuls of Indian meal; four large table-spoonfuls of powdered sugar; and a grated nutmeg. Stir it hard; letting it boil a quarter of an hour after all the Indian meal is in. Then take it up, and set it to cool. While it is cooling, beat eight eggs as light as possible, and stir them gradually into the batter when it is quite cold. Butter some large teacups; nearly fill them with the mixture, set them into a moderate oven, and bake them well. Send them to table warm, and eat them with butter and molasses; or with butter, sugar, lemon-juice, and nutmeg stirred to a cream. They must be turned out of the cups.

Priceless Pudding.

933. Add to the yolks and whites of five eggs their weight in sugar, flour, and butter; first beating the butter to a cream, then adding the sugar, the eggs, and the flour, one after the other; lastly, a good hand-ful of raisins, and the rind of one lemon; beat all together, and boil it in a mould seven hours: serve with wine sauce in a boat.

German Pudding.

934. Two ounces of fine flour, two ounces of powdered sugar, two ounces of butter, eight eggs, leaving out four of the whites, a little orange-flower water, and white wine; melt the butter with some cream, mix all well together, and bake in small cups.

Another.—Half a pound of bread-crumbs, six ounces of butter, half a pound of brown sugar, half an ounce of mixed spice (the cinnamon should predominate), four eggs. Mix the bread-crumbs, sugar, yolk of eggs, and the butter (just melted), the spice, and a little salt, altogether in a large basin, then add the whipped white of eggs. Put it into a mould, and bake or steam in a moderate oven one hour.

The above ingredients are sufficient to make one large pudding or two small ones.

Another.—Take a piece of crumb of bread, as much as you think will fill a mould. Pour over it some boiling milk; when soaked, drain it on a sieve, and squeeze it in a cloth, then beat it quite fine with a fork. Put a lump of butter, some sugar, four or five eggs; whip the whites, flavour it with bitter almonds, do not make it too soft. Butter and paper your mould. Put in a rather deep layer the first, then a little preserve, then more of the mixture, until the mould is full. Do not put too much jam for fear it should run on the outside of the pudding, which would spoil the look of it. Tie it tight down, and steam it one hour and a half. Take it up five minutes before wanted, and make the sauce, for which see page 254.

ALBION PUDDING.

935. Take a quarter of a pound of almonds blanched and beaten, half a pound of loaf sugar, six eggs, and nutmeg to taste. Beat the eggs well up with the sugar over the fire till hot, but not boiling. When cold, add the almonds, and beat again; pour the mixture into a buttered dish and bake it.

SIR WATKINS' PUDDING.

936. Mix half a pound of suet chopped fine, half a pound of breadcrumbs, a quarter of a pound of orange marmalade, a quarter of a pound of sugar (moist), six eggs. Mix all the ingredients well, with the yolks of the eggs unbeaten; take the whites, and whisk them to a stiff froth; mix altogether. Clear it, and let it stand one hour; butter a mould, steam it two hours. Serve it with marmalade, or the syrup from preserved oranges, or with wine sauce.

CALVES-FOOT PUDDING.

937. Boil two calves feet till tender, then chop very fine and mix with the same weight of suet, grated bread, currants and sugar, an apple, a small nutmeg, and six well-beaten eggs. Bake in an oven till done.

YEOMANRY PUDDING.

938. Take three ounces of fine sugar, three ounces of butter melted, three eggs well beaten, leaving out half the whites; mix all together, and put them into a dish lined with paste; put apricot or any other preserve at the bottom, and bake it.

ADELAIDE PUDDINGS.

939. Beat the yolks of eight eggs and whites of two, and mix with six ounces of lump sugar and six ounces of butter just melted; butter

some cups, and put a little preserve or orange marmalade at the bottom
of each (the cups should be small). Bake twenty minutes. They
may be served with wine sauce.

VICTORIA PUDDING.

940. Pour a pint of boiling milk upon the crumb of a twopenny
French roll; cover it till nearly cold, then add a few sweet and bitter
almonds well pounded, a little sifted sugar, a table-spoonful of brandy,
and three yolks of eggs well beaten. Butter the basin or mould, lay
sweetmeats, citron, or raisins about it in any pattern you like. Pour
the pudding in quite cold, boil it well, and serve with wine sauce.

CREAM COCOA-NUT PUDDING.

941. Grate a large cocoa-nut fine. Stir together a quarter of a pound
of butter, and a quarter of a pound of loaf sugar till quite light. Beat
six eggs, and mix them gradually with one pint of cream, or cream and
milk mixed; stir all together well. Put the mixture into a dish and
bake it. Serve either hot or cold with sifted sugar: this pudding may
be baked in puff paste.

A SPOONFUL PUDDING.

942. One spoonful of flour, one of cream, one egg, a little nutmeg,
ginger, and salt. Mix them well together, and boil half an hour. A
few currants may be considered an improvement.

TOWER PUDDING.

943. Mix half a pound of grated bread, half a pound of apples
chopped fine, three ounces of suet, and half a pound of sugar; press it
hard into the dish, and either boil or bake it.

BARFORD PUDDING.

944. Take one pound of beef suet, one pound of raisins, five well-
beaten eggs, four spoonfuls of flour, six ounces of loaf sugar, half a
nutmeg, and a little salt; mix them well, put them in a basin, and boil
four hours.

CUMBERLAND PUDDING.

945. Mix six ounces of flour, six ounces of chopped apples, four
ounces of currants, and four ounces of suet, three eggs, a little nutmeg

and salt, boil it two hours, turn it out into the dish, and pour wine sauce over it.

CHESHIRE PUDDING (EXCELLENT).

946. Mix two table-spoonfuls of flour, and the yolks of three eggs with a pint of cream; stir it on the fire till it thickens; sweeten and flavour to taste, pour into a dish and bake. Before sending it to table, grate fine sugar over it, and brown it with a salamander.

HEREFORDSHIRE PUDDING.

947. Chop fine a quarter of a pound of suet, and mix it with a quarter of a pound of apples, a quarter of a pound of currants, half a pound of flour, a spoonful of sugar, two eggs, and half a pint of milk. Bake an hour.

CHOCOLATE PUDDING.

948. Scrape down very fine two ounces of prepared chocolate, and add to it a tea-spoonful of nutmeg and cinnamon mixed. Put it into a saucepan, and pour over it a quart of rich milk, stirring it well; cover it, and let it come to a boil. Then stir up the chocolate, and press out all the lumps; repeat this until it is quite smooth. Then stir in by degrees, while it boils, a quarter of a pound of sifted sugar, and set it to cool. Beat eight eggs very well, and pour through a strainer to the chocolate; stir well, and bake. This pudding should be eaten cold.

CHEESE PUDDING.

949. Take three ounces of grated cheese, a tea-cupful of grated bread, a good pinch of salt and white pepper, four eggs, leaving out two of the whites, and half a pint of good cream; beat all together, and put it into a mould lined with writing-paper. Half an hour will bake it; take it out of the mould, and send it to table in the paper in which it was baked.

THE ELEGANT ECONOMIST'S PUDDING.

950. Fill a pie-dish with slices of cold plum-pudding, within about an inch of the top, fill the dish up with a cold custard made of two eggs, three tea-spoonfuls of sugar, and the same of flour; let it stand to soak for an hour before it is put in the oven, and bake it about the same time as a bread and butter pudding.

A RICH PUDDING.

951. Line your dish with rich puff-paste, cover the bottom with preserved stoned cherries or any kind of dried fruit (or, as a substitute, Sultana raisins), with the grated rind and juice of a lemon; cover it with slices of roll buttered and cut thin, two or three more layers of preserve and roll to nearly the top of the dish, sifting sugar between each layer; just before baking pour over it seven eggs well beaten, a spoonful of cream, and plenty of brandy.

LADY MARY LOWTHER'S PUDDING.

952. Mix half a pint of water, four spoonfuls of wine, a little sugar and salt, the rind and half the juice of one lemon, and a quarter of a pound of butter; put these on the fire till dissolved; when nearly cold, add a quarter of a pound of flour, and mix thoroughly. When quite cold, add three eggs very well beaten, again put all on the fire, and then bake them in cups.

COLD PUDDING.

953. Take a pint of cream, the rind of one lemon, a blade or two of mace, and sugar to your taste, boil them together, take out the lemon peel and beat it in a mortar, put it through a sieve and then put the cream to it. Let it stand till nearly cold, then pour the cream gently over the yolks of eight or six eggs beaten up. Mix all well together, and put it into a mould with a lid upon it, then put it over a slow fire, and let it boil gently for half an hour. Turn it out of the mould while warm; let it stand till cold, and then pour some melted currant jelly over it.

A NUT PUDDING.

954. Grate two penny rolls and pound an equal weight of blanched small nuts steeped a night in cold water, add half a pound of chopped suet and marrow, half a pound of loaf sugar, a pint and a half of cream, the yolks of eight and whites of four eggs, flavour with a little nutmeg and a pinch of salt, and, if liked, add citron and orange peel. Bake it in a dish lined with puff-paste for one hour and a half.

NOVICE'S PUDDING.

Beat well the whites of eight eggs, and mix with them half a loaf-sugar by degrees. Stir the mixture into a pint of good milk (flavoured with vanilla or sherry) alternately with four ounces of flour, a spoonful at a time; beat it very hard, put it in rather a quick oven, and bake it well. Serve cold.

CURD PUFFS, OR PUDDINGS.

956. Turn a quart of new milk to a curd with rennet, drain in a cloth, and then rub through a sieve with a quarter of a pound of butter beaten; add two ounces of ground rice, *or* a quarter of a pound of bread-crumbs, a little nutmeg, grated lemon-peel, a spoonful of wine and brandy, and sugar to your taste. Bake a little more than half an hour in buttered cups.

SECT. 3.—DUMPLINGS.

BREAD AND SUET DUMPLINGS.

957. Take half a pound of grated bread, half a pound of suet cut small, the juice and grated rind of a lemon, a quarter of a pound of moist sugar, and two eggs. Mix all together, and make it into five dumplings; boil them in cloths half an hour, and serve with sweet sauce in the dish.

Another.—Take equal quantities of bread and suet, a little salt (some nutmeg or other spice), and a table-spoonful of white wine. Mix all well together, and roll them up; when the water boils throw them in, and let them boil for half an hour. Flour the hands well whilst rolling them. This quantity is for a penny loaf.

RICE BALLS.

958. To a quarter of a pound of rice add a pint and a half of milk, and boil it with a little cinnamon, sugar, and lemon-peel, until it is quite tender; allow it to remain till cold, and then make it into balls. Beat up an egg, and roll the balls in it, and afterwards in grated bread-crumbs. Fry them in lard, drain them on a piece of paper, and serve them up covered with sifted sugar.

LEMON DUMPLINGS.

959. Take the juice and rind of a lemon, and from four to eight ounces of bread; grate both very fine, and add a quarter of a pound of suet chopped fine, a quarter of a pound of moist sugar, and two eggs; mix all well together, put it in teacups tied on with cloths, and boil or bake them three-quarters of an hour.

SUET DUMPLINGS.

960. Make as for suet pudding (which see), and drop into boiling water, or into the boilings of beef; or they may be boiled in a cloth.

YEAST OR SUFFOLK DUMPLINGS.

961. Make a very light dough with yeast, as for bread, but with milk instead of water, and add salt. Let it rise an hour before the fire. Twenty minutes before they are to be served, have ready a large stewpan of boiling water, make the dough into balls the size of a middling apple, throw them in, and boil twenty minutes. To ascertain when they are done enough, stick a clean fork into one, and if it comes out clear, it is done. Before serving, tear them apart on the top with two forks, for they become heavy by their own steam. Serve with meat, or sugar and butter, or salt.

APPLE DUMPLINGS.

962. Pare large apples (codlins are the best), scoop out the core with a small knife, then cover with a thin suet or butter crust, made as for puddings, and tie up in a cloth, to boil for twenty minutes to half an hour. *Or*, they may be baked.

SMALL APPLE DUMPLINGS.

963. Pare the apples, scoop out the cores, fill up the space with moist sugar and lemon-peel. Boil them in cups with a thin paste round them; when done, pour custard upon them. Apples prepared in this way, with a thin paste round them and baked on flat tins, are excellent.

CURRANT DUMPLINGS

964. Are made as for suet pudding, mixing in with the flour about one quarter of its weight of foreign currants, picked and washed. After mixing, the mass is divided into dumplings, and boiled in cloths.

SECT. 4.—PUDDING SAUCES.

COMMON WINE SAUCE.

965. Make thin a few ounces of melted butter (see page 105), then add from a table-spoonful to two of coarsely pounded lump sugar, and a glass of sherry, with half a glass of brandy: a little grated lemon-peel or nutmeg, or both together, are improvements.

ARROWROOT SAUCE FOR PUDDINGS.

966. Mix a small tea-spoonful of arrowroot with a little cold water, and boil a large tea-cupful of sherry or raisin-wine with sugar enough to sweeten it. Make the arrowroot with this, and pour over the pudding. It is an improvement to rub a lump or two of the sugar on lemon-peel.

BURNT CREAM SAUCE.

967. Put two ounces of sifted sugar on the fire, in a small saucepan, stir it, and when quite brown pour slowly in a gill of thin cream, stirring it all the time. To be used as a sauce to custard, or batter pudding.

SWEET PUDDING SAUCE WITHOUT WINE.

968. This is made with melted butter, a little cream added, sweetened to the palate, and flavoured with nutmeg, cinnamon, or mace.

PLUM PUDDING SAUCE.

969. Add to four ounces of melted butter, or thick arrowroot, an ounce and a half of each of the following; viz., sherry, French brandy, and curaçoa; sweeten to the taste, and add also a little nutmeg and lemon-peel grated.

FRUIT SAUCES.

970. These are easily made for any plain puddings, by stewing the fresh fruit with rather less sugar than for preserving, and adding water till they are of the proper consistence for a sauce. Some cooks mix a little arrowroot with the water, and then strain before serving.

GERMAN SAUCE.

971. A quarter of a pint of white wine (hock is the best) with a little lemon-juice, the yolks of three eggs well beaten, and sweetened with loaf sugar to the taste. Put all into a jug; the wine first, to prevent the egg sticking. Let the jug stand in a saucepan of boiling water, whilst the sauce is melted and worked to a complete froth with a whisk or chocolate mill. If the water gets cool before the sauce comes to a froth, add more boiling water. The sauce (made only just before it is wanted) may be served in a sauce tureen, or over the pudding.

SAUCE FOR GERMAN PUDDING.

972. Take the yolks of two eggs, with a little sugar and a teacupful of sherry wine; whisk it over the fire, but do not let it get too hot or it will curdle, it should be stiff; whisk it until it is wanted, and pour it over your pudding.

BOILED TREACLE.

973. Boiled treacle is an excellent accompaniment to hasty pudding, or to arrowroot and milk the consistency of hasty pudding, or to yeast dumplings.

RASPBERRY SYRUP.

974. Raspberry vinegar and raspberry syrup are good as sauces to bread or batter puddings, and the latter also to arrowroot blancmange.

CHAPTER XX.—PANCAKES, SWEET OMELETS, AND SOUFFLÉS.

SECT. I.—PANCAKES AND FRITTERS.

975. Pancakes are made by forming a common batter, and then frying this in a thin layer. When of a large size they are called pancakes; and when so small as to allow of several being fried in the same pan, they are called fritters. These are often mixed with apples, currants, &c. Omelets are made in a similar way, the ingredients being slightly different, and being also fried in thicker layers as to substance. There is a little art in turning the pancake, which, by a clever cook, is "tossed" in the air and caught again as it falls; but this is not by any means necessary, as with the aid of a common fork the edge may easily be raised, and the whole turned over. The frying is conducted upon the principles described at page 54.

TO BEAT EGGS.

976. The following excellent remarks on the proper mode of effecting this apparently simple operation, are extracted from Miss Leslie's book on Cookery:—"Those who do not know the right way, complain much of the fatigue of beating eggs, and therefore leave off too soon. There will be no fatigue if they are beaten with the proper stroke, and with

wooden rods, and in a shallow, flat-bottomed *earthen* pan. The coldness of a tin pan retards the lightness of the eggs. For the same reason do not use a metal egg-beater. In beating them do not move the elbow, but keep it close to the side. Move only the hand at the wrist, and let the stroke be quick, short, and horizontal; putting the egg-beater always down to the bottom of the pan, which should therefore be shallow. Do not leave off as soon as the eggs are in a foam; they are then only *beginning* to be light. But persist till after the foaming has ceased, and the bubbles have all disappeared. Continue till the surface is smooth as a mirror, and the beaten egg as thick as a rich boiled custard; for till then it will not be really light. It is seldom necessary to beat the whites and yolks separately, if they are afterwards to be put together. The article will be quite as light, when cooked, if the whites and yolks are beaten together, and there will then be no danger of their going in streaks when baked. When white of egg is to be used without any yolk (as for macaroons, meringues, icing, &c.), it should be beaten till it stands alone on the rods, not falling when held up."

COMMON PANCAKES.

977. Make a light batter of three spoonfuls of flour, three eggs well beaten, and half a pint of milk, some of which, with the eggs, is to be mixed with the flour; to the other part, put three ounces of butter melted. Then mix altogether, and put into the frying-pan in a very thin layer. Fry with lard or dripping; but do not put any butter into the pan to fry them after the first frying, as they will give out enough afterwards to keep up the stock. Sugar and lemon should be served to eat with them. *Or*, when eggs are scarce, make the batter with flour, small beer, ginger, &c. *Or*, clean snow with flour and very little milk will serve, but not nearly as well as eggs.

RICH PANCAKES, FRIED WITHOUT BUTTER OR LARD.

978. Beat six fresh eggs extremely well, and mix when strained with a pint of cream, four ounces of sugar, a glass of wine, half a nutmeg grated, and as much flour as will make it almost as thick as ordinary pancake batter, but not quite. Heat the frying-pan tolerably hot, wipe it with a clean cloth; then pour in the batter to make thin pancakes, and watch them that they do not burn, which is to be prevented by turning them.

RICE PANCAKES.

979. Boil half a pound of rice to a jelly in a small quantity of water; when cold mix it with a pint of cream, eight eggs, a bit of salt and nutmeg; stir in eight ounces of butter just warmed, and add as much flour as will make the batter thick enough. Fry in as little lard or dripping as possible.

NEW ENGLAND PANCAKES.

980. Mix a pint of cream, five spoonfuls of fine flour, seven yolks and four whites of eggs, and a very little salt; fry them very thin in fresh butter, and between each strew sugar and cinnamon. Send up six or eight at once.

CREAM PANCAKES.

981. Take half a pint of cream, four eggs well beaten, two ounces of butter, a table-spoonful of brandy, and a little sugar and nutmeg; melt the butter in the cream, and mix all together with a spoonful of fine flour. Butter the pan for the first pancake, and let them run as thin as possible. Serve with sugar sifted between each pancake. This quantity will make about ten; the pan should be smaller than for common pancakes.

FRITTERS.

982. Make them of any of the batters directed for pancakes, by dropping a small quantity into the pan; or make the plainer sort, and put pared-apple sliced and cored into the batter, and fry some of it with each slice. Currants, or sliced lemon as thin as paper, make an agreeable change. Fritters for company should be served on a folded napkin in the dish. Any sort of sweetmeat or ripe fruit may be made into fritters.

SPANISH FRITTERS.

983. Cut the crumb of a French roll into lengths, as thick as the finger, in any approved shape. Soak in some cream, nutmeg, sugar, and pounded cinnamon, beaten up with an egg. When well soaked, fry of a nice brown, and serve with butter, wine, and sugar sauce.

POTATO FRITTERS.

984. Boil two large potatoes, mash them well, beat four yolks and

three whites of eggs, and add to the above with one large spoonful of cream, another of sweet wine, a squeeze of lemon, and a little nutmeg. Beat this batter half an hour at least. It will be extremely light. Put a good quantity of fine lard in a stew-pan, and drop a spoonful of the batter at a time into it. Fry them; and serve with a sauce composed of a glass of white wine, the juice of a lemon, one dessert-spoonful of peach-leaf or almond water, and some white sugar warmed together, or the common wine sauce (which see).

BREAD FRITTERS.

985. Pick, wash, and dry half a pound of Zante currants, and, having spread them out on a flat dish, dredge them well with flour. Grate some bread into a pan till you have a pint of crumbs. Pour over the grated bread a pint of boiling milk, in which has been stirred, as soon as taken from the fire, a piece of fresh butter the size of an egg. Cover the pan, and let it stand an hour. Then beat it hard, and add nutmeg and a quarter of a pound of powdered white sugar, stirred in gradually, and two table-spoonfuls of the best brandy. Beat six eggs till very light, and then stir them by degrees into the mixture. Lastly, add the currants, a few at a time; and beat the whole very hard. It should be a thick batter. If it turns out too thin, add a little flour. Have ready over the fire a hot frying-pan with boiling lard. Put in the batter in large spoonfuls (so as not to touch), and fry the fritters a light brown. Drain them on a perforated skimmer, or an inverted sieve placed in a deep pan, and send them to table hot. Serve them with wine and powdered sugar.

APPLE FRITTERS.

986. Mix together half a pint of milk, two large table-spoonfuls of flour, one of sugar, two apples chopped fine, and a very small quantity of carbonate of soda; put a dessert-spoonful into the pan, and fry them a light brown.

INDIAN MEAL FRITTERS.

987. Having beaten eight eggs very light, stir them gradually into a quart of rich milk, in turn with twelve large table-spoonfuls of yellow Indian meal, adding a salt-spoon of salt. When all is in, stir the whole very hard. Have ready over a clear fire, in a pot or a large frying-pan, a pound of fresh lard, boiling fast; drop the batter into it, a ladleful at a time. If you find the batter too thin, stir into it

S

little more Indian meal. As the lard boils away, replenish it with more. As fast as they are done, take out each fritter with a perforated skimmer; through the holes of which let the lard drip back into the pot. The fritters must all be well drained. Send them to table hot, and eat them with wine and sugar, or with molasses. In cooking these fritters, you may drop in three or four, one immediately after another; they will not run if the lard is boiling fast, and the batter thick enough, and made with the proper number of eggs.

RICE FRITTERS.

988. Boil three table-spoonfuls of rice in water until it swells to the full size, then drain it quite dry, and mix with it four eggs well beaten, a quarter of a pound of currants, a little grated lemon-peel, nutmeg and sugar to the taste. Stir in as much flour as will thicken it, and fry in lard. If they do not brown quickly add a little more flour.

CREAM FRITTERS.

989. Take four eggs well beaten, two ounces of fine sugar, a little cinnamon, ginger, nutmeg, and salt, half a pound of sponge biscuits grated, or, if you prefer stale bread-crumbs, more sugar must be used. Mix this with a pint of cream and flour, or bread crumbs, enough to make it thicker than batter for pancakes. Fill the frying-pan with lard, and when it boils throw in the fritters with a knife from a plate. Sift sugar over them and serve in a napkin, or squeeze orange juice upon the sugar over them, and pile them, on a dish without the napkin.

SECT. 2.—SOUFFLÉS AND OMELETS.

990. Soufflés are elegant and delicious preparations of eggs and milk, variously flavoured, the latter with cheese, and whisked into a froth, as directed at the beginning of this section. After which they are baked, the heat of the oven keeping up the frothing until the material of the egg is set; but great care is necessary to avoid the falling down of the soufflé as soon as it is removed from the oven, and some cooks stand guard over their handiwork with a salamander, until the moment when they enter the dining-room.

SWEET SOUFFLÉ.

991. Take a pint of milk and as much flour as will come to a thick paste over the stove; keep stirring it all the time, add six yolks of

eggs and a pinch of salt, as much sugar as you like. Beat eight whites
of eggs all to a froth, stir them all together. To be put into the oven a
quarter of an hour before wanting it—the oven must be quick. Glaze
it with white sugar, and send quickly to table. It may be made with
ground rice. The rind of a lemon grated, or lemon juice, gives it a
nice flavour.

SOUFFLÉ OF RICE AND APPLES.

392. Steep one and a half teacupful of rice in milk, add the pulp of
five good-sized apples, sweeten the whole, and put it into a dish.
Then beat the whites of two eggs with two ounces of sifted lump sugar,
and pour it over the rice; and, just before you put it in the oven, dust
a little sugar on the top of it.

STRAWBERRY OR APPLE SOUFFLÉ.

993. Stew the apples with a little lemon-peel, sweeten them, then lay
them pretty high round the inside of a dish; make a custard of the
yolks of two eggs, a little cinnamon, sugar, and milk. Let it thicken
over a slow fire, but not boil. When ready, pour it in the inside of the
apple. Beat the whites of the eggs to a strong froth, and cover the
whole. Throw over it a good deal of pounded sugar, and brown it of
a fine brown. Any fruit made of a proper consistence does for the
walls. Strawberries when ripe are delicious.

SOUFFLÉ OF POTATOES WITH LEMON.

994. Roast about ten potatoes; when they are done, open them, and
scoop out the floury part, and mix it with half a pint of cream that has
boiled, and in which has been infused the peel of a lemon; add some
butter, a pinch of salt and a little lump sugar, not too much, lest your
soufflé should not be light, but enough to give flavour. Add the yolks
of four eggs to the above. Then beat the whites of six eggs, and mix
with the rest. Pour it gently into a dish, and bake in a moderate
oven. When done, sift a little sugar over it, and brown with the
salamander. It should be served up immediately.

FRIAR'S OMELETS.

995. Prepare twelve apples as for sauce, and stir in a quarter of a
pound of sugar and a quarter of a pound of butter; when cold, add four
eggs well beaten, and fry in butter or lard made very hot, as for French
frying, or proceed as follows: Well butter a dish, strew bread-cr

or vermicelli over it, so as to make them stick to it, put in the mixture, then strew crumbs or vermicelli plentifully over the top; when baked, turn it out of the dish and strew sugar over.

FRENCH PROMISES.

996. Mix together half a pint of milk, two tea-spoonfuls of French brandy, one egg, and a little grated ginger. Make it with flour a proper thickness for pancakes, and drop into a frying-pan with the lard very hot.

A SWEET OMELET.

997. Mix and crush six macaroons with a little brandy and six ounces of sifted sugar; beat the yolks of six eggs smooth, and add the other ingredients to this gradually. Have ready the whites, beaten to a stiff froth, and stir in a little at a time; then melt four ounces of butter in an omelet pan, and put in the mixture, stirring to the last. When the omelet is hot, and has begun to colour, transfer it to a buttered dish, and bake from five to ten minutes, till it is puffed. Sift sugar over, and serve immediately.

OMELETTE SOUFFLÉ.

998. Beat the yolks of six eggs, put to them four spoonfuls of sugar and a little essence of lemon; work these well together, whip the whites of the eggs till they are firm, mix altogether; butter your frying-pan, put in the omelette, and set it on a slow fire, taking care that it does not burn. Turn it out upon the dish it is to be served in, glaze it by throwing sugar over it, put a little preserve on the top, fold it over, put it in the oven till risen, glaze and serve.

CHAP. XXI.—CREAMS, CUSTARDS, JELLIES, AND STEWED FRUIT.

SECT. 1.—GENERAL OBSERVATIONS.

999. Creams include in their ranks a variety of rich and delicious sweet dishes, chiefly made with a foundation of milk or cream, and either whipped into a froth or eaten in a solid state. Isinglass or gelatine, or calf's foot jelly, are used to stiffen them, together with eggs in some cases.

1000. COLOURING TO STAIN CREAMS AND JELLIES :—

For a beautiful *red*, boil fifteen grains of cochineal in the finest powder, with a drachm and a half of cream of tartar in half a pint of water, very slowly for half an hour; add in boiling a bit of alum the size of a pea. *Or*, use beet-root sliced, and some liquor poured over.

For *white*, use the almonds finely pounded, with a little drop of water. *Or*, use cream.

For *yellow*, yolks of eggs, or a bit of saffron steeped in the liquor and squeezed.

For *green*, pounded spinach leaves or beet-leaves; express the juice, and boil in a teacup placed in a saucepan of water to take off the rawness.

THE MIXTURE of two coloured jellies, or of blancmange or cream with jelly, is made by allowing the first layer in the mould to harden sufficiently to bear the succeeding one of a different colour without their intermixing; several colours may be added in this way.

THE BEST MODE OF MELTING ISINGLASS.

1001. To melt a quarter of a pound of isinglass, take a little more than a pint of water, into which throw in the twelfth part of the white of an egg; beat the water well till it becomes white; throw the isinglass into that water, and lay it on the stove over a very slow fire. If it is kept covered, it will melt more easily. Take care it does not burn, for then it can never be made clear, besides it would have an unpleasant taste. For a larger quantity put more water, but not more white of egg. If the isinglass is required to be particularly clear, squeeze into it the juice of a lemon.

TO RUN JELLY.

1002. In running jelly through the flannel bag, it is apt to become cold and refuse to run. To avoid this, it is a good plan to fix the bag to a couple of sticks stretched across a large furnace, in the bottom of which are a few quarts of boiling water, so that the proper temperature is maintained.

MOULDS.

1003. Moulds of various forms are required, for the purpose of making blancmange, jelly, &c. They are, however, so well known as scarcely to need description. In order to get the articles out, only necessary, when they are once quite cold, to loosen the edges with a knife and invert them, giving a shake or two.

SECT. 2.—CREAMS AND CUSTARDS.

TO WHIP CREAMS.

1004. Follow the directions given for beating eggs at p. 254.

TO WHIP FRUIT CREAMS.

1005. Rub a lump or two of sugar on the peel of a lemon, then sprinkle the juice of half a lemon on the sugar, and leave it for a time to melt (a table-spoonful of sugar is enough if the preserve is very sweet). Then mix the jam or jelly with the above; and lastly, add a pint of good cream by degrees to the whole, and whip it steadily till *thick;* sometimes this will be in five or ten minutes. Cease whipping as soon as it is thick enough. Some cooks add a spoonful of brandy.

Another Plan.—Put a little sifted sugar in some thick cream, and whip it very fast; when it is quite thick, put in some rough pieces in a glass dish, then put strawberries or raspberries about, or very nice gooseberries, putting more and more till you have a handsome dish full, taking care to place them with taste on the outside; or, flavour the cream with syrup of quinces, and put bits of preserved quinces in; and cream flavoured with lemon, or any fruit syrup, and whipped in this way, and put in glasses, gives you a nice sweet in a few minutes.

RASPBERRY CREAM.

1006. Boil an ounce of isinglass in three pints of milk a quarter of an hour; strain it; when cool, add half a pint of raspberry syrup, stir it well, and sweeten it; add a glass of brandy, and, when nearly cold, put it into a mould.

PINE-APPLE CREAM.

1007. Infuse some foreign pine-apple cut in slices (or the *rind* only will do) in boiling cream, and proceed as is usual for other fruit creams (par. 1005).

SWISS CREAM OR TRIFLE.

1008. Grate the rind of a lemon into a pint of cream (first taking from the cream as much as will mix four tea-spoonfuls of ground rice to a smooth batter), add a small piece of cinnamon, sweeten with six ounces of loaf sugar, place it over a clear fire or hot hearth; when it boils, stir in the batter and simmer it five minutes, stirring it gently without ceasing, then pour it out; when it is quite cold, mix with it by degrees the juice of two lemons and two large table-spoonfuls of brandy, then pour it into a glass dish in which you have previously placed a quarter of a pound of macaroons and ratafias soaked in brandy; when set, it can be ornamented with almonds, citron, or preserved ginger.

APPLE TRIFLE.

1009. Scald as much fruit as required, pulp it smoothly; add sufficient sugar to sweeten it, and the grated rinds of two lemons; lay this thickly at the bottom of the dish. Mix a pint of cream, a pint of new milk, and the yolks of three eggs well beaten ; put it over the fire, stirring it until it is just upon the boil; sweeten it with white sugar, and let it grow cold; then put it over the apples with a spoon, and afterwards lay upon the whole a fine whip of cream, made some hours previously.

CODLIN CREAM.

1010. Pare and core twelve good-sized codlins ; beat them quickly and thoroughly in a mortar; then stir in a pint of thick cream, adding, as it becomes well mingled, the crumb of a stale sponge-cake, a glass of white wine, and powdered white sugar to taste. This is a deliciously cool preparation to partake of in the summer time, when codlins are in season.

ORANGE CREAM.

101½. Shred candied orange peel (about an ounce and a half, or to taste) as fine as you can, and boil it well in a pint and a half of thick cream till dissolved. If it is to be solid, add an ounce of isinglass and put it into a mould.

Another.—Boil the rind of a Seville orange till very tender; beat it fine in a mortar; put to it a spoonful of the best brandy, the juice of a Seville orange, four ounces of loaf-sugar, and the yolks of four eggs ; beat all together for ten minutes; then, by gentle degrees, pour in a pint of boiling cream; beat till cold; put into custard-cups set in a deep dish of boiling water, and let them stand till cold again. Put at the top small strips of orange-peel cut thin, or preserved chips.

ALMOND CREAM.

1012. Beat four ounces of sweet and a few bitter almonds in a mortar, with a tea-spoonful of water to prevent oiling, both having been blanched. Put the paste to a quart of cream, and add the juice of three lemons sweetened; beat it up with a whisk to a froth, which take off on the shallow part of a sieve; fill glasses with some of the liquor and the froth.

FRUIT CREAM.

1013. Whip up a thick cream with a little pounded sugar; then put into a glass dish a layer of cream and a layer of strawberries, or any other fresh or dried fruits alternately till the dish is piled high. Lay wafers round the outside.

PINK CREAM.

1014. Mix a quart of cream with a pint of red-currant juice or jelly, beat it with a whisk till quite thick, and serve it in a glass dish.

SOLID CLOUTED CREAM.

1015. String four blades of mace on a thread; put them to a gill of new milk, and six spoonfuls of rose-water; simmer a few minutes, then, by degrees, stir this liquor strained into the yolks of two new eggs well beaten. Stir the whole into a quart of *very* good cream, and set it over the fire; stir it till hot, but not boiling hot; pour it into a deep dish, and let it stand twenty-four hours. Serve it in a cream dish, to eat with fruits. Many people prefer it without any flavour but that of the cream; in which case use a quart of new milk and the cream, or do it as the Devonshire scalded cream.—(*Economical Housekeeper*, p. 47).

TO MAKE GOOSEBERRY FOOL.

1016. Take two quarts of unripe gooseberries, set them on the fire in one pint of water; when they begin to simmer, turn yellow, and begin to plump, throw them into a colander or sieve to drain; then press the pulp through a sieve into a dish; make it pretty sweet, and leave it till cold. Take two quarts of new milk, and four yolks of eggs beaten with a little nutmeg, stir it softly over a slow fire; when it begins to simmer take it off, and by degrees stir it into the pulp. If made with cream, the eggs may be omitted, and more gooseberries added if preferred thicker; a little brandy is a great improvement. It should be served cold. This quantity is sufficient to fill three ordinary glass dishes. *Or*, by some it is preferred to rub the gooseberries through a colander only, or merely to mash them after draining, so as to retain all the skins.

RHUBARB FOOL

1017. Is made as above, substituting the stalks of the rhubarb, cut in short lengths, for the gooseberries, and boiling them in a gill of water only.

APPLE FOOL.

1018. Pare the fruit, and either scald or bake it until sufficiently soft to pulp it through a colander; sweeten it agreeably to taste, and fill the glasses three parts full with it. Then plentifully sprinkle in some cinnamon and cloves in powder, put a good layer of rich scalded cream, and sift white sugar upon the top.

ORANGE FOOL.

1019. Mix the juice of three Seville oranges, three eggs well beaten, a pint of cream, a little nutmeg and cinnamon, and sweeten to the taste. Set the whole over a slow fire, and stir it till it becomes as thick as good melted butter, but it must not be boiled; then pour it into a dish, and set it by till cold.

POMMES À LA CHANTILLY.

1020. In a quart of good thick and very sweet cream, put the whites of four eggs strained, beat it until it becomes a stiff snow; then, while still beating it, add quite a pound of pulped apples, and a quarter of a pound of finely powdered sifted white sugar. Pile it high upon a dessert dish, and serve.

STONE CREAM.

1021. Add three-quarters of an ounce of isinglass to one quart of thin cream, previously dissolving the isinglass in a small quantity of water; then add the cream sweetened to taste, and let it boil from ten to fifteen minutes; meanwhile grate the rind of a small lemon into about half a pint of sherry or raisin wine, and put in the dish with preserved apricots or any light-coloured preserve. Stir the cream occasionally, and when almost cold pour it carefully over the preserve. In order that the two shall not mix, make the cream the day before.

Another Stone Cream.—Line a dish with orange marmalade, or some other preserve, squeeze on it the juice of a lemon, and grate upon it the peel. Then dissolve three-quarters of an ounce of extract of calves' feet, or half an ounce of isinglass dissolved in water, and add to it a pint of cream well sweetened. Pour this over the marmalade. It should be made the day before.

Another Stone Cream.—Lay some preserve of different sorts in the bottom of a deep glass dish, then pour some blancmange over it till the dish is rather more than half full. When *perfectly cold*, pour on the blancmange a *good thick* custard to fill the dish, and when that is also cold stick blanched almonds on the top.

LEMON CREAM.

1022. *Lemon Cream in Glasses.*—To the peel of one large lemon pared thin put the juice of two, half a pint of water, the whites of four eggs and yolk of one beaten well, and half a pound of lump sugar; stir it over a slow fire till it is the thickness of cream; strain it, and put it in glasses.

1023. *Lemon Cream without Cream.*—Take the peel of a large lemon and put it into a glass, then squeeze the juice of two lemons upon it, add to it half a pint of water and four eggs (leaving out three of the yolks) well beaten, and add half a pound of fine sifted sugar. Strain and set it over a slow fire, stirring it till it is as thick as a good cream.

1024. *Lemon Cream with Arrowroot.*—Dissolve and mix up two table-spoonfuls of arrowroot in a little cold water, add one and a half pint of boiling water, and boil it in a nice clean saucepan for a few minutes, stirring it all the time; add a couple of pinches of saffron (to colour it), and as much lemon juice and grated peel and lump sugar as will flavour and sweeten it; then add the yolks of five or six eggs well beaten up; stir the whole on the fire for a few minutes (but do not let it curdle), and cool. The above quantity will fill about twelve small glasses, and requires two or three lemons. It is not so good made with fewer eggs (*see* White Lemon Cream).

1025. *White Lemon Cream.*—Make the cream, as above, with the whites instead of yolks of eggs (leaving out the saffron). The whites must be well beaten, but not frothed, and an egg or two more is an improvement, making it whiter. If it should appear to curdle, the straining makes all right. In this manner three or four eggs will make six glasses of *white*, and six of yellow lemon cream.

CHOCOLATE OR ORANGE CREAM.

1026. Mix together two yolks of eggs, a pint of milk, sugar to the taste, a bit of butter twice the size of a walnut, a spoonful of dried and sifted flour, and sliced chocolate, which should be put to the milk cold; put all in a stewpan, and stir gently till it just boils. If you wish it flavoured with orange or lemon, chop some peel very fine, and put it in as you take it off the fire, and it retains a fresh flavour.

COFFEE CREAM.

1027. Boil a calf's foot in water till it wastes to a pint of jelly clear of sediment and fat, make a teacup of very strong coffee, clear it with a bit of isinglass. To be perfectly bright, pour it to the jelly with a pint of very good cream and as much lump sugar as is pleasant; give it one boil up, and pour it into the dish; it should jelly, but not be stiff.

RICE CREAM.

1028. Soak two and a half to three ounces of rice over night in water for a short time, then put in a sieve to drain and dry. Next morning to be half pounded, then boiled in half a pint of milk, and put in a basin to cool; add half a pint of cream, half an ounce of dissolved isinglass, and whip it to a strong froth; leave it in the mould all day, and add sweetmeats, or fresh fruits, or French prunes, in the middle.

BRANDY CREAM.

1029. To a pint of thick cream put a teacupful each of sifted sugar and brandy; add the juice of a lemon. Whisk till it thickens, and pour into a glass dish.

IMPERIAL CREAM.

1030. Take the juice of three large oranges or two lemons, sweeten it well with double-refined sugar pounded and sifted, put it into the dish you design to serve it up in, then take a pint of thick cream, sweeten it a little, boil it and stir it till it is milk warm; put it in a teapot with one spoonful of orange-flower water, and pour it very high on the juice, which will make it curdle, and look like a honeycomb.

APPLE SNOW.

1031. Take a pinch of powdered alum, with half a pound of the pulp of roasted apples, half a pound of powdered sugar, the juice of one good lemon, and the whites of three eggs. Whip all together for an hour, drop it lightly on a glass dish.

APPLE SPONGE.

1032. Boil half a pound of apples with a quarter of a pound of sugar and half a pint of water, and the rind of a lemon; when soft, pulp it through a sieve, then beat half a pint of thick cream to a strong froth, add half an ounce of isinglass melted in a little water; mix all together, and put it in the mould; if liked when turned out, pour a custard over

GATEAU DE POMMES.

1033. Boil one pound and a half of lump sugar in a pint of water till it becomes sugar again; then add two pounds of apples pared and cored, the peel and a little of the juice of two small lemons; boil it until *quite stiff*, and put it into a mould; when cold it should be turned out, and before being sent to table should have a thick custard poured round it. The cake will keep several months. It is less expensive if a larger proportion of apple is added, but does not stiffen so well.

PRUSSIAN CREAM.

1034. Whisk well the whites of four eggs and add them to four ounces of sugar (some lumps of which have been rubbed on the peel of a lemon), and one pint of cream; whisk again for three minutes, and set it on a stove, whisking gently till it boils. Then pour it into a dish and serve it cold.

A FRENCH CHARLOTTE.

1035. Soak well half a pound of macaroons in sherry, have ready a mould formed of the bottom and sides of an almond sponge-cake with the inside cut away, leaving the walls an inch thick, lay the dissolved macaroon at the bottom, over them a thick layer of preserve, and fill up with stiff whipped cream heaped high in the centre— ornament the edge with icing.

VELVET CREAM.

1036. Dissolve one ounce of isinglass in a breakfast-cup full of raisin wine, and a little brandy; add the juice of two small lemons, on which rub some lumps of sugar to obtain the essence. When the isinglass is quite dissolved strain it into a basin, and, when quite cool, but not set, stir into it gradually a pint of cream, and then put it into a mould.

SOLID RASPBERRY CREAM.

1037. Dissolve one ounce and a half of isinglass in a pint of new milk, strain it and add a pint of cream, and as much raspberry jelly or jam as will make it a fine colour; strain it altogether, and put it into moulds, which must not be of tin.

VENETIAN CREAM.

1038. Dissolve half an ounce of isinglass in a pint of cream (if much wasted, add a little more cream); pour the cream on three ounces of ratafias and macaroons mixed, sweeten with raspberry jelly (or lemon and sugar), whisk it ten or fifteen minutes; put it in a mould, and it will turn out next day.

APPLE AND CUSTARD.

1039. Prepare apples as for sauce, only *stiffer;* allow them to remain till cold. Put them into a simple mould to give a shape to them, or pile them in the centre of your dish and pour a custard over them.

MACARONI AND CUSTARD.

1040. Into nearly a quart of new milk when boiling fast, put by degrees a quarter of a pound of pipe macaroni. Simmer by the fire till nearly tender. Add two or three ounces of lump sugar, a *small* quantity of isinglass (and either lemon or cinnamon flavouring if liked). Then simmer the whole till the pipes are soft and swollen to their full size. Press it in a mould, and when quite cold turn it out into a deep glass dish, pouring over it enough of a rich custard to fill the dish—a little brandy is an improvement to the custard.

LÈCHE CRÈMA.

1041. Beat up three eggs, leaving out two whites, add to them a pint of new milk, and mix very carefully a table-spoonful of flour, with a little finely grated lemon-peel; boil this over a slow fire, constantly stirring it. Prepare a shallow dish, with some ratafia cakes at the bottom soaked in brandy and sherry, or covered with preserve; then, when the crema is boiled pretty thick, pour it over the cakes. To be sent to table cold.

FLOATING ISLANDS.

1042. Whip up two spoonfuls of jelly or jam with one of white of egg; beat well; then drop it with a spoon on a dish of cream.

SIR WALTER SCOTT'S WASSAIL BOWL.

1043. Crumble sponge-cakes with ratafias and macaroons into a glass dish, and cover them with rich raisin-wine, and a glass of brandy. The juice of a lemon should first be squeezed over the crumbled cake. Have a rich thick custard ready made, and pour it upon the whole *warm,* but *not hot.* If approved, add a little raspberry jam.

TRIFLE.

1044. Soak sponge-biscuits, macaroons, and ratafias, &c., in a dish with one pint of raisin-wine and about a glass of brandy, in the morning; then lay upon it a layer of preserve, and upon that the whip given below, reserving a little to put on just before sending it to table.

1045. *Whip for Trifle.*—Put two wine-glasses of white wine, with a stick of cinnamon, lemon peel, and a blade of mace, into a saucepan over the fire till it simmers, then strain it, and put it to stand until nearly cold, then add another glass of wine, with one of brandy, and an equal quantity of cream and milk; sugar to your taste. Beat it well with a whisk, and as the froth rises take it off and lay it on a sieve, the hollow part down. If for the evening, make this whip the first thing in the morning.

1046. *Solid Syllabub for Trifle, or to put into Glasses.*—A quart of cream, one glass of brandy, two glasses of raisin wine, the juice of two lemons, and the essence of the peel taken by rubbing lumps of sugar upon them. Sweeten to the taste, and whip it all together. A pint is enough for a trifle.

1047. *An Excellent Trifle.*—Lay macaroons and ratafia drops over the bottom of a dish, and pour in as much raisin-wine as they will suck up; which, when they have done, pour on them cold rich custard, made with plenty of eggs and some rice flour; it must stand two or three inches thick. On that put a layer of raspberry-jam, and cover the whole with a high whip, made the day before of rich cream, the whites of two well-beaten eggs, sugar, lemon-peel, and raisin-wine, well beaten with a wire whisk. If made the day before it is used, it has quite a different taste, and is far better.

1048. *Gooseberry or Apple Trifle.*—Scald such a quantity of either of these fruits as, when pulped through a sieve, will make a thick layer at the bottom of the dish; if of apples, mix the rind of half a lemon grated fine, and add to both as much sugar as will be pleasant; if of gooseberries, a little nutmeg and brandy. Mix half a pint of milk, half a pint of cream, and the yolk of one egg; give it a scald over the fire, and stir it all the time; do not let it boil; add a little sugar only, and let it grow cold. Lay it over the apple with a spoon, and then put on it a whip made the day before, as for other Trifle.

1049. *Chantilly Cake, or Cake Trifle.*—Bake a rice cake in a mould. When cold, cut it round about two inches from the edge with a sharp knife, taking care not to perforate the bottom. Put in a thick custard, and some teaspoonfuls of raspberry jam, and then put on a high whip.

LEMON SOLID.

1050. Mix the rind of one lemon grated, and the juice squeezed in, with one pint of cream, half an ounce of isinglass boiled in a little water, and six ounces of sugar boiled with the cream. When the cream and isinglass are almost cold, pour it on the lemon.

Another Lemon Solid.—Grate the peel of a large lemon, and put the juice into a basin, with brandy and sugar to the taste. Boil a quart of cream and pour it on the lemon, stirring it till it is cold.

NEIGE À LA GILETTE.

1051. Divide your eggs from the whites as for custards, about six to a pint of milk. Put the milk on the fire, and, while boiling, beat the whites up till they stand pretty firm, then take a quantity of the white on an egg slice and put it on the milk; when it is swollen and has boiled for half a minute, turn it on to the other side and do the same. Then put it on a dish and do the same with the rest of the whites; it will make about six lots, and you need not be afraid of putting one upon another. It looks just like snow. Make a custard with the rest of the eggs, milk, and sugar; flavour and serve as you like. Place in a dish, with the snow on the top, and custard round; or the snow lightly placed on the custard; or, snow on one dish and custard on another.

CRÈME À LA VANILLA (OR MAURITIUS CREAM).

1052. Take three table-spoonfuls of arrowroot and mix smoothly with three of cold milk: add a pint of boiling milk quickly stirred in. Whip well the yolks of six eggs and add to the arrowroot and milk; then boil gently over the fire until it becomes a rich yellow colour; but be very careful—for a little *boil* too much, and your cream is spoilt; flavour with a teaspoonful of the best vanilla. When nearly cold, add two teaspoonfuls of brandy, and pour the cream into a crystal dish. Whisk the whites of six eggs till they are as light as possible, and whip in six table-spoonfuls of sifted sugar. Pile it up rockily or plain, as you please, on the cream when cold, ornamenting with ratafias and pink sugar according to taste.

BLANCMANGE.

1053. Boil two ounces of isinglass in three half-pints of water half an hour; strain it through fine muslin into a pint and a half of cream; sweeten, and add a few bitter almonds pounded. Let it boil once up; if not wanted very stiff, a little less isinglass will do. Stir the blancmange occasionally while cooling, but let it settle before pouring into the moulds, or the blacks will settle in the moulds, and show themselves at the top when turned out.

Another Blancmange.—Infuse for an hour, in one pint and three-quarters of milk, the thin rind of a small lemon, and eight bitter almonds blanched and bruised; add two ounces of sugar and one ounce and a half of gelatine; boil them over a slow fire, stirring until the isinglass or gelatine is dissolved. Take off the scum. Stir in half a pint of rich cream, and strain the blancmange into a bowl. It should be moved gently with a spoon till nearly cold, to prevent the cream from rising to the top; add by degrees a wine-glassful of brandy, and when nearly cold pour it into a mould.

ARROWROOT BLANCMANGE (*excellent*).

1054 To a quart of new milk add a quarter of a pound of arrowroot sweetened to taste, and a pennyworth of cinnamon water; stir it well whilst on the fire, boil ten minutes, pour it into a mould, and let it stand twenty-four hours. Many prefer the flavour of lemon-peel or laurel-leaf to the cinnamon.

RICE BLANCMANGE.

1055. Take three table-spoonfuls of very finely ground rice, stir it gently into three gills of good new milk; add lump sugar to the taste, but not too much, or it will prevent its setting. Flavour it with lemon-peel or almond essence; set it on the fire, and let it boil thoroughly, stirring it and beating it extremely well for rather more than half an hour, and then pour it into a mould that has been soaked in cold water.

1056. *Improved Rice Blancmange.*—Mix three ounces of ground rice and one ounce of arrowroot with one quart of new milk, to which a little cream has been added. Sweeten it to the taste, and flavour it with laurel-leaf, cinnamon, or orange essence in the usual way. The addition of the arrowroot makes it eat much more tender and pleasant.

RICE FLUMMERY.

1057. Chop or grate the rind of half a lemon very fine, and pound half an ounce of bitter almonds; mix them together; then take a quart of new milk, a quarter of a pound of loaf sugar, and the same of ground rice, stirring the latter.

CHOCOLATE OR COCOA BLANCMANGE.

1058. Boil six ounces of cocoa or chocolate in a pint of cream, with six ounces of sifted sugar; let them boil five minutes; then add one ounce of isinglass dissolved in milk. Mix well and pour into the mould.

RATAFIA BLANCMANGE.

1059. Pour a quart of cream or rich milk, boiling hot, over half a pound of crushed macaroon ratafias, mix it well, and let it stand, stirring it occasionally till the ratafias are dissolved. Then add one ounce of isinglass dissolved in a gill of lukewarm water. Stir well, pour into a mould, and set it to cool.

SPANISH BLANCMANGE.

1060. Powder half a pound of loaf-sugar, having rubbed the rind of a lemon on some of it. Mix with it one pint of cream, the juice of the lemon, and half a pint of water. Stir it till all is dissolved, then stir in another pint of cream; dissolve one ounce of isinglass in a quarter of a pint of water; mix with the other lukewarm, and give the whole a good stirring; pour into a mould, and turn out when cold.

VANILLA BLANCMANGE.

1061. Dissolve one ounce of isinglass in a gill of water; boil a vanilla bean in a pint of milk till the flavour is well extracted. Whip a quart of cream to a stiff froth. Beat stiff the whites of four eggs, then the yolks separately, and beat in a quarter of a pound of sifted sugar; mix the cream and vanilla milk, then beat in by degrees the yolk, then the white, and lastly the melted isinglass, beating and stirring them; pour into your moulds, and set to cool; if it will not turn out, just slip the moulds into lukewarm water.

SUPPER DISH.

1062. Line a mould with any kind of preserves except raspberry, the greater variety the better; soak sponge cake with hot custard, and put it in the middle; then pour over a thin blancmange to bind the whole together; when cold, turn it out.

JAUNE MANGE.

1063. Put into one pint of water, the night before it is to be made, three-quarters of an ounce of gelatine and a little lemon-peel. The next day put into a pint-cup the juice of two lemons and one wine-glass of brandy; fill up the cup with good raisin-wine or sherry; pour these with the mixture into a saucepan, and add to them the yolks of

T

seven eggs well-beaten, and sufficient lump-sugar to sweeten it; set it on a slow fire, stirring it till it boils; strain it, and stir it occasionally until nearly cold, when it should be put into the moulds.

Another Jaune Mange.—Dissolve one ounce of isinglass in half a pint of boiling water; beat the yolks of six eggs, and mix them with half a pint of raisin or sherry wine, the juice of a lemon, and sugar to the taste (the peel of the lemon should be rubbed with some of the lumps of sugar to extract the essence). Stir all well together, and boil ten minutes. Strain, and when nearly cold put it into a mould first dipped in cold water.

Another Jaune Mange.—Stew half an ounce of isinglass in half a pint of water; add the rind of a lemon pared thin, after having rubbed two or three lumps of sugar on it to extract the essence for the jaune mange. When the isinglass is dissolved, squeeze the juice of the lemon into it, and add five table-spoonfuls of white wine. Stir into it by degrees the yolks of three eggs well beaten, and then set it over the fire and stir it one way till it boils. Strain it, and continue stirring till almost cold. Put it in a mould or glasses; when the eggs are mixed with it, sugar must be added to the taste. (This makes a very small quantity.)

LEMON CREAM IN SHAPE.

1064. Dissolve three-quarters of an ounce of Light's extract of calves' feet, or gelatine, in a quarter of a pint of water. Strain it, squeeze the juice of three lemons with the grated peel of one, sweeten with sifted lump sugar, and when you have added about three-quarters of a pint of good cream, or a little more, whisk it well till it becomes a strong froth. Then add the isinglass, cooled sufficiently, but not set; and mix it well. When it begins to set, put it into your mould, and in an hour or two it will be sufficiently firm to turn out. This quantity should fill a quart mould. This cream may be varied by adding before it sets a few dried or preserved cherries, greengages, &c., with a little candied peel, and colour it with a little cochineal.

Another.—Simmer three-quarters of an ounce of gelatine in a little milk until dissolved; strain and set it to cool; put the juice of three lemons and some sugar to a pint of cream; whisk them well together, pour in the gelatine by degrees, whisk it again, and pour it into a mould.

LEMON CHEESE.

1065. Mix one quart of cream, the juice of three lemons, a little of the peel, a large glass of brandy, and powdered sugar to taste; stir all well together, then whisk it to a strong froth, place it in a sieve with a piece of thin muslin in it, and it should then stand till the whey has entirely left it; after this it may be put into a mould, turned out, and ornaménted to fancy. The cheese is better if made two days before it is wanted. The muslin should be rinsed through cold water. The above proportions make but a small cheese, but may easily be increased at pleasure.

LEMON SPONGE.

1066. Take half an ounce of isinglass, dissolve it in a little boiling water, then take the juice of eight lemons, and put sugar to your taste; whisk it together until it becomes a sponge, then wet the mould and put it in; when set turn it out. The mixture ought to be nearly cold to whisk well.

POMMES AUX MARRONS.

1067. Boil some chestnuts until they are soft; pulp them, and add a little white sugar and lemon-juice. With this line the inside of a tart-shape, or cake-mould, thickly buttered; then put in a good layer of pulped apples, sweetened and seasoned with powdered cinnamon and nutmeg; over this spread more chestnut paste, and again some apple; proceed thus until your mould is full; squeeze in some lemon juice to fill up the interstices, and bake in a quick oven. Turn it out as you would a cake.

POMMES À LA VESUVE.

1068. Pile some apple marmalade high in a dish. Get ready some macaroni boiled in water, but well drained, and afterwards sweetened with white sugar and flavoured with brandy; cut it into short lengths, but do not mince it; lay it as a bordering round the mountain of marmalade; plentifully dust the whole over with powdered white sugar, and on the apex form a crater with about half a dozen good-sized lumps of sugar; pour a good gill of brandy over the top, and immediately before serving set fire to it, and introduce it at table flaming.

RASPBERRY CREAM, SOLID.

1069. Take full half a pound of raspberry jelly or jam, with the seeds taken out; whisk quickly three-quarters of a pint of rich cream, to which has been added the juice of a lemon. The jam must be sweetened with sifted lump-sugar, and may be coloured with a very little cochineal; three-quarters of an ounce of "extract of calves' feet," or gelatine, must be previously dissolved in rather less than a quarter of a pint of water, and added to the cream at last. It must be put into the mould as soon as it begins to set. If required to be kept, it should be put into a crockery mould, that the colour may be preserved.

CREAMED RICE.

1070. Boil a large handful of rice in a pint of new milk till very thick and tender; when about half done, put in half the rind of a small lemon cut very small, and a little nutmeg or laurel leaf. Sweeten to the taste; put it in the moulds, and when quite cold turn it out, and pour over it some thick cream or custard, or place round it some jam or preserved fruits; if wanted for dinner, it should be prepared the previous day.

A SHAPE OF RICE.

1071. A teacupful of rice well washed. Put it into a stewpan with half a teacupful of water. Add to it a pint of new milk; let it boil till soft. Turn into a mould till cold, then serve it in a dish with jam or cream.

ITALIAN CREAM.

1072. Grate the peel of two lemons, squeeze the juice on the peel, add some sifted sugar—it should be made pretty sweet—then pour over it one pint and a half of cream; stir it well that it may not curdle, beat it with a whisk till it is as thick as batter; put a piece of muslin into a tin mould (to be pierced full of holes), and pour the cream into it. The tin should be placed across a dish, that it may stand hollow. Fill up the mould as the whip subsides.

A CHARLOTTE RUSSE.

1073. Take a plain mould, pour in a little calves' foot jelly to cover the bottom of the mould. When set, take finger biscuits, cut them straight to fit in the mould, and add a little more jelly, coloured with cochineal. Then take a little cream, put it in a basin, add a little lemon juice and loaf sugar pounded, with a glass of brandy flavoured to the taste; then whisk it stiff, melt half an ounce of isinglass *if the mould is large*, if a small one less will do; stir the isinglass in the cream, and pour it in the mould.

TO MAKE CUSTARD.

1074. Set a saucepan of water to boil, and, while it boils, put all the ingredients for the custard into a jug; viz., a pint of thin cream, five yolks of eggs well beaten (*no* white), sugar and laurel leaf to the taste. Set the jug in boiling water, and keep stirring till it is the proper thickness. Then take it out, and stuff a clean cloth into the jug to prevent its skinning over, and let it stand till quite cold, and then add some brandy. If in a hurry, the cream and laurel leaves may be made warm before adding the sugar and eggs, but the custard is not quite so thick in this case.

1075. *Boiled Milk Custard* should be made with four eggs to a quart of new milk; flavour with sugar and nutmeg, if liked; pour it boiling over some thin slices of roll or cake, and eat it either hot or cold.

1076. *A Less Rich Custard.*—Mix a quarter of a pint of cream with a quarter of a pint of milk, leaving a little out to mix with a tea-spoonful of arrowroot; pour the other boiled and sweetened over it; and add the yolks of two eggs and a little brandy when cold.

VANILLE CUSTARD FROTHED.

1077. Sweeten and flavour one pint of milk with vanilla. Beat the *whites* of seven or eight eggs to a stiff froth; and, when the milk boils, take out a table-spoonful of the froth and let it set in the milk, turning it once. Put it on a sieve to drain, then another, and another. When there is a sufficient quantity, strain the milk and make it into custard in the usual way, eight or nine eggs to a pint of milk. Put the custard when cold into a glass dish, and place the frothed whites upon it.

SPANISH CUSTARD.

1078. To a quart of milk put a little sugar; when boiled, take it off the fire, and shake three table-spoonfuls of arrowroot into it, add half a tea-spoonful of noyau or essence of almonds to it, and about half an ounce of isinglass; set it over the fire again, stirring it one way, then pour it into a mould, which must first be wetted, and when cold turn it out, and stick it with blanched almonds; mix the arrowroot with a little cold milk.

LEMON CUSTARDS.

1079. Beat the yolks of eight eggs till they are as white as milk; then put to them a pint of boiling water, the rinds of two lemons grated, and the juice sweetened to the taste. Stir it on the fire till thick enough; then add a large glass of rich wine and half a glass of brandy; give the whole one scald, and put it in cups, to be eaten cold.

ALMOND CUSTARD.

1080. Take three bitter almonds with a little cinnamon, and rub some fresh lemon-peel grated on two ounces of lump-sugar, put them in a pint of milk or cream, and simmer them for a quarter of an hour, then strain and stir till cool. After this mix with the milk the yolks of four eggs well beaten, simmer again until it becomes a thick custard, then add an ounce of sweet almonds beaten smooth with rose water.

TIPSY CAKE.

1081. Take a stale sponge-cake of full size, pierce it with holes, making them with a knitting-pin. Pour over by degrees with a spoon half a pint of raisin-wine and a wine-glass of brandy mixed. When this quantity is soaked up, which will require the wine to be ladled up from the bottom, stick it thickly over with blanched almonds cut in points or spikes. Just before it goes to table pour over it a thick custard, or whipped cream. Seven or eight sponge biscuits may be boiled up and done the same way, or, by way of variety, the cake may be sliced with preserve spread between each layer, and then finish as above.

TURNED-OUT CUSTARD.

1082. Mix with one pint of sweet milk half an ounce of shred isinglass, the yolks of four eggs well beaten, nine pounded bitter almonds; stir all well over a slow fire till the isinglass is dissolved; strain through a fine sieve or muslin, and pour into a shape. When cold, turn it out.

SECT. 3.—JELLIES.

1083. For directions to run jellies, see the *Economical Housekeeper*.

CALF'S FEET JELLY.

1084. Put a set of calf's feet well cleaned into a pan with five quarts of water, and let them boil gently till reduced to two quarts. Then take out the feet, let the jelly become quite cold, skim the fat off clean, and clear the jelly from the sediment. Beat the whites of eight eggs to a froth, then add one bottle of raisin-wine or sherry, squeeze in the juice of from eight to twelve lemons, and the peel of five or six. Sweeten it to the taste (about two pounds and a quarter of loaf sugar). When the stock is boiling, take three spoonfuls of it and keep stirring it with the wine and eggs, to prevent it from curdling; then add a little more stock and still keep stirring, and then put it into the pan; let it boil twenty. minutes, and about the middle of the time pour in half a teacup of cold water; pour it into a flannel-bag, and let it run into a basin. Keep pouring it back into the bag gently till it runs clear. Let it settle a little after boiling before pouring it into the bag, and be nearly cold before going into the mould. The eggs and wine must be carefully mixed, or it will curdle. If loosening the edges and shaking the jellies or blancmange is not sufficient, try dipping the mould for *one instant* into *very* hot water, or lay under it a cloth that has been dipped in hot water.

JELLY WITH GELATINE.

1085. Take two ounces and three quarters of gelatine dissolved in about a quart of water, four lemons, one pound of loaf sugar, nearly half a bottle of raisin-wine, or a little brandy and less of the wine, as little white of egg as is neccessary to clear it, as the egg takes from the stiffness of the jelly. Boil altogether, strain through a jelly-bag, and put into a mould.

OX FEET JELLY.

1086. To three ox feet, made into very stiff stock, allow two pounds and a half of brown sugar, the juice of six lemons, a bottle of table-beer, seven eggs (yolks and whites), a few cloves, about one quarter of an ounce of isinglass, and a tea-cupful of vinegar. Boil all these ingredients together a quarter of an hour; take the pan off the fire, and let it stand on the fender for five minutes before putting it through the jelly-bag.

WINE JELLIES (MADE WITH GELATINE).

1087. Put full three-quarters of an ounce of gelatine in a pint of water the night before making the jelly, with a bit of lemon peel and twelve ounces of sugar; squeeze in a pint measure the juice of four lemons, add a glass and a half of brandy, some orange flavouring or spirit of punch, fill up with good raisin-wine, and whites and yolks of two eggs beaten; boil gently till the scum separates, and pass through a jelly-bag.

LEMON JELLY (*most excellent*)

1088. Pare very thin the rind of two lemons, put it into a cup, and pour a little boiling water over it. Dissolve one ounce of gelatine or of Light's extract of calves' feet in a pint of water, add to that the juice of six lemons, the water in which the rind has been steeped, one tea-spoonful of brandy, one tea-spoonful of rum, and one tea-spoonful of orange flavouring, with water enough to make up a quart; add half a pound of lump-sugar. Give it a boil up, and strain through a muslin; when nearly cold pour it into the mould.

TAPIOCA WINE JELLY.

1089. Take a quarter of a pound of tapioca, and wash it in two or three waters; then add a pint of cold water, and let it soak twelve hours or more; simmer it in the same water with the rind of a lemon until it becomes quite clear; then add the juice of the lemon, with wine and loaf sugar to taste, and put it in the mould at once.

APPLE JELLY.

1090. Put one pound and a half of apples, after being pared and cored, in a quart of water; boil them till the apples are in a pulp; put them into a hair sieve to drain, but do not *rub* through. Measure the juice, and to every pint put half an ounce of isinglass (or the extract of calves' feet) and the juice and peel of a small lemon, sugar to taste; boil altogether five or ten minutes. Pour it through a flannel bag, and stir it till nearly cold before it is put into a mould.

RED APPLES IN JELLY.

1091. Pare and core some well-shaped apples—pippins or golden rennets, if you have them, but others will do; throw them into water as you do them; put them into a preserving-pan, and with as little water as will only half cover them; let them coddle, and, when the lower side is done, turn them. Observe that they do not lie too close when first put in. Mix one or two grains of pounded cochineal or a tea-spoonful of the tincture with the water, and boil with the fruit. When sufficiently done, take them out on the dish they are to be served in, the stalks downwards. Take the water and make a rich jelly of it with loaf-sugar, boiling the thin rind and juice of a lemon. When come to a jelly, let it grow cold, and put it on and among the apples; cut the peel of the lemon in narrow strips, and put it across the eye of the apple.

ORANGE JELLY.

1092. Peel lightly six oranges, and throw the peel into a little water,

which lay on the corner of a stove without allowing it to boil, lest it
should taste too bitter. Cut the oranges in two, have a lemon
squeezer and silk sieve to squeeze the oranges (which dip in water to
prevent waste); squeeze the oranges into an earthen pan, and pour
into it through the sieve the infusion of peel. Next clarify a pound
of sugar or so, and then pour in the orange juice. The heat of the
sugar will clarify the jelly. Do not let it boil, but as soon as you
perceive a yellow scum skim it, and pour the jelly into a bag. Next
mix some melted isinglass, either hot or cold. This jelly must not be
made too firm. If the oranges are too ripe, mix a little lemon-juice
to make them more acid. Eighteen oranges are requisite to make a
good jelly. Lemon jelly may be made in the same way.

Another Way.—To two quarts of calf's feet or cow-heel stock made
stiff, add the juice of twelve China oranges and the peel of six, the
juice of two lemons and peel of one; pare the oranges and lemons
very thin. Boil all together for half an hour, and sweeten to the taste.
Strain through a piece of muslin.

Another Way.—Boil two ounces of isinglass in a pint of water,
three-quarters of a pound of loaf sugar in another pint of water.
Squeeze eight oranges, add the juice and rind of one lemon, and grate
the peel of some of the oranges. Mix all the ingredients together,
and let it boil a quarter of an hour. Strain it through a flannel bag,
and put it into the mould.

CHERRY JELLY.

1093. The best method of making cherry jelly consists in clarifying
the sugar, and when it has been skimmed properly and boils, throw
the cherries into it; take them off the fire, and, when the decoction is
cold, throw in a little liquid clarified cold isinglass. Squeeze three or
four lemons into it. Strain through a bag, and put it into an earthen
mould.

PUNCH JELLY.

1094. Take a pound of loaf sugar, one ounce and a half of isinglass,
the juice of four Seville oranges and four lemons, a wine glassful of
brandy, and one of rum. Melt the isinglass in a pint or more of boiling water, then strain it quite hot through a fine sieve upon the punch.
Stir it, and put it in a mould.

Another Punch Jelly.—Dissolve an ounce and a half of isinglass in a
pint or more of water, with the peel of a lemon. To a quarter of a
pint of brandy, and half that quantity of rum, add the juice of two

lemons, sweeten it with a pound and a quarter of loaf sugar. Strain the water in which the isinglass has been dissolved through a sieve upon the punch, then place it on the fire to heat, not to boil. Let it stand to settle, and pour it into the mould.

RASPBERRY JELLY.

1095. Dissolve one ounce of gelatine in half a pint of water, add three-quarters of a pint of raspberry syrup (with a spoonful of lemon juice, or fifteen grains of tartaric acid), boil and skim, and pour it into the mould.

EXCELLENT RED JELLY.

1096. Dissolve one ounce of isinglass in three-quarters of a pint of water, and add the eighth part of the white of an egg well beaten. When nearly dissolved put in one pound of loaf sugar broken, and a third of a spoonful of cochineal powdered. Ten minutes before taking off the fire, put in the grated rind of three lemons. Strain it through muslin, and add a cupful of Madeira, or any other good white wine, and the strained juice of four lemons. If it looks thick, give it one boil up. Let it cool before it goes into the mould. The pan should be kept covered all the time it is boiling.

GELATINE DE POMMES.

1097. In a pint of water, boil one pound and a half of white sugar until it is reduced to a very thick syrup; then add two pounds of Newtown pippins, pared, cored, and cut into slices; squeeze in the juice of three lemons, and simmer gently until it is almost a paste; then pour it into a mould, and, when cold, it will turn out a solid jelly. Serve it surrounded with scalded cream in a deep dish.

SECT. 4.—STEWED FRUITS; TO STEW NORMANDY PIPPINS.

1098. Soak a dozen pippins in a quart of cold water, and let them stand all night. Strain off the water, and add to it six ounces of powdered loaf sugar, six cloves, a glass of Madeira or light wine, and a little thin lemon-peel cut in very narrow pieces; boil it up to a syrup. Put in the apples, and let them simmer very gently till tender. If tied down in a jar, they will keep good a fortnight.

Another.—Soak them all night in cold water; next day pour the water from them, and to three-quarters of a pound of pippins put half a pound of loaf sugar and a large teaspoonful of grated lemon peel.

Stew slowly till they are quite tender and much swollen, keeping them well under the syrup. If not previously soaked a syrup must be made of the sugar with water, in which to stew the pippins.

STEWED APPLES, CALLED BLACK CAPS.

1099. Take large French pippins, or golden rennets; cut them in half, and lay them with the flat side downwards in a dish. Put a little currant wine and some fine sugar over them, and put them into a quick oven for half an hour. Boil some currant wine, or other sweet wine, with a little lemon-peel cut in long thin pieces, a small quantity of gelatine, a little lemon-juice, and some sugar together, till the gelatine or isinglass is dissolved; put the apples in a dish, and pour it over them. The jelly should be set before they are sent to table.

STEWED APPLES.

1100. Pare evenly any good boiling apples of a pretty large size; take out the core with a scoop, and put them into a stewpan, with water enough to cover them. Add a little sugar, lemon-peel, and juice, if the apples require it. Stew them gently till quite tender, taking care not to break them. Take them out of the water, to which add sugar enough to make a rich syrup, and a peach leaf or teaspoonful of capillaire; boil it, and, when as thick as cream, pour it in the dish round the apples. A little colouring may be given to one side of the apple with cochineal, or the juice of red beet-root.

TO SCALD CODLINS.

1101. Wrap each in a vine-leaf, and pack them close in a stew-pan; and when full pour as much water as will cover them. Set it over a gentle fire, and let them simmer slowly till done enough to take the thin skin off when cold. Place them in a dish, with or without milk, cream, or custard; if the latter, there should be no ratafia. Dust fine sugar over the apples.

POMMES À L'IMPERATRICE.

1102. Take some apples, do not pare them, but score them length-wise with a sharp knife; cut a good piece off the stalk ends, and remove the cores; fill the apples with quince marmalade, apricot, or green gage jam, and put them, with the flat end downwards, into a baking dish, with a pint of chablis and two table-spoonfuls of sugar.

Baste them frequently, and when done serve hot or cold in the syrup.

MIROTON DE POMMES.

1103. Scald six large apples, and when soft enough to do so, pulp them, and, after sweetening a little, pile them upon the dish you purpose serving them in. Take a teacupful of the liquor in which they were dressed, and boil the finely shred rind of a lemon, and three ounces of white sugar; then beat well the yolks of three eggs, and the white of one; add a dessert-spoonful of fine flour, the same of brandy, and two ounces of fresh butter. Mingle these ingredients well together in a saucepan, over a moderate fire; when perfectly smooth take them off, and pour over the apples; then whisk the whites of the two eggs into a stiff froth, put it upon the miroton, sifting a little sugar over it. Place it for ten minutes in a slow oven, and serve hot or cold.

POMMES À L'ALLEMANDE.

1104. Peel, and cut the fruit into quarters; take away the pips; put the apples into a stewpan of boiling butter; shake them for five minutes over a brisk fire, letting them become nicely browned; then dust them plentifully with flour, add a little water or Rhine wine, and sugar agreeably to taste. Let them simmer for half an hour, and serve with the syrup, which should be thickened with a well-beaten egg.

POMMES À LA HOLLANDAISE.

1105. Pare some rather small apples, prick them carefully all over, and, as you do them, throw them into a syrup made with equal quantities of water and white sugar. Put them on a slow but not smoky fire, and, as soon as they boil, remove them to a little distance from the fire, so that they may absorb the syrup, and become gradually clear without breaking. When they are done, put them into a glass dessert dish, and empty a small flask of Eau de Vie de Dantzig into the syrup. Mix well, and pour it over the apples. Should you not have this Eau de Vie, take a sufficient quantity of refined Hollands, and having procured a gilder's leaf of gold, mingle it with the syrup by bruising it with a spoon. The principal attraction of this elegant preparation is its beautiful transparency, which renders it a recherché ornament upon the dessert tables of continental dinner-givers of celebrity.

POMMES SANTÉES.

1106. Peel some very small and prettily shaped apples, but do not take off their stalks; put them into a stewpan of boiling butter, and shake them over a brisk fire until they are of a nice brown colour; drain them, and arrange them neatly, with their stalks upwards, upon a thick layer of white sugar in a dish. Serve them either warm or cold.

RED APPLES IN JELLY.

1107. Take some prettily formed apples of the pear main, or non-such kind, put them into a stewpan, with enough water to cover them; add a spoonful of powdered cochineal, and simmer gently; when the fruit is done take it out, and put it into a dessert dish. Make a syrup of the liquor by adding white sugar and the juice of two lemons; when boiled to a jelly put it with the apples, decorating the dish with the lemon peel cut into thin slips.

PLAIN BAKED APPLES.

1108. Choose some nice sizeable apples, rather large; prick them very well with a coarse needle to prevent their bursting, lay them nicely in a baking dish, with their stalks upwards. As they are be-ginning to get warm rub a little butter over each, and, when done, serve either warm or cold, with the addition of some pounded sugar strewed upon them.

APPLES TO STEW OR BAKE FOR FAMILY USE.

1109. Take any moderate-sized good cooking apples, and put them, in a jar, either into a cool oven or water bath with a little water, moist or loaf sugar, and lemon-peel; stew till tender, and serve when cold. The lemon-peel may be either taken out or laid in long narrow strips across the apples when served.

ROASTED APPLES.

1110. Select the largest apples; scoop out the core without cutting quite through, fill the hollow with fine brown sugar, and butter if approved; let them roast in a slow oven, and serve them up with syrup.

TO STEW PEARS.

1111. Pare and halve the fruit, and lay them in a bright tin or enamelled iron saucepan. Then strew over them some lump sugar and a few cloves; pour over them some water (not more than a tea-cupful for a large quantity of pears). Fill the saucepan with the parings laid closely in layers, and cover with the lid. Let gently till the pears are tender, and then either boil gently or simmer for five or six hours till the colour is a deep crimson. When done, and the pears are taken out, add a lump of sugar, previously well rubbed on the rind of a lemon, and a little lemon juice to the syrup. Give it a boil up, and pour it a few times over the pears to give them the same flavour. Should there not be plenty of lump sugar, the pears are much longer in acquiring their proper colour.

1112. *Stewed Pears (another Receipt, less rich).*—After paring and halving one pound of pears, put them into a well-lined pan with three ounces of lump sugar, two-thirds of a pint of water, and a few cloves. Stew until quite tender.

BAKED PEARS.

1113. These need not be of a fine sort; some taste better than others, and often those that are least fit to eat raw. Wipe, but *do not* pare, lay them on tin plates, and bake them in a slow oven. When soft enough to bear it, flatten them with a silver-spoon. When done through, put them on a dish. They should be baked three or four times, and very gently.

To STEW QUINCES FOR SYRUP OR JELLY.

1114. Stew them in a little water, but they must not be too long boiled, or the juice will become red. When quite tender, leave them in their own liquor in a bowl till the following day, when their juice will be rich and clear.

STEWED PEACHES.

1115. Prepare a thin syrup of about six ounces of sugar to half a pint of water, with a little lemon juice and a few blanched kernels. Pare six peaches, and stew them for twenty minutes gently in the syrup. Lay the fruit in a dish; boil up the syrup till it is thick, then pour it and the kernels over the peaches. Should the fruit be unripe, it should be simmered in boiling water till the skin can easily be removed. The above may be served hot at dinner, or cold at supper or dessert.

POMMES À LA FRANGIPANE.

1116. Take some Ribston pippins, pare and bake them until they are thoroughly tender, then pulp them into a deep dish, and put over them a thick layer of Frangipane, which is prepared as follows :—Mix four eggs and four table-spoonfuls of flour well together, dilute it with a quart of new milk sufficiently sweetened with white sugar, add six macaroons powdered finely, and a gill of orange flower water. Place this mixture upon the fire, and as it gets thick stir it well, and pour it over the apples. Bake it in a gentle oven for half an hour.

CHARTREUSE DE POMMES.

1117. Well boil half a pound of the best Carolina rice in a quart of fresh milk, taking the greatest pains to prevent it from catching at the bottom of the saucepan. Pare seven large or nine middling-sized Kentish pippins, take out the cores without cutting the fruit quite through, put a little raspberry jam into each hole, and fill up with cream. Edge a deep pie-dish with a rich light paste; lay in the apples, and level up the spaces between them with the boiled rice. Brush it over with the yolk of an egg, dust it well with pounded loaf sugar, decorate it with a few pieces of candied lemon or orange peel, and bake it for about forty minutes in a brisk oven. This dish is better eaten hot.

CHAP. XXVI—FRENCH COOKERY, AND MISCELLANEOUS RECEIPTS.

SECT. 1.—FRENCH COOKERY, AS COMPARED WITH THE ENGLISH SCHOOL.

1118. For many years our opposite neighbours have looked down upon the cookery of this country with the greatest contempt, considering it in a barbarous condition. This low opinion may have been well founded in the last century, but I much question whether at present we may not have it in our power to return the compliment; though I am ready to admit that we owe a great deal to the French for our existing knowledge of the art of cookery. I am not, however, attempting to settle the question depending upon the relative inventive powers of the two nations, but that connected with the *present modes* of preparing their food. Let any one sit down to a dinner cooked by a first-rate French cook, and say if it is not true that all the dishes worth eating are cooked on English principles, although, perhaps, dignified with high-sounding French names; while, on the other hand, the veritable French dishes, however beautiful and tempting to the eye they may be, are, when tasted, by no means of first-rate flavour. I am not now speaking from my own particular experience, because I

know that the taste of an individual is no criterion by which to judge
of those belonging to the multitude; but from close observation I
should decidedly say, that the large proportion of the English who
have the choice of both kinds, prefer genuine English dishes to those of
French preparation. Of course, it will happen that those who have
only an occasional opportunity of gratifying their fancy for novelty by
partaking of strange fare, profess to like what to them is a rarity; but
this is no rule to guide in the choice, and it is only needful in reality
to consider whether the French have discovered any methods of
cookery more *economical,* more *wholesome,* or more *palatable,* than
ours. Here issue must join, and I boldly maintain that they have not.
I know full well that the French can, and do, live upon less than the
English in point of animal food, but they make up for this abstinence
by indulging largely in salads and vegetables; and in bulk, as well as
most probably in weight, of food they equal, if they do not go beyond,
the usual allowance of the English. But do they, or do they not,
cook this said animal food in a more wholesome mode than we do?
If it is maintained that they do, I must ask in what way? Is it in
their soups? We have the same. Is it in their fish? I maintain
that plain boiled turbot is more wholesome than a *vol-au-vent de turbot.*
With regard to their *entrées* and *entremets,* they are only other names
for our side and corner-dishes, confectionery, and sweets—none of
which are certainly to be recommended for their suitability to the
stomach. If these facts are really what I say, then French cookery
can only claim a superiority in point of flavour; and here the matter
cannot be settled, since every one will judge for himself. But in every
other respect I maintain that, with the aid of the old English cook of
the early part of this century, we may live quite as economically, and
in a *more* wholesome way than even by the aid of Soyer himself. To
the French system of frying I have given due credit under the section
treating of that department, but beyond that I know of little real improvement which they can claim; excepting, perhaps, the mode of
boiling their fresh beef (*bouilli*), which would not bear to be presented
in English style. The plan, however, is a good one, and might certainly be adopted in this country with advantage. The English mistake has been, not so much in the poverty of their cookery, as in the
abuse of its abundance of good things. If fine meat were more plenti-
ful in Paris, we should see it more frequently produced *au naturel;*
but, with their tough and stringy beef and mutton, and melancholy-
looking veal, they are compelled to have recourse on all occasions to

those dishes which we only need employ occasionally. English receipts for stews, hashes, harricots, fricassees, &c., originally French
though they may be, are numerous enough, and, when well made, equal
in flavour to many of the much-vaunted modern French entrées; but
when ill-made, the fault lies not in the cookery, but in the cook, who is
thought nothing of if she confines her attention to English dishes, and
consequently neglects them in the attempt to reach beyond her limited
powers. Do we ever see a Frenchman refuse a fine haunch of mutton or
venison when he has the chance? It is true that he requires a
differently-flavoured sauce to that which is the customary one in this
country; but it is not against these that the complaint is made, but
against our barbarous method of roasting and boiling *joints*. Plain
melted butter may be his abomination, and so it is of many English-
men; nevertheless, it is the foundation in France, as well as in England, of very many good sauces. What I wish to have understood by
those who now submit to be called barbarous in cookery, is the fact,
that, except in making too free use of our splendid butcher's meat, we
are not in point of *science* behind the French. Our *principles of cookery*
are quite as well-founded as theirs (saving always the aforementioned
frying-pan); and we have no reason to submit to the alleged superiority which they claim. They are fonder of acids than we are; but
that is no scientific discovery. They also indulge in a greater variety
of flavours than we do; but that, again, is no improvement in science,
for it only tempts the stomach to do that which the Englishman is
already too prone to do without—namely, to eat too much. I am,
therefore, at a loss to know in what the pre-eminence consists; and I
can only come to the conclusion that it is undeserved. The English
of the last century were bigoted in thinking themselves superior to
all other nations; but in the latter half of this they seem determined
to run into the opposite extreme, and come to the conclusion that
they are only fit to wash the dishes for their neighbours' *chefs de cuisine.*

1119. The argument which I have maintained in the preceding
paragraph is still farther supported by the fact, that almost all the
French terms used in their cookery are easily translated into English
by synonyms, showing that they have had a previous or parallel existence, and been named in this country as well as in France. If it were
otherwise, instead of being merely adopted here by the cook and his
patrons, they would become part of the English vocabulary, in the
same way as many French words in other departments, such as *enve-
lope, ennui, hauteur,* &c.

VOCABULARY OF FRENCH COOKING TERMS TRANSLATED.

Atelets, small silver skewers.

Assiettes, dishes with four compartments, for the use of the cook (old English).

Assiette volante, dish handed round.

Au naturel, plain.

Bain-marie, a water-bath.

Beignet, a fritter.

Blanc, a white broth.

Blanquette, a kind of fricassee (French only).

Braising, (a peculiar kind of stewing (long used in England, see page 55).

Boudin, a French dish, formed of expensive forcemeats, poached and broiled.

Bouilli, boiled *fresh* beef, peculiar to France.

Bouillon, broth.

Buisson, a high standing dish of pasty.

Casserole, a stewpan.

Casserole, a rice-crust.

Compôte, a mixture of fruits, also a white mixture or ragout of small birds or pigeons.

Compotice, lowest dish to hold the compôte.

Court bouillon, a preparation of wine, &c., in which fish is boiled.

Consommé, a strong gravy (clear).

Coulis, cullis, or rich brown gravy.

Croustade, a hollow crust of bread formed to hold minces, &c.

Croquettes, savoury minces.

Crouton, a sippet fried.

En papillotte, in paper (oiled).

En couronne, in the shape of a crown.

Emincé, minced.

Entrées, corner or side dishes served with the first courses.

Entremets, ditto, with the second and third courses.

Feuilletage, puff-paste.

Friture, frying-pan.

Farce, forcemeat.

Fricandeau, a stew of veal (see Fricandeau).

Gateau, cake.

Gras, made with meat.

Gratiner, to make crisp, to grill.

Liaison, a mixture of cream and egg to thicken white soup.

Maigre, without meat.

Marinade, a liquor prepared with vinegar for boiling fish, &c.

Matelote, a kind of stew of fish.

Meringue, a very light cake, made of sugar and white of egg beaten up.

Miroton, a meat dish (see Miroton).

Nouilles, a paste made of egg and flour.

Noix de veau, the part of the fillet of veal near the udder.

Panieres, dressed with bread-crumbs.

Passer, to fry lightly.

Piqné, larded on the surface only.

Poêle, a liquor concocted to boil fowls in

Pot-au-feu, an economical dish (page 81.)

Potage, broth or soup.

Purée, meat, fish, &c., pounded and pressed through a purée presser and sieve to remove the lumps.

Quenelles, a kind of forcemeat.

Rissoles, small fried pastry, both savoury and sweet.

Ragout, a rich kind of stew or sauce with sweetbreads, &c.

Roux, a thickening of flour or butter.

Salmi, a hash of half-dressed game.

Saute, fried in the French style (page 51).

Singer, to flour the stewpan.

Tamis, a strainer or sieve of woollen canvas.

Timbale, a pie made in a peculiar mould.

Tourte, a species of tart.

Vanner, to take up a sauce with a spoon in a peculiar manner.

Veloute, a rich sauce.

Vol-au-vent, a raised crust of ornamental puff paste.

After carefully examining the above list, which, I believe, comprehends nearly all the terms used in the French *cuisine,* it is ridiculous to attempt to maintain that, except in the arrangement of the letters, they have any thing peculiar. Their words are composed of different changes of the members of the alphabet, but they are nearly all represented in our tongue by corresponding ones as good as theirs; and it might be just as well maintained that a fine roasted Norfolk turkey *is* improved by giving it the name of *dindon roti,* as to allege that *potage* is better than soup, or a *vol-au-vent* more scientific than a patty. By all means adopt improvements, whether French, German, Italian, or Russian; but do not take the bad with the good; nor is it necessary to despise our own really wholesome and appetizing dishes because they are our own. I fully admit that the French, as individuals, are more inventive than we are, and generally take to cookery better than the English, but that their national cookery is superior to ours, I as fully deny.

SECT. 2.—MISCELLANEOUS COOKERY RECEIPTS.

To Boil Eggs.

1120. Boil some water in a small saucepan; put in the eggs carefully with a spoon, taking the time by a clock or watch; boil for two minutes and a half to three and a half, according to the taste of the consumer. The first-mentioned time scarcely turns the white all through, while the last almost hardens the yolk. Three minutes boiling will be preferred by most people, as the whites are then just set, and the yolks a little thickened in consistence. If the weather is very cold, it is better to warm the eggs a little before boiling them, or they are very apt to crack from the sudden expansion by heat.

To Poach Eggs.

1121. Set a stewpan of water on the fire; when boiling, slip an egg, previously broken in a cup, into the water; when the white looks done enough, slide an egg-slice under the egg, and lay it on toast and butter, or spinach. As soon as enough are done, serve hot. If not fresh laid, they will not poach well, and without breaking. Trim the ragged parts of the whites, and make them look round.

Buttered Eggs, or Egg Toast.

1122. Beat four or five eggs, yolk and white together; put a quarter of a pound of butter in a basin, and then put it in boiling water, stirring it till melted; pour the butter and eggs into a saucepan; keep a basin in the hand, just holding the saucepan in the other, over a slow part of the fire, shaking it one way as it begins to warm; pour it into the basin and back; then hold it again over the fire, alternately stirring it constantly in the saucepan, and pouring it into the basin, more perfectly to mix the egg and butter, until they shall be hot without boiling. Serve on toasted bread, or in a basin, to eat with salt fish or red herrings.

Scotch Eggs.

1123. Boil hard five pullets' eggs, and, without removing the white.

cover completely with a fine relishing forcemeat, in which let scraped ham or chopped anchovy bear a due proportion. Fry of a beautiful yellow brown, and serve with a good gravy in the dish.

To Boil Eggs Hard.

1124. Boil them ten minutes, moving them gently to change the under side, and put them by to get cold.

Oatmeal Porridge (*a genuine Scotch receipt*).

1125. Put as much water as will make as much porridge as is wished into a saucepan, let it boil; then take a handful of meal in the left hand, letting it fall gently into the water while stirring the meal and water quickly round with the right, with a wooden stirrer or spoon; do this till it is the thickness of thick gruel, then salt to the taste; let it boil for ten minutes, add a little more boiling water, and boil it other five minutes, which makes it quite smooth and very digestible (boiling it well is the great secret for making it digestible and nourishing for invalids). It is poured out in pudding dishes for each member of a Scotch family, and they dip each spoonful into a jugful of milk, and thus make a hearty and nourishing breakfast. The poorer class of children often have it for their evening meal too, and in this way it forms the principal food for Scotch children, who seldom ever tire of it till they grow up.

Rice Porridge.

1126. On half a pound of rice pour three quarts of boiling water; let it swell till it becomes quite a jelly. Add one quarter (or half) a pound of oatmeal, mixing it first with cold water; stir it well together, add one ounce of onions chopped fine, half an ounce of bacon fat, butter, or lard, salt and pepper to taste; boil all together, stirring all the time.

Flour Milk

1127. Is made by mixing up a table-spoonful of wheat-flour in water to a thin paste, then stirring it into a pint of boiling milk till it thickens. It may be eaten with sugar or treacle.

Rice and Sago Milks

1128. Are made by washing the grains nicely, and simmering with milk over a slow fire till sufficiently done. The former sort requires lemon, spice, and sugar; the latter is good without any thing to flavour it.

BREAD AND MILK.

1129. Cut or break stale bread into fragments, then boil in milk for a quarter of an hour.

FRUMETY.

1130. Boil a quarter of a pint of wheat for three or four hours, then add one quart of milk, with two spoonfuls of flour mixed with it, two eggs, three parts of a small teacupful of raisins and currants, a little lemon-peel and cinnamon. Boil for a quarter of an hour, and serve.

Another.—Bake wheat in water till every corn is broken and completely swelled out, adding more water as it is taken up by the wheat. Then add some milk, sugar, and nutmeg to taste, either with or without currants and raisins; just give it a boil up, adding at the last a little cream thickened with flour.

CURDS AND CREAM.

1131. Put three or four pints of milk into a pan a little warm, and then add rennet or gallino. When the curd is come, lade it with a saucer into an earthen shape perforated, of any form you please. Fill it up as the whey drains off, without breaking or pressing the curd. If turned only two hours before wanted, it is very light; but those who like it harder may have it so, by making it earlier, and squeezing it. Cream, milk, or a whip of cream, sugar, wine, and lemon, to be put in the dish, or into a glass bowl, to serve with the curd.

Another Way.—To four quarts of new milk warmed put from a pint to a quart of buttermilk strained, according to its sourness; keep the pan covered until the curd is of firmness to cut three or four times across with a saucer; as the whey leaves it, put it into a shape, and fill up until it is solid enough to take the form. Serve with plain cream, or mixed with sugar, wine, and lemon.

GALLINO CURDS AND WHEY, AS IN ITALY.

1132. Take a number of the rough coats that line the gizzards of turkeys and fowls; clean them from the pebbles they contain; rub them well with salt, and hang them to dry. This makes a more tender and delicate curd than common rennet. When to be used, break off some bits of the skin, and put on it some boiling water; in eight or nine hours use the liquor in the same way as other rennet.

BUTTERMILK.

1133. This, if made of sweet cream, is a delicious and most wholesome food. Those who can relish sour buttermilk, find it still more light; but it is not generally liked. Buttermilk, if not very sour, is also as good as cream to eat with fruit, if sweetened with white sugar, and mixed with a very little milk. It likewise does equally for cakes and rice-puddings, and therefore it is economical to churn before the cream is too stale to make buttermilk fit for nothing but to feed pigs.

LONDON SYLLABUB.

1134. Put a pint and a half of port or white wine into a bowl, with nutmeg grated, and a good deal of sugar, then milk into it near two quarts of milk, frothed up. If the wine is not rather sharp, it will require more for this quantity of milk.

STAFFORDSHIRE SYLLABUB.

1135. Put a pint of cider, and a glass of brandy, sugar, and nutmeg into a bowl, and milk into it; or pour warm milk from a large teapot some height into it.

SOMERSETSHIRE SYLLABUB.

1136. In a large china bowl put a pint of port, and a pint of sherry or other white wine; sugar to taste. Milk the bowl full. In twenty minutes' time cover it pretty high with clouted cream; grate over it nutmeg, and put in pounded cinnamon and nonpareil comfits.

DEVONSHIRE JUNKET.

1137. Put warm milk into a bowl; turn it with rennet; then put some scalded cream, sugar, and cinnamon on the top, without breaking the curd. Many people add a little brandy and rum in equal proportions.

POSSET SYLLABUB.

1138. Mix a quart of thick cream with one pound of lump sugar and a pint of white wine; rub a few lumps of sugar upon the rind of two or three lemons to extract the essence, and pour upon them the juice of three lemons; add this to the cream, and whisk it one way for half an hour, or till thick.

EVERLASTING SYLLABUB.

1139. Take half a pint of thick cream, half a pint of white wine, a little brandy, the juice of a small lemon, and the essence of the rind rubbed off upon lumps of sugar, and, added to the juice, half a pound of lump sugar sifted; mix the whole well together, and whisk until quite thick.

BUTTERMILK CURDS.

1140. Take three pints of buttermilk and put it in a broad basin; take a pint and a half of new milk, and boil it with half a nutmeg till it relishes; pour it hot on the buttermilk, and let it stand two or three hours, till the whey is cleared from the curds; put it on a thin cloth, and let it hang till the whey is all drained from it. Serve it up with cream, sugar, and grated nutmeg.

TO POT CHEESE.

1141. Take two pounds of cheese, one of Cheshire and one of Gloucestershire; to this add three spoonfuls of mountain wine and two spoonfuls of made mustard; beat all these together in a marble mortar, and then put it into pots for use.

Another Way.—Cut and pound four ounces of Cheshire cheese, one ounce and a half of fine butter, a tea-spoonful of white pounded sugar, a little bit of mace, and a glass of white wine; press it down in a deep pot.

TOASTED CHEESE.

1142. Lay a slice of cheese on toasted bread buttered on both sides; put it to the fire, and, when the cheese begins to toast, mix some beer, pepper, and salt, and pour over it. The beer should be sufficient to moisten the bread.

TOASTED CHEESE TO COME UP AFTER DINNER.

1143. Grate three ounces of fat Cheshire cheese, mix it with the yolks of two eggs, four ounces of grated bread, and three ounces of butter; beat the whole well in a mortar with a dessert-spoonful of mustard, and a little salt and pepper. Toast some bread, cut it into proper pieces, lay the paste, as above, thick upon them into a Dutch oven, covered with a dish, till hot through; remove the dish, and let the cheese brown a little. Serve as hot as possible.

MELTED CHEESE.

1144. Take two ounces each of good Cheshire and of Parmesan cheese, grate them, and add about double the weight of each in beaten yolks of eggs and melted butter; mix them well together, add pepper and salt to the taste, and then put to it the white of the eggs, which

have been beaten separately; stir them lightly in, and bake it in a
deep dish filled but half full, as it will rise very much. Serve when
quite hot.

WELSH RABBIT.

1145. Toast a slice of bread on both sides, and butter it; toast a
slice of Gloucester cheese on one side, and lay that next the bread,
and toast the other with a salamander; rub mustard over, and serve
very hot, and covered.

CHEESE TOAST.

1146. Mix some fine butter, made mustard, and salt into a mass;
spread it on fresh-made thin toasts, and grate or scrape Gloucester
cheese upon them.

ANCHOVY TOAST.

1147. Bone and skin six or eight anchovies; pound them to a
mass with an ounce of fine butter till the colour is equal, and then
spread it on toasts or rusks.

Another Way.—Cut thin slices of bread into any form, and fry them
in clarified butter; wash three anchovies split, pound them in a mortar
with some fresh butter, rub them through a hair-sieve, and spread it
on the toast when cold; then quarter and wash some anchovies, and
lay them on the toast. Garnish with parsley or pickles.

FINGERS OF CHEESE.

1148. Half a pound of flour, half a pound of grated cheese, half a
pound of butter, half a tea-spoonful of cayenne dissolved in a teacup full of hot milk. Mix all well together with the hand, roll it out
and cut it into the size and shape of finger biscuits, and bake them
in a quick oven, taking care not to scorch them.

MACARONI.

1149. Wash one ounce of macaroni, and soak it in one pint of new milk
six hours, then stew it in the milk; or drop it at once into the milk, and
stew it till quite tender for about one hour and a half. Lay it in the
dish, grate cheese finely over it with some butter and bread crumbs,
brown with a salamander or in a Dutch oven.

FAIRY BUTTER.

1150. Take two ounces of butter, two ounces of sugar, the hard yolks of two eggs, and one Naples biscuit; beat all these well in a mortar, add a little orange or other flavouring, press it through a sieve, and garnish with biscuits round it. The Naples biscuit may be omitted.

CHESTNUTS TO ROAST FOR DESSERT.

1151. First boil them for eight or ten minutes, then prick the shells, or cut off a small portion from the pointed end, to prevent their bursting. Before they are cool, lay them to roast in an oven or before the fire for nearly a quarter of an hour. They must be tried to see if well done; and served very hot in a napkin.

SECT. 3.—CONFECTIONER'S RECEIPTS.

MOCK ICE.

1152. Dissolve half an ounce of isinglass in a breakfast cup of hot water; beat up a pot of strawberry or any other preserve with a pint of cream, pass it through a sieve, add the juice of a lemon and a teacupful of sugar, then add the isinglass when nearly cold, whisk it together, and when it begins to thicken put it in a mould.

Another Mock Ice.—Dissolve one ounce of isinglass in a little water, let it strain and cool. Put the juice of three lemons, or half a pint of fruit jelly or fruit to one pint of cream, with some sugar—whisk, and add the cooled isinglass. Whisk again well, and pour into moulds.

FRUIT DROPS OF LEMON JUICE.

1153. Mix a quantity of lemon juice with sifted sugar, nearly thick enough for a spoon to stand upright in. Put it in a deep pan and make it quite hot on the fire, stirring it all the time, but do not let it come to a boil, then mix in a small quantity more sugar. Warm it, then chalk the spout of the pan, and with a small stick drop it on tin or pewter plates in small drops. When cold, take them off the plates, and put them in the stove or sieves to dry.

GINGER DROPS (*a good Stomachic*).

1154. Beat two ounces of fresh candied orange in a mortar with a little sugar, to a paste; then mix one ounce of powder of white ginger with one pound of loaf sugar. Wet the sugar with a little water, and boil altogether to a candy, and drop it on paper, as for lemon drops.

PEPPERMINT DROPS.

1155. Pound and sift four ounces of double-refined sugar, beat it with the whites of two eggs till perfectly smooth, then add sixty drops of oil of peppermint, beat it well, and drop on white paper as above, and dry at a distance from the fire.

Ratafia Drops.

1156. Blanch and beat in a mortar four ounces of bitter and two of sweet almonds, with a part of a pound of sugar sifted, then add the remainder of the pound of sugar, and the whites of two eggs, making a paste; of which put little balls, the size of a nutmeg, on wafer-paper, and bake gently on tin plates.

Toffy.

1157. Mix one pound of coarse sugar, half a pound of treacle, a little butter, one tea-spoonful and a half of ginger, the same of mixed spice, let it boil for half an hour, grease a pewter plate and pour it in, then let it cool.

Everton Toffy.

1158. Mix one pound of sugar, a quarter of a pound of treacle, half a pound of butter, with the rind of half a lemon; boil all over a slow fire an hour, and pour it upon tins well buttered.

Barley Sugar.

1159. Dissolve a pound and a half of lump sugar in half a pint of water, with the white of half an egg; when it is at candy height (see *Economical Housekeeper*) add a tea-spoonful of strained lemon-juice, and boil it quickly till it recovers its previous condition. Pour it over a marble slab, and when it becomes stiff cut it into strips, and twist it.

To Prepare Fruit for Children in a more Wholesome Way than in Pies and Puddings.

1160. Put apples or pears sliced, plums, currants, gooseberries, &c., into a stone jar, and sprinkle as much Lisbon sugar as is necessary among them; set the jar on a hot hearth, or in a saucepan of water, and let it remain till the fruit is perfectly done. Slices of bread or rice may be either stewed with the fruit, or added when eaten; the rice being plain boiled.

Fruit Meringues or Cakes.

1161. Take either raspberries, apricots, or plums; infuse them in water till they are soft, then pulp them through a sieve, and to one pound of pulp put ten ounces of powdered lump sugar, and three whites of egg; beat them well with your hand for two hours, then drop them on cards with the edges turned up, or sheets of paper, on a baking tin. Sift sugar on the cards or paper before dropping them. Dry them gently on a stove, and when they slip off the paper they may be stored away in tin cases.

MERINGUED APPLES.

1162. Pare and core some large pippin apples, but do not quarter them; wash them in cold water, and put them wet in a deep baking dish, not touching; pour in enough water to prevent burning, and bake them till tender, but not broken; take them out and set them to cool, removing any juice; when cold, fill the core-hole with preserve or jelly, and cover them all over with a meringue put on in table-spoonfuls, and smooth it with the blade of a knife dipped often in water; then dredge the surface with sifted sugar, and put in a cool oven till the meringue is hardened. A meringue or icing is made of beaten white of egg, thickened with sifted sugar (in the proportion of the whites of four eggs to one pound of sugar), the egg being beaten to a stiff froth, then the sugar beaten in, a spoonful at a time; flavour it with lemon juice or rose water.

DRIED APPLES À L'ANGLAISE.

1163. Put them into a very slack oven, three or four days succes-sively, and as they become soft gently flatten them, by keeping a slight weight over them when they are out of the oven. The heat may be rather increased towards the last.

POMMES PRALINEES.

1164. Squeeze the juice of two or three lemons into a small pipkin or enamelled saucepan. Take some apples (the smallest you can get), peel them, remove the cores, and cut them lengthwise into thin slices, throw them into the boiling lemon juice, shake them well for a minute or two over the fire, take them off and put them aside to absorb the lemon juice as much as possible. When quite cold, put them into a syrup of boiling sugar, let it simmer until the syrup is turned to sugar again; take out the fruit and let it become dry.

APPLES À L'AMERICAINE.

1165. These are dried by taking some baking apples, paring and coring them, and cutting all up into thin slices, which are threaded upon string, and hung in dry airy places, where they soon get perfectly dry, and are used for sauces, &c., by dressing them in syrup.

APPLE CHOCOLATE.

1166. In a quart of new milk boil a pound of scraped French chocolate, and six ounces of white sugar. Beat the yolks of six eggs, and the whites of two, and, when the chocolate has come to a boil, remove it from the fire, gradually add the eggs, stirring well at the time. Have ready a deep dish, at the bottom of which you have placed a good layer of pulped apples sweetened to taste, and seasoned with powdered cinnamon; pour the chocolate gently over it, and place the dish upon a saucepan of boiling water. When the cream is set firmly it is done. Sift powdered sugar over it, and glaze with a red-hot shovel, if you have nothing better. This preparation is not only very delicious, but exceedingly salutary, on account of the apples being a corrective to the too great richness of the chocolate.

CIDER CUP.

1167. To two quarts of cider add two glasses of sherry, one of brandy, and one of curaçoa, the peel of half a lemon, pared very thin, sugar, ginger, and nutmeg to the taste; when all is mixed, add a bottle of soda-water; garnish with a branch of borage.

PLAIN CIDER CUP.

1168. To one quart of cider put two table-spoonfuls of moist sugar, one tea-spoonful of ginger, and a little nutmeg with a piece of toasted bread put in hot.

A COLD CUP.

1169. One quart of cider, a quarter of a pint of sherry, two wine glasses of brandy, half a pound of loaf sugar, the peel of one lemon pared thin, and half a lemon sliced in, with the rind of another lemon rubbed on lumps of sugar, a little nutmeg and ginger, and some sprigs of borage and balm. In hot weather, put in a few lumps of ice.

APPLE POSSET.

1170. Boil some slices of fine white bread in a pint of milk; when quite soft take it off the fire, sweeten it with sugar, and put in a spoonful of powdered ginger; pour it into a bowl, and gradually stir in the pulp of three or four nicely baked apples.

CHAP. XXIII.—COOKERY FOR THE POOR.

SECT. 1.—REMARKS.

1171. THE OBJECT OF THIS CHAPTER is twofold—1st, To enable those who are anxious to benefit their poorer neighbours, to cook for them occasionally soups, puddings, &c., which may be nourishing and wholesome, and yet their cost may be so trifling as not to be felt in a moderately large establishment; and, 2nd, To afford such information as may be imparted by oral teaching, on the kinds of cookery and general management of food most suitable for those who are obliged to live upon a very small weekly stipend. Economy is the keystone of each; but it is very differently applied in the one from the other. Thus, many things in a large establishment are useful to the poor man, and yet he cannot procure them by purchase, even if so disposed. Such are the boilings of meat, what are called "broken victuals" or "scraps," and many other things which are not made use of by those who can afford to despise them; but which to the badly-fed child or adult are positive luxuries, because they consist of articles which their systems call for in the most urgent manner. "Waste not what your neighbours want," is an adage which the rich man should treasure up and act upon; and if so, many a cottage which is now rarely gladdened with the sight of animal food, would be made comfortable at times, if not always so.

SECT. 2.—THE RICH MAN'S SUPERFLUITIES.

BOILINGS.

1172. The cook should be charged to save the boilings of every piece of meat, ham, tongue, &c., however salt; as it is easy to use only a part of them, mixed with an equal or double quantity of fresh water; and by the addition of more vegetables—the bones of the meat used in the family—the pieces of meat that come from table on the plates—and rice, Scotch barley, or oatmeal—there will be some gallons of nutritious soup two or three times a week. The bits of meat should be only warmed in the soup, and remain whole; but the bones should be boiled in the digester till they yield their nourishment. If the things are ready to put in the boiler as soon as the meat is served, it will save the fresh fire for second cooking. Should the soup be poor of meat, the long boiling of the bones and different vegetables, will afford better nourishment than the laborious poor can obtain; especially as they are rarely tolerable cooks, and have not fuel to do justice to what they buy. In every family there is some superfluity; and, if it is prepared with cleanliness and care, the benefit will be very great to the receiver, and the satisfaction no less to the giver. In times of scarcity, ten or fifteen gallons of soup could be dealt out weekly at an expense not worth mentioning, even though the vegetables were bought; and if, in any village containing ten gentlemen's houses, the quantity of ten gallons were made in each, there would be a hundred gallons of wholesome and agreeable food given weekly for the supply of forty poor families, at the rate of two gallons and a half each.

Refuse Vegetables.

1173. Take turnips, carrots, leeks, potatoes, the outer leaves of lettuce, celery, or any sort of vegetable that is at hand; cut them small, and throw in to any quantity of boilings, with the thick part of peas, after they have been pulped for soup; or grits, or coarse oatmeal, which have been used for gruel; or bread-crumb and refuse pieces of bread.

Skimmed Milk.

1174. Where cows are kept, a jug of skimmed milk is a valuable present, and always a very acceptable one where there are children; while in a gentleman's house it is only fit for pig's wash, or at all events it is used for that purpose wherever cows are kept sufficient to make butter for the family.

A Cheap Pudding.

1175. When the oven is hot a large pudding may be baked, and given to a sick or young family; and when made as follows, the trouble and cost are little:—Into a deep tin or pan put half a pound of rice, four ounces of coarse sugar or treacle, two quarts of skim milk, and two ounces of dripping; set it cold in the oven. It will take a good while, but is an excellent solid food.

Crumb Pudding.

1176. Serve all the crumbs left upon the cloth during the week, add to these any waste pieces of bread. Put them into a basin with two ounces of treacle mixed up with them. Soak them in enough water to make them swell. Then tie them in a cloth in the usual way, and boil half an hour. Hundreds of poor children would be glad of such a pudding.

A Sopped Toast.

1177. A very good meal may be thus easily made :—Cut a very thick upper crust of bread, and put it into the pot where salt beef is boiling and nearly ready; it will attract some of the fat, and, swelled out, will be no unpalatable dish to those who rarely taste meat.

An Excellent Pudding for the Poor.

1178. One pound of common rice stewed four hours in four quarts of water, then add half a pound of treacle and a little salt. Simmer half an hour after this, and stir it up well.

A Savoury Baked Dish.

1179. Put a pound of any kind of meat cut in slices; two onions, two carrots, ditto; two ounces of rice, a pint of split peas, or whole ones if previously soaked, pepper and salt, into an earthen jug or pan, and pour on two quarts of water. Cover it very close, and bake it with the bread.

Good but Plain Plum Pudding, suited for Christmas or any Festive Occasion.

1180. Mix three-quarters of a peck of flour, six large loaves, eight pounds of suet, six pounds of raisins, six pounds of currants, ten eggs, three pounds of brown sugar, one ounce of allspice, a quart of old ale, a bottle of raisin wine, and milk enough to make it of a proper consistence. Whether made into two puddings or more, it should be boiled for full twenty hours; if made some little time previously, it may be hung up in a dry place, and if boiled again a few hours before serving it will be all the better.

Sect. 3.—The Poor Man's Cookery.

1181. Under this head will be included directions suitable for the poor man's guidance, or rather for that of his wife, in conducting his humble cookery. I have already observed, that experience and instinct are, in the main, pretty sure guides to man in selecting his diet; but there are numberless exceptions to this rule, and none more marked than in the case of the poor man. With the pittance which he has at his command, he is often tempted to spend too much in ways which do not bring him the best return for his money. Thus, he will buy nine-pennyworth of *fine white* bread in preference to eight of a superior quality in reality; but being more brown in appearance, and not patronized by his employers, he fancies it is not as good, and decides against it without giving it a trial. Again, in his desire for present happiness (or freedom from care the sensation should perhaps be called), he spends a day's wages in beer or gin, which would, if laid out in meat, make all the difference to him for the next week between the food which his system requires and that which he can then procure. Lastly, the poor man in his ignorance is led to mistake the promptings of his palate for an infallible guide, and thus is tempted to buy *fat* bacon or mutton to eat with his potatoes instead of such lean parts as will supply the nitrogen in which they are deficient. It is chiefly in this neglect of azotized food that the poor are mistaken, and the reason is that its effects are not immediate, like those of alcoholic stimulants, nor is it in small quantities so full of flavour as fried fat, and therefore it is no wonder that both the one and the other should be preferred to it. Besides these reasons for choosing certain kinds of food peculiar to himself, it is unfortunately a fact that the labouring-man and his family seldom have their stomachs overloaded with food, and consequently it is of no importance to them to avoid that which is in itself too bulky; potatoes, therefore, are less objectionable in large quantities than they are to the overloaded stomach. But if with their potatoes, which contain very little nitrogen, they could mix lean meat or its juice, together with some gelatine, it would be of far more benefit than the fat which they select with so much care. With bread, abounding in nitrogen, fat bacon or mutton is the proper mixture, or with beans, peas, or cabbage; but with potatoes —milk, buttermilk, gravy, or meat should be the proper flavouring material. It is of great importance, whenever the educated man is anxious to benefit his poorer neighbours, that these facts should be well known, so that he may be able to afford useful advice in the selection of the proper kinds of food. It may be here as well to repeat the various articles of food suited to the poor man, and to give them under the respective heads of *azotized* and *non-azotized*, so that he may have recourse to any of the former list to supply the deficiency in the azote of the latter, or *vice versâ.*

VARIOUS KINDS OF CHEAP FOOD SUITABLE TO THE POOR MAN.

AZOTIZED.	DEFICIENT IN AZOTE.
Bullock's, pig's, calf's, or sheep's liver, melt, or kidney.	Potatoes.
Pig's blood for black puddings.	Rice.
Inferior pieces of beef.	Fat (dripping).
Sheep's trotters.	Lard.
Sheep's head and pluck.	Bacon fat.
Cheap fish.	
Peas and beans	
Mushrooms.	

Cabbages, cauliflower, brocoli, oatmeal, bread, milk, and buttermilk, may be considered as containing a proper proportion of the four elements, and merely requiring any flavouring matter mixed with them to suit the palate. It will therefore be necessary to adapt the diet in this list; so that, for instance, potatoes, as the cheapest of all foods, may be mixed with some one or other articles in the opposite list; while peas and beans, again, require the addition of dripping, lard, or bacon, to make them in the same way suitable to the demands of the system. In the first place, then, we will see how liver, pig's blood, ox cheek, or sheep's head and trotters, may each be cooked to advantage, so as to make a good and cheap meal, with *potatoes* or *rice*, for the poor man. It must be remembered that we have not only to consider what is the *best* food for the labourer, but what is the *best for his money;* and, if this precaution is neglected, it only leads to his rejecting other and perhaps really useful advice, by the idea that the adviser is not practically acquainted with his necessities. In a very well-intended little book on Domestic Economy, lately published by one of her Majesty's Inspectors of Schools, the first item given under the head of "Recipes for Economical Cookery," is a *cheap* mode of making Irish stew, in which "good beef sausages and a little dripping" are ordered, with potatoes, to replace a neck of mutton, which is the usual animal part of the concoction. Now, every one knows that beef sausages are sold at nearly, or in some places quite, double the price of necks of mutton and the coarse parts of beef, which would also answer better for the stew than the expensive sausages; so that a stew made of them would, instead of being economical, be quite the reverse, and such a recommendation would at once condemn all the consecutive pieces of advice in the judgment of the person who tried the receipt, although they might be, and are, really useful. But with

X

this caution the following savoury compounds may be adopted, which shall, at the same time, be as cheap as such messes can be made, provided they contain sufficient nourishment of both kinds.

BULLOCK'S LIVER FRIED WITH POTATOES.

1182. This dish requires very peculiar management, as it is very apt to be made hard in the dressing. Two or three pounds of liver, *in one lump*, are to be stewed in a very small quantity of water for at least three hours; then take it out and stew an equal quantity of potatoes and of cabbages, carrots, or turnips, in the liquor, adding pepper and salt to the taste; when nearly done, but not quite, take them out of the liquor, and break them into small pieces about the size of a pigeon's egg; after which, having heated a little lard or dripping in a frying-pan, they, with the liver sliced thin, are to be put in and fried till they are sufficiently done. Lastly, after taking out the whole, the liquor is put into the pan, thickened with a little flour, and warmed up, when, on being poured over the liver, &c., the dish is complete, and is a very savoury one when properly prepared according to the above directions. The cost being as below, varying of course in certain localities, in some of which, for instance, bullock's liver is scarcely to be had at any price, and there these remarks will not apply. When, however, the prices are ascertained, the proper correction can readily be made.

									s.	d.
3 lb. bullock's liver	...	...	...	...	...	...	...	...	0	6
2 lb. potatoes	...	...	...	...	...	...	...	...	0	1½
1 lb. cabbage or carrots	...	...	...	...	...	...	...	...	0	0½
2 oz. lard or dripping	...	...	...	...	...	...	...	...	0	1
Spice, flour, and salt	...	...	...	...	...	...	...	...	0	0½
									0	9½

This will make, with one or two pounds of bread, a dinner for a labouring-man and his wife, together with from five to six children, according to their ages; the whole cost, with the bread, not exceeding one shilling, independently of the firing. If a smaller proportion of liver is used, the cost will be still less.

BULLOCK'S LIVER AND RICE.

1183. Soak three pounds of liver for half an hour in water to get out the blood, then boil it gently in three quarts of water with one pound of rice; add two or three onions, a little parsley, and, towards the last, pepper and salt to the taste, together with four table-spoonfuls of vinegar. At the time of adding the spice, cut the liver into slices,

and the addition at that time of a rasher or two of bacon is a great improvement. This is sufficient for the same number of persons as the
last, when eaten either with plain boiled potatoes or bread—the cost
being also about the same.

LIVER PUDDING.

1184. Stew a pound and a half of liver in a very small quantity of
water for an hour and a half, then cut it up into small squares, season
with pepper and salt, and add either some pieces of bacon-fat, beef-fat,
or mutton-fat. Make a crust of dripping and flour, as directed at
page 199, and line a quart basin; put in the liver and fat, well mixed
together, pour in the gravy remaining in the stew-pan, and cover with
crust; then boil in a cloth for two hours. This, with three pounds of
potatoes, will go as far as (1182) or (1183). The prices being—

	s.	d.
1½ lb. of liver...	0	3
4 oz. of bacon, or fat	0	3¼
Flour and dripping...	0	3
Spice	0	0½
3 lb. of potatoes	0	2¼
	0	11¼

BEEF KIDNEY

1185. Is capable of being used in the same way as liver; but it
requires long soaking in very weak vinegar and water after cutting it
open, to deprive it of the strong flavour peculiar to the kidney or
the ox.

THE MELT,

1186. Which is extensively used even in well-furnished kitchens, is
also by the poor sometimes made available as follows:—It must be
prepared by soaking it for three hours in salt and water, with the
addition of a spoonful or two of vinegar, then let it be dried with a
cloth, and made into a thick mass by tying together alternate layers
of it and thin slices of bacon, with a seasoning of sage and onions,
parsley, and a little of either thyme or marjoram, according to fancy.
Put on the top a lump of dripping or lard, and bake, or put in a
Dutch oven in front of the fire, dredging it well in either case. The
price of a melt varies from 2d. to 6d.

1187. WHEN PIG'S, CALF'S, OR SHEEP'S LIVER OR KIDNEY can be
obtained at a low price, they are superior to the above in flavour; but
they are seldom to be bought for less than double or treble the price
of beef liver.

PIG'S BLOOD

1188. Is generally to be had for nothing, when it is obtainable at all, or at all events the price is very low. Cottagers who kill their own pigs would do well to exchange with their neighbours a portion of the blood, as it is generally more than they can use themselves, and black-puddings may readily be made without the skins. The directions given at page 112 are sufficient, and need not be repeated here. This is a very cheap and nourishing dish, and, when made without the skins, it may either be plain boiled or fried, with boiled potatoes and lard, or dripping.

COW-HEEL,

1189. As sold in the shops, is already boiled and deprived of a large proportion of its nourishment. It is not, in this condition, at all an economical dish, as one of them has not more than half a pound of gelatinous matter upon it, and they are sold at from fourpence to six-pence a-piece. If, however, a *raw* cow-heel can be got at that price, it is cheap enough, as there is a large amount of nutritious matter in it which it loses in the preparation at the tripe-shop. It only wants four or five hours' slow simmering, and in that time it will give out a quantity of excellent soup, besides the same amount of solid matter that it contains when bought ready prepared. The hoofs merely require putting into boiling water for a few minutes to get them off, together with the hair remaining on the skin attached to them, after which the feet are ready for boiling.

SHEEP'S TROTTERS.

1190. These in the country compose a most nourishing and cheap dish, but in London they are so highly valued that they are not to be bought at a correspondingly low price. In the latter city, besides, they are not to be obtained in their raw state, but always boiled and deprived of half their value, while at the same time the cost is doubled. Nevertheless they are eagerly sought for at the tripe-shops in the poor neighbourhoods, the price being from a farthing to three-farthings a-piece. On the other hand, in the country, they are neglected, and are generally to be bought of the tanners who collect the skins at the rate of eight or ten for a penny, and often as many as a dozen may be had for that sum. A trotter, after cleaning, will generally average two ounces; so that here we have *more than a pound of nutritious matter and bone for one penny,* the bone not weighing any thing like half of the whole, and being also full of gelatine. They are prepared by first scalding them in boiling water; and, if this is scarce, it is better to put them into a saucepan with the water previously made boiling, and simmer them for ten minutes, as, unless the proportion of water to trotters is great, the temperature is lowered too much to have the proper effect of loosening the hoofs and hair. It is, however, easy to try one, and, if the hoof and hair do not come off, put them on the fire and boil till they do. When this is found to be the case, it is only necessary to remove them with a knife, taking one at a time and scraping it; then, after washing it clean in cold water, the whole are to be simmered till they fall to pieces, when the bones are taken out, and pepper and salt added, with any onions, parsley, or other garden-stuff which may be readily available. With this, as a foundation, a most savoury and nourishing mess may be made. Boiled rice or potatoes may be added to them in the pot, or eaten separately. The cost, for a large family, of a substantial meal made in this way is as follows :—

	s.	d.
30 trotters...	0	3
6 lb. potatoes, or 1½ lb. rice....	0	4½
Onions, parsley, &c.	0	1
Pepper, salt, &c.	0	0½
	0	8½

1191. MEAT SOUP WITH PEAS :—

	s.	d.
Half an ox cheek, or a sheep's head	0	6
8 lb. of potatoes...	0	2
1 pint of split peas	0	3
2 onions, 2 turnips, and a stick of celery	0	1
Salt and pepper...	0	0½
Water, 7 quarts		
	1	0½

This will produce about five or six quarts of good soup by the following method of proceeding :—Wash the cheek or head, peel the potatoes very thin, and boil all together for six hours; then take out the cheek or head, strip off the meat and put by, and return the bones, which are to be gently stewed for another six hours in a Papin's digester, if at hand, or if not, in the saucepan, with a part of the liquor. The fire required is not more than the small one always necessary for warming a cottage. When the bones are stewed for this second period, they may be taken out, and the liquor from them added to the previously boiled vegetables and meat, after which the whole is warmed up and served.

1192. Meat Soup with Rice, &c.

								s.	d.
1½ lb. of coarse gravy beef	...	...	...	...	...	...	...	0	5½
½ lb. of rice	...	...	...	...	...	...	...	0	1½
¼ lb. of Scotch barley ...	...	...	...	...	...	...	...	0	1½
An onion and seasoning	...	...	...	...	...	...	...	0	0½
6 quarts of water									
								0	9

This will, at the above cost, produce about nine or ten pints of good broth, but not equal to the former soup in quality

1193. Pea-soup without Meat:—

								s.	d.
Half a pint of peas	...	...	...	...	...	...	...	0	1½
A carrot and turnip, a head of celery, and two onions	...	...	...	0	1½
Dripping	...	...	...	...	...	...	...	0	1
Pepper and salt ...	...	...	...	...	...	...	...	0	0½
Water, three quarts									
								0	4½

This produces about two quarts of very palatable soup, when managed by boiling the peas in the water for three hours, and then adding the vegetables, previously cut up and fried in the dripping; after which the whole is to be boiled slowly an hour and a half, and seasoned with pepper and salt towards the last.

1194. Barley Broth without Meat:—

								s.	d.
Half a pint of Scotch barley	...	...	...	...	...	...	...	0	1½
Ditto of oatmeal	...	...	...	..	...	...	...	0	1½
Two ounces of dripping...	...	...	...	...	...	...	...	0	1
Vegetables, as for (1176)	...	...	...	...	...	...	...	0	1½
Seasoning	...	...	...	...	...	...	...	0	0½
Water, five quarts									
								0	6

Making about three quarts and a half of broth, costing about as much per quart as the pea-soup.

Baked Rice Pudding.

1195. Put half a pound of rice into three pints of skim milk, sweeten with three ounces of sugar, add an ounce of good beef or mutton dripping, and a laurel leaf. Nutmeg, lemon-peel, or allspice is an improvement when at hand. This, when baked, will produce about four pounds of good solid pudding, at a cost of—rice 1½d., sugar 1d., milk 3d., dripping ½d., total 6d.

Sprats or Herrings (both Fresh and Cured),

1196. When fried in dripping or lard, with potatoes and onions,

make a very cheap and nourishing dish—that is to say, they can be obtained at a low price.

RICE AND APPLE DUMPLINGS.

1197. Boil half a pound of rice, tied up loosely in a cloth, until the grains will stick together; then surround some apples previously pared with a layer of this; tie up in a cloth and boil for half an hour. When, as is often the case, apples can be had for little or nothing, this dish costs only the price of the rice and a little sugar or treacle to be eaten with it.

OATMEAL PORRIDGE.

1198. This, as made in Scotland, is a very useful dish, and is there the chief food of the labouring classes. The receipt for its concoction is given at page 292, and the cost is merely that of the meal and the milk eaten with it. A quarter of a pound of oatmeal, costing about three farthings, will make more than a quart of porridge, the quantity of meal required varying with its quality. With this food a good breakfast or supper may be made for one penny.

RICE PORRIDGE.

1199. Rice porridge described at page 292, is also another very economical dish, which may be useful to the poor.

KOLCANNON (*an Irish dish*).

1200. Boil separately equal quantities of potatoes and cabbages; when the former are fit to peel, take off their jackets, and mix the two together in a saucepan after pouring off the cabbage liquor, then beat them up together, and add an ounce of lard or dripping to each pound of potatoes. Season with pepper and salt, and most people add to the cabbages an onion or two.

INDIAN MUSH.

1201. Have ready on a clear fire a large saucepan of boiling water; take in one hand the mush-stick (a strong round stick, nearly half a yard long, and flattened at the lower end), and with the other hand throw in *gradually* sufficient Indian-meal to make a very stiff porridge, stirring it all the time with the stick; add a *very* little salt. After the mush is sufficiently thick and smooth, boil it one hour more, stirring it frequently from the bottom to prevent its burning; then cover the pot closely, and let it simmer for an hour. Its goodness depends upo'

1192. Meat Soup with Rice, &c.

										s.	d.
1½ lb. of coarse gravy beef	...	...	...	...	...	...	...	...	0	5½
½ lb. of rice	...	...	...	...	...	...	...	...	0	1½
½ lb. of Scotch barley	...	...	...	...	...	...	...	...	0	1½
An onion and seasoning	...	...	...	...	...	...	...	...	0	0½
6 quarts of water										
									0	9

This will, at the above cost, produce about nine or ten pints of good broth, but not equal to the former soup in quality

1193. Pea-soup without Meat:—

									s.	d.
Half a pint of peas	...	...	...	...	...	...	...	...	0	1½
A carrot and turnip, a head of celery, and two onions		...	...	...	0	1½
Dripping	...	...	...	...	...	...	...	...	0	1
Pepper and salt	...	...	...	...	...	...	...	...	0	0½
Water, three quarts										
									0	4½

This produces about two quarts of very palatable soup, when managed by boiling the peas in the water for three hours, and then adding the vegetables, previously cut up and fried in the dripping; after which the whole is to be boiled slowly an hour and a half, and seasoned with pepper and salt towards the last.

1194. Barley Broth without Meat:—

									s.	d
Half a pint of Scotch barley	...	...	...	...	...	...	...	0	1½
Ditto of oatmeal	...	...	...	...	...	...	...	...	0	1½
Two ounces of dripping	...	...	...	...	...	...	...	0	1
Vegetables, as for (1176)	...	...	...	...	...	...	...	0	1½
Seasoning	...	...	...	...	...	...	...	...	0	0½
Water, five quarts										
									0	6

Making about three quarts and a half of broth, costing about as much per quart as the pea-soup.

Baked Rice Pudding.

1195. Put half a pound of rice into three pints of skim milk, sweeten with three ounces of sugar, add an ounce of good beef or mutton dripping, and a laurel leaf. Nutmeg, lemon-peel, or allspice is an improvement when at hand. This, when baked, will produce about four pounds of good solid pudding, at a cost of—rice 1½d., sugar 1d., milk 3d., dripping ½d., total 6d.

Sprats or Herrings (*both Fresh and Cured*),

When fried in dripping or lard, with potatoes and onions,

make a very cheap and nourishing dish—that is to say, they can be obtained at a low price.

RICE AND APPLE DUMPLINGS.

1197. Boil half a pound of rice, tied up loosely in a cloth, until the grains will stick together; then surround some apples previously pared with a layer of this; tie up in a cloth and boil for half an hour. When, as is often the case, apples can be had for little or nothing, this dish costs only the price of the rice and a little sugar or treacle to be eaten with it.

OATMEAL PORRIDGE.

1198. This, as made in Scotland, is a very useful dish, and is there the chief food of the labouring classes. The receipt for its concoction is given at page 292, and the cost is merely that of the meal and the milk eaten with it. A quarter of a pound of oatmeal, costing about three farthings, will make more than a quart of porridge, the quantity of meal required varying with its quality. With this food a good breakfast or supper may be made for one penny.

RICE PORRIDGE.

1199. Rice porridge described at page 292, is also another very economical dish, which may be useful to the poor.

KOLCANNON (an Irish dish).

1200. Boil separately equal quantities of potatoes and cabbages; when the former are fit to peel, take off their jackets, and mix the two together in a saucepan after pouring off the cabbage liquor, then beat them up together, and add an ounce of lard or dripping to each pound of potatoes. Season with pepper and salt, and most people add to the cabbages an onion or two.

INDIAN MUSH.

1201. Have ready on a clear fire a large saucepan of boiling water; take in one hand the mush-stick (a strong round stick, nearly half a yard long, and flattened at the lower end), and with the other hand throw in *gradually* sufficient Indian-meal to make a very stiff porridge, stirring it all the time with the stick; add a *very* little salt. After the mush is sufficiently thick and smooth, boil it one hour more, stirring it frequently from the bottom to prevent its burning; then cover the pot closely, and let it simmer for an hour. Its goodness depends upo'

1192. MEAT SOUP WITH RICE, &c.

		s.	d.
1½ lb. of coarse gravy beef	... ...	0	5½
½ lb. of rice	... ...	0	1½
¼ lb. of Scotch barley ...	... ...	0	1½
An onion and seasoning	... ...	0	0½
6 quarts of water			
		0	9

This will, at the above cost, produce about nine or ten pints of good broth, but not equal to the former soup in quality

1193. PEA-SOUP WITHOUT MEAT:—

		s.	d.
Half a pint of peas	... ...	0	1½
A carrot and turnip, a head of celery, and two onions	... ...	0	1½
Dripping	... ...	0	1
Pepper and salt	... ...	0	0½
Water, three quarts			
		0	4½

This produces about two quarts of very palatable soup, when managed by boiling the peas in the water for three hours, and then adding the vegetables, previously cut up and fried in the dripping; after which the whole is to be boiled slowly an hour and a half, and seasoned with pepper and salt towards the last.

1194. BARLEY BROTH WITHOUT MEAT :—

		s.	d.
Half a pint of Scotch barley	... ...	0	1½
Ditto of oatmeal	... ...	0	1½
Two ounces of dripping...	... ...	0	1
Vegetables, as for (1176)	... ...	0	1½
Seasoning	... ...	0	0½
Water, five quarts			
		0	6

Making about three quarts and a half of broth, costing about as much per quart as the pea-soup.

BAKED RICE PUDDING.

1195. Put half a pound of rice into three pints of skim milk, sweeten with three ounces of sugar, add an ounce of good beef or mutton dripping, and a laurel leaf. Nutmeg, lemon-peel, or allspice is an improvement when at hand. This, when baked, will produce about four pounds of good solid pudding, at a cost of—rice 1½d., sugar 1d., milk 3d., dripping ½d., total 6d.

SPRATS OR HERRINGS (*both Fresh and Cured*),

1196. When fried in dripping or lard, with potatoes and onions,

make a very cheap and nourishing dish—that is to say, they can be obtained at a low price.

RICE AND APPLE DUMPLINGS.

1197. Boil half a pound of rice, tied up loosely in a cloth, until the grains will stick together; then surround some apples previously pared with a layer of this; tie up in a cloth and boil for half an hour. When, as is often the case, apples can be had for little or nothing, this dish costs only the price of the rice and a little sugar or treacle to be eaten with it.

OATMEAL PORRIDGE.

1198. This, as made in Scotland, is a very useful dish, and is there the chief food of the labouring classes. The receipt for its concoction is given at page 292, and the cost is merely that of the meal and the milk eaten with it. A quarter of a pound of oatmeal, costing about three farthings, will make more than a quart of porridge, the quantity of meal required varying with its quality. With this food a good break-fast or supper may be made for one penny.

RICE PORRIDGE.

1199. Rice porridge described at page 292, is also another very economical dish, which may be useful to the poor.

KOLCANNON (an Irish dish).

1200. Boil separately equal quantities of potatoes and cabbages; when the former are fit to peel, take off their jackets, and mix the two together in a saucepan after pouring off the cabbage liquor, then beat them up together, and add an ounce of lard or dripping to each pound of potatoes. Season with pepper and salt, and most people add to the cabbages an onion or two.

INDIAN MUSH.

1201. Have ready on a clear fire a large saucepan of boiling water; take in one hand the mush-stick (a strong round stick, nearly half a yard long, and flattened at the lower end), and with the other hand throw in *gradually* sufficient Indian-meal to make a very stiff porridge, stirring it all the time with the stick; add a *very* little salt. After the mush is sufficiently thick and smooth, boil it one hour more, stirring it frequently from the bottom to prevent its burning; then cover the pot closely, and let it simmer for an hour. Its goodness depends upo'

its being thoroughly boiled, and sufficiently smooth and thick; if kept
three or four hours over the fire, first boiling and then simmering, it
will be better. Send it to table hot in a deep dish, and eat it with
either milk, buttermilk, cream, butter, and sugar, or butter and treacle.
Cold mush may be cut in slices and fried.

Indian Hasty Pudding.

1202. Place on the fire three quarts of boiling water, with a little
salt; stir in by degrees three quarts of Indian-meal and a quarter of a
pound of butter; it should be stirred till quite thick. Serve it hot,
and eat it with milk or cream, treacle or sugar.

Plain Indian Breakfast-cake.

1203. Mix over-night one quart of yellow sifted Indian meal, one
handful of wheat-flour, and one spoonful of salt; pour on gradually
one quart of warm water, and stir it so as to form a soft dough; cover
the pan closely, and set it by till morning, when dissolve in one pint
of warm milk and water a salt-spoonful of carbonate of soda, and with
this mixture reduce the dough into a batter, stirring it very hard;
cover, and place it before the fire for a quarter of an hour; have ready
over the fire a frying-pan or griddle; grease it well with lard or fresh
butter, and bake the cakes in the shape of small crumpets. When
brown on one side, turn them with a knife. These cakes may be
eaten with dripping, butter, or treacle.

Indian-meal Gruel

1204. Sift some Indian-meal, then mix in a quart basin two spoonfuls of the meal with three of cold water; stir it till quite smooth;
then pour in gradually a pint of boiling water, stirring it well, and add
a pinch of salt; next put it on the fire, and let it boil half an hour,
still stirring it to prevent its burning, and skimming it. It should be
eaten warm, and sweetened with sugar, or a little nutmeg and white
wine if approved. This is excellent for invalids.

Hominy

1205. Is Indian-corn shelled from the cob, and divested of the
yellow skin, so as to be perfectly white, and then dried. Having
washed it well through two or three waters, put it in a pan, pour over
boiling water, and cover it; let it soak for several hours. Drain it,
then put it in a clean saucepan, allowing two quarts of water (cold or

hot) to every quart of hominy, and boil for five or six hours, stirring it frequently. Drain it *dry* though a sieve or colander, and put it in a deep dish; add a little butter, pepper, and salt; serve it hot to eat with any sort of meat, particularly with beef, pork, or bacon. If properly prepared, it is very wholesome and strengthening. What is left may be re-boiled next day for one hour, or it may be made into flat cakes, adding a little wheat-flour, and fried in lard or butter.

INDIAN DUMPLINGS.

1206. Mix three pints of Indian-meal with half a pound of finely-chopped suet, dredged with wheat-flour; add one small tea-spoonful of salt; put in gradually sufficient milk to make it into a stiff dough, and knead it; divide the dough into equal portions, and then, having floured the hands, make each portion into a ball the size of a small orange; flatten them with a rolling-pin, and beat on both sides to make light and flaky. Tie them up loosely in small cloths previously soaked in hot water and floured, put them in boiling water, and boil for two hours. When done, dip each dumpling in cold water before the cloth is untied. Send them to table hot. They may be eaten with boiled fresh or salt meat, or as sweet dumplings, with treacle, or butter and sugar.

1207. With the above dishes a poor man's wife may manage to make a few shillings go a great way, varying them with dried fish and potatoes, or the same fried. In the above calculations, it has been assumed that there is a family of four to six children; but when this is the case, two or three will always be able to earn a little, in order to help the wages of the father. Altogether it may be assumed that the whole family will earn about 15s. per week, and that the rent and clothing are paid by the garden and pig, which ought to be the case with good managers; there will then remain, after allowing 3s. for coals, wood, schooling, and emergencies, 12s. per week to be spent in food. Of this, 1s. 2d. may be allowed for beer, which will give nearly three gallons per week if brewed at home, and 10s. 10d. for food. The breakfasts and suppers may be made at about 1d. per head, or 6d. per day, which per week will be 3s. 6d., leaving 7s. 4d. for the dinners, which, as I have shown, may be furnished in the most ample manner for that money, as follows:—Sunday, with bread, 1s.; Monday, soup (1191), four quarts, 8d., and bread, 4d.; Tuesday, trotters, prepared (1190), 8¾d.; Wednesday, bacon fried, 1 lb., potatoes, 3 lb., 1s. 0½d.; Thursday, soup, with rice (1122), 9d., bread, 4d.;

Friday, same as Sunday, 1s.; Saturday, rice pudding, 6d., and black-puddings, or some other dish with bread. The outlay altogether being below the allotted sum.

1208. IT HAS THUS BEEN SHOWN that the family of a labouring man may be kept in a good and wholesome way, upon viands which are appetizing enough to those who use strong exercise, for a sum which will barely suffice to purchase bread and potatoes. Thus, supposing the family to consist of seven in number, they would eat at least sixty pounds of bread, and as much of potatoes, costing 13s.; and if cheese or bacon is added, at least 7s. more. In point of economy, the bread diet so much practised by the poor is a very extravagant one; and in point of nutrition, potatoes when used alone, as by the very poor, are of very inferior value, and not adapted for the hard-working man. But with the above diet, costing no more money, he may be kept in full health.

CHAP. XXIV.—INVALID COOKERY.

1209. IN COOKING FOOD, &c., FOR THE INVALID, great art is required, because the palate is morbidly acute, or disinclined to strong flavours of any kind. Thus it often happens that seasoning which is relished in a state of health is loathed under disease; and the cook who is not aware of this fact will be almost sure to displease her employers. Hence it is that the nurse who understands the kind of cookery which is fitted for the sick will generally succeed better than the most finished cook, because she knows by experience that all rich flavours are sure to turn the stomachs of her charge. Chicken is for this reason so generally liked by the sick, because its flavour is mild; while the dark and high-flavoured meat of game or ducks would be turned out of the room as soon as submitted to the nose, without even having the honour of a taste. Fat should be most carefully avoided in all animal broths, such as mutton-broth or beaf-tea; onions, garlic, and other herbs, except perhaps parsley, are also objectionable in the sick-room; and even the faintest flavour of the first in bread sauce will seldom be tolerated. Pepper may be used to some extent when not forbidden, and also salt, but beyond these seasonings it is seldom safe to venture far. Cloves and cinnamon, as well as nutmeg, are liked by some and disliked by others, as also are the flavours of caraways and all-spice. Lemon-peel gives a clean flavour, as does orange-peel, and may generally be used for the purpose of giving a slight taste to sweets, or puddings; but even of these a smaller quantity than usual will suffice. With regard to adding wine in making jellies, it must always be ascertained whether it is forbidden; for in many cases jelly without wine would be advantageous, while the addition would be altogether wrong. The following list of receipts comprises those which are peculiarly applicable to the invalid; those which are also employed in ordinary cookery being to be found in the chapters devoted to that subject.

BEEF-TEA.

1210. Take one pound of lean beef, pick all the fat off; cut it into small pieces the size of the end of the thumb, and score it still further to let out the gravy; put it in an enamelled saucepan with a quart of water, two cloves, eight to twelve peppercorns, and half a tea-spoonful of salt. Simmer for three or four hours, and skim it *as long* as either scum or fat rises, or else it curdles. In cases of *extreme* debility, one pound and a half of beef may be used. Before serving, absorb every globule of fat with silver paper.

Another Mode (very grateful in convalescence, when there is no tendency to diarrhœa). Put in a preserving jar alternate layers of beef, cut into small pieces, and sliced turnips; when the jar is filled, place it in a water-bath, or slow oven, and let it remain for two or three hours; then drain off all the tea, using a little pressure to assist the operation, and let it stand till cold, when any fat may be taken off, or, if wanted directly, it may be removed while hot with silver paper.

Another (*quickly made*).—Take a piece of skirtings of beef, of the size of a walnut, scrape it well, then pour a tea-cup of boiling water upon it, and it is fit to drink when cool.

To MAKE KNUCKLE BROTH.

1211. Take ten or twelve knuckles from legs or shoulders of mutton, put them into water for two or three hours. Rub them with a little salt, and wash them *well*. Boil in four quarts of water two hours. Skim it clear, and add two ounces of hartshorn shavings, and the under crust of a penny loaf. Boil again till reduced to three pints; strain. When cold, remove the fat. Take half a pint as hot as you can drink it before you rise in the morning, the same quantity in bed at night. Make it fresh twice a week in winter, and three times in summer.

SOUP FOR INVALIDS.

1212. Take six pounds of shin of beef, six pounds of any wʰ···

meat, seasoned, and an onion, if liked; put it in a stone jar, and tie down with bladder; let it boil twelve hours in a large saucepan of water, then strain it off. A tea or table spoonful is enough for an invalid, if taken several times during the day. (It is well to know, that what remains after the soup has been strained, makes excellent common stock with additional water.)

STRONG MEAT JELLY FOR WEAK PERSONS.

1213. Take about two pounds of lean beef, cut in pieces, with a hock of ham of the same weight, and a knuckle of veal of eight or ten pounds, a small quantity of salt and mace, without any other spice; cover it with water and stew seven hours. Strain, and when cold take off the fat; clear it with whites of eggs, and pass it through a jelly-bag. The produce of jelly from the above proportions should be about five quarts; to be taken warm or cold, as best suits the patient.

TEA-KETTLE BROTH.

1214. Cut some small squares of crumb of bread into a broth basin, and some finely chopped parsley, with enough of salt to flavour it; pour over it some boiling water, softening the whole with a spoonful or two of cream or milk. Some invalids like the flavour of mint, and peas when in season; and, if this can be allowed by the medical man, the water used must have a few young peas, or pea-pods, and a leaf of mint boiled in it, before pouring it over the bread; without this addition, it is often much liked by invalids, as being so free from grease, and so clean-tasting. A little clear gravy from under the dripping-pan may sometimes be added with advantage. Pepper may be used or omitted, according to the palate or the nature of the illness.

GRAVY-BREAD FOR INVALIDS.

1215. Cut deeply into a joint of beef, or leg of mutton, while roasting; fill the opening with a thick slice of crumb of bread, and leave it there for half an hour, or till completely saturated with the gravy; then sprinkle upon it a little salt, with or without pepper, as is recommended, and serve hot.

TOAST SANDWICHES FOR INVALIDS.

1216. Toast carefully a very thin slice of bread; cut off the crust; spread two slices of thin bread and butter, also cutting away the crust, seasoning each with a very little made mustard and a sprinkle of salt; lay the toast in the middle, serving it as a sandwich.

JELLY OR BLANCMANGE FOR INVALIDS.

1217. Take the bones of a knuckle of veal, well scrape *all* the meat from them, and stew them four or five hours in two quarts of water; after it is cold, skim it clear from all fat and sediment; melt it, and flavour with home-made wine and a little lemon-peel. If for blancmange, the stock must be still more reduced, to bear the addition of some milk, flavoured with laurel-leaf and lemon-peel: the addition of a little wine or brandy will of course improve it.

COW-HEEL BAKED IN MILK.

1218. Clean well a cow-heel, and put it with two quarts of milk into an earthen jar; let it stand in a slow oven for five or six hours. The heel may be taken out, and served with a little parsley and butter, or eaten with mustard and vinegar; and the milk, which resembles blancmange, skimmed when cold, then melted and flavoured, as in the above receipt.

SOOTHING NOURISHMENT IN CONSUMPTION.

1219. Beat up a table-spoonful of oatmeal, and a table-spoonful of honey, with the yolk of an egg; pour upon it a pint of boiling water; then boil altogether for a few minutes.

TO RENDER MILK DIGESTIBLE IN ILLNESS,

1220. Pour a bottle of soda-water on half a pint of boiling milk, and re-bottle it.

MILD CHOCOLATE FOR INVALIDS.

1221. Take one square of chocolate (the sixth part of a cake), shave it, and boil a pint of water five minutes; then add a pint of skimmed milk; boil them together a little while; then add a tea-spoonful of arrowroot wetted with cold water, and boil it very slowly for five minutes longer.

A STRENGTHENING JELLY FOR INVALIDS.

1222. One ounce of isinglass, half an ounce of gum arabic, a pint of port-wine; sweeten with sugar-candy or loaf-sugar, and then flavour with cinnamon, or a little nutmeg and lemon-peel. The cinnamon may be boiled in a quarter of a pint of water for an hour; strain, and add the isinglass with another quarter of a pint of water; strain when it is dissolved, and add the other ingredients. Take a wine-glassful the first thing in the morning and the last at night, melted; or eat it cold, taking a piece the size of a nutmeg occasionally.

Another.—Take three ounces of isinglass, two ounces of candied eringo root, and one ounce each of conserve of roses, pearl-barley, and rice. Put them in two quarts of water, and simmer about five hours till reduced to less than a pint. Put a spoonful of it into tea or any other liquid food, or take it alone.

MUTTON CUSTARD FOR BOWEL COMPLAINTS OR CONSUMPTIVE CASES.

1223. Take two ounces of fresh mutton suet shred fine, and half a drachm of cinnamon, or some grated nutmeg, and boil in rather more than a pint of milk: when boiled, to be set by the fire till the scum rises, which should then be carefully taken off. Half a tea-cupful may be given, warm or cold, as the patient prefers, three or four times a day. It should be continued till the complaint is quite cured.

FRESH FRUIT JELLY.

1224. Dissolve one ounce of isinglass in half a pint of water, then add a pint and a half of fruit juice of any kind, and from half to three-quarters of a pound of sugar, according to the taste. Boil for a few seconds, and use when cold. There is no necessity for a jelly-bag in this case.

A LIGHT INVALID'S PUDDING.

1225. Take a slice of bread an inch or two in thickness (with or without the crust), wrap it in a cloth, and boil it gently for a quarter of an hour; when brought on table, sugar and white wine may be added according to fancy.

TO STEW TAPIOCA.

1226. To make a breakfast-cupful, take a small teacup of tapioca, soak it for ten minutes in cold water, let it simmer *very gently* about an hour (adding a little more water if it become too thick), then add milk enough to make it a proper thickness, and warm it altogether, stirring it all the time: flavour with sugar, nutmeg, lemon, or wine as may be approved.

BAKED FLOUR (*Infants' food*).

1227. Put a basin of flour with a paper tied over it, into the oven with the bread; bake it till the bread is drawn, and use it as you would biscuit powder. It is strengthening and good for weak bowels.

BEER CAUDLE.

1228. Make your gruel with pretty good beer instead of water, and flavour with ginger and allspice, and sweeten with moist sugar; a quarter of an ounce of ginger, and a tea-spoonful of all-spice, to two quarts.

WINE CAUDLE.

1229. Make two or three pints of oatmeal gruel, and flavour with half a pint of either port or sherry wine, add a clove or two, and, if desired, the yolks well beaten of two or three eggs. Sweeten with white or brown sugar.

CURRANT GRUEL (*rather Aperient*).

1230. To a quart of half-made water gruel, put in two ounces of Zante currants well washed; add sugar, but no spice, and finish boiling. To this simple water gruel, the addition of a spoonful of cream is a great improvement. The gruel may be made of water in which the currants have been boiled, if the currants are not approved.

BRANDY GRUEL.

1231. Boil the rind of half a lemon thinly pared, and four large lumps of sugar in a quarter of a pint of fresh milk; then mix one dessert spoonful of fine oatmeal and a salt spoonful of salt in four table spoonfuls of *cold* milk till quite smooth, and pour it into the boiling milk. Stir without ceasing, and allow it to boil for full five minutes. Put it into a basin, and add to it a piece of butter about the size of a common nut, and one wine-glass and a half of brandy.

A REFRESHING FEVER DRINK.

1232. Pour boiling water on some black currant jam, sweeten with coarse moist sugar, and add a little raspberry vinegar if approved. The poor are very fond of this.

TO MULL PORT.

1233. Put half a pint of water into a clean saucepan, with three ounces of sugar and a little nutmeg and cloves; boil all together for a few minutes; then add from six to twelve glasses of *rich* port wine;

do not allow it to do more than boil for a moment, and pour out in a jug ready for use.

To Mull Claret.

1234. Boil gently the sugar and spice in just enough wine for the purpose; then add the remainder, and boil as above for a second or two.

To Make White Wine Whey.

1235. Boil a pint and a half of skimmed milk, and two glasses of raisin or sherry wine, fifteen grains of purified nitre, and lemon-juice enough to turn the milk; boil it up, and then set it aside until the curd subsides; strain it, and add enough sugar to make it pleasant; one half to be taken on getting into bed, the other ten minutes afterwards.

Egged Wine.

1236. For each half-pint of egged wine intended to be made, take two eggs, beat them up thoroughly in a small basin with an ounce and a half of white sugar (fine moist will do), and a little powdered nutmeg and cloves. While doing this, heat half a pint of sherry and water in equal quantities, or stronger of the sherry, if desired, and when boiling hot stir it into the eggs; after which pour the whole backwards and forwards, from the saucepan into the basin, and *vice versâ*, until it thickens. If this, from the coldness of the atmosphere, does not take place, it must be put on the fire again, and constantly stirred till it does, which never fails in a few minutes.

Egg Flip.

1237. This is made in the same way as egged wine (par. 1236), substituting good ale for the sherry and water, and occasionally adding a little brandy, if the ale is not strong enough.

Rice Water

1238. Is used in diarrhœa as the only drink which will not increase the mischief. It is made by boiling a spoonful of washed Carolina rice in a pint of water for two or three hours, reducing this with more water until it is thin enough to suit the palate. A little lemon-peel may be added towards the last to give flavour; and it should be sweetened to the taste. It makes a very pleasant drink. Nutmeg is liked by some people, and cloves or cinnamon by others, as an additional flavour.

LEMONADE.

1239. Pare two tolerably sized lemons as thin as possible, put half of the rind of one into a pint of hot, not boiling, water, and cover it over for three or four hours. Rub some fine sugar on the lemons to absorb the essence, and put it into a china bowl, into which squeeze the juice of the lemons, adding sugar enough to sweeten to the palate, and when cool it is fit to drink.

CONCENTRATED LEMONADE.

1240. Take one drachm of essence of lemon, one ounce and a half of citric acid, two and a half pounds of loaf sugar, and one pint of water. To make the syrup, put the sugar into the water when cold, and let it boil gradually, then pour it hot on the acids. To make the beverage, put a table-spoonful of the lemonade into a tumbler of water.

ORANGEADE.

1241. Squeeze the juice from a dozen of fruit, pour boiling water on the peel of four, and cover close. Boil water and sugar to a thin syrup, and skim it. When all are cold, mix the juice, the infusion, and the syrup, with as much more water as will make a rich sherbet; strain through a jelly-bag, and cool.

CRANBERRY WATER.

1242. Bruise a cupful of cranberries, mixed with a cupful of cold water. Boil two quarts of water with a table-spoonful of oatmeal and the rind of a lemon; then stir in the cranberries, and add two ounces of Lisbon sugar and a quarter of a pint of white wine; simmer for a quarter of an hour; then strain, and leave to cool.

RASPBERRY VINEGAR AND WATER.

1243. No draught is more agreeable to a feverish patient than a dessert-spoonful of raspberry vinegar mixed in a tumbler of cold water. It should never stand in any metal or glazed vessel, for the acid would act upon their surfaces to an injurious extent.

RHUBARB SHERBET (*a Refreshing Drink*).

1244. Boil six or eight sticks of clean rhubarb ten minutes in a quart of water; strain the liquor into a jug, in which is the peel of a lemon cut very thin, and two table-spoonfuls of clarified sugar; let it stand five or six hours, and it is fit to drink.

APPLE WATER.

1245. Cut two large apples in slices, and pour a quart of boiling water on them, or on the same roasted; strain two or three hours after, and sweeten lightly.

IMPERIAL.

1246. Scald a jug, and put in it from a quarter to half an ounce of cream of tartar; then add a quart of boiling water, flavour it with a little lemon-peel, or essence of lemon, and sweeten to the palate.

GINGER BEER.

1247. Put into a large pan two pounds of loaf sugar, two ounces of bruised ginger, and two gallons of cold water. Boil the whole for half an hour, skimming it well; then pour out into a large earthenware jar, adding a lemon sliced, and half an ounce of cream of tartar. Let it cool to new milk heat, then add a tea-cupful of yeast, and allow it to ferment for two days; strain it, and bottle in small stone bottles, with the corks firmly tied down.

CURRANT WATER.

1248. Currant water is made by dissolving a small table-spoonful of currant jelly in a tumbler of water, and adding from ten to fifteen grains of tartaric acid.

BLACK CURRANT DRINK.

1249. Scald out a glass, then put into it two or three spoonfuls of black currant jelly or preserve. Add a little boiling water, and stir up the jelly, then fill with more water, and drink as hot as possible. Useful for common coughs and hoarseness.

CHAP. XXV.—PLAN OF HOUSEKEEPING, AND BILLS OF FARE.

CALCULATION OF ANNUAL EXPENDITURE.

1250. In order to manage the details of a household in an economical manner, it is, before all things, necessary that the manager shall know what sum may be spent in each department, as well as the total expenditure which may safely and properly be incurred. When this is once settled, the next thing is to cut down the expenses of each department to the proper figure in proportion to the whole expenditure, and here there is room for considerable variation, according to the extent of the income, and the numbers of the family to be provided for. Generally speaking, about one-half of a moderate income must be set apart for the supplies of the house (and stables, if any), the other moiety to be devoted as follows:—one-eighth of the whole to rent and taxes—one-eighth to clothing—one-eighth to illness, parties, and other amusements—and the remaining eighth to wages and incidental expenses, including those charities over and above the superfluities of the household. This rule applies tolerably to those who spend £500 or £1000 a-year; but with those who have only the smaller sums of £250 and £100, the proportion for wages, amusements, and incidental expenses must be reduced, and the subtracted sums added to those for housekeeping. On this scale, therefore, according to the several sums already specified as treated of in this book, there will be the following division of income under the several heads attached.

TABLE OF EXPENDITURE.

	ANNUAL INCOME.			
	No. 1, £1000.	No. 2, £500.	No. 3, £250.	No. 4, £100.
	£ s.	£ s.	£ s.	£ s.
Housekeeping:—				
Butcher's meat and bacon	75 0	40 0	30 0	18 0
Fish and poultry ...	30 0	10 0	7 0	—
Bread	20 0	16 0	14 0	10 0
Milk, butter, and cheese	20 0	18 0	16 0	8 0
Grocery	30 0	20 0	18 0	8 0
Italian goods	8 0	5 0	8 0	—
Green-grocery	20 0	12 0	10 0	6 0
Beer	20 0	12 0	10 0	5 0
Wine and spirits ...	50 0	15 0	8 0	1 0
Coals	25 0	15 0	12 0	5 0
Chandlery	12 0	7 0	7 0	2 0
Washing	40 0	30 0	15 0	2 0
	350 0	200 0	150 0	65 0
Carriage and horses ...	150 0	50 0	—	—
Rent and taxes	125 0	62 10	31 5	12 10
Clothing	125 0	62 10	31 5	12 10
Wages & incidental expenses	125 0	62 10	18 15	5 0
Illness and amusements	125 0	62 10	18 15	5 0
	£1000 0	£500 0	£250 0	£100 0

This calculation is made on the supposition that in each case there is a family of four children, together with the parents, and the servants usually allotted to the several incomes. The rule given above, upon which it has been framed, has been strictly carried out in Nos. 1 and 2, while it has been modified in Nos. 3 and 4, by adding to "House-keeping" £25 and £15 respectively, deducting the amounts from the two lowest items in the table. It will also be seen, in analyzing the details for housekeeping, that the allowances for each article have been varied according to the necessities of the case. Thus, the charge for bread in No. 1 does not bear the same ratio to Nos. 2, 3, and 4, that £350 bear to £250, £200, and £65 respectively, because this article is required in a proportionably larger amount in the poorer man's family than it is in that of the man with an expenditure of £1000 a-year; and the same remark will apply to many other items, though not to the same extent as in the "staff of life."

WEEKLY EXPENSES.

1251. The calculation of the weekly expenses is readily made from the above table of annual expenditure by dividing each item by 52. Of course, every manager will find he (or she) must vary the items to suit particular circumstances, inasmuch as in many situations milk is dearer in proportion than bread, while it is an invariable rule that green-grocery in towns is double the price which it bears in the country; so that the calculation must only be received as an average one, and as serving to show the mode of arriving at the several details. But when the manager has carefully set about her task, and after putting down the whole sum to be spent, and dividing it into items, has proceeded to consider whether the fifty-second part of each of these will serve her for a week, she begins to see her way through her task, and at once is able to accommodate herself to circumstances, and to raise one, and lower another, accordingly. The great thing is, *to make the calculation on paper, and when that is done, to determine to adhere to it somehow or other.* But, without this weekly estimate, it is scarcely possible to check the expenditure until it has gone so far as to trench severely upon the whole sum to be laid out in the year.

1252. When the manager has proceeded thus far, the next thing is to lay in a stock for the week, or in some articles for a longer period, in-·cluding in the latter those which improve by keeping, or which may be bought to advantage in larger quantities than are required for the seven days. But, until she has gained some experience in housekeep‑ ing, it is perhaps better in all cases either to buy a week's consumption, or that for a month, or a quarter, or half a year, so that it may be divided into distinct portions, one of which may be easily set apart for each week. This is not possible with all the articles used in house‑ keeping, nor can the rule be as strictly carried out in the affairs of the house as it can in a large mercantile establishment, because, in order to do this, stock must be taken at the end of each week, which would be a difficult and tedious affair. Besides which, some articles are not used invariably in the same quantities in each week, such as poultry and fish; but these may be considered as exceptions to the rule, and treated accordingly. Coals and candles, again, are in much greater demand in the winter than in the summer; so that usually in the latter season one-half or one-third at least may be subtracted from the weekly sum, and put by to be afterwards added to that demanded in the winter months. The remedy, however, is simple enough; for though the expenses of each single week are not to be taken as the exact fifty-second part of the whole annual cost, yet after a time it will be found that one week will correct another, and that the cost of thirteen will give as nearly as may be the fourth part of the year's expenses, and, by proceeding further on the same principle, the outlay made in four weeks will show, though not so accurately, the thirteenth part of the annual expenditure.

1253. The task relating to the provisioning for the week is affected by so many causes, that no rule can possibly apply. Thus, at a dis‑ tance from market, many articles are of necessity purchased at intervals, which would be bought as they are wanted where the proximity to good shops admitted of such a convenient mode. In the country it is often impossible to procure butcher's meat, or even butter, except on market-days; so that, even in the sultry weather of midsummer, a stock sufficient for the interval must either be laid in at those times, or they must be altogether dispensed with. It must not therefore be assumed, that because the week's provisions are here indicated as purchased on the Saturday, the caterer should always do so on that day, but that she should comply with the rule in principle, and should only depart from it when some valid reason exists, as a matter of course substituting any other day of the week which may be the local market-day. The limits of this book will necessarily prevent a statement of the actual details in each separate income; and therefore what is given can only be received as a sr men of the plan generally to be adopted, which must be modified according to the circumstances already alluded to. In the higher incomes, also, there is less necessity for extreme care and anxiety, because the amounts set apart for them are on a liberal scale; and they will therefore be omitted in the calculation, the attention being confined to that most difficult problem comprised in the catering for a family upon the confined scale of expenses given under the third and fourth columns.

A Week's Catering for an Expenditure on Housekeeping of £150 a-Year.

1254. By the adoption of the above plan, and by subdividing the amounts given in the table of expenditure, the result is, that the mistress will have 18lb. of meat, 2s. worth of fish, 30lb. of bread, 2lb. of flour; 6s. worth of milk, butter, and cheese; 7s. worth of grocery; 3s. 10d. worth each of green-grocery and beer; and 5s. 9d. to spend in materials and female help in washing and ironing. She therefore goes to market and buys, we will say, a leg of mutton and a piece of the buttock of beef, together weighing 18lb., which, allowing for one day's dinner on fish, will be 3lb. per day on the whole. The bread will allow of three-quarters of a pound per head per day, with 2lb. of flour for puddings during the week; and, if it is made at home, there will be an extra quantity, or a saving to the extent of about 6d. The breakfast must be confined to oatmeal porridge or flour-milk, alternately with bread and butter or dripping for the children, and also tea and sugar; for which last item 6d. may be allowed for breakfast and tea, and 6d. for the sugar, rice, raisins, &c., used at dinner for puddings. About 6½d. is allowed per day for green-grocery and beer respectively, which is quite enough for these items; so that the chief difficulty lies in the management of the meat, which must be eked out with some care, and made to go as far as possible. Three pounds are allowed per day, or, in other words, the leg of mutton and piece of beef must each last three days, which, with a family of four children, is not a very easy task. Many people do this by filling their stomachs with heavy pudding in the first place; but this, I believe, to be wrong in point of health and economy. Whatever is considered a treat, will be eaten by children after they have already had enough of other articles of food. The better plan is to tell them that so much will be given of meat and no more, and then let them have their pudding afterwards. In this way the following dinners may be arranged :—

Sunday.—Leg of mutton; roast potatoes and greens; Yorkshire pudding.

Monday.—Cold mutton; potatoes and salad; rice pudding.

Tuesday.—Hashed mutton; fried potatoes; cauliflower; apple dumplings.

Wednesday.—Boiled beef; carrots and potatoes; suet pudding.

Thursday.—Pea-soup made from the mutton bones and beef boilings; fish and potatoes; currant dumplings.

Friday.—Cold boiled beef; potatoes and salad; bread-and-butter pudding, made with fruit preserve.

Saturday.—Bubble and squeak; potatoes; yeast dumplings.

In this plain way it is undoubtedly possible to keep a family of four children in good health on the above sum; and, what is more, there is not a particle of waste in the method of cookery. It is quite absurd to suppose that more can be done with the materials in point of economy. They may, no doubt, be made into more palatable dishes; but as, in the case of healthy children, due justice will generally be done to the above fare, it is useless to make the attempt on their account alone. While at the same time, if parents have this limited income, and have also a family of the number described above to keep, they must content themselves with this plain fare, or else they must pinch the stomachs of their children in order to pamper their own.

A WEEK'S CATERING FOR AN EXPENDITURE OF £65 PER ANNUM ON HOUSEKEEPING.

1255. The manager has here a much more difficult task to perform, as she has to support the same family upon a smaller allowance of the most expensive articles, and cannot, therefore, afford butcher's meat every day. She will have the following materials to go to work upon —viz., about 11lb. of meat or bacon, 20lb. of bread, and 3lb. of flour; 3s. worth of milk, butter, and cheese; 3s. worth of grocery; 2s. worth of green-grocery; 1s. 10d. for beer; and 9d. a week for washing materials, the labour for which she must find herself. All these contracted items will, therefore, demand great care, as the quantities furnished are scarcely sufficient for the wants of nature. Unless, by good fortune, there is a garden to supply potatoes, or they can be purchased at a low rate, it is impossible to effect a full diet on this scale, as three pecks of potatoes per week are the utmost which can be obtained for the money, on the average, throughout England. This will allow nearly half a peck a day, or say 6lb., which gives one pound of potatoes per head for dinner, with nearly half a pound of bread each per day for breakfast and tea, to be eaten with one quarter of a pound of salt butter among the family, divided between the morning and evening meal. One quart of milk will also be allowed, but no cheese, as I believe it to be an extravag article of food. The next thing, therefore, to consider, is as to the dinners, which may be as follows :—

Sunday.—Sheep's head roasted with chopped liver, and roast potatoes.

Monday.—Remainder of sheep's pluck fried, with dish of fried potatoes.

Tuesday.—Half a pound of bacon fried with cabbage, and eaten with boiled potatoes; suet pudding.

Wednesday.—Bouilli (page 81); cabbage and potatoes.

Thursday.—Pot-au-feu (page 81); potatoes and yeast dumplings.

Friday.—Two pounds of beef stewed with carrots or potatoes, as Irish Stew.

Saturday.—Pea-soup made without meat, or from part of pot-au-feu : fried potatoes and suet pudding.

These remarks might be indefinitely extended ;. but the natural intelligence of every individual must be exercised in arranging different kinds of cheap food, so as to suit the ever-varying circumstances connected with the locality. Much that would be useful to the man with only £65 a year to spend in this way, may be found under Cookery for the Poor (page 304), if he is not too proud to make use of it; but the prevailing error in this country is, that the man who is cramped in his means will not make up his mind to bend his diet low enough in materials to suit his purse. We are all too apt to try and imitate the manners of our superiors just above us; and in this way much misery and inconvenience is occasioned, which might be avoided by a timely submission to our lot.

ECONOMICAL FARE FOR A VERY SMALL FAMILY.

1256. When a smaller family than the above requires a very economical fare, the case is still more difficult, because less variety can be obtained from those joints which are well known to be the only really economical ones. Nevertheless, a good deal may be done by management; and even in the case of a leg of mutton, the dinners for a whole week may be obtained from it without having any two exactly alike, and without extra cost in any way. The following is the method proposed, which may be often useful to a married couple without children or servant, or to two sisters living by themselves.

1st Day.—Cut some steaks off the large end and broil them.

2nd Day.—Cut off a small knuckle and boil it, to be served with caper or nasturtium sauce.

3rd Day.—Cut some cutlets off the side next the knuckle, and fry with egg and bread crumbs.

4th Day.—Bone and stuff the fillet, which is to be roasted.

5th Day.—Hash part of the remainder.

6th Day.—Eat part cold, with salad.

7th Day.—Mince the remainder, and cover with bread crumbs. (See par. 531).

1257. A sirloin of beef may be treated nearly in the same way, but does not admit of quite so much variety. Thus—

1st *Day*.—Cut off the thin end, and stew with peas or carrots, and potatoes.

2nd *Day*.—Cut a thin steak off one side, and broil.

3rd *Day*.—Roast.

4th *Day*.—Hash part of remains.

5th *Day* —Eat part cold.

6th *Day*.—Mince part with carrots (see par. 531).

1258. The following bills of fare, arranged to suit an expenditure of £1000 a year, on the calculation that the materials of each dinner will cost about 8s., which is the sum allowed in the table at page 323, exclusive of beer and wine.

BILLS OF FARE FOR £1000 A YEAR.

JANUARY.

(a) Pea-Soup.

Remove—Boiled rabbit smothered in onions.

Mashed potatoes.   Stewed celery.

Roast leg of mutton.

Bread-and-butter pudding.

Mince pies.   Stewed pears.

Brace of partridges.

(b) Minced mutton, browned.

Fried potatoes, garnished with plain boiled potatoes.   Brocoli.

Cod's head and shoulders.

Remove—Sirloin of beef

Leamington pudding.

Glasses of custard   Preserved fruit in glasses.

Hot apple tart.

FEBRUARY.

(c) Boiled turkey.

Mashed potatoes.   Jerusalem artichokes.

Cold roast beef.

Semolina pudding.

Arrowroot blancmange.   Stewed apples.

Macaroni.

(d) Cod-fish, fricasseed, with wall of potatoes.

Potatoes.   Sea-kale.

Roast griskin of pork.

Rolly-polly pudding, baked or boiled.

Fruit tart.

MARCH.

(e) French soup.

Remove—Veal cutlets, garnished with bacon.

Brussels sprouts.   Potatoes.

Roast loin of mutton.

Apple soufflé pudding.

Open tart.

(f) Boiled beef, garnished with carrots and parsnips.

Ham garnished with greens.   Potatoes.

Roast fowls, garnished with sausages.

Custard pudding.

Remnant of open tart.   Stewed pears.

Boiled apple-dumplings.

APRIL.

(g) Hashed pork.

Potato balls.   Mashed Jerusalem artichokes.

Mutton en masquerade.

Lemon dumplings.

Pancakes.

(h) Boiled leg of mutton.

Potatoes.   Brocoli.

Cutlets of soles.

Prussia puffs.

Fruit tart.

MAY.

(i) Onion soup.

Potatoes.   Asparagus.

Stewed breast of veal.

Ground-rice pudding.

Rhubarb tart.

(j) Eggs and spinach,

Mashed turnips   Potatoes.

Stewed beef.

Custard pudding.

Creamed rice.

Orange fritters.

JUNE.

(k) Potatoes. Mutton cutlets. Asparagus.
Roast fillet of veal.
—
Rhubarb pudding.
Macaroni, with cheese grated over it.

(l) Potatoes. Turbot. Spinach.
Quarter of lamb.
—
Bread pudding.
Custards in glasses. Cheese-cakes.
Gooseberry tart.

JULY.

(m) Young potatoes. Boiled lamb. Peas.
Roast ducks.
—
Ground-rice pudding.
Red-currant tart.

(n) Young potatoes. Hashed duck. Stewed French beans.
Turbot.
—
Cabinet pudding.
Jelly.
Open tart.

AUGUST.

(o) Potatoes. Chicken pie. Stewed cucumbers.
Bubble and squeak.
—
Macaroni pudding.
Black-currant tart.

(p) Potatoes. Hodge-podge. Stewed peas.
Lamb cutlets.
—
Strawberry soufflé.
Stewed currants.

SEPTEMBER.

(q) Potatoes. Brace of grouse. Vegetable marrow.
Roast leg of mutton.
—
Oxford puddings.
Whipped cream.
Plum tart.

(r) Potatoes. Boiled bacon. Broad beans.
Beef-steak pie.
—
Friar's omelet.
Apple charlotte.

OCTOBER.

(s) Pea-soup.
Remove—Hashed mutton.
Potatoes. French beans.
Ribs of beef.
—
Bread-and-butter pudding.
Tartlets. Stewed apples.
Brace of partridges.

(t) Savoury rice. Boiled chicken. Mashed potatoes.
Stewed beef.
—
Sponge-cake puddings.
Custard.
Apple tarts.

NOVEMBER.

(u) Potatoes. Rabbit curry. Jerusalem artichokes.
Roast spare-rib of pork.
—
Baked hasty-pudding
Macaroni and cheese.

(v) Peas-pudding. Minced mutton. Potatoes.
Boiled pork.
Lemon suet pudding.
Potato fritters.

DECEMBER.

(w) Potatoes. Wild ducks. Stewed Portugal onions.
Roast leg of mutton.
—
Swiss pudding.
Mince pies.

(x) Potatoes. Cod's head and shoulders. Mashed turnips.
Sirloin of beef.
—
Plum pudding.
Apple tart.

1259. THE ANNEXED BILLS OF FARE are suited to an expenditure of £500 a-year, in which, on the calculation made in the table given at page 323, 4s. 6d. per day will be about the sum allotted for the dinners.

BILLS OF FARE FOR £500 A YEAR.

JANUARY.

(a) Yorkshire pudding.

Potatoes.   Jerusalem artichokes, mashed.

Leg of mutton.
Ground rice pudding.

(b) Minced mutton.   Mashed potatoes.
Brussels sprouts.

Stewed beef-steaks.

Remnant of pudding.
Hot apple tart.

FEBRUARY.

(c) Soles.   Parsnips.
Potatoes.

Irish stew.

Poor Knight's pudding.
Tartlets.

(d) Carrot soup.
    Mashed potatoes, garnished with browned ditto.
Greens.

Roast pork.

Pancakes.

MARCH.

(e) Carrots.   Potatoes.
Mashed turnips.
Boiled beef.

Baked apple dumplings.

(f) Pea-soup.
Potatoes.
Bubble and squeak.

Rice and apple soufflé.

APRIL.

(g) Ham or bacon.   Mashed potatoes.
Jerusalem artichokes.
Fillet of veal.

Rhubarb tart.

(h) Poached eggs and bacon.
Cabbage.   Fried potatoes.

Veal cutlets.

Arrowroot pudding.
Cheese-cakes.

MAY.

(i) Hashed mutton.
Potatoes.   Brocoli.

Roast leveret.

Baked tapioca-and-rhubarb pudding.

(j) Potatoes.   Asparagus.
Quarter of lamb.

A baked jam roll pudding.

JUNE.

(k) A brill.
Potato-balls.   Cabbage.
Veal cutlets.

Milk custard in glasses.
A green apricot tart.

(l) Ham.   Peas.
Young potatoes.
Boiled fillet of veal.

Gooseberry fool.
Arrowroot blancmange.

JULY.

(m) Soup Julienne.   Potatoes.
Peas.
Lamb cutlets.

Remnant of some sweet.
Currant tart.

(n) A marsden.
Potatoes.
Hodge-podge.

Strawberries and cream.
Rice pudding.

AUGUST.

(o) Vegetable soup.
French beans.
Potato pie.

Custard pudding.
Stewed fruit.

(p) Shoulder of mutton.
Broad beans.   Potatoes.
Bacon.

Raspberry and currant tart.

SEPTEMBER.

(q) Chicken pie.

Stewed French beans.   Potatoes.

Cold roast beef.

Carrot pudding.

(r) Cod's head and shoulders.

Potatoes.   Stewed mushrooms.

Beef stewed with peas.

Baked batter pudding with damsons.

OCTOBER.

(s) Brace of partridges.

Potatoes.   Vegetable marrows.

Harico.

Potato fritters.

(t) Roast sirloin of beef.

Potatoes—Spinach.

Milk custard.
Damson pudding.

NOVEMBER.

(u) Goose.
Potatoes.

Swiss Pudding.

(v) Peas-pudding.
Potatoes.
Boiled leg of pork.

Bread pudding.
Tartlets.

DECEMBER.

(w) Pig's puddings.

Potatoes.   Jerusalem artichokes.

Hare.

Apple charlotte.
Rice pudding.

(x) Turkey.

Potatoes.   Brocoli.

Chine.

Plum pudding.
Mince pies.

1900. IN SEARCHING FOR VARIETY, the housekeeper may receive some assistance from the following list of articles in season in the different months throughout the year.

SEASONAL TABLE.

JANUARY.

MEAT.—Beef, mutton, pork, and house-lamb.

POULTRY AND GAME.—Pheasants, partridges, hares, rabbits, woodcocks, snipes, wild fowl, turkeys, capons, pullets, fowls, chickens, pigeons, and larks.

FISH.—Carp, tench, perch, lampreys, eels, pike, cod, soles, flounders, plaice, turbot, skate, smelts, whitings, lobsters, crabs, crayfish, prawns, oysters

VEGETABLES.—Cabbage, savoys, colewort, sprouts, brocoli, sea-kale, leeks, onions, beet, sorrel, endive, spinach, celery, garlick, potatoes, parsnips, turnips, shalots, lettuces, cresses, mustard, herbs of all sorts, dry or green.

FRUIT.—Apples, pears, nuts, walnuts, medlars, oranges, and grapes.

FEBRUARY AND MARCH.

MEAT AND FOWL as in January, with the addition of ducklings and chickens; which last are to be bought in London throughout the year, but are now very dear.

FISH.—As the last month; except that cod is not thought so good from February to July, but may generally be bought; and salmon is coming in, though very scarce.

VEGETABLES.—The same as the former months, with the addition of forced kidney-beans.

FRUIT.—Apples, pears, oranges, and forced strawberries.

APRIL, MAY, AND JUNE.

MEAT.—Beef, mutton, veal, lamb, and venison in June.

POULTRY.—Pullets, fowls, chickens, ducklings, pigeons, rabbits, leverets.

FISH.—Carp, tench, sole, smelts, eels, trout, turbot, lobsters, chub, salmon, herrings, mackerel, crayfish, crabs, prawns, shrimps.

VEGETABLES.—As before. In May, early potatoes. In June, peas, radishes, kidney-beans, carrots, turnips, early cabbages, cauliflowers, asparagus, artichokes, and all sorts of salads forced.

FRUITS.—In June, strawberries, cherries, melons, green apricots, currants, and gooseberries for tarts. In July, cherries, strawberries, pears, melons, gooseberries, currants, apricots, grapes, nectarines, and some peaches. But most of these are forced, and sold at a high price.

JULY, AUGUST, AND SEPTEMBER.

MEAT, as before.

POULTRY AND GAME.—Pullets, fowls, chickens, rabbits, pigeons, green geese, turkey poults, leverets. Two first months, plovers, wheat-ears; geese in September, and also partridges in that month, and grouse after August 12. Hares all through; quail and landrails.

FISH.—Cod, haddock, flounders, plaice, skate, thornback, mullets, salmon, till the 25th September, pike, carp, eels, shell-fish—except oysters. Mackerel the first two months of the quarter, but not good in August.

VEGETABLES.—Of all sorts. Beans, peas, French-beans, &c. &c.

FRUIT.—In July—Strawberries, gooseberries, pine-apples, plums (various), cherries, apricots, raspberries, melons, currants, damsons. In August and September, peaches, plums, figs, filberts, mulberries, cherries, apples, pears, nectarines, grapes. Latter months, pines, melons, strawberries. Medlars and quinces in the latter months. Morella cherries, damsons, and various plums.

OCTOBER.

MEAT as before, and doe venison.

POULTRY AND GAME—Fowls as in the last quarter. Pheasants from the first of October; partridges, grouse, larks, hares, dotterels. At the end of the month, wild-ducks, teal, snipes, widgeon.

FISH—Dories, smelts, pike, perch, halibut, bril, carp, barbel, gudgeon, tench, shell-fish.

VEGETABLES.—As in January. French-beans, last crops of beans, &c.

FRUIT.—Peaches. pears. figs, bullace, grapes, apples, medlars, damsons, filberts, walnuts, nuts, quinces, services.

NOVEMBER.

MEAT. — Beef, mutton, veal, pork, doe venison.

POULTRY AND GAME as in last month.

FISH as in last month.

VEGETABLES —Carrots, turnips, parsnips, potatoes, onions, leeks, shalots, cabbage, savoys, colewort, spinach, cresses, endive, celery, lettuces, salad, herbs, pot-herbs.

FRUIT —Pears, apples, nuts, walnuts, bullace, chestnuts, medlars, grapes.

DECEMBER.

MEAT.—Beef, mutton, veal, house lamb, pork, and doe venison.

POULTRY AND GAME. — Geese, turkeys, pullets, pigeons, capons, fowls, chickens rabbits, hares, snipes, woodcocks, larks pheasants, partridges, guinea-fowl, wild-ducks, teal, widgeon, dotterels, dun-birds, grouse, and ptarmigan.

FISH.—Cod, turbot, halibut, soles, gurnets, carp, pike, gudgeons, eels, dories, shell-fish.

VEGETABLES.—As in the last month, and asparagus forced, &c.

FRUIT as in the last month.

CHAP. XXVI.—PRINCIPLES OF CARVING.

1261. The general principles upon which carving is, or ought to be conducted, are very plain, and the only real difficulty consists in the necessity for practice, to enable the carver to hit the joints either between the several bones of a piece of mutton or veal, or in any of the various kinds of poultry or game. Each of these must, therefore, be separately considered; but, with regard to butcher's meat, one rule may be laid down as almost, but not quite, invariable, and that is—always to cut across the fibres of the meat, and not in the same direction. This ensures a short grain, and avoids those long strings in the mouth, which are by no means pleasant. If, therefore, the carver will only examine into this point, and ascertain the direction of the grain or fibres of the meat, he will at once be able to cross them with the knife, and gain the desired advantage. The exception alluded to is the under side of the sirloin of beef, which is always cut in the direction of its fibres, though I really do not see why, as it is much improved in flavour by cutting it in the same direction as the upper side, that is, parallel with the bones. This, however, is not a ver easy task with a bad knife, as the meat is apt to slip from the bone. The next rule to be observed is to make the knife and fork assist each other—that is to say, the fork should steady the joint for the knife, or where the fork is used as the means of division in removing the leg of a fowl, the knife must take the office of steadying the body of the bird, and the same remark applies to the carving of a hare or rabbit, or any other kind of poultry or game; and, thirdly, it is very important, in an economical point of view, to cut all slices, either of meat, game, or poultry, completely down to the bone, so as to leave no ragged portions behind.

CARVING BY THE BUTLER IN LARGE PARTIES.

1262. In parties of any size or pretensions, it is now the fashion for the butler to carve all the dishes on the side-table; but this requires a servant equal to the task, with assistants in proportion, and also a dining-room large enough to admit of a side-board devoted solely to this purpose. In small quiet parties, and in the home circle, the carving will still be carried out by the master or mistress of the house, and therefore it is necessary to make some remarks on the subject in this place.

KNIVES AND FORKS.

1263. The carving knives and forks are made specially for each article; thus, for fish they are of silver or plated ware, with a large massive blade for the knife, and the fork also large and massive, with five prongs, so as to raise a large flake of the flesh without breaking it. Again, for large joints, such as beef, mutton, or venison, a long steel blade is required, which should be made very sharp with the steel, applied in the true butcher's mode, and in addition a two-pronged fork; and lastly, for game, the handles are long, to give a good purchase in twisting off the leg, while the blade of the knife is small and pointed, so as to be easily insinuated between the small bones at the wing, the fork being also two-pronged.

A COD'S HEAD AND SHOULDERS

1264. Is a most troublesome dish to carve, because, if well boiled, it looks whole until touched, and then tumbles to pieces in the most trying way to the inexperienced carver. As in the salmon, so here, the thick and the thin parts are not equally prized by all, and should be served according to choice. There is, also, a part on the head behind the eye which is much relished, and called the cheek, together with many other tit-bits about the head. Close to the back-bone is the sound, the flavour of which is patronised by most people, though

Fig. 138

Fig. 139

Fig. 140

Fig. 181

Fig. 182

Fig. 183

not by all, as is the case with the liver also; each of which should be divided into portions suited to the size of the party, and their respective wishes on the subject. Thus, draw the knife from B to D (*fig.* 138), then meet this line by cutting from A to B, and from C to D; or, if necessary, smaller slices may be cut according to the party, but always in these directions. The thick is the part here cut—the thin is below the longitudinal line.

To Carve Salmon,

1265. It is only necessary to take care to avoid breaking the flakes unnecessarily, by attempting to divide them at right angles with the long axis of the fish. There is a great difference in the flavour of the back or thick part, and that of the thin part of the fish, and therefore most people like to be asked which they prefer. This being done, the knife is carried down to the bone longitudinally, and removes a thick slice of either or both, according to the choice. (See directions for codfish, par. 1264.)

Turbot

1266. Requires peculiar carving, because, unlike other fish, its skin and fins are thought a great delicacy. It is only necessary to carry the blade of the knife down to the bone along the middle, and then to make similar deep and clean cuts at right angles to this, each way to the fins, a portion of which should be separated and *kept* with each square of fish, so as to avoid that hacking of the fins into pieces afterwards, which is by no means sightly. When this part is not approved of, it is very easy to leave the fin attached to the bones below (see *fig.* 139).

Brill, Soles, and Plaice,

1267. Are carved much in the same way as turbot when they are of any size; but small soles are completely divided into two or three portions by the knife, which requires a slight twist in order to do this with ease. Many ladies with weak wrists have great difficulty in effecting this seemingly simple operation; but though strength will enable any bungler to do it, yet a little knack will make up for the deficiency in this ingredient, and place the delicate lady's hand on a level with that of the most powerful man. The exact method, however, can scarcely be described, and must be watched and imitated, in order to insure its being caught by the learner. Some people prefer to remove the whole of the flesh in the same way as in carving turbot, but this only answers for large soles.

MACKEREL.

1268. Mackerel arc split at the tail, and the upper half raised at that part from the bones, after which the bone is removed from the lower half of the fish, and that in its turn is served either in one piece or divided into two, according to its size.

SMALL FISH.

1269. Most other small fish are carved much in the same way, that is, either by serving them whole, or dividing them with the knife into sections, according to size.

LOBSTERS.

1270. For the mode of serving lobsters and crabs, see page 70. The sketch at *fig.* 140 will shew the way in which lobsters and crabs are arranged on the dish for table.

THE HAUNCH OF MUTTON OR VENISON

1271. Is carved very differently by different people. The usual plan is to cut through the flesh between the leg and loin, and then to run the knife from this to the lower end of the loin, cutting parallel slices in that direction. A much better plan, however, consists in making these cuts in one sweep, carrying the knife directly from the outside of the leg to the end of the loin, and thus getting a beautiful long slice of lean with the fat at the end (see *fig.* 176, A B). There is, also, a delicious mine of kidney-fat in the loin of mutton *under* the flank, which is often too high in venison; but, if fresh enough, is even more rich and palatable in that meat than in mutton.

SADDLE OF MUTTON.

1272. The saddle of mutton is carved in three different ways—1st, by longitudinal slices along each side of the bone, by which the lean and fat do not come in the same slice; 2nd, by transverse slices, taking in the bones, and which therefore must be thick and clumsy; and 3rd, by oblique slices, slightly curved, which is far the best plan, in which the knife begins at the bone near the tail, and, after cutting off the outside, takes a series of parallel slices all through the joint (see *fig.* 177).

LEG OF MUTTON.

1273. The leg of mutton is capable of being carved in two modes, the choice of which must depend greatly upon the number of the party ᵥ be served. Thus, for a small one, it is better to cut the leg in the ᵗction A B, *fig.* 178; but this only admits of a small number of good

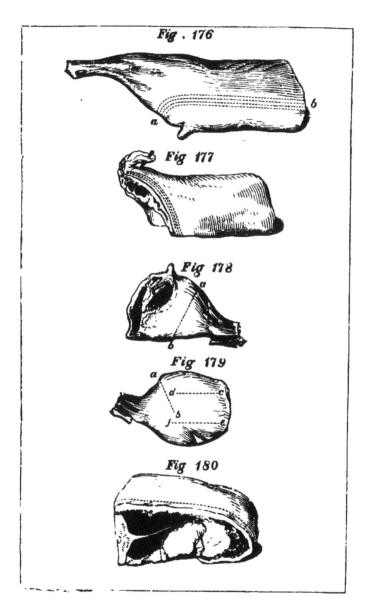

Fig . 176

Fig 177

Fig 178

Fig 179

Fig 180

slices, beyond which they are of loose and coarse fibre. But by turning up the leg, and cutting it exactly on the plan shown in the figure
of the haunch, a much greater proportion of handsome slices may be
obtained, and consequently a larger party may all be equally gratified.

SHOULDER OF MUTTON OR LAMB.

1274. In carving a shoulder of mutton or lamb, the first thing for
the young housekeeper to ascertain is the position of the bone, which
is near the edge on one side at A, *fig.* 179. Here the knife must not
be inserted, because it would be stopped at once; but by trying the
opposite side a deep cut may be made, and from its two surfaces
slices are readily obtained. When this part is exhausted, slices may
be procured along the sides of the bladebone at (c d) and (e f), and
again on the under-side some few good cuts will be met with.

FORE-QUARTER OF LAMB.

1275. The fore-quarter of lamb must be commenced by separating
the shoulder from its bed, carrying the knife all round it, and raising
it with the fork; after which a lemon should be squeezed into the cut
surface, and a little pepper and salt then sprinkled over it; but all
this may be much better done in the kitchen than on the dining-table.
In order to carve this part, the same directions will apply as are
given in the last paragraph; and for the remaining portion it is only
necessary to separate the thin part, called the brisket, from the ribs,
and then divide each into transverse sections. One rib is usually
served to each plate, and with this many people like a small division
of the brisket; but the question ought always to be asked before giving
either or both.

A BREAST OF VEAL.

1276. A breast of veal is carved in the same way as the bed of the
fore-quarter of lamb after the shoulder is removed.

THE FILLET OF VEAL.

1277. The fillet of veal merely requires successive horizontal slices
of meat to be taken off with a sharp knife, serving with each a small
portion of fat and forcemeat, unless disliked by the person for whom
it is intended.

A LOIN OF VEAL.

1278. A loin of veal is usually divided into two portions, the chump
end and the kidney end. The latter merely requires to be divided

z

into portions at right angles with its length, every other one of which contains a bone, and the intermediate one is of meat only. Most people like some of the fat on the under side, round the kidney, spread on toast and seasoned, when it eats like marrow. The CHUMP END has the tail attached to its upper side, and this must be taken off horizontally, after which successive slices of meat are served without any bone, which is all in one piece, and therefore not capable of being divided.

SHOULDER OF VEAL.

1279. The shoulder of veal is carved like the shoulder of mutton by some people; but the best plan is to begin on the under-side, and then cut slices from the thick edge opposite the bone, and parallel with it. When stuffed, a portion must be served on each plate.

SIRLOIN OF BEEF.

1280. The sirloin of beef is usually carved by cutting the upper side in slices parallel with the bone, and commencing at the edge, the brown of which forms the first slice. On the under side the knife is generally made to cross the grain, cutting through the middle down to the bone, and removing slices on each side. This part, however, tastes much better if cut on the same plan as the upper side, that is, by commencing at the edge; but in this way the slices are small, and do not look so handsome, for which reason the ordinary mode is generally preferred (see *fig.* 180).

RUMP AND H-BONE.

1281. The rump and h-bone are carved by commencing to cut from the surface of the meat in such a direction that the grain is cut across; by attending to which a mistake may always be avoided.

THE ROUND.

1282. The round of beef requires the same management as the fillet of veal, the slices being cut in the direction A B C, *fig.* 181.

INFERIOR JOINTS.

1283. The inferior joints of beef must all be cut according to the principles alluded to at par. 1238—that is to say, by cutting across the grain. The brisket is no exception to this rule, the bones being neglected in carrying it out.

TONGUE.

1284. The ox tongue, when sent to table without rolling, is carved

꙼y cutting it nearly in the middle, leaving a small portion at the bot-
om to keep the two parts together. Many people like a little fat
served with the lean, but others do not like its flavour. When rolled
and pressed, as directed at page 117, the knife is carried horizontally,
as in carving a fillet of veal.

HAM.

1285. A ham may be carved in three ways—1st, it may be commenced at the knuckle, and gradually worked up to the other end;
2nd, it may be cut in the middle, and each side taken from until exhausted, taking care to carry the knife down to the bone in a perpen-
dicular direction (A B, *fig.* 182); or, 3rd, a hole may be scooped out in
the middle, and thin circular slices removed from around it (o, *fig.* 182).
In any case the slices ought to be thin and regular, which requires
some little practice; for the third method great art is demanded.

PIG.

1286. A sucking pig requires very little carving, as the knife may
be carried through any of its bones with little force. It is usual to
divide it into sections about two inches broad, and including about
three ribs in the middle, and a part only of the fore and hind-quarters
at each end (A B—B C, *fig.* 183).

CALF'S HEAD.

1287. A calf's head merely demands the careful use of the knife in
cutting off longitudinal slices of the gelatinous skin, carrying the
blade straight down to the bone.

POULTRY AND GAME.

1288. Poultry and game require all the art of the experienced carver
to do justice to them, inasmuch as they may be made to look extremely
inviting if nicely separated, or they may be hacked to pieces by the
bad manager of the carving-knive. One of the chief advantages of the
present fashionable method of serving a dinner consists in the avoid-
ance of this mistake, which is alike annoying to the giver of a good
dinner and to the guests. The mistress cannot always allot the task
to a person who is skilful at this craft, and, if the reverse takes place,
she is annoyed at his bungling for his sake as well as her own. As
far as possible, the fork should only be inserted once, and not continually driven in, and then removed to try a fresh place. This constant
stabbing disfigures the bird, and looks awkward and unsightly in the

carver, besides which it is seldom or never necessary. The following
special directions may assist the young carver, but nothing short of
actual observation and trial will make him accomplished in the art.

TURKEY.

1289. A roast or boiled turkey may be made to serve a great number
of people if carved with judgment, or it may be used so extravagantly
as to be expended before half the guests have been served. A sharp
knife should be passed clearly down to the bone, almost close to the
wing, and then a thin slice is taken out from between this and the
breast, continuing the same plan until the whole side is exhausted,
after which the other side is served in the same way. A portion of
the force-meat is also placed in each plate; and, if there are sausages
or balls, a part of each of them. When both sides of the breast are
used up, and the party are not all served, the legs must be taken off
by carrying the knife backward between them and the body, until it
is stopped by the joint, when by means of the fork stuck in the leg it
is severed from the body, the knife completing the removal by its edge.
If possible, however, the carver should endeavour to avoid having
recourse to the legs; and it is usually either a reproach upon the mistress for not procuring a sufficiently large bird, or upon his own
powers of carving, if such an expedient is unavoidable. In dividing
the leg into its two portions, the knife should be used against the
inside of the joint, where it enters with much less difficulty than on
the outside. After this, in a large bird, the meat is cut off in sections
for serving.

CHICKEN.

1290. The roast or boiled chicken, when carved hot, is generally
cut into separate joints, consisting of—1st, the wings; 2nd, the legs;
3rd, the merrythought; 4th, the neck-bones; 5th, the breast; 6th,
the back and its side-bones; 7th, the neck. But, excepting for family
use, it is seldom customary to use more than the wings, merrythought,
and breast, or sometimes in addition the legs. The plan of proceeding is, to stick the fork into the breast firmly, then draw the knife
steadily along the line between the leg and body, continuing it forward until it has separated a slice of the breast with the wing-bone.
If the carver is dexterous, he hits the joint at once; and some can
remove a wing as if there were no bone at all, the art consisting in
guessing at the exact situation of the joint. As soon as the two
wings are removed, the knife is carried down in front of the breast-

bone, scooping out the merrythought, and readily separating it from its bony attachments. If the legs are now to be removed, the fork is taken out of the breast, and by sticking the prongs in the leg, with the knife laid flat against the side, they are readily lifted out of the sockets, and torn as it were from the body. The neck-bones are now twisted off with the fork, after which the breast is removed whole by cutting through the ribs with the knife, and then a separation of the back-bone in the middle divides the remaining part of the body into the back and neck. The former of these may again have its side-bones easily removed with the knife, each containing a delicious morsel in a sort of spoon-shaped cavity, which is much prized by the gourmand.

COLD ROAST FOWL.

1291. When a cold roast fowl is to be served at a breakfast or supper party, it is often the custom to carve it up completely with a sharp knife, and then put the joints together again, keeping them in their places by means of white ribbon tied in bows. This is a very good expedient in such a case, as it prevents the exhibition of bad carving, and facilitates the rapid serving of the guests, which is essential to success in such matters.

GEESE AND DUCKS.

1292. Geese and ducks are carved much on the same principle as the turkey and fowl, excepting that there is very little meat on the merrythought, which is also more difficult to get off. In the goose the best parts will be found in the breast, which is, however, not so meaty as that of the turkey, and the slices are much more shallow. Ducks are cut in slices when large, or if small they are disjointed like fowls. If these are dressed with seasoning, it should not be distributed on the plates without ascertaining that it is agreeable to the tastes of the party to be served.

PARTRIDGE AND GROUSE.

1293. The partridge is so small that it will scarcely admit of disjointing, and it is usual to separate at once into the breast portion and the back and legs, which may readily be done without cutting, by inserting the fork in the former, and raising it while depressing the latter. When this is done the knife may be carried longitudinally through the breast, so as to divide it into two equal portions, after which the back and legs may be halved in the same way. Some

people, however, divide the partridge differently, by cutting off a leg
and a wing together, and leaving a small breast, so as to make either
three or five portions out of this bird. The grouse is carved in the
same way as the partridge.

PHEASANT.

1294. A pheasant may be sliced on the breast like a turkey, after
which, if the party require it, the plan of carving similar to that practised on the roast fowl must be adopted.

WOODCOCK.

1295. The woodcock is carved like the partridge, distributing it into
four, or sometimes two portions only, and giving out the toast in the
same way, equally to each plate; the thigh is usually considered the
most delicate part of this bird.

SNIPE.

1296. The snipe is only large enough to divide into a breast and
back, with the legs. The toast is the same as for the woodcock.

PIGEONS, LARKS, FIELDFARES, &c.

1297. These are divided into two portions, as described for the
partridge.

HARE.

1298. The hare is rather difficult to manage nicely, especially if it
is an old one. When the carver has a strong wrist, the most advantageous way is to carry the knife along on each side of the back-bone,
all the way from the shoulder to the tail, and leaving a useless piece
of back in the middle about half an inch wide, with a good fleshy fillet
on each side, and the legs ready for subdivision. After this primary
division, the side-slices are readily served in separate portions by cutting them across. In default of this strong-armed method, some
carvers cut fillets off the back, and serve them, proceeding to do the
same with the legs, which may or may not be previously raised out or
their sockets. A third plan consists in removing the legs, and serving
them in two portions each, then dividing the back into sections of
about two or three inches in length, and finally removing the shoulders, and serving them also. If this plan is preferred, and the hare is
to be carved by a person deficient in strength of wrist, the prominent
part of the back-bone should be removed by the cook from the inside

before roasting. A portion of the forcemeat must of course accompany each plate. The back is considered the best, then the legs, and lastly the shoulders, which, however, some people prefer to any other part.

CHAP. XXVII.—HOUSEKEEPING ACCOUNTS, AND TOTAL ORDINARY EXPENDITURE.

1299. The accounts in housekeeping should be kept with great accuracy and circumstantiality, for many reasons, not the least of which is, that in most cases there are two people concerned, who sometimes may take different views of the result; and, if a reference to details cannot be given, it is extremely difficult to show that the total expenditure is correct. Besides this, unless there is an account kept against each tradesman, it is impossible to check him, and an error made either wilfully or by mistake, can neither be detected, nor remedied if surmised. No one, however, can possibly deny the advantage of keeping good accounts; and the only objection consists in the trouble they give, which will be small if the task is performed with regularity.

1300. THE BEST MODE OF KEEPING ACCOUNTS for a house is to have a daily entry book, in which every item of expenditure is put down, either opposite a printed form or otherwise. Many people use printed books in which a list is given for each day, with ruled columns; but this seems a very useless expense, as a plain ruled book is all that is necessary for the purpose. In my opinion, the weekly account should always be kept, and the daily one need not then be attempted; but by putting down each item paid during the week *seriatim*, and then adding up the total, the week's expenses are readily arrived at.

1301. BUT, BESIDES THE WEEKLY ACCOUNT, there should be a ledger account kept, in which each tradesman should be entered under a separate head. Thus, it is well to procure a small ledger, in which the whole book is "lettered"—that is to say, it is divided into twenty-six portions, each having a letter of the alphabet assigned to it, and marked on the margin. In this the manager enters under the letter D the butcher's account as it is paid, so that at the end of a month, quarter, or year, she can tell the whole outlay in that article. Bread, also, will come under the same letter. Fish will of course be posted under the letter F, and so on.

TOTAL ANNUAL EXPENDITURE.

1302. In this way there is an opportunity of arriving at—first, the weekly expenditure, which will vary in some trifling degree; and, secondly, the total cost of each item set down in the table given at page 323. The plan is exceedingly simple, and only requires a knowledge of compound addition to carry it out, as the entries are all made in the same amounts as are stated on the weekly bills, or those paid at longer or shorter intervals. These may be either left open, to be added up at the end of the year, or they may be added up quarterly, or even monthly, if desired; but less than the quarter seldom gives an exact idea of the yearly cost of the house.

TABLES OF WEIGHTS AND MEASURES.

1303. For the convenience of reference, the following tables of measures and weights are introduced, together with an account of the modes by which the exact capacity has been determined by Act of Parliament.

1304. Measures are either—1, of length; 2, of surface; 3, of solidity or capacity; 4, of force or gravity, or what is commonly called, weight; 5, of angles; 6, of time; and their respective standards are, in Britain—*a yard, square yard*, or *the* 1-4840*th of an acre, a cubic yard, a gallon, pound weight, degree, minute.* The British Act, for establishing uniform measures throughout the. realm, and called the *Act of Uniformity*, took effect January 1, 1826. The system thus established is called the *Imperial* system. Its *rationale* is as follows :—Take a pendulum which will vibrate seconds in London, on a level of the sea, in a vacuum, divide all that part thereof which lies between the axis of suspension and the centre of oscillation into 39,1393 equal parts; then will 10,000 of those parts be an imperial inch, twelve whereof make a foot, and thirty-six whereof make a yard. The standard yard is " that distance between the centres of the two points in the gold studs in the straight brass rod, now in the custody of the Clerk of the House of Commons, whereon the words and figures 'Standard Yard, 1760,' are engraved, which is declared to be the genuine standard of the measure of length called a yard; and, as the expansibility of the metal would cause some variation in the length of the rod in different degrees of temperature, the Act determines that the brass rod in question shall be of the temperature of 62 degrees Fahrenheit. The measure is to be denominated the *Imperial Standard Yard*, and to be the only standard whereby all other measures of lineal extension shall be computed." Thus the foot, the inch, the pole, the furlong, and the mile, shall bear the same proportion to the imperial standard yard as they have hitherto borne to

the yard measure in general use. The Act also makes provision for
the restoration of the standard yard in case of loss, destruction, or
defacement, by a reference to an invariable natural standard, which is
to be that proportion which the yard bears to the length of a pendulum
vibrating seconds of time, in the latitude of London, in a vacuum at
the level of the sea; which is found to be as thirty-six inches (the
yard) to 39·1393 (the pendulum); thus a sure means is established to
supply the loss which might by possibility occur. Take a cube of one
such inch of distilled water, at 62 degrees of temperature by Fahrenheit's thermometer, let this be weighed by any weight, and let such
weight be divided into 252,458 equal parts, then will 1000 of such
parts be a troy grain, and 7000 of those grains will be a pound avoirdupois, the operation having been performed in air. Ten pounds such
as those mentioned of distilled water, at 62 degrees of temperature,
will be a gallon, which gallon will contain 277 cubic inches, and
274-1000th parts of another cubic inch. The standard pound is
determined to be that standard pound troy weight made in the
year 1758, in the custody of the Clerk of the House of Commons;
such weight is to be denominated the *Imperial Standard Troy
Pound*, and is to be "the only standard measure of weight from
which all other weights shall be derived, computed, and ascertained;
and one-twelfth part of the said troy pound is to be an ounce, and
one-twentieth part of such ounce a pennyweight, and one-twenty-
fourth part of such pennyweight a grain; so that 5760 such grains
shall be a pound troy, and 7000 such grains a pound avoirdupois, and
one-sixteenth part of such ounce a drachm. If the standard pound
shall be lost, destroyed, or defaced, the act directs that it shall be recovered by reference to the weight of a cubic inch of water; it having
been ascertained that a cubic inch of distilled water, weighed in air by
brass weights, at the temperature of 62 degrees Fahrenheit, and the barometer at thirty inches, is equal to 252·458 grains; and as the standard
troy pound contains 5760 such grains, it is therefore established that the
original standard pound may be at any time recovered, by making
another weight to bear the proportion just mentioned to a cubic inch
of water. The standard gallon is determined by the Act to be such
measure as shall contain ten pounds avoirdupois of distilled water
weighed in air, at the temperature of 62 degrees Fahrenheit, and the
barometer at thirty inches; and such measure is declared to be the
Imperial Standard Gallon, and the unit and only standard measure of
capacity to be used, as well for wine, beer, ale, spirits, and all sorts of
liquids, as for dry goods not measured by heaped measure; and all

other measures are to be taken in parts or multiples of the said imperial standard gallon, the quart being the fourth part of such gallon.
and the pint one-eighth part, two such gallons making a peck, eight
such gallons a bushel, and eight such bushels a quarter of corn, or
other dry goods not measured by heaped measure. The standard for
heaped measure for such things as are commonly sold by heaped measure, such as coal, culm, lime, fish, potatoes, fruit, &c., is to be "the
aforesaid bushel, containing eighty pounds avoirdupois of water, as
aforesaid; the same being made round, with a plain and even bottom.
and being nineteen and a half inches from outside to outside;" and
goods thus sold by heaped measures are to be heaped "in the form of
a cone, such cone to be of the height of at least six inches, the outside
of the bushel to be the extremity of the base of such cone." Three
such bushels are to be a sack, and twelve such sacks a chaldron.

STRICKEN MEASURE.

1305. The last-mentioned goods may be sold either by the heaped
measure, or by the standard weight, as before mentioned; but for every
other kind of goods not usually sold by heaped measure, which may
be sold or agreed for by measure, the same standard measure is to be
used, but the goods are not to be heaped, but stricken with a round
stick or roller, straight, and of the same diameter from end to end.
Copies and models of the standard of length, weight, and measure
are to be made and verified under the direction of the Treasury, and
every county to be supplied with them for reference whenever required. Existing weights and measures may be used, being marked
so as to show the proportion they have to the standard measures and
weights. Tables of equalization of the weights are to be made by the
Treasury; tables, also, for the Customs and Excise, by which the
duties will be altered so as to make them equal to what they are at
present, in consequence of the alterations in the weights and measures.

1306. IMPERIAL MEASURES OF CAPACITY for all liquids, and for all
dry goods, except such as are comprised in the next division:—

				Cubic in. nearly.
4 gills	=	1 pint	=	34¾
2 pints	=	1 quart	=	69¼
4 quarts	=	1 gallon	=	277½
2 gallons	=	1 peck	=	554¾
8 gallons	=	1 bushel	=	2218 1-5th

				Cubic ft. nearly.
8 bushels	=	1 quarter	=	10¼
5 quarters	=	1 load	=	51½

The four last denominations are used for dry goods only. For iquids, several denominations have been heretofore adopted—viz., for beer, the firkin, of nine gallons; the kilderkin, of eighteen; the barrel, of thirty-six; the hogshead, of fifty-four; and the butt, of one hundred and eight gallons. These will probably continue to be used in practice. For wine and spirits, there are the anker, runlet, tierce, hogshead, puncheon, pipe, butt, and tun; but these may be considered rather as the names of the casks in which such commodities are imported, than as expressing any definite number of gallons. It is the practice to gauge all such vessels, and to charge them according to their actual contents.

Imperial measure of capacity for coals, culm, lime, fish, potatoes, fruit, and other goods, commonly sold by heaped measure :—

				Cubic in. nearly
2 gallons	—	1 peck	—	704
8 gallons	—	1 bushel	—	2815¼
				Cubic ft. nearly
3 bushels	—	1 sack	—	4 8-9ths
12 sacks	—	1 chaldron	—	58⅔

1307. AVOIRDUPOIS WEIGHT :—

27 11-32nds grs.	—	1 dr.		
16 dr.	=	1 oz.	—	437½ gr.
16 oz.	—	1 lb.	=	7000 ,,
28 lb.	=	1 qr.		
4 qr.	—	1 cwt.		
20 cwt.	—	1 ton.		

This weight is used in almost all commercial transactions, and in the common dealings of life.

1308. PARTICULAR WEIGHTS BELONGING TO THIS DIVISION :—

		cwt.	qr.	lb.
8 pounds = 1 stone, used for meat and fish.				
7 pounds = 1 clove				
14 pounds = 1 stone	=	0	0	14
2 stone = 1 tod	=	0	1	0
6½ tod = 1 wey	=	1	2	14
2 weys = 1 sack	=	3	1	0
12 sacks = 1 last	=	39	0	0

8 pounds = 1 clove	} used for cheese and butter.
32 cloves = 1 wey in Essex.	
42 cloves = 1 wey in Suffolk.	
36 pounds = 1 firkin.	

DINNER AND EVENING PARTIES.

1309. In giving parties, it is often the case that a larger stock of glass, china, and plate is required than is possessed by the lady of the house. To meet this demand, the vendors of glass and china let out services to the public; and the silversmiths have generally in large towns an assortment of plate at their service. Chairs and tables may also be hired in most places.

1310. PASTRYCOOKS are in the habit of undertaking to supply all kinds of pastries and the other materials for refreshing the inward man, together with, if desired, plate, china, glass, table-cloths, and all the *etceteras* required. When, therefore, there is a deficiency these articles, or when the party is not likely to be often repeated, the plan may be economical, as well as a relief in point of trouble and anxiety. A breakfast or supper party (without wine) may in this way be given at about 4s. to 10s. per head, the former sum finding a very good array of dishes, and the latter being sufficient to insure a very splendid set out. The charge for dinner parties varies from 12s. to £1, 1s. per head, according to the kind of dinner required.

1311. In the present day it is too often the case that dinner parties, as well as those given in the evening, are carried to such an extravagant extent that a serious outlay is involved, which may not always be agreeable to those invited, some of whom are neither able, nor, if able, willing to return such a display. It will, I believe, be found that on the whole more pleasure is afforded if less expensive feasts are offered, and they are made more frequent, with a smaller number of guests, so as to insure cordiality and comfort. No one should attempt in a dinner party to entertain more guests than the table and room will conveniently accommodate, or than the servants can wait upon without awkwardness; nor should an expense be incurred which will produce an inconvenience to the giver, or entail it upon the receiver when it has to be returned. In this country people do not seem to feel happy until their stomachs are satiated; so that it is in vain to expect the continental receptions to attain popularity. But still a comparatively plain dinner, if nicely cooked, will always be appreciated; while a prettily set out, but inexpensive, supper, is often more attractive than a heavy, though costly, effort of the adjacent pastrycook, or of the home establishment.

COST.

1312. The average cost of an economical dinner party for twelve persons, when of frequent occurrence, and exclusive of the wine, may be taken at £5. Many people spend ten times that sum upon a grand

" spread," but for really agreeable and social dinner parties, the above is sufficient to procure what is wanted, calculating the residue as useful for the house, and as coming in to the ordinary expenditure. The actual dinner, it is true, costs more than the above sum ; but as the remains will feed the household for a week, the difference from the usual whole weekly expenditure will not be more than £5 or £6, unless every delicacy of the season is considered indispensable. At all events, it is a fact that many people, celebrated for the pleasantness of their dinner parties, confine themselves to the above sums.

BILLS OF FARE FOR PARTIES.

1313. The following bills of fare are introduced as a guide to those who are anxious to follow out the present fashion. The first may be considered as a specimen of the style adopted in the highest circles of London society, being in fact very similar to those introduced at the *very highest* tables in the present year. The dessert may or may not be placed on the table, some people disliking the smell of fruit ; besides which the silver is, to a certain extent, hidden or eclipsed by it. The fish and top-dishes are usually carved on the side table, and handed round by the servants ; also the mutton, venison, chickens, game, &c. ; the tureens are left on the table till the puddings are put on. Many have only two sweets and two vegetables for corners ; the sweets being handed, while the puddings are being brought in by the servants. Others, again, merely deviate from the above plan by ornamenting the table with dried fruits and pyramids in addition to the usual display of silver, and have the top dishes put on the table for a few seconds only, and then removed to be carved at the side-table, and the fresh fruit brought in after the cheese has been handed round. A third plan consists in having nothing but dessert on table, and a bill of fare to every two guests, the dishes being all from the first placed and carved on the side-tables, which saves much trouble in garnishing. Many who adopt this style have only three or four *entrées* for sixteen or eighteen guests. Even in all those cases where the dishes are placed on the table, flanks are seldom now introduced. Ice is becoming every year in greater request, both as pure ice placed in the glasses, and in the shape of water and cream-ices, as well as ice puddings. The two first of these are introduced as a part of the dessert, and are handed round by the servants before they leave the room, the last being made a part of the usual sweets. The ARRANGEMENT OF

BREAKFASTS depends greatly upon the season of the year, ornamentation with natural flowers being the chief means employed for decorative purposes. Epergnes, vases, small flowering plants, and fruits in pots, are introduced on the table with a very light and elegant effect. The sweets are also thickly garnished with flowers, and sometimes wreaths are placed round them. This, however, depends so much upon the opportunities for obtaining choice flowers and fruit, and upon the taste of the parties concerned, that no minute directions can be here given. Every thing is cold, excepting tea, coffee, and chocolate, and the rolls and fancy breads, which are served hot. Sugar and cream are placed at short intervals round the table, so as to be within the reach of all the guests. LUNCHEONS, in their arrangements, are very similar to breakfasts, except that they are not ornamented with flowers to the same extent; and that, instead of tea and coffee, a hot top and bottom, and also a principal dish of sweets are introduced, with hot vegetables handed round. TEA and COFFEE are served soon after dinner, the latter being introduced on the dinner-table for the gentlemen, and in the drawing-room it is handed round to the ladies. When tea is announced to the gentlemen, it is served both to them and the ladies in the drawing-room. Instead of dessert, a continental plan is sometimes now adopted in England, in which finger-glasses are placed on the table before each person, and when they have been used they are taken away, coffee being immediately handed round on a small tray, which is then left on the table, the servant retiring from the room. This plan is intended to supersede the English custom of sitting over the wine, as the gentlemen then leave the dining-room at once. It is, however, only suited to quiet family meetings, or those in which all are known to be averse to sitting long after dinner. For a large evening party, tea and coffee are made by the servants in a room devoted to the purpose, and partaken of by each guest before entering the reception-room, a long table or counter being generally put up, covered with a large table-cloth, and arranged with biscuits, small cakes, &c. SEVERAL BILLS OF FARE FOR SUPPER PARTIES are also shown in the following pages; but they are now generally given without seats, counters being arranged on two sides of the room, with servants behind. Hot soup is always given, and chickens, cut up and tied as described at par. 1291. Ice is not placed on the counters, but supplied by the servants as wanted, the doors being opened at an early hour of the evening, and the guests going in whenever they wish for refreshment.

(a) FASHIONABLE BILL OF FARE FOR A DINNER OF FROM 16 TO 28 COVERS:—

FIRST COURSE.

Clear soup.

Remove—Chickens and tongue.

Rissoles.   Lamb cutlets.

(Vase of flowers.)

Fish.   (Epergne.)   Fish.

(Vase of flowers.)

Sweetbreads.   Pureé soup.   Fillets of duck.

Remove—Saddle of mutton.

Vegetables on side-table. Fish and removes carved on side-table. Covers on tureens. (See remarks above.)

SECOND COURSE.

Partridges.

Vegetables dressed.   Tureen taken off for souffié.   Cream.

(Vase.)

(Epergne.)

Jelly.   (Vase.)   Pastry or lobster salad.

Grouse.

Cheese fondu or pastry.

Game carved on side-table.

(b) BILL OF FARE FOR A DINNER OF 8 COVERS IN JANUARY OR FEBRUARY:—

FIRST COURSE.

Jerusalem artichoke soup.

Remove—Boiled chickens.

Tongue.   (Epergne.)   Curried rabbit.

Cutlets of soles.

Remove—Haunch of mutton

Vegetables—mashed potatoes, brocoli, seakale, stewed white.

SECOND COURSE.

Leamington pudding.

Mince pies.   (Epergne.)   Blancmange.

Brace of partridges.

(c) BILL OF FARE FOR 12 COVERS IN JANUARY OR FEBRUARY:—

FIRST COURSE.

Hare soup.

Remove—Boiled turkey.

Slices of tongue stewed.   (Vase.)   Chicken curry.

(Epergne.)

Pork steaks, with apple sauce in the centre.   (Vase.)   Sausages.

Cod fish.

Remove—Sirloin of beef.

Vegetables—whole potatoes, potato balls, Jerusalem artichokes, on side-table.

SECOND COURSE.

Plum pudding.

Jelly   (Vase.)   Tartlets.

(Epergne.)

Mince pies   (Vase.)   Solid custard.

Brace of Pheasants.

(d) BILL OF FARE FOR 16 OR 18 COVERS IN JANUARY OR FEBRUARY:—

FIRST COURSE.

Turbot.

Remove—Turkey, garnished with sausages.

Stewed celery.	(Vase.)	Oyster patties.
Tongue.	(Epergne.)	Stewed ox cheek.
Egg balls.	(Vase.)	Mutton chops, with tomato sauce.

Gravy soup.

Remove—Haunch of mutton.

Vegetables—mashed potatoes, mashed carrots and turnips, brocoli, on side-table.

———

SECOND COURSE.

Partridges.

Remove—Cabinet pudding.

Jaune mange.	(Vase.)	Mince pies.
Potato chips.	(Epergne.)	Lobster salad.
Meringues.	(Vase.)	Italian cream.

Hare.

Remove—Fondu.

———

(e) BILL OF FARE FOR 8 COVERS IN MARCH:—

FIRST COURSE.

Onion soup.

Remove—Boiled calf's head.

| China. | (Epergne.) | Veal cutlets. |

Boiled whiting.

Remove—Loin of mutton.

Vegetables—potatoes, cabbage, on side-table.

SECOND COURSE.

Potato pudding.

| Arrowroot blancmange. | (Epergne.) | Lemon cream. |

Maccaroni.

———

(f) BILL OF FARE FOR 12 COVERS IN MARCH:—

FIRST COURSE.

Carrot soup.

Remove—Boiled calf's head.

Stewed sea-kale.	(Vase.)	Mutton cutlets.
	(Epergne.)	
Scotch collops.	(Vase.)	Eggs and spinach.

Brill.

Remove—Roast fillet of veal.

Vegetables—potatoes, brocoli.

———

SECOND COURSE.

Pound puddings.

Italian cheese.	(Vase.)	Curd cheese-cakes.
	(Epergne.)	
Open tart.	(Vase.)	Coffee cream.

Guinea fowls.

(g) BILL OF FARE FOR 16 OR 18 COVERS IN MARCH:—

FIRST COURSE.

White soup.

Remove—Stewed eels.

Remove—Stewed breast of veal.

Fish patties.	(Vase.)	Scalloped mutton.
	(Epergne.)	
Veal olives.	(Vase.)	White sweetbreads.

Boiled soles, garnished with smelts.

Remove—Saddle of mutton.

Vegetables — potatoes, Jerusalem artichokes, Brussels sprouts, on side-table.

SECOND COURSE.

Roast pigeons.

Chester pudding.

Calf's-feet jelly	(Vase.)	Apricot cream, in shape.
	(Epergne.)	
Blancmange.	(Vase.)	Cake and custard.

Pea-fowl.

Remove—Rhubarb tart.

(h) BILL OF FARE FOR 8 COVERS IN APRIL OR MAY:—

FIRST COURSE.

Clear gravy soup with asparagus.

Remove—Boiled leg of lamb.

Veal cutlets.	(Epergne.)	Lamb's fry.

Fried soles.

Remove—Stewed beef.

Vegetables—young rotatoes, asparagus, on side-table.

SECOND COURSE.

Prussia puffs.

Apples and custard.	(Epergne.)	Stewed pears.

Ramakins.

(i) BILL OF FARE FOR 12 COVERS IN APRIL OR MAY:—

FIRST COURSE.

French soup.

Remove—Boiled fillet of veal, with white sauce.

Face.	(Vase.)	Potatoe balls.
	(Epergne.)	
Rissoles.	(Vase.)	Sweetbreads.

Stewed lamperns.

Remove—Quarter of lamb.

Vegetables — young potatoes, asparagus, cauliflower, on side-table.

SECOND COURSE.

Selkirk puddings.

Solid syllabub.	(Vase.)	Potatoe cheese-cakes
	(Epergne.)	
Stewed Normandy pippins.	(Vase.)	Rice flummery.

Leveret.

2 A

(*j*) BILL OF FARE FOR 16 OR 18 COVERS IN APRIL OR MAY:—

FIRST COURSE.

Mock-turtle soup.

Remove—Stewed calf's head.

Rissoles.	(Vase.)	Curried salmon.
	(Epergne.)	
Lobster patties.	(Vase.)	Sweetbreads, stewed brown.
	Salmon.	

Remove—Quarter of lamb.

Vegetables—young potatoes, asparagus, salad and ham, on side-table.

——

SECOND COURSE.

Asparagus.

Remove—Marlborough pudding.

Trifle.	(Vase.)	Orange jelly.
Open tart.	(Epergne.)	Green apricot tart.
Gâteau de Pommes.	(Vase.)	Stone cream.

Three spring chickens.

———

(*k*) BILL OF FARE FOR 8 COVERS IN JUNE OR JULY:—

FIRST COURSE.

Green pea-soup.

Remove—Roast ducks.

Lamb cutlets.	(Epergne.)	Beans and bacon.

Stewed lamperns.

Remove—Fillet of veal.

Vegetables—young potatoes, peas, salad, on side-table.

SECOND COURSE.

Soufflé pudding.

Chocolate cream.	(Epergne.)	White clouted cream.

Green currant tart.

(*l*) BILL OF FARE FOR 12 COVERS IN JUNE OR JULY:—

FIRST COURSE.

Clear gravy soup, with thin pieces of carrot and French beans cut into it.

Remove—Boiled couple of chickens.

Tongue.	(Vase.)	Fish patties.
	(Epergne.)	
Sweetbreads, done white.	(Vase.)	Veal cutlets.
	Stewed lampreys.	

Remove—Quarter of lamb.

Vegetables—potatoes, French beans, peas, salad, on side-table.

——

SECOND COURSE.

Tea-cup puddings.

Lemon jelly.	(Vase.)	Stewed blackcaps.
	(Epergne.)	
Whipped cream.	(Vase.)	Cake and custard.
	Stewed pigeons.	

(*m*) BILL OF FARE FOR 16 OR 18 COVERS IN JUNE OR JULY:—

FIRST COURSE.

White soup with maccaroni.

Remove—Boiled breast of veal, done white.

Stewed cauliflower.	(Vase.)	Ham, garnished with greens.
Rabbit curry.	(Epergne.)	Chicken with rice.
Lamb chops, with potatoes in the centre.	(Vase.)	Stewed cucumbers.
	Salmon.	

Remove—Venison.

Vegetables—potatoes, peas, salad, on side-table.

SECOND COURSE.

Peas.

Remove—Ice pudding.

Gooseberry fool.	(Vase.)	Calf's-feet jelly.
Tart.	(Epergne.)	Lemon cheese-cakes.
Arrowroot blancmange, with strawberry cream.	(Vase.)	Whipped fruit cream.

Couple of ducks.

(*n*) BILL OF FARE FOR 8 COVERS IN AUGUST OR SEPTEMBER:—

FIRST COURSE.

Brown soup.

Remove—Mutton cutlets, with stewed mushrooms in the middle.

Tongue.	(Epergne.)	Vegetable marrow.*

Soles.

Remove—Fillet of veal.

* Cut in slices lengthways, put on a toast, and white sauce poured over.

Vegetables—potatoes, French beans, salad, on side-table.

SECOND COURSE.

Sweet omelet.

Trifle.	(Epergne.)	Tartlets.

Brace of birds.

(*o*) BILL OF FARE FOR 12 COVERS IN AUGUST OR SEPTEMBER:—

FIRST COURSE.

White soup.

Remove—Fowls.

(Vase.)

Ham.	(Epergne.)	Curry of rabbits.

(Vase.)

Cod.

Remove—Saddle of mutton.

Vegetables—potatoes, mashed vegetable marrows, on side-table.

SECOND COURSE.

Lemon apple pudding.

(Vase.)

Jelly.	(Epergne.)	Tipsy cake.

(Vase.)

Brace of birds.

(*p*) BILL OF FARE FOR 16 OR 18 COVERS IN AUGUST OR SEPTEMBER:—

FIRST COURSE.

Mock-turtle soup.

Remove—Chickens.

Lobster patties.	(Vase.)	Lamb cutlets, with stewed beans in centre.

(Epergne.)

Veal cutlets.	(Vase.)	Currie.

Turbot.

Remove—Neck of venison.

Vegetables—potatoes, peas, salad, on side-table.

SECOND COURSE.

Birds.

Jelly. (Tem.) Cheese-cake.

(Sponge.)

Shape cream. (Tem.) Apple cake, with custard.

Lemon cream.

(t) BILL OF FARE FOR 8 COVERS IN OCTOBER OR NOVEMBER:—

FIRST COURSE.

Vermicelli soup.

Remove—Veal cutlets, white.

Har-ico mutton. (Epergne.) Minced beef with wall of potatoes.

Brill.

Remove—Roast chickens.

—

Vegetables—potatoes and beans on side-table.

SECOND COURSE.

Pancakes.

Lèche crême. (Epergne.) Apple tart.

Hare.

(v) BILL OF FARE FOR 12 COVERS IN OCTOBER OR NOVEMBER:—

FIRST COURSE.

Ox-tail soup.

Remove—Hashed calf's head.

(Vase.)

Chickens. (Epergne.) Tongue.

(Vase.)

Cod.

Remove—Haunch of mutton.

Vegetables—potatoes, vegetable marrow, on side-table.

SECOND COURSE.

Marlborough pudding.

(Vase.)

Lemon cream. (Epergne.) Pastry.

(Vase.)

Charlotte russe. Ratifia cream.

Hare.

(u) BILL OF FARE FOR 16 OR 18 COVERS IN OCTOBER AND NOVEMBER:—

FIRST COURSE.

Mulligatawny soup.

Remove—Chickens, with tongue in the centre.

Oyster patties. (Vase.) Beef olives.

(Epergne.)

Stewed onions. (Vase.) Sweetbread.

Turbot.

Remove—Sirloin of beef.

Vegetables—beans, potatoes, &c. on side table.

—

SECOND COURSE.

Pheasant.

Remove—Soufflé.

(Vase.)

Jaune mange. Lemon cheese-cakes.

(Epergne.)

Tartlets. Sir Walter Scott's wassail bowl.

(Vase.)

Brace of partridges.

(f) BILL OF FARE FOR 8 COVERS IN DECEMBER:—

FIRST COURSE.

Jerusalem soup.

Remove—Boiled leg of mutton.

Rabbit curry. (Epergne.) Veal cutlets.

Brill.

Remove—Stewed beef.

Vegetables—potatoes, sea-kale, on side-table.

SECOND COURSE.

Adelaide puddings.

Apple jelly. (Epergne.) Solid custard.

Grouse.

(u) BILL OF FARE FOR 12 COVERS IN DECEMBER:—

FIRST COURSE.

Carrot soup.

Remove—Turkey.

Pork chops, with potatoes in the middle.	(Vase.)	Beef-steaks.
	(Epergne.)	
Ham.	(Vase.)	Stewed mushrooms.

Cod.

Remove—Haunch of mutton.

Vegetables—potato balls, brocoli, Jerusalem artichokes, on side-table.

SECOND COURSE.

Ramakins.

Lemon jelly.	(Vase.)	Mince pies.
	(Epergne.)	
Trifle.	(Vase.)	Blancmange.

Hare.

(v) BILL OF FARE FOR 16 OR 18 COVERS IN DECEMBER:—

FIRST COURSE.

Clear soup.

Remove—Turkey.

Harrico mutton.	(Vase.)	Stewed celery.
	(Epergne.)	
Vol au vent of Lobster.	(Vase.)	Ham.

Cod.

Remove—Roast beef.

Vegetables—potatoes, brocoli, on side-table.

SECOND COURSE.

Woodcocks.

Remove—Plum pudding.

Mince pies.	(Vase.)	Italian cheese.
	(Epergne.)	
Lemon sponge.	(Vase.)	Apple tart, filled up with custard.

Brace of pheasants.

LUNCHEON FOR 40 OR 50.

Turkey.

Pastry.	Cream.
Blancmange.	
Partridges.	Oyster patties.
Pickled salmon.	
Peaches.	Grapes.
Pheasants. (Epergne.)	Ham.
Grapes.	Nectarines.
Lobster salad.	
Pigeon-pie.	Partridges.
Jaunemange.	
Jelly.	Past—
Chickens and tongue.	

WEDDING BREAKFAST FOR 40, IN JULY.

Tongue.

Muffins.

Boiled custard.

Chicken pie (raised).

(Flowers.)

Fancy bread.

Honeycomb

CAKE
(in shape).

Peaches.

(Vase of flowers.)

Strawberries.

Sugar and cream.

Pastry.

Roast chickens.

Potted veal.

Butter.

Pressed beef.

Sugar and cream.

Breakfast cakes.

Wine jelly.

Lemon sponge.

Pigeons in jelly.

Butter.

Potted shrimps.

Cold salmon.

Lobster salad.

Purple grapes.

Cake.

White grapes.

Lobster salad.

Savoury pie.

Strawberries.

(Vase of flowers.)

Cherries.

SPONGE CAKE
(in shape).

Marmalade.

Fancy bread.

(Flowers.)

Ham, ornamented.

Potted beef.

Butter.

Calf's-head pie.

Italian cream.

Sugar and cream.

Wine jelly.

Butter.

Sugar and cream.

Potted veal.

Muffins.

Potted ham.

White chickens.

Breakfast cakes.

Pastry.

Blancmange.

Tongue.

Tea, coffee, and chocolate handed round.

STAND-UP SUPPER FOR FROM 60 TO 100, ARRANGED ON TWO COUNTERS, WITH SERVANTS BEHIND.

Pheasant.

Scalloped oysters.

(Vase of flowers.)

(Vase of flowers.)

Apple trifle.

Tipsy cake.

Lobster salad.

Tongue.

(Epergne of flowers.)

(Epergne of flowers.)

Chickens, cut up.

Turkey, cut up.

Oranges.

Grapes.

Pickled salmon.

Pheasants.

Solid syllabub.

Trifle.

(Vase of flowers.)

(Vase of flowers.)

Savoury pie.

Potted meat sandwiches.

Left counter side labels: Rolled ham. | Stone cream. | White soup. | Dried fruits. | Lemon sponge. | Lobster patties. | Oyster patties. | Italian cream. | Biscuits. | Whipped cream. | Potted meat.

Right counter side labels: Partridges. | Blancmange. | Orange jelly. | Meat cake. | Partridges. | Potted meat, in shape. | Wine jelly. | White soup. | Solid custard.

Glasses of custards, creams, and jellies to be placed about the table, and a supply of ices behind it. Some of the dishes should be garnished with crackers.

PLAIN SAVOURY SIT-DOWN SUPPER FOR 50.

Pheasants.	A ham, garnished with pasta.	Tongue.
Cheese-cakes.	Stone cream.	Oyster patties.
	Potted shrimps.	

Cold turkey or fowls.   Tipsy cake.   Wine jelly.   Cake.   (Epergne with flowers.)   Cake.   Orange jelly   Trifle.   Round of beef.

	Potted lobster.	
Veal patties.	Blancmange.	Tartlets.
Tongue.	Savoury pie.	Partridges.

Fill the vacant spaces of the table with jelly in glasses, custards or whipped cream, raspberry, lemon, &c., &c.

SIT-DOWN SUPPER FOR 12.

Potted shrimps.	Sponge cake.	Mixed biscuits.
	Glasses of jellies and cream.	

Chicken.   Jelly.   Sweet sandwiches.   Glasses of jellies and cream.   ORANGES.   Glasses of jellies and cream.   Tartlets.   Custards.   Tongue.

	Glasses of jellies and cream.	
Lemon creams.	Pigeon-pie.	Potted-meat sandwiches.

INDEX.

N

O

THE END.

M'CORQUODALE AND CO., PRINTERS, LONDON—WORKS, NEWTON.

Milton Keynes UK
Ingram Content Group UK Ltd.
UKHW021305100524
442539UK00005B/12